terra australis 37

Terra Australis reports the results of archaeological and related research within the south and east of Asia, though mainly Australia, New Guinea and island Melanesia — lands that remained terra australis incognita to generations of prehistorians. Its subject is the settlement of the diverse environments in this isolated quarter of the globe by peoples who have maintained their discrete and traditional ways of life into the recent recorded or remembered past and at times into the observable present.

List of volumes in Terra Australis

Volume 1: Burrill Lake and Currarong: Coastal Sites in Southern New South Wales. R.J. Lampert (1971)

Volume 2: Ol Tumbuna: Archaeological Excavations in the Eastern Central Highlands, Papua New Guinea. J.P. White (1972)

Volume 3: New Guinea Stone Age Trade: The Geography and Ecology of Traffic in the Interior. I. Hughes (1977)

Volume 4: Recent Prehistory in Southeast Papua. B. Egloff (1979)

Volume 5: The Great Kartan Mystery. R. Lampert (1981)

Volume 6: Early Man in North Queensland: Art and Archaeology in the Laura Area. A. Rosenfeld, D. Horton and J. Winter (1981)

Volume 7: The Alligator Rivers: Prehistory and Ecology in Western Arnhem Land. C. Schrire (1982)

Volume 8: Hunter Hill, Hunter Island: Archaeological Investigations of a Prehistoric Tasmanian Site. S. Bowdler (1984)

Volume 9: Coastal South-West Tasmania: The Prehistory of Louisa Bay and Maatsuyker Island. R. Vanderwal and D. Horton (1984)

Volume 10: The Emergence of Mailu. G. Irwin (1985)

Volume 11: Archaeology in Eastern Timor, 1966–67. I. Glover (1986)

Volume 12: Early Tongan Prehistory: The Lapita Period on Tongatapu and its Relationships. J. Poulsen (1987)

Volume 13: Coobool Creek. P. Brown (1989)

Volume 14: 30,000 Years of Aboriginal Occupation: Kimberley, North-West Australia. S. O'Connor (1999)

Volume 15: Lapita Interaction. G. Summerhayes (2000)

Volume 16: The Prehistory of Buka: A Stepping Stone Island in the Northern Solomons. S. Wickler (2001)

Volume 17: The Archaeology of Lapita Dispersal in Oceania. G.R. Clark, A.J. Anderson and T. Vunidilo (2001)

Volume 18: An Archaeology of West Polynesian Prehistory. A. Smith (2002)

Volume 19: Phytolith and Starch Research in the Australian-Pacific-Asian Regions: The State of the Art. D. Hart and L. Wallis (2003)

Volume 20: The Sea People: Late-Holocene Maritime Specialisation in the Whitsunday Islands, Central Queensland. B. Barker (2004)

Volume 21: What's Changing: Population Size or Land-Use Patterns? The Archaeology of Upper Mangrove Creek, Sydney Basin. V. Attenbrow (2004)

Volume 22: The Archaeology of the Aru Islands, Eastern Indonesia. S. O'Connor, M. Spriggs and P. Veth (2005)

Volume 23: Pieces of the Vanuatu Puzzle: Archaeology of the North, South and Centre. S. Bedford (2006)

Volume 24: Coastal Themes: An Archaeology of the Southern Curtis Coast, Queensland. S. Ulm (2006)

Volume 25: Lithics in the Land of the Lightning Brothers: The Archaeology of Wardaman Country, Northern Territory. C. Clarkson (2007)

Volume 26: Oceanic Explorations: Lapita and Western Pacific Settlement. S. Bedford, C. Sand and S. P. Connaughton (2007)

Volume 27: Dreamtime Superhighway: Sydney Basin Rock Art and Prehistoric Information Exchange. J. McDonald (2008)

Volume 28: New Directions in Archaeological Science. A. Fairbairn, S. O'Connor and B. Marwick (2008)

Volume 29: Islands of Inquiry: Colonisation, Seafaring and the Archaeology of Maritime Landscapes. G. Clark, F. Leach and S. O'Connor (2008)

Volume 30: Archaeological Science Under a Microscope: Studies in Residue and Ancient DNA Analysis in Honour of Thomas H. Loy. M. Haslam, G. Robertson, A. Crowther, S. Nugent and L. Kirkwood (2009)

Volume 31: The Early Prehistory of Fiji. G. Clark and A. Anderson (2009)

Volume 32: Altered Ecologies: Fire, Climate and Human Influence on Terrestrial Landscapes. S. Haberle, J. Stevenson and M. Prebble (2010)

Volume 33: Man Bac: The Excavation of a Neolithic Site in Northern Vietnam: The Biology. M. Oxenham, H. Matsumura and N. Kim Dung (2011)

Volume 34: Peopled Landscapes: Archaeological and Biogeographic Approaches to Landscapes. S. Haberle and B. David. (2012)

Volume 35: Pacific Island Heritage Archaeology: Identity & Community. J. Liston, G. Clark and D. Alexander (2011)

Volume 36: Transcending the Culture-Nature Divide in Cultural Heritage: Views from the Asia-Pacific Region. S. O'Connor, S. Blackwell and D. Byrne (2012)

terra australis 37

Taking the High Ground

THE ARCHAEOLOGY OF RAPA, A FORTIFIED ISLAND IN REMOTE EAST POLYNESIA

Edited by Atholl Anderson and Douglas J. Kennett

Australian
National
University

E PRESS

ANU
E PRESS

© 2012 ANU E Press

Published by ANU E Press
The Australian National University
Canberra ACT 0200 Australia
Email: anuepress@anu.edu.au
Web: http://epress.anu.edu.au

National Library of Australia Cataloguing-in-Publication entry

Title:	Taking the high ground : the archaeology of Rapa, a fortified island in remote East Polynesia / edited by Atholl Anderson and Douglas J. Kennett.
ISBN:	9781922144249 (pbk.) 9781922144256 (ebook)
Series:	Terra Australis ; Number 37.
Subjects:	Archaeology--Rapa Island.
	Rapa Island--Antiquities.
Other Authors/Contributors:	
	Anderson, Atholl.
	Kennett, Douglas J.

Dewey Number: 996.22

Series Editor: Sue O'Connor

Cover image: Tevaitau Fortification on Rapa Island. Photograph taken from south looking north, D. J. Kennett.

Back cover image: Tangarutu Shelter on Rapa Island. Photograph by Atholl Anderson.

Back cover map: Hollandia Nova. Thevenot 1663 by courtesy of the National Library of Australia.
Reprinted with permission of the National Library of Australia.

Terra Australis Editorial Board: Sue O'Connor, Jack Golson, Simon Haberle, Sally Brockwell, Geoffrey Clark

Contents

1 Archaeological research on Rapa Island, French Polynesia
Atholl Anderson, Douglas J. Kennett and Eric Conte   7

2 'Dwelling carelessly, quiet and secure': A brief ethnohistory of
Rapa Island, French Polynesia, AD 1791–1840
Atholl Anderson   25

3 Archaeology of the coastal sites on Rapa Island
Atholl Anderson   47

4 The archaeobotany of Rapan rockshelter deposits
Matiu Prebble and Atholl Anderson   77

5 Cordage from Rapan archaeological sites
Judith Cameron   97

6 Bird, reptile and mammal remains from archaeological sites on Rapa Island
Alan J. D. Tennyson and Atholl Anderson   105

7 Prehistoric fishing on Rapa Island
Yolanda Vogel and Atholl Anderson   115

8 The Tangarutu invertebrate fauna
Katherine Szabó and Atholl Anderson   135

9 Marine resource exploitation on Rapa Island: Archaeology, material culture
and ethnography
Katherine Szabó, Yolanda Vogel and Atholl Anderson   145

10 Palaeobotany and the early development of agriculture on Rapa Island
Matiu Prebble and Atholl Anderson   167

11 A Bayesian AMS ¹⁴C chronology for the colonisation and fortification
    of Rapa Island
        Douglas J. Kennett, Brendan J. Culleton, Atholl Anderson and John Southon   189

12 The archaeology of Rapan fortifications
        Douglas J. Kennett and Sarah B. McClure   203

13 Rapan agroecology and population estimates
        Jacob Bartruff, Douglas J. Kennett and Bruce Winterhalder   235

14 The prehistory of Rapa Island
        Atholl Anderson, Douglas J. Kennett and Eric Conte   247

    Appendices   257

1

Archaeological research on Rapa Island, French Polynesia

Atholl Anderson
Department of Archaeology and Natural History, Research School of Asian and Pacific Studies, The Australian National University, Canberra, Australia, atholl.anderson@anu.edu.au

Douglas J. Kennett
Department of Anthropology, The Pennsylvania State University

Eric Conte
Université du Polynésie Française

Introduction

This volume describes the results of archaeological and related research on Rapa Island, which lies at the southern extremity of French Polynesia. Notable for its numerous fortified sites atop the peaks of a spectacular volcanic landscape, Rapa has remained nonetheless an enigma in Polynesian prehistory. It has been linked, on the one hand, with its more famous and near-namesake Rapa Nui (Easter Island), in hypotheses of Amerindian migration and the dire impacts of deforestation and societal isolation, and, on the other hand, with settlement and fort construction in the similarly cool and remote nearest neighbour to the southwest, New Zealand. Our project set out to construct a cultural sequence and palaeoenvironmental context so that consideration of such issues might profit from the existence of a more diverse and comprehensive database.

Rapa Island is located in a remote position at $27^0 35S$, $144^0 20W$, in the subtropical South Pacific Ocean (Figure 1.1). In the form of a horseshoe, which reflects its origin as a breached caldera, Rapa has 38 km^2 of land area and, lacking any barrier or fringing reef, its outer coast rises abruptly out of the sea towards jagged peaks, products of erosion around the caldera rim (Figure 1.2), the highest of which is Mont Perau, at 650 m;

> Where the steep sides of the jagged peaks reach the coast they form great cliffs falling vertically to the sea. The coast is bold with deep caves worn in it by the sea. Except around the bays in the coast, which have sandy beaches at their heads, the island is inaccessible. (Haslam 1982:83)

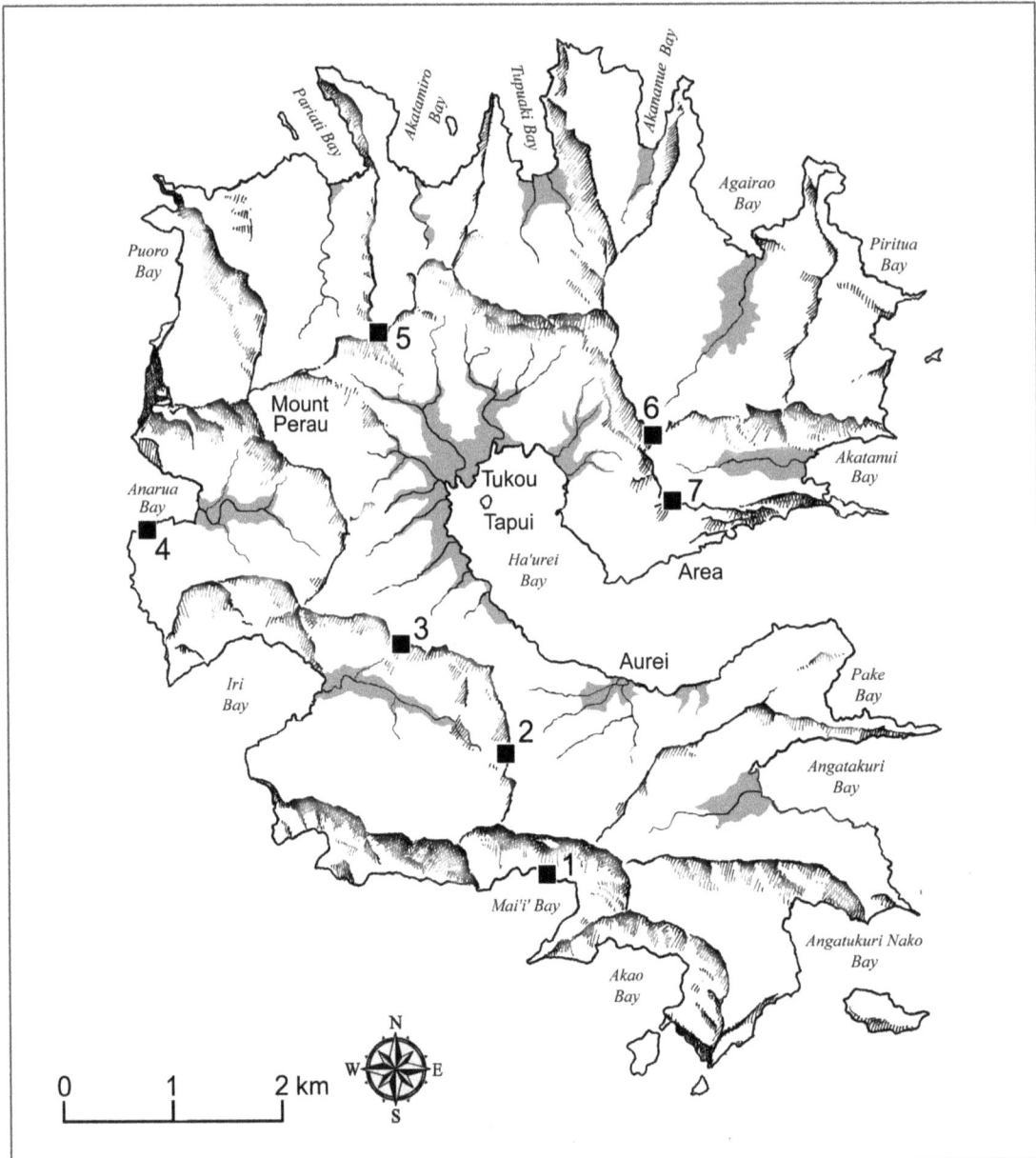

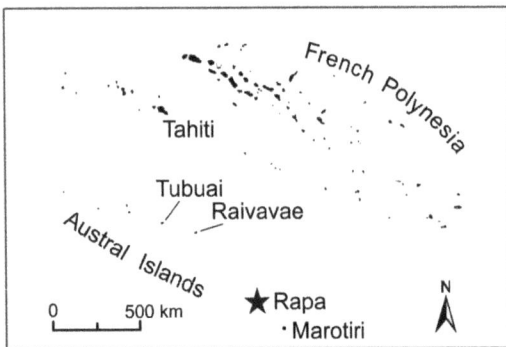

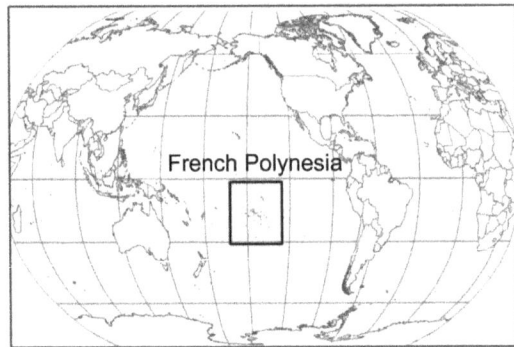

Figure 1.1. Rapa Island, showing the main topographical features and modern settlements.
Numbered squares indicate locations of previous research mentioned in this chapter: 1=Anapoiri Cave, 2=Tevaitau, 3=Moronga Uta, 4=Tangarutu Cave, 5=Kapitanga, 6=Potaketake, 7= Tapitanga. See Figures 3.1, 10.1 and 12.1 for the sites examined during the 2002 field season. Inset, the location of Rapa in the South Pacific Ocean and Austral Island group. Drafted by R. Van Rossman.

Figure 1.2. (a) The steep outer coast of Rapa near Akananue Bay. **(b)** Rapan cliffs on the northern coast.
Photographs A. Anderson.

Topographically, the redeeming feature of Rapa for human habitation is its large, protected harbour with relatively extensive low and fertile ground at its head (Figure 1.3). The harbour was called Aurai in the 1820s (Chapter 2) and it has been called Ha'urei or Ahurei since the 1940s at least (Naval Intelligence Division 1943:253). However, Stokes (n.d.) called it 'Tairirau' and on an early map published by Hall (1868) it is labelled 'Boukakika' (Figure 1.4). The two main settlements of historical times, and today, are located opposite each other on Ha'urei Harbour. They were written as Harea and Aruhei by Hall (Figure 1.5), and today are Area and Ha'urei or Aurei respectively. We use Area for the smaller community on the north side of Ha'urei Bay and Aurei for the larger community, located to the southwest, to distinguish it from the bay name itself. It is worth noting here, as well, that the spelling of Rapan names is quite varied because of the historical influence of Tahitian on the Rapan dialect. Thus we get Taga and Tanga, Angairao and Agairao, Iri and Hiri and so on. Neither we, nor other writers, have standardised the spelling.

About 83 km to the east-southeast of Rapa lie the bare, uninhabited Marotiri (Bass) Islets. They have about 2 km² of surface area, and bear some remains of stone-built structures (Ferdon 1965b:71). Rapa and Marotiri are part of the Austral archipelago, named by the French geographer Malte Brun (Ellis 1838:363), but they are sometimes separated out, and once were known as the Bass group, in recognition of their relative remoteness from the other Austral Islands (e.g. Naval Intelligence Division 1943; Kooijman 1972; Haslam 1982:82). The nearest inhabitable island to Rapa is Raivavae, 537 km to the northwest, but the administrative centre of the Australs is on Tubuai Island, 730 km from Rapa.

Figure 1.3. Ha'urei Bay, showing lowlands, taro plantations in the Tukou region and Tapui Island. Hilltop fortifications are visible on several of the highest peaks. Photograph D.J. Kennett.

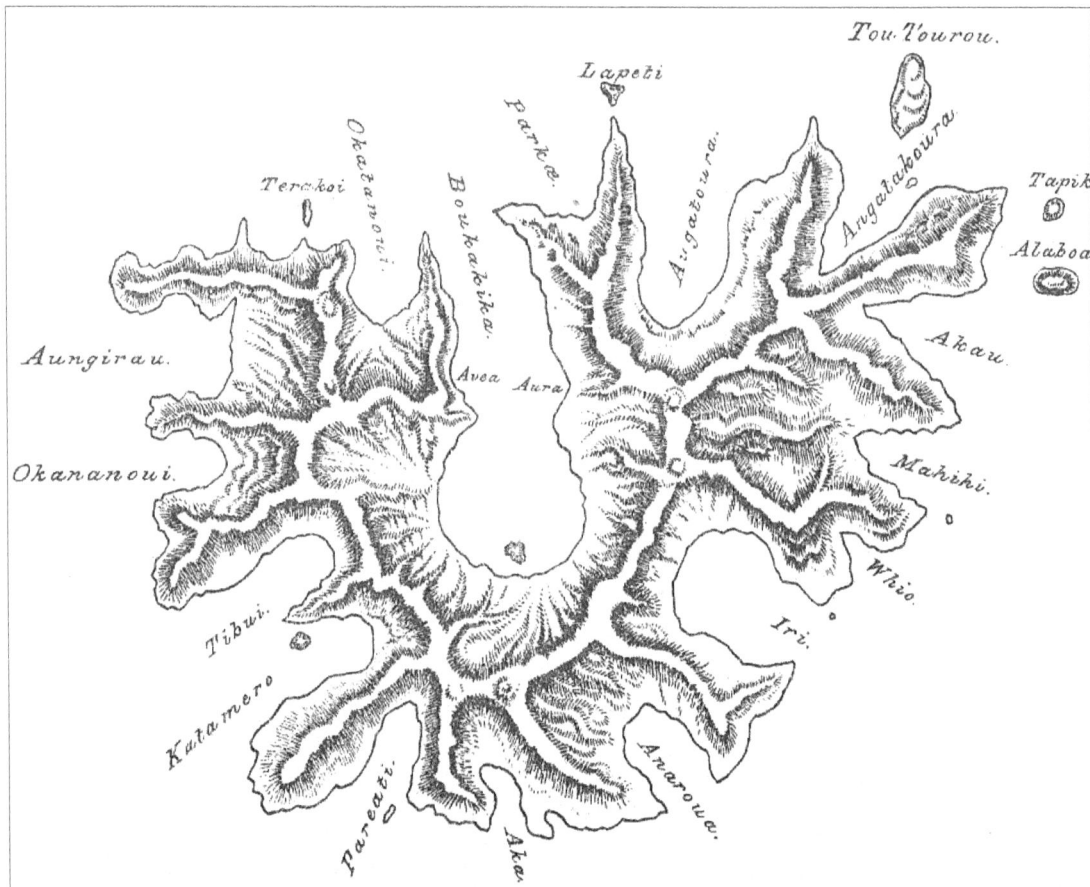

Figure 1.4. Map of Rapa published by Hall (1868:facing p. 80).

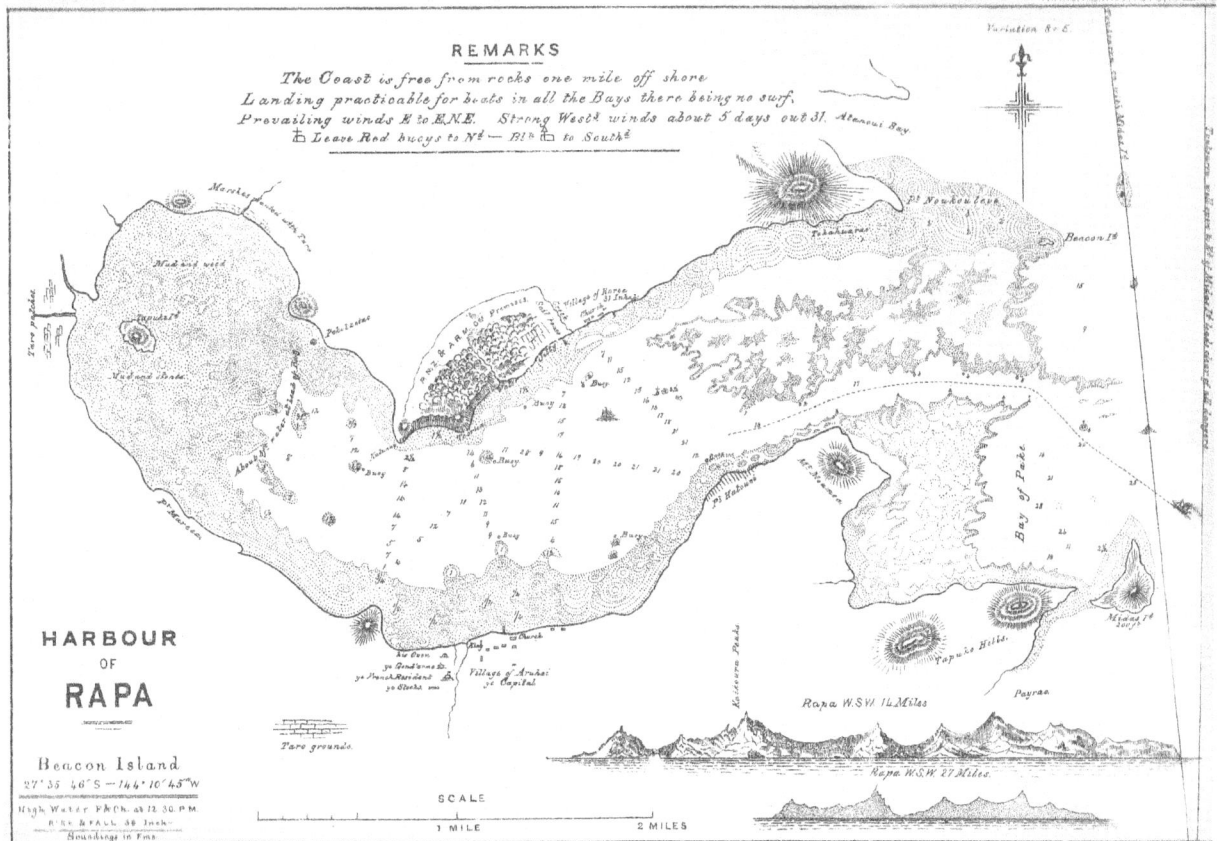

Figure 1.5. Plan of the harbour at Rapa, showing the main settlements (Hall 1868:facing p. 76).

The Rapan climate is relatively cool, cloudy and windy. Mean daily maximum temperatures at the coast vary from 26⁰C in February to 20⁰C in July, about 3⁰C below those elsewhere in the Australs. Rainfall is high, at 2840 mm per annum, and 156 days a year have more than 70% cloud cover. Rapa has mainly easterly conditions in the summer (60% of winds from an easterly quarter in February), but in the winter there are numerous westerlies (32% in July) that create cool, squally conditions (Haslam 1982:56). Wind directions change every few days and all winds from the east-northeast through south to the north-northwest are described by Rapans as 'cold and strong'; the only warm winds are from the north (Stokes n.d.:4).

Taken under French protection in 1867 and annexed in 1881, Rapa was once on the main shipping route across the Pacific between New Zealand and the Panama Canal. A coaling station was established in Ha'urei Harbour by the Panama–New Zealand & Australia Royal Mail Company (PNZARMC) in 1867, but as steamers were replaced by motor vessels, Rapa became more isolated again. It lacks suitable ground for an airfield, and is thus accessible only by sea. In recent times, the population has varied around a total of 400, most of it in Aurei village on the south side of Ha'urei Harbour (Figure 1.6). Cultivation of taro and fishing are the main subsistence pursuits, and there is also hunting of feral goats and cattle, along with some fowling along the cliffs, but the economy is subsidised heavily by the French Polynesian exchequer.

Discovering Rapan archaeology

The archaeological significance of Rapa has rested almost entirely upon its dramatic landscape of sculpted peaks along the mountain rim that almost encircles Ha'urei Harbour. These were observed as inhabited places during the first European visit in 1791, when they were described

Figure 1.6. Aurei village taken from the site of Ororangi just to the southeast and looking northwest up Ha'urei Bay. Photograph D.J. Kennett.

as 'fortified places resembling redoubts' and likened to New Zealand Maori pa (Vancouver 1791 in Lamb 1984:374). Ellis (1838:364) noted that the fortifications:

> are so constructed as to render them impregnable by any means which the assailants could bring against the besieged. Wars have not been frequent among them, and, when they have existed, have been less sanguinary than those among the islands to the northward.

By the late 19th century, the Rapan forts were being drawn into a popular discourse about ancient Polynesian history and ethnology that sought to link the remote islands of Polynesia to continental origins, either in Asia or South America, notably by reference to megalithic remains. This focused, of course, on Easter Island, but the apparent linguistic, and implicitly ancestral, connection of Rapa-nui (Big Rapa), as Easter Island was also known, to Rapa-iti (Little Rapa), as Rapa was then commonly called, coupled with massive structural remains in both places, encouraged speculation about ancient cultural connections between the two (see Smith 1910).

Captain John Vine Hall (1868:133) published a plan and drawings of two Rapan forts (Figures 1.7 and 1.8). The source of this material is unclear. He was on Rapa for only two days and did not visit any of the forts (Hall 1868:134). His information about them, and indeed most of his information about Rapa generally, seems to have come from his colleague in the PNZARMC, Captain McKellar, superintendent of the coaling station. Hall reported, nevertheless, that:

> On the summits of many of the steep hills are to be seen these square fortresses, some of very elaborate construction. But what is very singular, they are mostly solid within. The stones are well squared, of very large size, and well cemented. (Hall 1968:133)

Professor MacMillan Brown visited Rapa in 1917 (Best 1975:415), climbed up to the highest fort and found it a disappointingly rudimentary structure of small lava slabs, 'which had by long infiltration of some adhesive element almost solidified into the appearance of a natural rock'. Yet, distance lent enchantment to his view of others, for, like Captain Hall, he saw:

> ... away in the distance and across the harbour ... the outlines of much more elaborate forts, with terrace upon terrace, parapets and moats, and in almost every case there rose above all a similar solid tower which was evidently meant as an outlook into the valleys beyond. These forts were, in short, specimens of the rude megalithic masonry that I afterwards saw in the Society islands, and still more in the Marquesas, consisting of great stones roughly squared to fit their place without cement. (MacMillan Brown in Best 1975:415)

In 1921, the Routledges visited Rapa for 10 days while on a cruise of French Polynesia, with the object of finding traces of culture analogous to that of Easter Island (Routledge and Routledge 1921:438). They visited eight of the forts (known as *pare*, and recorded by them as *palé*) and described their general construction, noting that, far from being structures of stone blocks and cement, they were:

> ... in some cases little more than excavated terraces, of the nature of pure earthworks, but usually the summit of the hill has been turned into a round tower or keep. In such cases, the rock is sometimes utilized with no addition, or only a small amount of walling, but where this is not adequate the core has been faced ... with a dry masonry of basaltic fragments ... in all cases [the towers] are solid, and never contain apartments. (Routledge and Routledge 1921:454–455)

The *pare* each occupied one to three acres (0.4–1.2 ha) in extent and consisted of flights of terraces, up to six in a series, formed by simple cutting or by cut and fill with stone facings. Ditches restricted access into the fort. It was not clear to what extent the *pare* had been permanent villages, for:

> On the terraces of the forts there were never found buildings, nor foundations of buildings, nor even subterranean shelters worthy of the name; the only depression in the ground had evidently been excavated for purposes of cooking. Huts made of grass only would, no doubt, have disappeared, but would be peculiarly unsuitable for so exposed a position. It seems most probable that the forts were designed only to serve as a refuge for the inhabitants of the valley below in case of sudden raid or emergency. (Routledge and Routledge 1921:455)

As John Stokes (Chapter 2) was already at work on Rapa, the Routledges abandoned their plan to work there and moved to Mangareva. Stokes' (n.d.) notes and drafts for his proposed Bishop Museum monograph on Rapa show that he spent considerable time visiting the *pare* and locating other archaeological sites. The salient details of his work are noted in Chapters 2, 3 and 12.

Using Stokes' notes, Buck summarised the construction of *pare* thus:

> A ridge with a peak was selected and the summit levelled off to form the topmost terrace. The sides were cut down with digging implements of pointed wood and rude adzes of dyke basalt, until a second terrace could be formed of sufficient width to accommodate houses. The military architects of the day continued the plan of successive terraces, which necessitated high walls at the back. The razorback on the ridge leading to the peak was levelled off and the sides were cut to increase the steepness against assault. Deep ditches were cut across the main ridge on either side of the citadel to improve the defences. On the secondary ridges leading up to the main fort, further terraces were dug to provide house accommodation and outposts for defence. The back walls of the terraces, particularly near the citadel, were further

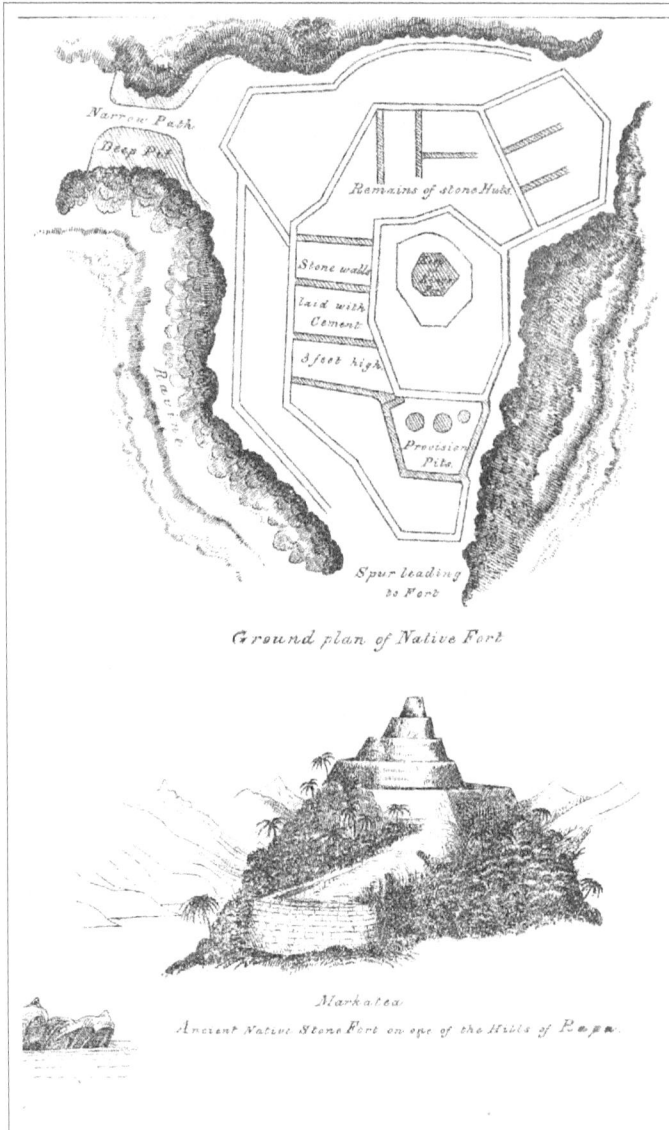

Figure 1.7. Drawing and plan of Markatea *pare* (Hall 1868:facing p. 80).

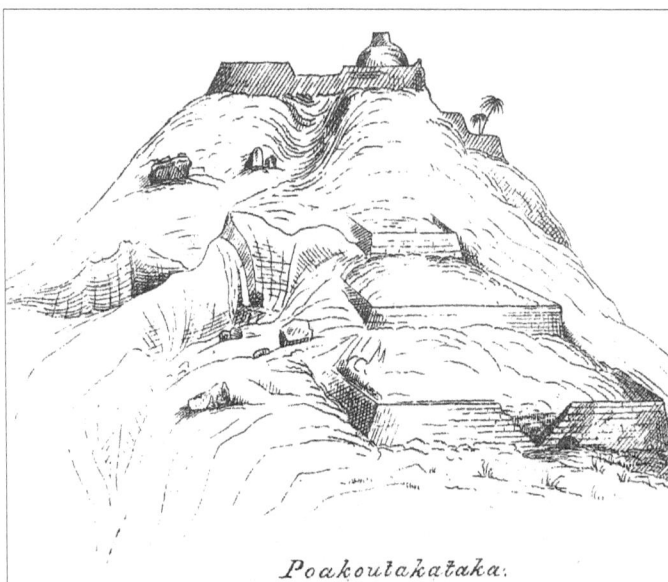

Figure 1.8. Sketch of Poakoutakataka fort (Hall 1868:facing p. 80).

reinforced with stone slabs carefully built in to protect the earth face against the detrition of wind and rain. Projecting stones formed footholds by which the defenders could retreat from terrace to terrace … On the topmost terrace of the citadel peak the high chief resided. (Buck 1954:183)

He went on to propose that, 'the peculiar geographical formation' of Rapa had induced the development of fortifications and, alluding to the similar pa of New Zealand, which he knew well, suggested that if he had managed to visit Rapa he might, 'have sensed an affinity that personal contact may convey with more subtlety than the written words of others' (Buck 1954:184). In later discussion, Buck (1954:288) implies a developmental sequence of fortifications in which the Rapan structures occupy a middle ground between ditched enclosures, as in Tonga, and more complex and permanently occupied Maori pa that combined terrace and ditch with palisades.

Earlier archaeological research

Although Stokes had cleared part of the *pare* Morongo Uta and put spade pits into a number of sites, the first systematic archaeological research on Rapa was by the Norwegian Archaeological Expedition to Easter Island and the East Pacific (1955–1956) organised by Thor Heyerdahl (Heyerdahl and Ferdon 1961, 1965). Ferdon (1965:12–13) recorded stone structures above the shore in Ha'urei Bay and surveyed the *pare* at Potaketake, Tapitanga and Kapitanga. Smith (1965a) investigated stone-outlined features which he thought had been houses and, from an exposed oven in a small terrace (R-16) at the head of Ha'urei Harbour, he took a charcoal sample that was radiocarbon dated to ca. AD 1337 (M-707), the earliest date obtained on Rapa at that time (Smith 1965a:83). Anapoiri, a burial cave, and an oven site were recorded in Mai'i' Bay. Historical and modern burials were also investigated by Smith (1965b), with scant regard to propriety or cultural sensitivity.

The main research was on the large *pare*, Morongo Uta (Mulloy 1965). This is a complex structure occupying several ridges and their junction. It consists mainly of terraces covering an area of about 5400 m²:

> For the most part they were constructed by excavating horizontal floors into the steep slopes and shoring up the front sides of these with dry masonry walls, or planing the ridge-tops and surrounding rectangular areas with masonry. On most of these terraces presumably stood houses of perishable materials. (Mulloy 1965:23)

The entire site was cleared, overburden – generally from terraces higher up – was removed and many of the displaced stones were used to repair damaged terraces. Mulloy (1965:25) determined that the site had been built from its core outward, beginning with the tower, and suggested that it was first constructed as a fort and then developed later into a fortified village. Basalt prisms were used preferentially in walls and facings, but as these became locally scarce, other stones were used as well. Low walls or parapets lined the outer edges of some terraces and other low walls acted as terrace partitions. The terraces or enclosures, approximately 85 in all (Mulloy 1965:53, cf. Stokes n.d., Chapter 2), are assumed to have been platforms for perishable houses. Fourteen stone-kerbed fireplaces, complete with ash and charcoal, were found, but the very wet weather that prevailed for much of the short field season precluded a systematic search for post holes.

Recovered on the terraces were 60 each of adzes (whole and fragmentary) and pounders. There were also some anvils and polishing stones, several probable sling stones and the charred remains of a net or netting bag. Mulloy (1965:57) commented on the scarcity of evidence for storage of food or water, and of deep midden deposits, suggesting that occupancy might have been temporary. Two samples produced radiocarbon dates of 310 ± 300 bp and 210 ± 200 bp (Mulloy 1965:59), which are essentially modern. They lend support to the Rapan belief that the site was occupied until the European era.

In summary, Ferdon (1965) proposed that the *pare*, as all the fortified peaks can be called (Ferdon (165:69) saw little in the distinction made by Stokes (n.d.) between fortified villages and refuge villages), were all built quite rapidly by large groups of organised labour and according to fairly simple architectural principles founded on the idea of a central fort surrounded by defended house terraces with defensive ditches externally and internally, and outlying clusters of undefended or lightly defended settlement (*auga*). Within the *pare*, small niches in the back walls of terraces held two lines each of four to seven small vertical stones, and a few similar features were recorded out on the open house terraces. These are almost certainly remains of shrines (Ferdon 1965:74–75).

The Rapan results of the Norwegian expeditionary research were soon brought into Heyerdahl's more general thesis of Polynesian origins. The *pare* were seen initially as 'mysterious pyramids' (Heyerdahl 1958:288) and, on excavation of Morongo Uta, as fortified villages, once occupied by oval huts, 'suspiciously reminiscent of Easter Island' (Heyerdahl 1958:341). Heyerdahl thought that the *pare* and other signs of habitation on the ridge-tops were evidence that the Rapan population feared an external enemy, perhaps from Easter Island, and that having 'built themselves curved reed houses and rectilinear stone ovens … instead of rectilinear houses and round earth ovens as on all the islands in the neighbourhood' (Heyerdahl 1958:343), they had come from Easter Island as refugees at the time of the traditional wars. It was implicit in this view that *pare* were built more or less at once by the colonising population, rather than later in the settlement sequence.

In 1984, in the course of a French survey of the Rapan environment, a radiocarbon date of 370 ± 60 bp was obtained from Tangarutu Cave, in Anarua Bay (Walczak 2001:250). In 1997, a French doctoral student, Jérôme Walczak (2001:297–303, 2003) undertook some small excavations at the site (Chapter 3). He also surveyed the remains of a number of the abandoned village sites and other structures on the low ground around Ha'urei Bay, in particular, which, added to some similar work by the Norwegian expedition, has helped to balance the early emphasis on forts.

However, the focus of Walczak's (2001, 2003) research in Rapa remained the nature of the *pare*: whether they were simply refuge forts necessitated by chiefly competition driven by population growth, which was the prevailing model, as articulated by Hanson (1974), or whether they had more complex functions, including ritual significance. Walczak discusses the latter proposition:

> Ces *pare* peuvent selon nous être assimilés à des villages d'altitude. Cet terrasses sont dominées par un promontoire central, qui pourrait être un centre religieux comparable à ce quétaient les *marae* dan d'autres îles de la Polynésie orientale. (Walczak 2003:30)

Assuming that the relatively young age of occupation at Tangarutu represents the era of early settlement, then the age of *pare* construction cannot have been much later, in which case, he concludes, it is unlikely to have been compelled by population pressure, and more probably reflects the needs of ritual use.

Enlarging on this theme, Walczak emphasises the difference between public religious cults, sustained largely by chiefs, and domestic religious observances, and proposes that it was not so much depopulation *per se*, but chiefly rejection of the public cults that led to post-European abandonment of those *pare*, or the higher levels of *pare*, that were associated with public ritual functions, while some *pare* or parts of them, remained in use until the later 19th century by the common people; Tevaitau being one (Walczak 2001:276). He concludes that *pare* were essentially symbolic in function, perhaps modelled on the form of the burial island of Tapui in Ha'urei Harbour. Consequently:

> Grâce à cette hypothèse, nous pouvons expliquer leur unité de style architectural, leur situation surélevée, leur configuration en réseau – voire en complexes – et l'absence de murallie ou de fossé protecteur. (Walczak 2001:277)

There are, therefore, several competing hypotheses concerning the origins and functions of fortified settlements in Rapa, as there are elsewhere, and an implication that they may have occupied more complex roles in Rapan society than purely defence.

The 2002 expedition

Although previous research had produced substantial information about Rapan archaeology, notably about the hill forts and associated material culture, there was little context in 2002 to interpret these impressive sites. Indeed, the archaeology of Rapa was essentially a story about castles in the air; coastal occupation and the concerns of life in the valleys had been barely noticed, much less investigated. The age of Rapan colonisation was unknown, the age of fort construction was largely unknown, the sequence of settlement pattern was based on a plausible proposition, but one that remained untested, and the human impact on the island environment and its possible consequences for settlement pattern and social development remained unexplored. Each of these issues is important, not only to understanding the prehistory of Rapa, but also in the wider contexts of East and South Polynesian prehistory. The project was organised, consequently, into three research areas: island colonisation, the origins of fortification, and trends in environmental change. This had the coincidental advantage of dividing fieldwork into the three main zones, respectively, of the Rapan landscape: the bays and harbour, the high ground, and the valleys and swamps.

Island colonisation

The key issue of East and South Polynesian colonisation, though far from the only one, was the chronology. Earlier research (see summary by Kirch 1986; Kirch and Kahn 2007) had reached a consensus that colonisation began in the early first millennium AD, if not earlier, in tropical East Polynesia and there were arguments for exploration of New Zealand about the same time (Sutton 1987; Holdaway 1999). Yet, renewed chronological research on samples from the same provenances of key sites regarded as early, such as Haatuatua and Hane in the Marquesas (Rolett and Conte 1995; Anderson and Sinoto 2002), Vaitootia-Faahia and Maupiti in the Societies (Anderson et al. 1999; Anderson and Sinoto 2002), South Point in Hawaii (Dye 1992), Anakena on Easter Island (Steadman et al. 1994) and Papatowai and Wairau Bar in New Zealand (Anderson and Smith 1992; Higham et al. 1999), produced manifestly later dates, suggesting no colonisation of East Polynesia before about AD 900–1000 (Anderson and Sinoto 2002), nor of South Polynesia before AD 1200 (Anderson 2000, 2006), or possibly later (Wilmshurst et al. 2011). As Rapa is both unusually remote and well south of central East Polynesia, it was a moot point whether its colonisation chronology was closer to that of South or that of East Polynesia, an issue that has interesting implications for early migration pace and patterning.

In addition to chronology, we wanted to know about the behaviour of the early settlers. Where did they live on Rapa and was there evidence of houses and other structures? Did agriculture begin with colonisation or somewhat later? Was there evidence of faunal depletion or extinction, of land birds especially? Were turtles, marine mammals, and large fish and shellfish proportionately more common in early habitation levels? Were the rather distinctive Rapan adzes an early development? Was there any evidence of distant contacts, in the form of obsidian or other exotic materials or artefacts?

Based on research in other Pacific Island groups, we predicted that early colonists would have preferred settling on the coast in relatively sheltered bays with easily accessible fishing, reliable freshwater sources and near prime agricultural lands. We focused first on Ha'urei Bay, which stands out as meeting those criteria and which is, of course, the preferred locus of modern habitation and gardening. We travelled around the outside coast of Rapa in several expeditions by open boat, and also by walking over the ridges from the harbour, in order to investigate each bay for potential evidence of early settlement (Chapter 3). The results of this research, almost entirely around the coast, are described in Chapters 3–9.

Origins of fortification

Competition for resources is an important driving force in the development of social and political complexity (Kennett and Kennett 2000) and it has been argued repeatedly that it played a crucial role in the development of Pacific Island chiefdoms (Kirch 1984; Rechtman 1992; Ladefoged 1993; Field 1998, 2004; Kuhlken 1999). Fortified hilltop villages in remote Oceania provide the most obvious archaeological evidence for warfare prior to European contact and indicate that inter-village conflict was an important component of social and political life (Green 1967; Best 1993; Kirch 1994; Burley 1998), although recently a more nuanced understanding of the complex roles of fortified sites has begun to emerge (Walczak 2001; Sutton et al. 2003).

The hyper-fortified nature of Rapa has often been used as an example of Polynesian inter-village hostilities (Kirch 1984:212). But these fortifications had not been investigated in sufficient depth to understand their age, origins or development. The archaeological studies by the Norwegian expedition (Heyerdahl and Ferdon 1965) revealed the remains of house platforms, hearths and habitation debris at the *pare*, but a basic chronological framework, necessary to understand the development of these villages, was lacking. In addition, artefact analysis was confined to large objects and no detailed midden constituent work was conducted.

The primary objective of our fieldwork was to recover organic material suitable for constructing a radiocarbon chronology of fortification on Rapa. We mapped and tested (auger probes and small sample test units) 14 hilltop fortifications to recover organic material for AMS radiocarbon dating (see Chapters 11 and 12). We also excavated larger test units at four hilltop village sites (Tevaitau, Ororangi, Potaketake and Tapitanga) to obtain additional information about the distribution of artefacts and ecofacts (Chapter 12). IKONOS and Quickbird satellite imagery and a laser transit were used to map the domestic and defensive features at these locations. Based on previous excavations at Morongo Uta, it appeared that the deposits were relatively shallow (ca. 1 m, Mulloy 1965). A standard bucket auger was used to probe subsurface deposits for concentrations of organic material (shell or charcoal) necessary for AMS radiocarbon dating. When concentrations of material were encountered, small test units (50 x 50 cm, larger if necessary) were excavated to obtain samples from stratigraphically intact deposits.

Palaeoenvironmental change

Recovery and analysis of sedimentary cores for inorganic and organic materials indicative of former environments is a long-established and well-proven technique in palaeoenvironmental research. Debate about its application to Polynesian issues (e.g. Kirch and Ellison 1993; Parkes

1998; McGlone and Wilmshurst 1999; Kirch 2007 *contra* Anderson 1994, 1995; Prebble 2007) highlighted some problems in interpretation and dating which have been addressed in more recent research. As Rapa was once covered by temperate rainforest but at some point in the prehistoric past became almost completely denuded of forest, pollen analysis was the most suitable approach to that sequence. Pollen analysis of shifts in plant communities provides a basis for the detection of anthropogenic influence in deforestation and provides a proxy for the history of agricultural expansion (Hope 1996; Hope and Pask 1998).

The general strategy of the Rapan project in this matter was to focus on the wetlands around the head of Ha'urei Harbour, on the assumption that they, as the largest and most readily accessible area of coastal flats, would have been the first choice for introduction of agriculture and then for later development of intensive taro cultivation. Other bays where wetlands were cored included Angatakuri, Iri, Anarua, Pariati, Agairao and Akatanui. The methods and results of our field and analytical research are described in Chapter 10.

Limitations

The data reported here come from small samples, particularly the archaeological data that arose from excavations, which, in other circumstances, might be regarded as hardly more than test pits. Another field season, at least, would have been desirable in several respects: to extend excavations in the main coastal site at Tangarutu, to investigate terraces and other features, especially around the harbour, which appear to represent former villages and isolated houses, to extend excavations on the extensive *pare* sites, and to undertake systematic research on the agricultural systems. However, as the project occurred at a time when archaeological funding for Polynesian projects was especially scarce and the attention of the principal investigators was being drawn elsewhere, this was just not possible. This monograph, then, should be regarded as an interim description of the prehistory of Rapa.

Acknowledgements

The field team (Figure 1.9), consisted of Atholl Anderson and Matiu Prebble (The Australian National University), Douglas Kennett, Yann Doignan, Sarah McClure and Nathan Wilson (University of Oregon), and Roti (Rosine) Oitokaia (Université de Polynésie Française). Eric Conte (Université de Polynésie Française) was involved in the development of the project and organised the expedition travel from and to Tahiti, but he was unable to participate in the fieldwork. Including several days in Papeete, and also in Tubuai, the expedition was from July 1 to August 25, 2002, of which 43 days were spent on Rapa.

The expedition was funded primarily by the National Geographic Society (Grant 7059–01), to which our gratitude is due, and we also thank the universities represented for their supporting subventions. For a research permit, and permission to remove material temporarily from French Polynesia, we thank the Mission d'Aide Financière et de Coopération Régionale of the Haut-Commissariat de la République en Polynésie Française, and also Martine Rattinassamy (Le Chef de Service) and Tamara Maric of the Service de la Culture et du Patrimoine in Tahiti.

On Rapa, we received permission to undertake our research from the Mayor and Council. Our stay was made both profitable and pleasurable by our generous hosts, Annette and Freddy Riaria and Faraire Cerdan. For assistance in particular matters, we thank Freddy Riaria for arranging travel by boat around the island, and Teraura Oitokaia for information on traditional fishing, fowling and shellfishing.

For collaboration in post-fieldwork research we thank: Alan Tennyson (Te Papa, National Museum of New Zealand), Yolanda Vogel (New Zealand Historic Places Trust and University of Otago), Katherine Szabó (ANU and University of Wollongong), Judith Cameron (ANU), Jacob Bartruff (University of Oregon), Virginia Butler (Portland State University), Bruce Winterhalder (University of California, Davis) and John Southon (University of California, Irvine). We are also grateful for Rusty Van Rossman's assistance with drawings, graphics and maps, and for comment on the manuscript by Terry Hunt (University of Hawaii at Manoa), and Richard Walter (University of Otago).

Figure 1.9. The 2002 Rapan field team on Tubuai Island before embarking for Rapa. Left to right, back row Atholl Anderson, Yann Doignan, Douglas J. Kennett, Matiu Prebble; front row Nathan Wilson, Sarah B. McClure, Rosine Oitokaia.

References

Anderson, A.J. 1994. Palaeoenvironmental evidence of island colonization: a response. *Antiquity* 68:845–847.

Anderson, A.J. 1995. Current approaches in East Polynesian colonization research. *Journal of the Polynesian Society* 104:110–132.

Anderson, A.J. 2000. The advent chronology of south Polynesia. In: Wallin, P. and Martinsson-Wallin, H. (eds), *Essays in honour of Arne Skjolsvold 75 years.* Occasional Papers of the Kon-Tiki Museum 5:73–82.

Anderson, A.J. 2002. Faunal collapse, landscape change and settlement history in Remote Oceania *World Archaeology* 33:375–390.

Anderson, A.J. 2006. Retrievable time: prehistoric colonization of South Polynesia from the outside in and the inside out. In: Ballantyne, T. and Moloughney, B. (eds), *Disputed Histories: imagining New Zealand's pasts,* pp. 25–41. University of Otago Press, Dunedin.

Anderson, A.J. and Smith, I.W.G. 1992. The Papatowai site: new evidence and interpretations. *Journal of the Polynesian Society* 101:129–158.

Anderson, A.J., Conte, E., Clark, G.R., Sinoto, Y. and Petchey, F.J. 1999. Renewed excavations at Motu Paeao, Maupiti Island, French Polynesia: preliminary results. *New Zealand Journal of Archaeology* 21:47–66.

Anderson, A.J. and Sinoto, Y.H. 2002. New radiocarbon ages of colonization sites in East Polynesia. *Asian Perspectives* 41:242–257.

Best, E. 1975. *The Pa Maori.* Government Printer, Wellington.

Best, S. 1993. At the Halls of the Mountain Kings. Fijian and Samoan Fortifications: Comparison and Analysis. *The Journal of the Polynesian Society* 102(4):385–447.

Buck, Sir P.H. 1954. *Vikings of the Sunrise.* Whitcombe and Tombs, Christchurch.

Burley, D.V. 1998. Tongan Archaeology and the Tongan Past, 2850–150 B.P. *Journal of World Prehistory* 12(3):337–392.

Dye, T. 1992. The South Point radiocarbon dates thirty years later. *New Zealand Journal of Archaeology* 14:89–97.

Ellis, W. 1838. *Polynesian Researches, during a residence of nearly eight years in the Society and Sandwich Islands.* Volume III, Fisher, Son and Jackson, London.

Ferdon, E.N. 1965a. Report 2: A reconnaissance survey of three fortified hilltop villages. In: Heyerdahl, T. and Ferdon, E.W. (eds), *Reports of the Norwegian Archaeological Expedition to Easter Island and the East Pacific,* Volume 2 Miscellaneous Papers, pp. 9–21. Monographs of the School of American Research and the Kon-Tiki Museum, 24 Pt. 2, Esselte AB, Stockholm.

Ferdon, E.N. 1965b. Report 4: A summary of Rapa Iti fortified villages. In: Heyerdahl, T. and Ferdon, E.W. (eds), *Reports of the Norwegian Archaeological Expedition to Easter Island and the East Pacific,* Volume 2 Miscellaneous Papers, pp. 69–87. Monographs of the School of American Research and the Kon-Tiki Museum, 24 Pt. 2, Esselte AB, Stockholm.

Field, J.S. 1998. Natural and Constructed Defenses in Fijian Fortifications. *Asian Perspectives* 37:32–58.

Field, J.S. 2004. Environmental and climatic considerations: a hypothesis for conflict and the emergence of social complexity in Fijian prehistory. *Journal of Anthropological Archaeology* 23:79–99.

Green, R.C. 1967. Fortification in Other Parts of Tropical Polynesia. *New Zealand Archaeological Association Newsletter* 10:96–113.

Hall, J.V. 1868. On the island of Rapa. *Transactions of the New Zealand Institute* 1:128–134.

Hanson, F.A. 1970. *Rapan Lifeways: society and history on a Polynesian island.* Little and Brown, Boston.

Haslam, D.W. 1982. *Pacific Islands Pilot, Volume III.* Hydrographer of the Navy, Taunton.

Heyerdahl, T. 1958. *Aku-Aku: The Secret of Easter Island.* Allen and Unwin, London.

Heyerdahl, T. and Ferdon, E.W. (eds), 1965. *Reports of the Norwegian Archaeological Expedition to Easter Island and the East Pacific,* Volume 2 Miscellaneous Papers. Monographs of the School of American Research and the Kon-Tiki Museum, 24 Pt. 2, Esselte AB, Stockholm.

Higham, T.G.F., Anderson, A.J. and Jacomb, C. 1999. Dating the First New Zealanders: the chronology of Wairau Bar. *Antiquity* 73:420–427.

Holdaway, R.N. 1999. A spatio-temporal model for the invasion of the New Zealand archipelago by the Pacific rat *Rattus exulans*. *Journal of the Royal Society of New Zealand* 29:91–105.

Hope, G.S. 1996. Quaternary change and historical biogeography of Pacific Islands. In: Keast, A. and Miller, S.E. (eds), *The Origin and Evolution of Pacific Island Biotas, New Guinea to Eastern Polynesia*. SPB Publishing, Amsterdam.

Hope, G.S. and Pask, J. 1998. Tropical Vegetational Change in the late Pleistocene of New Caledonia. *Palaeogeography, Palaeoclimatology, Palaeoecology* 142:1–21.

Kennett, D.J., Anderson, A.J., Prebble, M. and Conte, E. 2003. La colonization et les fortifications de Rapa. In: Marchesi, H. (ed), *Bilan de la recherché archeologique en Polynesie francaise*, pp. 165–170. Dossier d'Archéologie Polynésienne 2. Service de la Culture et du Patrimoine, Punaauia.

Kennett, D., Anderson, A.J., Prebble, M., Conte, E. and Southon, J. 2006. Prehistoric human impacts on Rapa, French Polynesia. *Antiquity* 80:1–15

Kennett, D.J. and Kennett, J.P. 2000. Competitive and Cooperative Responses to Climatic Instability in Coastal Southern California. *American Antiquity* 65:379–395.

Kirch, P.V. 1984. *The Evolution of the Polynesian Chiefdoms*. Cambridge University Press, Cambridge.

Kirch, P.V. 1986. Rethinking East Polynesian Prehistory. *Journal of the Polynesian Society* 95:9–40.

Kirch, P.V. and Ellison, J. 1994. Palaeoenvironmental evidence for human colonization of remote Oceanic islands. *Antiquity* 68:310–321.

Kirch, P.V. and Kahn, J.G. 2007. Advances in Polynesian Prehistory: Assessment of the Past Decade (1993–2004). *Journal of Archaeological Research* 15:191–238.

Kooijman, S. 1972. *Tapa in Polynesia*. B.P. Bishop Museum Bulletin 234, Honolulu.

Kuhlken, R. 1999. Warfare and Intensive Agriculture in Fiji. In: Gosden, C. and Hather, J. (eds), *The Prehistory of Food: Appetites for Change*. Routledge: Taylor and Francis Group, New York.

Ladefoged, T.N. 1993. Evolutionary Process in an Oceanic Chiefdom: Intergroup Aggression and Political Integration in Traditional Rotuman Society. Unpublished PhD Dissertation, University of Hawaii.

Lamb, W.K. (ed), 1984. George Vancouver, *A Voyage of Discovery to the North Pacific Ocean and Round the World 1791–1795*, Volume I. The Hakluyt Society, London.

McGlone, M.S. and Wilmshurst, J.M. 1999. Dating initial Maori environmental impact in New Zealand *Quaternary International* 59:5–16.

Mulloy, W. 1965. Report 3: The fortified village of Morongo Uta. In: Heyerdahl, T. and Ferdon, E.W. (eds), *Reports of the Norwegian Archaeological Expedition to Easter Island and the East Pacific*, Volume 2 Miscellaneous Papers, pp. 23–68. Monographs of the School of American Research and the Kon-Tiki Museum, 24 Pt. 2, Esselte AB, Stockholm.

Naval Intelligence Division 1943. *Pacific Islands. Volume II Eastern Pacific*. B.R. 519 B (Restricted) Geographical Handbook Series. United States Navy, Washington DC.

Parkes, A. 1998. Environmental change and the impact of Polynesian colonization: sedimentary records from central Polynesia. In: Kirch, P.V. and Hunt, T.L. (eds), *Historical Ecology in the Pacific Islands: prehistoric environmental and landscape change*, pp. 166–199. Yale University Press, New Haven.

Paulding, H. 1831. *Journal of a cruise of the United States Schooner Dolphin, among the islands of the Pacific Ocean* etc. G. & C. & H. Carvill, New York.

Prebble, M.J. 2005. Islands, Floras and History: an environmental history of plant introductions and extinction on the Austral Islands, French Polynesia. Unpublished PhD dissertation, The Australian National University, Canberra.

Rechtman, R.B. 1992. The Evolution of Sociopolitical Complexity in the Fiji Islands. Unpublished PhD dissertation, University of California, Los Angeles.

Rolett, B.V. and Conte, E. 1995. Renewed investigation of the Haatuatua Dune (Nuku Hiva, Marquesas Islands): a key site in Polynesian prehistory. *Journal of the Polynesian Society* 104:195–228.

Routledge, S. and Routledge, K. 1921. Notes on some archaeological remains in the Society and Austral Islands. *Journal of the Royal Anthropological Institute of Great Britain and Ireland* 51:438–455.

Smith, C.S. 1965a. Report 5: Test excavations and surveys of miscellaneous sites on the island of Rapa Iti. In: Heyerdahl, T. and Ferdon, E.W. (eds), *Reports of the Norwegian Archaeological Expedition to Easter Island and the East Pacific*, Volume 2 Miscellaneous Papers, pp. 77–87. Monographs of the School of American Research and the Kon-Tiki Museum, 24 Pt. 2, Esselte AB, Stockholm.

Smith, C.S. 1965b. Report 6: The burial complex on the island of Rapa Iti. In: Heyerdahl, T. and Ferdon, E.W. (eds), *Reports of the Norwegian Archaeological Expedition to Easter Island and the East Pacific*, Volume 2 Miscellaneous Papers, pp. 89–95. Monographs of the School of American Research and the Kon-Tiki Museum, 24 Pt. 2, Esselte AB, Stockholm.

Smith, S.P. 1910. Easter Island (Rapa-Nui) and Rapa (Rapa-Iti) Island. *Journal of the Polynesian Society* 19:171–175.

Steadman, D., Vargas, P. and Cristino, C. 1994. Stratigraphy, chronology and cultural context of an early faunal assemblage from Easter Island. *Asian Perspectives* 33:79–96.

Stokes, J.F.G. n.d. *Ethnology of Rapa Island*. Unpublished draft of B.P. Bishop Museum Bulletin of the Bayard Dominick Expedition. Five unbound volumes with multiple pagination (page numbers used here are generally the circled numbers). B.P. Bishop Museum, Honolulu.

Sutton, D.G. 1987. A paradigmatic shift in Polynesian prehistory: implications for New Zealand. *New Zealand Journal of Archaeology* 9:135–155.

Sutton, D.G., Furey, L. and Marshall, Y. 2003. *The Archaeology of Pouerua*. Auckland University Press, Auckland.

Walczak, J. 2001. Le peuplement de la Polynésie orientale. Une tentative d'approche historique par les exemples de Tahiti et de Rapa (Polynésie française). Unpublished PhD dissertation, University of Paris I – Pantheon Sorbonne, Paris.

Walczak, J. 2003. Presentation des données actuelles sur la préhistoire de Rapa Iti (archiple des Australes-Polynésie Française). In: Orliac, C. (ed), *Archéologie en océanie insulaire: peuplement, sociétés et paysages*, pp. 28–45. Editions Artcom, Paris.

Wilmshurst, J.M., Hunt, T.L., Lipo, C.P. and Anderson, A.J. 2011. High-precision radiocarbon dating shows recent and rapid initial human colonization of East Polynesia. *Proceedings of the National Academy of Sciences* 108(5):1815–20.

2

'Dwelling carelessly, quiet and secure'
A brief ethnohistory of Rapa Island, French Polynesia, AD 1791–1840

Atholl Anderson

Department of Archaeology and Natural History, Research School of Pacific and Asian Studies,
The Australian National University, Canberra, Australia, atholl.anderson@anu.edu.au

Introduction

In 1826, the first European missionary to Rapa, the Rev. John Davies, quoted Judges 18:7 in seeing the Rapans as 'dwelling carelessly, quiet and secure, and having no business with any man' (in Stokes n.d.:28; an idiomatic rendering of the passage). It was to some extent, possibly to a great extent, quite illusory. Rapa was certainly isolated by comparison with most of East Polynesia, and it was small, mountainous and relatively cold, but even the first European visitors found that Rapans exhibited evidence of contact with the outside world, and within Rapan traditions, historical observations and ethnographic data which together form the stuff of ethnohistory, the theme of contact and change is illustrated continually.

Rapan society was East Polynesian in ancestry and culture. Rapans spoke an East Polynesian language, but its closest affinities were puzzling for a long time. The earliest historical contacts with Rapans showed that they found both Hawaiian and Tahitian largely unintelligible and later characterisation of Rapan by European scholars was confused because of the early introduction of Tahitian by missionaries and, after 1863, of other Polynesian languages by Tongans, Tokelauans and Cook Islanders, whose descendants came eventually to represent nearly half of the population (Stokes 1955). Samuel Stutchbury had observed, presciently, in 1826 (in Richards 2004:5) that the Rapan language was 'something resembling the Marquesan', but Horatio Hale (1968:141), about 1840, 'obtained at Tahiti, from a native of Rapa, a brief vocabulary of the language spoken there, which turns out to be, with a few verbal exceptions, pure Rarotongan, and this in its minute peculiarities', while the missionaries William Ellis (1838) and M. Russell (1852:205) thought that Rapan was closer to Maori than Tahitian. In the event, modern analysis shows that Rapan is part of the group of languages that also includes Mangarevan, east Tuamotuan and Easter Island, and probably once included languages on Pitcairn and Henderson islands, which derive from 'proto Southeastern Polynesian'. This group was probably the first to be differentiated within proto East Polynesian (Fischer 2001), quite probably because of the relative remoteness of the southeastern islands from the central archipelagos.

Rapan social organisation was divided historically (as described by Hanson 1970:19–22; Hanson and Ghasarian 2007:59–60) among clans or ramages (*kopu*), each of which normally occupied a single valley and adjacent fishing waters, the territory being commanded by a hill fort or fortified village (*pare maunga, pare tamaki* or *pa tamaki*). The clans recognised membership by unrestricted cognatic descent (i.e. through lineages of both parents) and access to land and other resources by primary, active (*arakaa*) and secondary, latent (*moekopu*) rights. Primary rights devolved both by descent and residence and held the clan together as a land-holding and defending unit. Such groups of territorial definition and ambilateral descent are also called 'ramages', the term Hanson (1970) prefers, but 'clan' is used in the historical sources and will be adopted here. The Rapan clan was headed by an *ariki* whose spiritual authority arose primogeniturally from the clan ancestor, but whose practical authority in peace and war was mediated through the consensus of family elders, the *hui ragatira* (Hanson 1970:22). The Rapan traditions of pre-European events reflect the competitive development of the historical clans, of which perhaps 18–22 existed by the arrival of Europeans (Hanson 1970:19).

Rapan traditions

During his stay on Rapa (April 1921–January 1922), as part of the Bayard Dominick Expedition to the Austral Islands by the B.P. Bishop Museum, John Stokes (n.d.:Preface), accompanied by his wife Margaret Stokes, collected historical traditions, mainly it seems from the official island chief, Pataritari. In addition, Stokes collaborated with the linguist, Frank Stimson, who checked Stokes' material with Rapans living in Papeete. These included Teraau, son of the last main 'king' of Rapa, Terakau III, who died in 1887 (Queen Ruirau had succeeded but was deposed after several months when Rapa was annexed to France in June 1887). Teraau, born 1862, traced his descent primarily from the Gaitapana line, but he and his relatives, living in Tahiti, were also descended from the clan Takatakatea, which Gaitapana had eclipsed. Others who assisted Stokes were the Rapan men, Kareka (born 1867), Faaora (born 1865) and Gariki, plus Mato, 'a native of Fakaho' (Fakaofo in the Tokelaus) who arrived on Rapa in 1864 as part of a group of Polynesians returning from Peru, and whom Stokes regarded as his most reliable informant. Stokes' account of Rapan traditions is the fullest available, but differs in its assignment of some clan origins to multiple landfalls with that of Caillot (1932), who regarded all pre-European Rapans as descendants of a single population (Hanson 1970:23 concludes that the data are inadequate to decide the matter).

Accounts of initial colonisation obtained by Stokes (n.d.:1–28, 918–924, 951–954) said that the first man to arrive on Rapa was Tiki (a common Polynesian mythological ancestor, often regarded as the first man), who came from Avaiki (Hawaiki) in the Tuamotus and married a Rapan woman. This is essentially a creation myth. They had two daughters, who also produced a male and female child by Tiki, and these became the progenitors of all Rapans, but the boy, Tamatiki, sailed off to Easter Island. There are other accounts of voyages to Easter Island or New Zealand, by Temarago, and of Hotumatua, the Easter Island ancestor, as having been king of Rapa.

The first settlers of Rapa included several peaceful peoples, such as the legendary Mana'une, who were discovered by the East Polynesian ancestral figure, Hiro (or Iro). Hiro stayed briefly in Rapa, and may have left a son there, while moving around the other Austral islands. By genealogical reckoning, in which Stokes (n.d.) used the Rarotongan traditions accumulated by

J.B. Stair (1895) and S.P. Smith (1899), this Hiro is thought most likely to have been the cousin of the equally well-travelled Tangiia, and is dated to about AD 1250, or possibly to about AD 1100. Buck (1954:119) has Tangiia searching for the son of Hiro, reputedly on Rapa, in the mid-13th century. While Stokes (n.d.:26) accepted the Hiro story as well-documented by 19th century sources, he doubted the historical validity of others, including those collected in his day from informants who were 'liable to include in the record what they think at the time and are frequently unaware of the necessity of segregating ancient and modern information'.

Nevertheless, Stokes' (n.d.:700–709) arrangement of accounts of the inter-clan history of Rapa, although noting disputed stories by informants of opposing lineages at various points, is probably as close to a chronicle of traditional, and putatively historical, events as we may get on the surviving evidence. He says that some of Hiro's followers remained on Rapa, intermarrying with the indigenous people and forming the Mato clan, which lived in the northern lands centred on Tupuaki Bay. About the same time, ancestors of the Takatakatea clan arrived at Anarua or Iri on the west coast and, by intermarriage, expanded into the southern and eastern areas, contesting with Ngate Mato the ownership of the flat land at the head of Ha'urei Harbour. No *pare* (hill forts) were built at this time.

The early ascendant clan was Takatakatea. Sometime after it, ancestors of the Taukina clan arrived on the western coast and settled among Takatakatea, but eventually disagreements arose and warfare began. Takatakatea was driven out of the northwestern bays and constructed *pare* at Karere, Paoreore, Motu and Rekie, then later at Mititipeiru, Napiri, west Pukutaketake, Pukumaga and Nogoorupe. The expanding Taukina people, represented by their descendant clans of Tipi and Okopou, continued to move southeast. Okopou occupied the Ha'urei lands in the main harbour, and a strip across the main ridge to their earlier base at Iri Bay. The clan wrested control of *pare* at Nogoorupe and Takitaga from Takatakatea, who then re-took them, and, by managing to hold on to Morongo Uta and Pukutaketake, created an uneasy stalemate in the west. The Tipi clan moved east and built *pare* at Ruatara and Vairu. At this point, Rapa was divided into a Takatakatea territory in the south and southwest, with Tipi and its allies in the north and east, and a small group of the Mato clan at Taratu, between them. The Tipi a Manumanu (Tipi a Tepaiamarama) clan was the strongest and to it is attributed the first historical high chief, Temarogo.

Several generations later, the Aureka people, who claimed descent from Tiki but probably included new arrivals as well, formed a clan based on the eastern stronghold at Pukumia and sought to bring the other clans under their control. Aureka built the *pare* at Tevaitau and from it defeated Okopou in their nearby stronghold at Napiri, and then the Tipi clans at Anarua. The Aureka clan, known later as Gaitapana, began its own kingly line with Aurariki I, dated about 1600–1650, and that dynasty persisted until 1887 through, successively, Aurariki II–VII and then Terakau I (AD 1775–1825), who lived through the period of European discovery and arrival.

European discovery

The European discovery of Rapa began on December 22, 1791. Captain George Vancouver, HMS *Discovery*, sailing a wide northeasterly track from New Zealand, saw three small islands that, as he sailed closer, coalesced into Rapa Island (Figure 2.1). Vancouver was familiar with Polynesians, having sailed on Cook's second and third voyages (1772–75, 1776–79), and he had no hesitation in seeking contact with the inhabitants. At 3 pm, about three nautical miles off the western shore, three canoes arrived, their crews unwilling to board the ship but signalling the ship's crew towards land. Vancouver then sailed nearer to shore and several canoes paddled out, from one of which a man boarded the *Discovery*, touched noses with Vancouver, and was given an iron adze. Soon many men boarded and exchange began (Figure 2.2):

> They all seemed perfectly well acquainted with the uses to which they could apply iron, and how to estimate its value amongst themselves; as also in the manner in which it was regarded by Europeans. They made no scruple, even with some force, to take articles of iron out of our hands; and in lieu of them with great courtesy and address presented, in return, some few fish, fishing-hooks, lines, and other trifles, which they seemed to wish should be accepted as presents, and not received in exchange. Looking-glasses, beads and other trinkets of little importance, at first attracted their attention, and were gladly accepted; but no sooner did they discover that articles made of iron were common amongst us, than they refused all other presents, and wanted to barter every other gift for iron. I could not prevail on any of them to accept a few medals.
>
> Their visit seemed prompted only by curiosity, as they were completely unarmed, and brought with them (except the few fish &c) neither articles of food nor manufacture. A few spears and a club or two, were seen in one or two of the canoes only; two or three indifferent slings for stones were also noticed; with which they parted without the least reluctance. (Vancouver in Lamb 1984:372–373)

The Rapan men attempted to carry off anchors, cannons and other large iron articles, the weight of which surprised and frustrated them. They also stole what they could but had little means of concealment. Some opened the shirts of sailors, evidently to see whether they were women (Lamb 1984:372). Vancouver thought that the men most resembled Tongans. An Hawaiian lad, Towereroo, on board *Discovery* was hardly able to understand the Rapan language, but he had been in England since 1789. Vancouver attempted, with some difficulty and eventual uncertainty, to obtain the name of the island; 'at length I had reason to believe the name of the island was Oparo; and that of their chief *Korie*' (Lamb 1984:373). At 5 pm, after only two hours of contact, *Discovery* sailed off to the north, the officers noticing part of the north coast of the island as she departed. Vancouver summarised his impressions of Rapa thus:

> Its principal character is a cluster of high craggy mountains, with perpendicular cliffs nearly from their summits to the sea [high cliffs are especially prominent on the northwest coast] … the vacancies between the mountains would more probably be termed chasms than vallies, in which there was no great appearance of plenty, fertility or cultivation; they were chiefly clothed with shrubs and dwarf trees. Neither the plantain nor other spontaneous vegetable productions common to the inhabited tropical islands, presented themselves. The tops of six of the highest hills bore the appearance of fortified places, resembling redoubts [George Hewett, Surgeon's First Mate on the *Discovery* thought these were probably, 'like the hippahs of New Zealand' (Lamb 1984:374, fn 3)]; having a sort of block house, in the shape of an English glasshouse, in the centre of each with rows of pallisadoes a considerable way down the sides

Figure 2.1. A sketch of Rapa drawn on the *Discovery* expedition 1791 (Lamb 1984 Volume 1:Plate 18 'The island of Oparo'). Published with the permission of the Hakluyt Society and the State Library of New South Wales (item MRB/Q910.4/6 A/1).

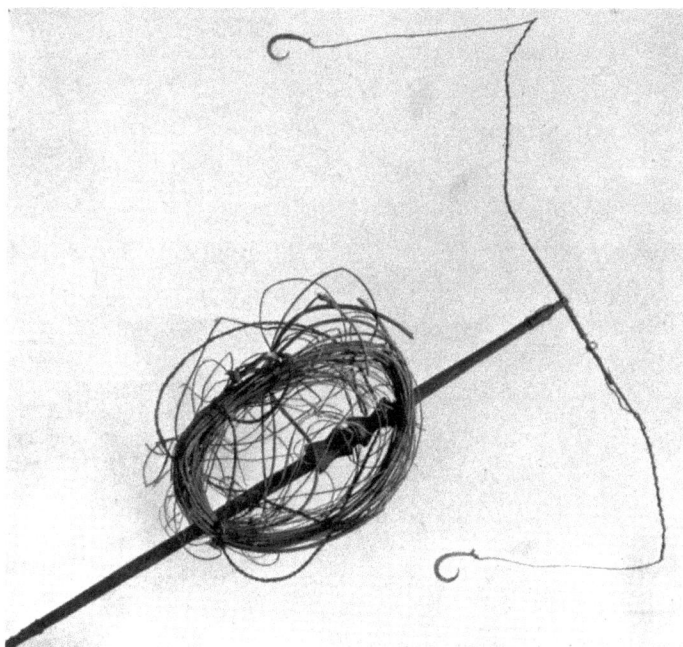

Figure 2.2. A fishing device collected at Rapa on the Vancouver expedition, 1791 (Beasley 1928:Plate LXXII). It consists of a fibre strip line, a wooden spreader, and two small shell bait hooks, which are attached by cordage.

of the hills, nearly at equal distances. These, overhanging, seemed intended for advanced works, and apparently capable of defending the citadel by a few against a numerous host of assailants. On all of them we noticed people, as if on duty, constantly moving about ... [the block houses] were sufficiently large to lodge a considerable number of persons, and were the only habitations we saw. Yet from the number of canoes that in so short a time assembled around us ... [we could infer] ... that the shores and not those fortified hills which appeared to be in the center of the island [Vancouver was unaware of the central harbour] would be preferred for their general residence. We saw about thirty double and single canoes, though most of them were of the double sort: the single canoes were supported by an outrigger on one side, and all built much after the fashion of the Society Islands, without having their very high sterns, though the sterns of some of these were considerably elevated; and their bows were not without some little ornament. They were very neatly constructed, although the narrowest canoes I ever saw. (Vancouver in Lamb 1984:374)

Vancouver (Lamb 1984:374) remarked that the canoe builders 'are nearly destitute of iron, and possessed of very few implements of that valuable metal'. This comment, and his earlier description of the behaviour of the men who came aboard *Discovery*, suggest that he saw evidence to imply that iron had reached Rapa before his arrival. Of the canoes he wrote:

The island did not appear to afford any large timber; the broadest planks of which the canoes were made, not exceeding twelve inches ... Some of the stoutest double canoes accommodated from twenty-five to thirty men, of whom, on a moderate computation, three hundred were supposed to have been seen near the ship. These were all adults and apparently none exceeding middle-age; so that the total number of inhabitants on the island can hardly be estimated at less than fifteen hundred. In this respect it must be considered prolific, notwithstanding its uncultivated appearance. The natives, however, appeared to be exceedingly well fed, of middle stature, extremely well-made. (Vancouver in Lamb 1984:375)

The plank-built construction of early Rapan canoes, evident in the various canoe planks found in rockshelters by Stokes (n.d.:Preface) gave way later to dugout construction, as introduced trees produced larger timbers (Haddon and Hornell 1975:147–151).

The Rapan men made every effort to get the *Discovery* crew to go ashore:

On their departure they took hold of the hand of everyone near them, with a view to get them into their canoe. They all had their hair cut short; and, excepting a wreath made of a broad, long-leaved, green plant, worn by some about the waist, they were intirely without clothing. Although the custom of tatowing prevails so generally with all the islanders of this ocean, these people were destitute of any such marks.

Independent of the protection their fortified retreats may afford, it did not appear that they were subject to much hostility, as scarcely any scars from wounds or other marks of violence were observed on their bodies. Their elevated fortified places ... led some of us to conjecture, that they were frequently annoyed by troublesome neighbours from some other islands not far distant. But, as the canoes we saw were not even furnished with sails nor had any appearance of having been equipped for an expedition beyond their own coast, it may reasonably be inferred, that they were not accustomed to voyages of any length. Yet, on the other hand, when the small extent of their island is taken into consideration, it is hard to reconcile that it is not the fear of foreign enemies, but the apprehension of domestic insurrection, that has induced the laborious construction of their fortified retreats. (Vancouver in Lamb 1984:375)

Archibald Menzies, botanist and surgeon on *Discovery*, was another experienced eyewitness of the first meeting, having earlier sailed around the northwest Pacific, including to Hawaii. He adds some useful details to Vancouver's narrative. His impression of the forts was that 'each bore some resemblance to a large block-house fenced round at a little distance with a high wall of stone or turf' (Shineberg 1986:66). The Rapans on board *Discovery* were prevailed upon:

... to count their numerals to ten, which we found to agree exactly with those of Otaheite, & a few other words which they repeated convinced us that they spoke a dialect of the same general language, but so modified from their local situation that even Toowowero [above] could understand very little of what they said. This being the case I think it is probable that Oparoo may not be the real name of the Island, though it was often their answer to our interrogation on that head and therefore adopted ... They suffer their beards to grow long, but their hair which is naturally straight was croppd short round about the nape of the neck & their ears were perforated though we saw them wear no ornaments in them excepting the nails they got from us. (Menzies in Shineberg 1986:67)

No signs of tattooing were observed, and 'the only cloathing they wore were a narrow strip of cloth made from the bark of a tree which passed around their waist and between their legs' (Shineberg 1986:67). Menzies thought the cloth was probably scarce because many men simply wore bunches of *Dracena* leaves attached to a girdle (Prebble 2005:156 suggests the bark cloth was more likely from *Hibiscus tiliaceus* than paper mulberry (below), and that *Dracena* was probably *Cordyline*). Turning to the Rapan canoes, Menzies described them as:

... small & narrow but neatly formed, rising a little at each end to a sharp point with outriggers fitted to them – similar to the generality of Canoes in this Ocean. They had also double canoes with Sails constructed in the same manner, & though we observed no wood or Timber on the Island of a size capable of making their canoes, yet they did not seem to be a scarce article among the Natives, for at one time we counted no less than 30 canoes about the ship & between us & the Shore, eight or nine of them were double canoes each of which had upwards of 20 men, & few of the single canoes had less than five men, many of them had more, so that we estimated that the number of people that came off in these Canoes from this Bay to be about 300, and as there were no women, children or any very old people seen amongst them I think it may be safely inferrd that they were not one fifth of the Inhabitants of this little Valley, which from whence would amount to upwards of 1500. But I would not conclude from this that the Island is very numerously inhabited, perhaps the environs of this Bay may contain one-half of the whole number. (Menzies in Shineberg 1986:68)

Both Vancouver and Menzies thought there might be other inhabited islands to the south of Rapa, and these could explain both the need for fortification and the existence of so many canoes in the apparent absence of substantial trees.

Menzies noted that 'excepting a few small fish, none of these canoes brought off any kind of refreshments – either Hogs Poultry or Vegetables, so that we remain entirely ignorant of the produce of this Island' (Shineberg 1986:68). Looking into the bay off which the *Discovery* lay, he could see scattered bushes among which were 'the habitations of the Natives & some little signs of Cultivation'. Otherwise, the island appeared fairly open. On the south slopes of the bay were some scrubby trees, especially in the hollows, and on the north side only grass. No coconut palms were seen.

The *Discovery* observations

Although the result of barely two hours contact, the *Discovery* observations provide an immensely useful picture of late 18th century Rapa. It seems that the Rapans had some iron but their evident wonderment on boarding *Discovery* – 'their attentions & curiosities absorbd with everything they saw' (Menzies in Shineberg 1986:67) so that it was very difficult to obtain their compliance in answering questions – was such that it is very unlikely that any earlier European voyagers had called in there. The iron must have come by travel to or from islands nearer to earlier European contact. Don Thomas Gayanagos, *Aguila*, discovered Raivavae, the nearest island to Rapa, in January 1775, and, in a brief encounter, traded some knives and nails with the inhabitants (Corney 1915:179). Cook, accompanied by Omai, found Tubuai in 1777 but was unable to induce anybody to step on board the *Resolution*. However, as the Societies had experienced extensive contact with Europeans since discovery by Wallis in June 1767, it is quite probable that iron had been traded into the Australs for 10–20 years before 1791. The Rapans, at the end of the line, had much less than they wanted, and no idea initially, on boarding *Discovery*, that they had chanced upon a fabulously rich source.

It is not certain just where the *Discovery* lay off the coast. As it sailed up from the southwest, the six forts seen (five being visible at one time) were almost certainly six of the seven which lie along the skyline of the west coast: south to north these are: Ungarere (Ororangi?), Ngapiri, Tevaitau, Morongo Uta, Puketaketake, Noogurope and probably Kapitanga. Puketaketake and Noogurope overlook Anarua Bay, which, as the only bay on the northwest coast, must have been 'the small Bay on the Northwest side of the island' (Menzies in Shineberg 1986:66) off which *Discovery* lay. As the valley runs directly inland behind the sandy bay-head, the *Discovery* crew would have had a good view of the inhabited landscape at a distance of about 1 km, and while sailing up the coast, the forts would have been seen at 2.5 km to 4 km away, no great distances for telescopic inspection.

European observations of the Rapans suggested that they were thought somewhat shorter and darker and more robustly built than the generality of East Polynesians, and that their language, although clearly East Polynesian, was a distinct dialect. It is difficult to understand what the Rapans meant by referring repeatedly to 'Oparo' in response to enquiries about the island, but it is possible that they interpreted those as questions about where they had come from and replied that they were 'Opare', meaning inhabitants of the forts. More speculative still is the possibility that 'paro' (stray or wander) and 'korie' or kore (absent, destroyed, annihilated), if these meant the same in Rapan as Maori (Williams 1971), were references to the fate of the people to whose place the Europeans were pointing. The name 'Rapa', it might be conjectured, is an allusion to Ha'urei Harbour as a vagina, the means by which mediation between ordinary and supernatural were negotiated with each passage (cf. Hanson and Hanson 1983:86–94).

Only men were seen, and there are no observations of differences in rank, either by deference or appearance. The men had short, straight hair and probably no topknots, unlike at Raivavae, for example (Corney 1915:179). There was little sign of weapons, there was no tattooing and pierced ears held only nails. Clothing was restricted to breech-cloths and similar coverings, some of them made from bark cloth, possibly from *aute*, the paper mulberry (*Brousonettia papyrifera*), and bunches of *ti* (*Cordyline* sp.) leaves. The *Discovery* lay inshore long enough, and was visited by sufficient canoes, that had there been local men of obviously substantial status then it is hard to imagine they would not have made themselves known, as was the case elsewhere in East Polynesia when Europeans arrived.

Other than the people who came aboard, the forts attracted most attention. The *Discovery* observations clearly suggest that the six western skyline forts were in existence in 1791 and perhaps that they were all inhabited. There is, at least, no comment to the effect that some appeared abandoned or in disrepair. The description of these sites indicates that a large building – possibly a communal house – had been erected in a central position, where it was surrounded by a stone or turf wall and, at regular intervals away from the centre, by rows of outward-leaning palisades. People were seen moving about within the defences.

Menzies saw structures that were possibly habitations, though they might have been garden sheds, in the valley, but relatively little sign of cultivation, although the land was very largely cleared. However, the European view of the valley floor of Anarua Bay, if that was the place, would have been somewhat obscured by a dune system above the beach. Nevertheless, Menzies saw no sign of pigs or poultry (or dogs, it can also be assumed, though he did not mention them). Coconut palms and bananas were absent to view and neither vegetables nor fruits were brought out to the ship.

Discussion of population size by the *Discovery* officers is particularly interesting. Vancouver, evidently reporting observations other than his own, said that 300 men were seen about the ship and the island population could hardly have been less than 1500, an estimate which has been widely used in the subsequent literature on Rapa. However, Menzies is more specific, and seemingly from direct observation. He describes the canoes, on which the population estimates depended, in greater detail, noting that some double canoes had sails of a common Polynesian type (as Vancouver seems not to have seen these, and as the *Discovery* lay close inshore, they were perhaps furled around spars in the bilges of the canoes and may, thus, have been of the form used by Maori), and the number of men in canoes of different type. Most importantly, he says these canoes came out from the bay inshore of *Discovery* and so his estimate of a total population of 1500 is for the bay alone. He was reluctant to extrapolate his data to the whole island, suggesting it had perhaps 3000 people, but then he had seen only the west coast at close range and knew nothing of Ha'urei Harbour or the large bays elsewhere on Rapa.

Early 19th century contact at sea

As European interest in the Pacific grew apace during the late 18th and early 19th centuries it seems quite probable that Rapa was visited on various occasions during that period, especially after the publication in 1798 of the first edition of *Voyage of Discovery* (Lamb 1984:267). However, there are few confirmed data. The Sydney trader, Captain Roger Simpson probably visited Rapa in 1802, Stephen Reynolds in the *New Hazard* sailed by it in 1813, and the Sydney vessel *Endeavour* clearly made contact with Rapans in July 1815, when it found, 'the Roppa Islanders to be pilferers of anything they could lay their hands on on deck' (Richards 2004:4. This seems to be the earliest reference to 'Rapa'). Captain John Powell of the *Queen Charlotte* was becalmed near Rapa in 1815 or 1816 and a number of canoes came off but none of the men would go onboard. Instead, about 50 of them jumped into the sea and, grabbing a loose rope at the stern of the ship, began swimming towards land, 'labouring and shouting with all their might, as they supposed they were drawing the vessel towards the shore'. An ensuing tug-of-war with the ship's crew and the fortuitous arrival of a breeze ended the encounter (Ellis 1838:369–370).

The *Queen Charlotte* returned to Rapa with William Ellis of the London Missionary Society (LMS) on January 27, 1817. While sailing slowly along the western coast, 30 canoes came around the ship:

> The men were not tataued, and wore only a girdle of yellow ti leaves round their waists. Their bodies, neither spare nor corpulent, were finely shaped; their complexion a dark copper colour; their features regularly formed; and their countenances often handsome, were shaded by long black straight or curling hair. (Ellis 1838:365)

A crayfish, lying in the bilge of a canoe among some spears, was exchanged for fish hooks. A man then came aboard, carefully sniffing Ellis' hand as he did so. Many others then boarded and began to take anything they could make off with, including a kitten. The crew eventually produced long knives to drive off the remaining Rapans who, not understanding the nature of the weapons, tried to seize them by the blade and were badly cut in their hands.

In the winter of 1820, Bellingshausen in command of the *Vostok* and Lazarev with the *Mirnyi* reached Rapa on a passage from New Zealand. They came up from the southwest and stood off the northern coast at a distance of at least 4.5 sea miles, in light and fickle winds. Fewer canoes ventured out than had been seen by Vancouver: 15 containing 80 people on June 29 (although another report says 23 canoes with at least five men in each on the first day; Barratt 1988:211), and 22 with about 110 people on June 30. The canoes, fastened with twisted bark cordage, and some of them 7.6 m long, showed no decoration (see Barratt 1988:Plate 26). There were double canoes and some large canoes with double outriggers (Simonov in Barratt 1988:205). No sails were mentioned.

At noon on June 29, several canoes, each with five to seven men (Figure 2.3), came out and greeted the *Vostok* with a speech of 'much heat and volume'. Coming on board, the Rapans presented 'us with sea crabs and some sort of fermented dough' (Barratt 1988:201). The dough was almost certainly *tioo* (fermented taro) and the sea crabs appear from later description to have been crayfish. One islander wore a bark sash, which he exchanged for a fish hook. Taro roots were presented, and cooked and eaten by the Russians, who enjoyed them as much as they abhorred the bitter taro dough. Shellfish, 'a dried pumpkin which had nowhere been cut through' (Barratt 1988:211) and was very probably a gourd, and bast cords, probably of *hau* bark, worn around the neck, were also in evidence.

The appearance of the Rapans (Figure 2.4) was much as it had seemed to Vancouver except that by now there were signs of earlier sexual relations with Europeans, including a half-caste youth (see Barratt 1988:Plate 27). On this occasion also a chief was recognised – indeed he was the first to go aboard – and given appropriate privileges and presents. Rapan thievery remained a problem but it was evident that the Rapans now understood the use of guns. The Russians asked for fish, poultry and pigs, showing examples of the domestic animals to their visitors, but none were produced. Looking at the island through telescopes, the Russians could see the forts, 'within which huts were visible' (Barratt 1988:217) and narrow paths running up to them. Yellowish-red and red patches on the hill slopes were surely signs of soil erosion (Barratt 1988:212, 216).

These later contacts at sea served to widen European knowledge of Rapans and, of course, knowledge of Europeans by Rapans. They showed the first indications of varied status in Rapan society and of a growing awareness of European things, including guns. Evidence arrived of the prominent means of subsistence, notably of taro in several forms and perhaps the gourd, but conversely, of the probable absence of domestic animals. A new form of canoe, the double outrigger, was seen, or at least asserted (it seems improbable given the western Pacific distribution of this type). Otherwise, Rapans looked and behaved as they had done in the late 18th century.

Early 19th century observations ashore

Between 1825 and 1830, Rapa was pulled into the European colonial world of industry, religion, commerce and disease. The first extended contact began in July 1825 when a cutter, the *Snapper*, owned by Tati, a Tahitian chief, but under the command of Captain Shout (Davies in Newbury 1961:279 has him as I. Shant), the first European to set foot on Rapa, arrived on passage from the Tuamotus to Tahiti. Two Rapans were on board when the captain, feeling under threat by many more canoes arriving, sailed off to Tahiti. There the two men, Paparua and Aitareru, attended school and church under the supervision of the LMS missionary, John Davies and, in October 1825, they were returned to Rapa, 'loaded with presents and accompanied by two Tahitians [Hota and Nene], who were sent to gain more accurate information relative to their country, and the dispositions of its inhabitants … the captain of the cutter procured some tons of sandal-wood and when he left, the Tahitians [also] returned' (Ellis 1838:372).

The successful visit to Tahiti by the two Rapan men, 'tho they did not understand much Tahitian' (Davies in Newbury 1961:280), and their congenial homecoming, during which Teraau (also recorded as Teranga and Terakau), the 'head chief of the island', desired the Tahitians to return (Davies in Newbury 1961:280), encouraged John Davies to begin a mission on Rapa. The mission station was established 'in Aurai [Ha'urei] harbour' in January 1826. On the brig *Governor Macquarie* Davies took Hota and Nene and their wives, plus Mahana (a schoolmaster) and Pauo (a tradesman and boat-builder):

> They carried with them not only spelling-books, and copies of the Tahitian translations of the scriptures, but also a variety of useful tools, implements of husbandry, valuable seeds and plants, together with timber for a chapel, and doors &c. for the teachers' houses … Mr Davies … was pleased with his visit, and, upon the whole, with the disposition of the people, although some appeared remarkably superstitious, and, as might be expected, unwilling to embrace Christianity. This arose from an apprehension of the anger of their gods, induced by the effects of a most destructive disease, with which they had been recently visited.

Figure 2.3. Drawing of a Rapan canoe with six crew produced from a sketch by Pavel Nikolaevich Mikhailov, June 29, 1820 (which shows faint sketches of seven crew; Barratt 1988:Plate 26). The canoe shows similarities to Maori craft, including, on the sternpiece, a shape that resembles the seated ancestral figure sometimes carved on the Maori sternpiece (taurapa) of a war canoe (Debenham 1945:Plate XVIII). Published with the permission of the Hakluyt Society and the State Library of New South Wales (item MRB/Q98/32 A1).

Figure 2.4. Drawing of a young Rapan man by Pavel Nikolaevich Mikhailov, June 30, 1820 (Barratt 1988:Plate 27), published with the permission of the Hakluyt Society and the State Library of New South Wales (item MRB/Q98/32 A1). The man is probably wearing leaves in his ear, as noted of some Rapan visitors, and it is his only form of decoration, as common among Rapans at that time.

The gods, they imagined, had thus punished them for their attention to the accounts from Tahiti. (Ellis 1838:373)

There had been 'a great mortality amongst the people since they were visited by the Snapper' and among the dead was Teraau, upon whose land the original chapel at Papara was re-erected (Newbury 1961:280), presumably at the request of Teraau's son, Koinikiko, who supported the mission and gave it land and taro patches (Stokes n.d.:24). Davies was impressed with the plantations of taro:

> which are well laid out and display a degree of skill and contrivance, evinced in nothing else we saw. The houses are miserable huts about five feet high, with holes to creep in, about two feet square. The natives have neither maraes nor altars, but only a few rude stones placed in the ground, which denote a va'i tapu or sacred place. These stones (they say) are mea mana nui, i.e. things of great power. There seems to be no images worshipped. Everything exceedingly rude; their stone adzes &c. are similar to those found in other islands, but more rude and uncouth. They do not tatau their bodies, and till they were visited by the Snapper and Minerva were all without clothing … [Davies then says the two Rapans who had been to Tahiti told their countrymen that nakedness was disliked and since then the Rapan chiefs, at least, had worn clothes in the Tahitian fashion]… The vegetable productions of Rapa, with few exceptions,

resemble those of Tahiti and the Society Islands. There are found the various kinds of taro that are cultivated at Tahiti, one kind of *meia* or banana, the *umara* or sweet potato, and a species of yam; the *ahia* also, or red apple, but there is no bread-fruit nor cocoa-nut, neither the vi nor mountain-plantain. One cocoa-nut tree, indeed, was found by Hota and Nene, when they were here before, growing on the west side of the island; but this had been thrown up by the seas, and the natives did not then know what it was. Abundance of wild celery grows here in the moist grounds similar to that of New Zealand. (Davies in Stokes n.d.:25–26)

Davies comments usefully on the name of the island: 'the natives call it Rapa only. The name occurs in some of the old traditional songs of Tahiti', and he wrote that the population, 'is supposed to be upwards of 2000, or nearly as many as those in Raivavae' (Stokes n.d.:27). His investigations of Rapan belief established that:

Puoero Poere is one of the chief gods of the Eriki, or chiefs, but their gods in general seem to be the spirits of departed ancestors. I wrote down the names of about forty of them, with a collection of Rapa words, but I has mislaid or lost the manuscript of them. That the natives of this island are of the same general origin as their neighbours, their language, customs, and superstitions afford sufficient proof. They have, however, many words not used at present in Tahiti, and retain the consonants k, g, ng, not used here [i.e. in Tahiti]. On the other hand they reject both f and h. Their numerals are nearly the same. (Davies in Stokes n.d.:28)

Davies reiterated his good impression of the state of taro cultivation, and observed that, 'The planting, weeding, baking of it altogether the work of the women. In making canoes the Rapa-men do not excel' (Stokes n.d.:29).

Although the early services, being in Tahitian, were 'unintelligible' to the Rapans, two mission stations had been established by June 1826. By 1829, the LMS missionaries, Pritchard and Simpson:

found that four chapels had been erected in different stations [Moturi, Tupuai, Iri, Aurai] at which, by native Missionaries, religious instruction was statedly imparted. The inhabitants manifested a pleasing attention during service, and their advancement in knowledge exceeded the expectations of their visitors. (Ellis 1838:374)

They also found that 'the various seeds and plants that had been taken to the island from Tahiti did not thrive, the climate being much colder than that of Tahiti' (Newbury 1961:281). Their observations on Rapan belief amplified those of Davies. They found that Paparaa or Paparua and Poere were the principal gods:

Paparaa was made of the coconut husk, neatly plaited in the form of a cask [Ellis 1838:364, reporting similar information, says it was 'a kind of cylinder, full in the centre, and smaller at the ends']. Its length is from 2 to 3 inches. To this god they prayed for victory in war, for the recovery of the sick, and for an abundance of turtle in the harbour. Poere was a piece of stone from 12 to 15 inches long. This was planted in the ground, and worshipped at the launching of a canoe, at the opening of a new house, praying that in it there might ever be an abundance of food; and that they might have much water in the springs … no sacrifice was offered except fish. (Stokes n.d.)

As for the mountaintop forts, Pritchard and Simpson heard that:

Their wars were not so frequent, nor so cruel, as in some of the neighbouring islands. There are still remaining, several old castles, built on the tops of the highest mountains, to which the vanquished repaired, and continued the siege for a long time. These fortifications appear to have been standing for ages. It is now a long time since they have been used. Some of the oldest people say that they have no recollection of war in their time. (Stokes n.d.:31)

From Tahiti, had been brought fowls, pigs, kumara, pumpkins, melons, papaw, cabbages, onions, pineapples and potatoes. Breadfruit, mountain plantain (*fei*) and coconut, also introduced, did not thrive, according to Pritchard and Simpson. Three Europeans who had some ability in Polynesian languages, which they had used, reputedly, to recruit slaves, lived on Rapa for a short period about this time, probably 1827–1829. They were occupied particularly in distilling spirits from *ti* (Stokes n.d.:29).

Pritchard and Simpson baptised 251 people in 1829. Another missionary, Mr Darling, visited in June 1831 on the *Rarotonga*, and another 140 people were baptised (75 men, 65 women; a later note by Davies (Newbury 1961:282) says it appears that Darling baptised 147 people (76 men, 71 women) and also 44 boys and 51 girls of baptised parents). At the latter time, the names of the entire Rapan population were written down; there were 357 adults and 243 children, 600 in all (Davies in Newbury 1961:281). Among them was a Mangarevan man, Mapuagua, who was the only survivor of seven Mangarevans whose raft had drifted to Rapa many years earlier. Four had later set out in a strong westerly wind to attempt to sail back. Mapuagua died in 1829 (Ellis 1838:374; Richards 2004:5).

The mission had arrived in Rapa in 1826 with a sandalwood expedition by Captain Samuel Henry on the *Snapper* and Captain Thomas Abrill (or Ebrill) on the *Minerva*, which was owned by the Tahitian 'king' Pomare III. Sandalwood (*Santalum insularum*) was in limited supply on Rapa, but up to 20 tons were taken, and this encouraged the British Consul to send a Mr Young with some Tuamotuan labourers to Rapa, on the brigantine *Active* (Captain Elley), to cut more sandalwood and collect *beche-de-mer*. They were unsuccessful (Richards 2004:5), but Mr Young remained on Rapa for at least six months, certainly until June 1826. The Pacific Pearl Company's ships, *Sir George Osborne* and *Rolla*, visited Rapa briefly in April and June 1826, unsuccessfully, but the expedition leader, Samuel Stutchbury, made some interesting observations. He noted that 'the natives subsist on taro which is very abundant. They also have the Ti root … Rats appeared innumerable and exceeding bold' (in Richards 2004:5). From Mr Young, Stutchbury heard that the Rapans were:

> … very peaceable, living entirely upon fish and taro, and that the females [were] remarkably chaste, if a man dies or is driven away from the island in his canoe which sometimes happen as they fish a great distance out to sea, the widow will ascend one of the highest and most precipitous mountains and hurl themselves down … When a person dies, they place the body in a rude kind of wicker coffin or basket and carry it to the top of one of the mountains, the relatives and friends assemble, and lament and cut themselves for many days continuance, after some weeks of exposure on the mountain, they will place the body or bones in an old canoe, tow it a considerable way out to sea, then fix on a number of large stones, and let it sink. If it is a chief, they will sometimes bury the body on shore. The generality of the natives go about perfectly naked. (Stutchbury in Richards 2004:6)

In June 1826, the US Navy schooner, *Dolphin*, seeking yams and taro, visited several small bays on the north and east coasts of Rapa, finding huts and taro patches in each, but was directed by inhabitants to the main harbour, where Mr Young piloted it in, somewhat inexpertly. The First Officer, Lt. Hiram Paulding, found that taro 'was planted everywhere, in large patches, where there was a small valley through which a stream of water [flowed] … the hills were green with another species we had not before seen, called mountain tarrow. The latter is superior … and will keep longer at sea' (Paulding 1831:252; Prebble (2005:162) suggests 'mountain tarrow' was either the common taro, *Colocasia esculenta*, or *Alocasia macrorrhiza*). The Rapans permitted the *Dolphin* crew members to dig as much taro as they wanted, perhaps because they were unable to do so themselves. An epidemic disease seems to have been in progress and the people 'had a sickly look, almost without an exception' (Paulding 1831:253). They were dressed in:

... a heavy mat of grass, weighing from ten to fifteen pounds, which was thrown over their shoulders, and another light mat, of the same material for their loins. Their deportment was modest and retiring, and they evinced a disposition to have but little intercourse with us. A few of their houses were scattered about on the hills. They were extremely miserable ... long and narrow, about three or four feet high, so that when one entered them, it was necessary to go down on hands and knees. (Paulding 1831:254)

Two whaleships visited Rapa in July 1826, and the British naturalist, Hugh Cuming, visited on May 17, 1828. Cuming was ashore for only four days but he took good note of what he observed of the Rapan people. Their dress consisted of:

Two pieces the size and shape of a very large door mat, thickly thrumbed. One of those they fasten over the neck which reaches the loins. The other is made fast to the loins so that the upper one covers the lower one a few inches. These species of cloaks are very heavy, are made of a large bush with the rind taken off, woven by hand with the leaves of the Te [ti or *Cordyline* sp.] Plant split in fine threads ... they can withstand the rain for a month. (Cuming in Richards 2004:7)

Cuming implies, very plausibly, that this was the traditional winter dress of the Rapans. Their summer dress was made in the same form, 'only it is made entirely from the leaves of the Te Plant finely drawn into threads and much longer than the winter dress, yet it is not above half the weight' (Richards 2004:7). There were also mortuary cloaks, some fragments of which have been recovered from cave sites (Buck 1925).

The Rapans did not like the mission plan of houses set out in rows of 12 to 14, preferring 'to live in their ancient sites and dwellings close to their taro grounds' in dispersed dwellings (Cuming in Richards 2004:7). Their houses were about 14 feet (4.3 m) long, 10 (3 m) broad and 3 (1m) high, with an entrance at each end, two small windows and a fireplace at one end. They were shaped like the top of a covered wagon, which presumably means rounded rather than ridged, and thatched to a thickness of about 0.6 m (Cuming in Richards 2004:7). Cuming could find nobody who knew much about the forts, except that they were places of refuge when Rapa was divided between two warring chiefs:

The losing party then had to fly to these mountain fortresses for safety as every male that was taken in the battle or afterwards was slain. The females and children was not molested and was permitted to carry up to their relatives, food until they made peace with the conquerors which was soon effected by the females. Most of those strongholds are square, the walls very thick about ten or eleven feet high with some rugged stones by which they could get up on the platform. On the top was an immense heap of large stones which they threw upon their pursuers. The mountains I ascended appeared to have steps cut in the mount, winding several times around it ... [the Rapan weapons, according to Cuming, were] ... a lance eighteen feet [5.5 m] long, very rudely made, and a short ugly unadorned club. Their fish hooks were made of the roots of trees bent and hardened by fire. Their household furniture consist of a low stool cut out of the solid wood [or possibly a wooden pillow], a stone knife and a few stones to keep the fire together ... Their food consisted of fish and tara. (Richards 2004:7)

The Belgian trader, Jacques-Antoine Moerenhout (1837) visited Rapa in 1834 to bring back Rapan men whom he had employed as pearl divers. He remarked that, 'fish and taro were the only food formerly. Tiao [tioo] was made of taro, in place of breadfruit as in the islands to the north' (in Stokes n.d.:33). *Tioo*, or fermented taro, was a particularly important Rapan food made by packing cleaned taro corms, or mashed raw taro, into pits lined with grass and leaves, which were then covered with earth. It would keep for six months during which it turned into a sour, pungent, but much esteemed paste (Stokes n.d.:24–26. *Tioo* storage pits (*rua tioo*) of 2–4.5 m in diameter and more than 2 m deep were recorded around and on many *pare* by Stokes n.d.:277). Moerenhout was offered provisions of cabbage, onions, taro, chickens and pigs, an indication of the extent of change in agriculture. He heard that the trunk of the candlenut or tiairi (*Aleurites triloba*), the largest type of tree on the island, was used for canoe building, and its nuts for lighting, and he was struck by the extent that men were evidently tabu and fed by their wives. Moerenhout thought that cultivation, cooking and other domestic tasks and crafts were the responsibility of women, while men made nets, presumably fished, and built canoes and houses.

European contact continued after the 1830s, of course, and with growing frequency, but observations were becoming repetitive and they were, increasingly, of Rapan behaviour modified by close European contact (e.g. Lucett 1851, who visited in 1843 and 1844; Hall 1868 in that year), which is largely irrelevant to this volume. Most importantly, Rapan society had been deeply transformed by a demographic catastrophe during the early 19th century.

Contact ashore had, predictably, a much greater impact on Rapan society than that at sea. Much of this remains effectively invisible. For example, it is impossible to be sure of the nature of the original Rapan pantheon. Later scholars remarked on the apparent absence of such major East Polynesian gods as Rongo, Tane and Tangaroa (Buck 1954:179), but how much this owed to the rapid destruction of the pagan belief system before it was recorded is unknown. Arrival of Europeans ashore, and doubtless disputes over women, brought violence, as in 1826 between Rapans and the crew of the *Minerva*, in which it seems some Rapan men were killed. Much more lethal, however, was disease, but it is difficult to estimate its full impact without knowing the approximate size of the Rapan population about AD 1790. In the light of discussion above, it is apparent that the popular estimate of 1500 people was not intended by Menzies to represent the entire population, which he put, extremely conservatively in the light of his method of calculation, at only 3000, twice that estimated for a single bay, probably Anarua. On the other hand, it is very improbable that the eight most habitable outer bays plus Ha'urei Harbour each supported an average population of 1500, making a total of more than 13,000. Eugène Caillot (1932:24), who visited Rapa in 1912, reports a Rapan estimate of a former population of 6000.

Stokes (n.d.:35, 436–440) attempted an estimate for the late prehistoric population using his detailed archaeological records of *pare* and coastal settlements. For each of 25 *pare*, he established the number and size of habitation terraces and allowed an average of five people for each (four to 10 according to size). For Morongo Uta this produced a population of 390, for Ororangi 280, and 215 for Tapitaga, but most supported fewer than 100 people. The *pare* total was 2377 people, and with 10 coastal settlements added on the same basis, the overall total was 3027 people. Bartruff et al. (this volume) calculate the maximum sustainable population according to an agricultural production model at around 2000, which is similar to the first recorded estimate of 'upwards of 2000' made by Davies in 1826 (above), but he reported that disease had already taken its toll.

It might be reasonable, therefore, to assume that the maximum population size in the early 1820s was close to 3000. It was nearer 2000 by 1826 and Darling's first census in 1831 recorded only 600 people. Stokes (n.d.:3) says that 85 per cent of the population disappeared in the eight years following missionary arrival in 1826. In 1836, Darling's census totalled 453 (more than the 300 estimated by the French trader Armand Mauruc in 1834, Caillot 1932:25; MacArthur 1968:307). By the 1860s, especially after the landing in February 1863 of Polynesians sick with smallpox and cholera, who were being returned from Peru, the population had plummeted to 100–150 people, from which it began a gradual climb in the 1880s to reach more than 450 today. As early as the mid-19th century, the demographic catastrophe had begun to transform the social basis of landholding into an unrestricted cognatic system that, in time, conferred virtually universal rights upon everybody (Hanson and Ghasarian 2007).

Additional evidence from Stokes' informants

All of the informants upon whom Stokes relied had been born in the late 19th century, and not all of them were Rapan (above), so it is necessary to treat their observations about life before the arrival of Europeans with caution. On some subjects, Stokes found them unreliable. For example:

> the opinions of the natives are very diverse on the subject of the original native house, even to the point of absurdity … the older natives are in agreement that the huts were small and low, but none of them had seen one completed. The one point never disputed is that the thatch was of *ti* leaves. (Stokes n.d.: 333, 340)

There was some agreement that houses usually had a fireplace, although Stokes found this to be rarely in evidence on the house terraces of the *pare*, where only a few small stone-kerbed rectangular hearths were seen. Floor mats were evidently never made, the floors and sleeping areas being covered only in dried grass (Stokes n.d.:341). Tapa cloth was always plain according to Stokes' informants, and only plain fragments have been recovered from rockshelters (n.d.:342). Gourds were used to store water and for utensils; no wooden vessels were made because of the absence of suitable timber, and stored food was normally wrapped in packages of *ti* or *kiekie* leaves and suspended from the rafters (Stokes n.d.:342; Figure 2.5).

On religious structures, Stokes found little coherent information. Some areas of rudimentary paving, including several raised and terraced rectangular areas, were described as marae, but

Figure 2.5. Packages of food, probably *poi*, suspended to dry. From a framed photo in the Mairie at Ha'urei, and with the permission of the Maire. The provenance of this is unclear, but it might be from the Stokes expedition.

without particular details of ritual or deities beyond reference to cannibalism etc. There are several monoliths around the shores of Ha'urei Harbour that appeared to Stokes (n.d.:901–903) to have been boundary markers, although he thought they, and some cavities in the walls of terraces, might also have had ritual significance. No putatively prehistoric stone images or carvings were recorded. Routledge and Routledge (1921:454), who visited Rapa while Stokes was there, said:

> No marae or ceremonial structure of any kind was seen by us. That name is given to three monoliths which stand on the main bay … [and] … which, it seems most probable, were boundary stones or had reference to the fish ponds, which are numerous. We could gain information about one building only, termed a marae, which was in one of the exterior bays we were unable to visit. It was said to be an insignificant enclosure, perhaps 20 ft. square, surrounded by a low wall about 2 ft. 6 in. in height, and having at one end a semi-circular platform of the same height. It is debatable whether the present inhabitants of Rapa really know what constitutes a marae.

Stokes found that Rapans recalled three types of canoes. Two were used in fishing: a single outrigger called *vaka* (or *kami'a*, a term otherwise found only in Mangareva), and the ordinary double canoe, *taurua*. A special double canoe (*taurua tamaki*) that could carry up to 40 men was used in war. His informants had no knowledge of former sails, nor did they use them in sailing the canoes and whaleboats of the 1920s. Stokes recovered pieces of canoes from caves on Rapa and deduced from them that the construction had consisted of strakes built up on a round-bottomed [dugout] hull, the latter generally requiring several pieces to be butted together because of the absence of large trees. By 1925, the Rapan outriggers had taken the form customary in Tahiti (in Haddon and Hornell 1975:147–148).

Rapan subsistence economy and crafts are known only sketchily from historical observations, but their scope can be amplified, with caution, from the records obtained by Stokes. In regard to plant foods, the Stokes' informants were generally agreed (Stokes n.d.:197 indicates minor disagreement) that at least one variety of sweet potato and one of banana (*tautau maori*) were grown prehistorically, along with taro, gourd (*koali*) and *Cordyline* (*karokaro*, of which the edible root was known as *ti*). The paper mulberry (*aute*) was also cultivated for making tapa cloth. Introduced in the missionary era were: sugarcane, arrowroot, manioc, the *ufi* form of yam (although it seems not to have thrived in Rapa), and a range of bananas, sweet potato and taro, among other Polynesian and European crops. The manufacture of *poi* or *popoi* from crushed and pounded taro (Figure 2.6) was probably introduced from Tahiti, although Stokes (n.d.:180–183) suggests some contrary evidence.

Cultivated plant foods were supplemented with native sources. The most important of these (Stokes n.d.:204–210) were *para* (stem bases of an edible fern), *aki* (tree fern starch) and *'omeka* (a type of wild yam). Others were the *Pandanus* (*kai'ara*) from which the juicy bases of the keys were eaten, but not the kernels, the *magu* (fruit of *kiekie*, *Freycinettia* sp.) *matoe* (a wild cliff taro), *poporo* (*Myoporum* sp.), *makiri* (the aerial tubers of wild yams of *Dioscorea* spp.) and *paraira* (or *puparira*, the stem bases of a sedge). Three kinds of edible seaweed were also collected.

The most commonly eaten shellfish according to Stokes' observation of the middens on *pare* was the *pa'ua* (*Chama* and possibly *Spondylus* spp.). Other species included *pipi* (*Tellina rugosa*), *mitata* (*Circe pectinata*), *ka'i* (*Asaphis* spp.), *tupere* (*Venus* spp.), *piu'u* (*Modiolus* sp.), *akaikai* (*Arca* sp.), *pangi* (*Patella* spp.), *i'i* (*Nerita morio*), *pu* (*Triton* sp.), and also *Trochus*, *Cerithium*, and various sea urchins. At least six kinds of crabs were caught, also the crayfish (*koura*), and river shrimps, and octopus and squid (Stokes n.d.:212–215).

Fishing from canoes with hook and line produced, primarily, the *rari*, described as a large-

Figure 2.6. Women sitting beside a stream pounding and kneading taro to make *poi*. From a framed photo in the Mairie at Ha'urei, and with the permission of the Maire. The provenance of this is unclear, but it might be from the Stokes expedition.

mouthed red fish like a rock cod, with large anal spines. Bagnis et al. (1974:105) identify *rari* as *Cephalopholis coatesi*, a much-esteemed species caught on the outer slopes of coral reefs. It is probably the six-spot grouper, *C. sexmaculata*, in Lieske and Myers (1994:25). Two carangids (*matu, maaki*), which were probably trevallies (Caranx spp.), were also mentioned, and the *uhu* (a generic term for parrotfish species), which was speared near the shore (Stokes n.d.:212). Freshwater eel occurred commonly but was not eaten. In 2002, large freshwater eels were abundant in the streams and taro ponds and still were not eaten. Local people have a legend about a guardian spirit in the form of a blonde-haired woman who changes into an eel, which accounts for it not being killed or eaten. The turtle ('*onu*) was much sought after but not common. Several informants told Stokes (n.d.:153) that several kinds of seals (*kumi*) had once occurred abundantly in Rapa. In fact, they still occur, one being seen near Anarua while we were on the island in 2002.

There were several methods of fishing. Large seines (*rau*) of suspended *ti* leaves were dragged in the shallows of the main harbour, and fish were also driven into them by men in canoes, splashing the water. The tough, heavy wood of the *mairari* shrub (*Dodonea viscosa*) was used to make large and medium-sized bait hooks by training the branches to grow in the required shape. Small hooks were made from candlenut shell (*tuitui*) by using coral files. They were used to catch small fish called *gaga* and *komokomo*. A hook of *mairari* wood with a *tuitui* point was used to catch albacore (*ahi*). Temporary hooks were tipped with *rari* anal spines (Stokes n.d.:259–262). Pearl shell was absent at Rapa, but turtle shell and whale bone may have been used in earlier days. Basket traps ('*inaki ika*), generally made from *kiekie*, were also used for fishing and crayfishing, and fish were speared in shallow water, especially parrot fish. Marine eels were snared in the coral-reef shallows by women. They used two sticks, one of which held a bait, and the other a slip noose. Stone fish traps (*pa ika*), regarded as of ancient origin, can be seen along the margins of east coast bays (Stokes n.d.:265–280).

The native rat (*kiore*) was seldom eaten, but birds of all kinds were hunted. Noted by Stokes' (n.d.:211) informants were (using identifications in Fontaine et al. 1999) a dove (*turuturu,* possibly the Tahitian ground dove of that name), spotless crake (*kotokoto*), grey duck (*mokora*), snipe or lesser golden plover (*torea*), blue-grey noddy (*paraki*), brown noddy (*n'goi'o*), common fairy-tern (*taketake*), little shearwater (*kakikaki*), Kermedec petrel (*ke'a*) and red-tailed tropic bird (*tavake*), which by legend brought fire to Rapa and was hunted on the cliffs. The latter remains a common activity today, both birds and eggs being taken.

Stokes' informants (n.d.:446–454) also added to the spare list of weapons in the historical data. They described a form of wooden pike with a blade at each end (*omore* or *komore*), a wooden dart (*ie*), of which a broken example has been recovered, and a fighting axe or adze (*tapu te toki*), which was possibly of a form similar to the Maori *patu*. Such an implement, described by Stokes (n.d.:448) variously as a 'truncheon', 'two-edged cleaver', or 'hand mattock' formed from a thin broad prism of basalt with a pecked handle, was found at Angairo. The former military use of pitfalls and nets (*kupega tamaki*) was asserted and also of the bow and arrow, which Stokes doubts.

Conclusions

Rapa was small and isolated and its period of pre-European habitation was probably quite brief, perhaps beginning in the 12th or 13th centuries, judging, very imprecisely, by the genealogical reckoning of traditionalist scholars. Through the pre-European era, and especially in the past few hundred years, inter-clan competition seems to have been endemic and fierce, even if the level of death and injury was relatively slight. It may have been driven by population growth which, on an island of few native resources and very little horticultural land, forced a change in settlement patterns from coastal habitation to hilltop defended settlements, with outlying groups of warriors on the lower hills above the plantations. Rapan social structure was similar to that in New Zealand. In both cases, cognatic descent defined membership of the clan (*kopu* in Rapa, *hapu* in New Zealand), and decisions taken mainly by family heads determined rights of residence and resource access. Before European discovery, it seems that control over Rapa had been consolidated into the dispensation of a single clan, in which a line of high chiefs had begun.

European discovery in 1791 was restricted to a fleeting encounter off the coast of Rapa with men that paddled out in outrigger and double-hulled canoes. These men were comparatively dark and stocky, unadorned, without tattoos, apparently of homogeneous status, and aggressively acquisitive of iron; their boats were well-made outriggers and double canoes, probably with sails on some, and capable of carrying more than 20 crew. Hill forts were seen surrounded by rows of palisades and had a large house at the centre. There was no sign of domestic animals and relatively little to be seen of cultivation, although much of the land had been cleared of forest.

By the early 19th century, more shipboard contacts disclosed the existence of chiefs and taro cultivation, and from 1825 when contact began ashore, the peculiarities of Rapan subsistence became clear. Taro was by far the most important cultivated plant, its wet-field plantations occupying nearly all of the coastal land; others were sweet potato, a banana, the gourd, paper mulberry and *Cordyline*. These were supplemented with pandanus, wild celery, edible ferns and other native plants. Strikingly absent were breadfruit, *ufi* yam, coconut, kava and most forms of banana. The pig, dog and chicken were also absent, but the Pacific rat (*Rattus exulans*) was abundant and tame. Fishing and shellfishing were important pursuits, the protein they provided being augmented by the capture of seabirds and collection of their eggs.

The reduced subsistence diversity compared with more tropical Polynesian islands was matched by a comparably narrower inventory of material goods and crafts, according to Stokes (n.d.). Weapons seem to have been confined to club, spear, sling, and one or two additional items. Along with an absence of tattooing, there were few ornamental items, no decoration of tapa cloth, no kava drinking, no use of fish poisons (despite the presence of suitable plants), no use of *Pandanus* in mat-making, and no featherwork. Despite the relatively late existence of high chiefs or 'kings', and the construction of impressive hill forts, there was very little development of constructed marae or shrines, or the maintenance of priests.

To what extent these features of Rapan society and culture can be ascribed to remoteness from most other islands in East Polynesia, a relatively cool climate, a small population (even if of relatively high density), scarcity of cultivable land, or some contingencies of history are issues that are addressed in the light of archaeological investigations discussed in this volume.

References

Bagnis, R., Mazellier, P., Bennett, J. and Christian, E. 1974. *Fishes of Polynesia*. Landsdowne Press, Melbourne.

Barratt, G. 1988. *Southern and Eastern Polynesia*. Volume 2 of *Russia and the South Pacific 1696–1840*. University of British Columbia Press, Vancouver.

Beasley, H.G. 1928. *Pacific Island Records Fish Hooks*. London, Seeley, Service & Co.

Buck, Sir P.H. 1925. Maori clothing, Part V. *Journal of the Polynesian Society* 34:87–88.

Buck, Sir P.H. 1954. *Vikings of the Sunrise*. Whitcombe and Tombs, Christchurch.

Caillot, A-C.E. 1932. *Histoire de l'Ile Oparo ou Rapa*. Librairie Ernest Leroux, Paris.

Corney, B.G. (ed), 1915. *The Quest and Occupation of Tahiti by Emissaries of Spain during the Years 1772–1776* etc. Volume II. Hakluyt Society, London.

Debenham, F. (ed), 1945. *The Voyage of Captain Bellingshausen to the Antarctic Seas 1819–1821*. Translated from the Russian. The Hakluyt Society, London.

Ellis, W. 1838. *Polynesian Researches, during a residence of nearly eight years in the Society and Sandwich Islands*. Volume III. Fisher, Son and Jackson, London.

Fischer, S. 2001. Mangarevan doublets: preliminary evidence for Proto Southeastern Polynesian. In: Stevenson, C.M., Lee, G. and Morin, F.J. (eds), *Pacific 2000: Proceedings of the Fifth International Conference on Easter Island and the Pacific*, pp. 417–424. Easter Island Foundation, Los Osos, California.

Fontaine, P., Fossati, O., Fossati, J., Mu-Liepmann, V., Raust, P. and Vernaudon, Y. 1999. *Manu: les oiseaux de Polynésie*. Manu: Société d'ornithologie de Polynésie française, Papeete.

Haddon, A.C. and Hornell, J. 1975. *Canoes of Oceania*. B.P. Bishop Museum Special Publications 27, 28 and 29. Bishop Museum Press, Honolulu.

Hale, H. 1968. *United States Exploring Expedition during the Years 1838, 1839, 1840, 1841, 1842. Under the Command of Charles Wilkes, U.S.N. Ethnography and Philology*. The Gregg Press, Ridgewood N.J.

Hall, J.V. 1868. On the island of Rapa. *Transactions of the New Zealand* Institute 1:128–134.

Hanson, F.A. 1970. *Rapan Lifeways. Society and History on a Polynesian island*. Little, Brown: Boston.

Hanson, F.A. and Ghasarian, C. 2007. 'The land belongs to everyone': the unstable dynamic of unrestricted cognatic descent in Rapa, French Polynesia. *Journal of the Polynesian Society* 116:59–72.

Hanson, F.A. and Hanson, L. 1983. *Counterpoint in Maori Culture*. Routledge and Kegan Paul, London.

Lamb, W.K. (ed), 1984. George Vancouver, *A Voyage of Discovery to the North Pacific Ocean and Round the World 1791–1795*, Volume I. The Hakluyt Society, London.

Lieske, E. and Myers, R. 1994. *Coral Reef Fishes: Indo-Pacific and Caribbean*. HarperCollins, London.

Lucett, E. 1851. *Rovings in the Pacific from 1837 to 1849*. Two volumes. Longmans, London.

MacArthur, N. 1968. *Island Populations of the Pacific*. The Australian National University Press, Canberra.

Moerenhout, J-A. 1837. *Voyages aux îles du Grand Océan*. 2 volumes. Bertrand, Paris.

Newbury, C.W. (ed), 1961. *The History of the Tahitian Mission 1799–1830, written by John Davies missionary to the South Sea Islands with supplementary papers from the correspondence of the missionaries*. The Hakluyt Society, Cambridge.

Paulding, H. 1831. *Journal of a cruise of the United States Schooner Dolphin, among the islands of the Pacific Ocean* etc. G. & C. & H. Carvill, New York.

Prebble, M.J. 2005. Islands, Floras and History: an environmental history of plant introductions and extinction on the Austral Islands, French Polynesia. Unpublished PhD dissertation, The Australian National University, Canberra.

Richards, R. 2004. The earliest foreign visitors and their massive depopulation of Rapa-iti from 1824 to 1830. *Journal de la Société des Océanistes* 118:3–10.

Routledge, S. and Routledge, K. 1921. Notes on some archaeological remains in the Society and Austral Islands. *Journal of the Royal Anthropological Institute of Great Britain and Ireland* 51:438–455.

Russell, M. 1852. *Polynesia: a history of the South Sea Islands, including New Zealand* etc. T. Nelson and Sons, London.

Shineberg, D. (ed), 1986. Archibald Menzies' account of the visit of the *Discovery* to Rapa and Tahiti, 22 December 1791–25 January 1792. *Pacific Studies* 9:59–102.

Smith, S.P. 1899. History and traditions of Rarotonga. *Journal of the Polynesian Society* 8:61–75, 171–175, 179–187, 242–249.

Stair, J.B. 1895. Flotsam and jetsam from the great ocean. *Journal of the Polynesian Society* 4:99–131.

Stokes, J.F.G. n.d. *Ethnology of Rapa Island*. Unpublished draft of B.P. Bishop Museum Bulletin of the Bayard Dominick Expedition. Five unbound volumes with multiple pagination (page numbers used here are generally the circled numbers). B.P. Bishop Museum, Honolulu.

Stokes, J.F.G. 1955. Language in Rapa. *Journal of the Polynesian Society* 64:315–340.

Williams, H.W. 1971. *A Dictionary of the Maori Language*. Government Printer, Wellington.

3

Archaeology of the coastal sites on Rapa Island

Atholl Anderson

Department of Archaeology and Natural History, Research School of Pacific and Asian Studies, The Australian National University, Canberra, Australia, atholl.anderson@anu.edu.au

Introduction

Archaeological research on the coastal landscape of Rapa was confined to remains of habitation and associated resource exploitation, leaving aside various kinds of structural remains (below). The objectives were to define the Rapan archaeological sequence, but primarily its beginnings (Kennett et al. 2006), to describe the use of coastal resources, and to characterise broad variation in coastal settlement patterns. On the basis of Pacific archaeological experience generally, and according to previous archaeological and ethnographic data from Rapa, it was assumed that pertinent evidence most probably would be found close to the shore. We focused on an approximately 300 m wide coastal strip, searching for open and rockshelter locations of habitation.

It should be conceded that this strategy leaves out some coastal sites that might eventually prove significant to an understanding of the Rapan archaeological sequence. The most immediately obvious are the valley systems of taro gardens. A few are currently under cultivation, but substantial areas of them are historical and archaeological. Several particular aspects of these features were examined in the palaeoenvironmental research (Chapters 3, 10), and considered in relation to palaeodemography (Chapter 13), but there was no systematic research on the archaeology of Rapan agriculture in our project. Associated with some former gardens are sets of putative house terraces that can be ascribed to historical villages, as at Tokoroa, near Aurei, and other more enigmatic structural remains, such as pit and terrace features, stone alignments and standing stones. There are also stone-built fish traps along the shoreline. Some of these diverse coastal remains, which are particularly abundant around Ha'urei Harbour, have been surveyed and investigated (Smith 1965; Walczak 2001, 2003), but the thorough research that they deserve will require a substantial archaeological project.

Our research began in the coastal margins of Ha'urei Harbour, then expanded into each of the external bays, with the exception of Mai'i' (inspected by the Norwegian Expedition) and Takao, both of which are cut off by high cliffs and have very little coastal land. We observed these southwest bays and the larger offshore islands (Karapoo and Tauturoo) from the sea, but were unable to land. The fieldwork consisted of searching all caves, shelters and exposed stream and wave-cut sections for early cultural deposits, using an auger and spade as needed. We also cored back-beach deposits, especially dunes and loam flats behind them, spade-tested terraces, and engaged in limited test-pitting by excavation. Forty-seven sites were recorded and in the 31 that were tested (Figure 3.1), we sampled for available radiocarbon dating materials, these generally

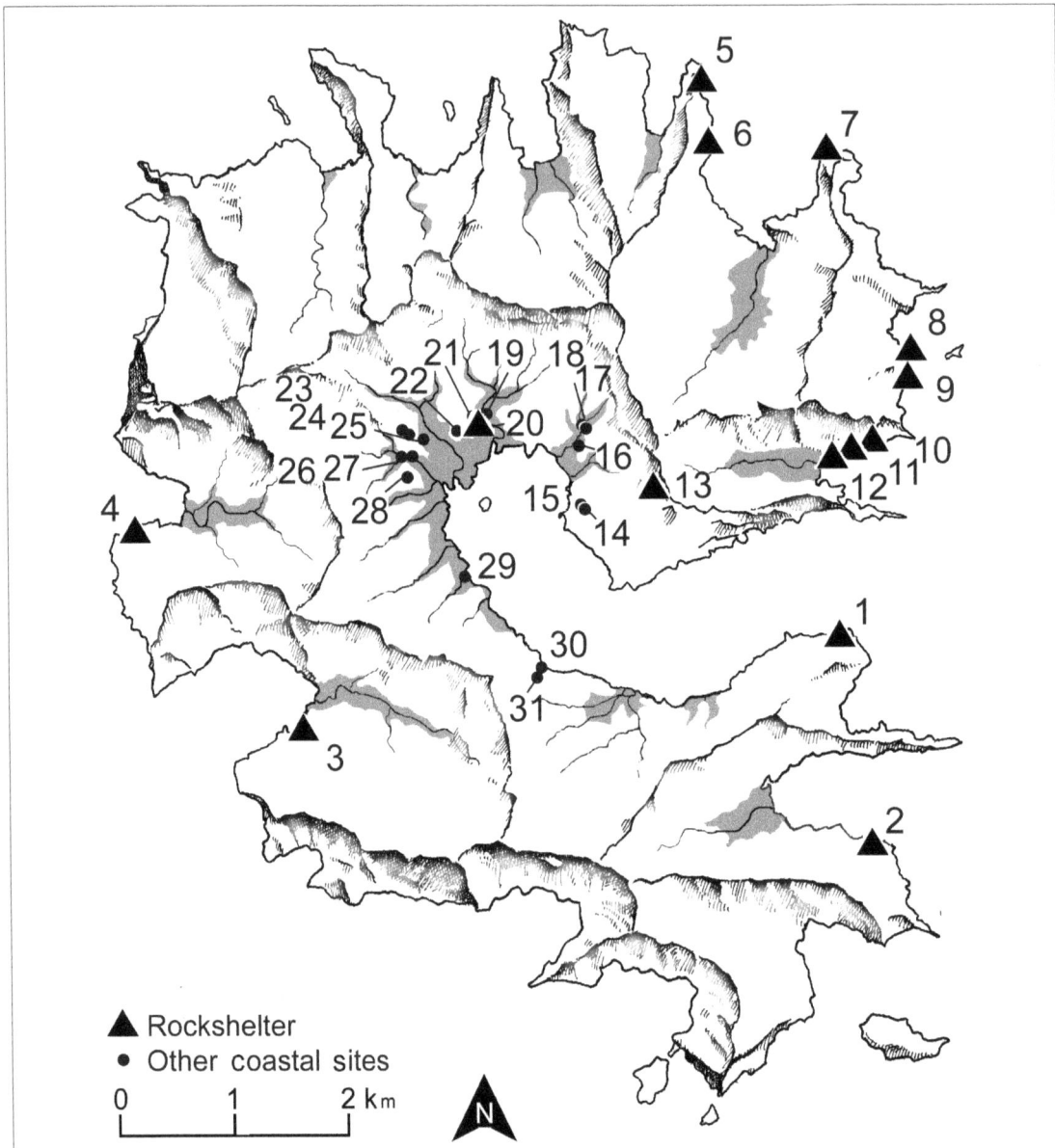

Figure 3.1. Map of Rapa Island showing location of bays and sites mentioned in this chapter.
1=R2002-30 south entrance shelter, 2=R2002-31 Anatakuri shelters, 3=R2002-33 Anakere shelter, 4=R2002-29 Tangarutu Cave, 5=R2002-34 Angairao shelter C, 6=R2002-36 Angairao shelter E, 7=R20002-38 Noogoriki shelter, 8=R2002-47 Taugatu shelter, 9=R2002-46 Autea shelter, 10=R2002-28 Akatanui Shelter 3, 11=R2002-27 Akatanui Shelter 2, 12=R2002-26 Akatanui Shelter 1, 13=R2002-44 Taga shelters, 14=R2002-20 Aitoke Oven 4, 15=R2002-25 Aitoke buried soil, 16=R2002-18 Aitoke Site 2 terrace, 17=R2002-17 Aitoke Oven 1, 18=R2002-19 Aitoke Oven 3, 19=R2002-45 Probable R16 terrace, 20=R2002-23 Tukou shelter, 21=R2002-24 Tukou Site 8 garden soil, 22=R2002-16 Tukou Site 7 terraces and walls, 23=R2002-13 Tukou Oven 4, 24=R2002-14 Tukou Oven 5, 25= R2002-15 Tukou Oven 6, 26=R2002-11 Tukou Oven 2, 27=R2002-12 Tukou Oven 3, 28=R2002-10 Tukou Oven 1, 29=R2002-7 Maraia Oven, 30=R2002-3,4,5 Tokoroa ovens, 31=R2002-8,9 Tokoroa ovens.

being restricted to charcoal because of the poor survivability of shell and bone in the damp volcanic soils of Rapa. We gave each site that we recorded a code number of R2002-n. Most of the sites recorded were small and evidently of single-phase usage, nearly all of them small earth ovens, but more complex sites exhibiting deep stratigraphy were also found, and excavated. The notes on archaeological sites collected by Stokes (n.d.) provided a valuable starting point.

Observations by Stokes

Stokes (n.d.:356) observed that flat land suitable for habitation was scarce on Rapa. The valleys are swampy and there is very little dry land at the bay heads; that which does exist is often stony. Nevertheless, he recorded a number of coastal habitation sites. He thought there might be older occupational remains under the 2.5 ha site of the modern village of Aurei. Other possible village sites mentioned by Stokes (n.d.:357–358) were at Angairao, Pairirao, Iri and Anarua. The last of these was the most promising. There are relatively extensive shore flats and low dunes, among which some patches of cobbles had the appearance of being arranged by hand and were possibly indicative of house floors. In addition, Stokes (n.d.:359) refers to,

> many shelter caves… along the shore and some are very large. They are now used for camping in mild weather, either by fishing parties or by field workers [i.e. people working on the taro plantations etc], and from native accounts they were also occupied in earlier days.

Stokes (n.d.:360–365) describes caves at Togorutu [Tangarutu], Tikaioe [Akatanui] and, in Agairao Bay, at Noogoriki. Two tiny shelters in Angairao, suitable only for sleeping in, occurred at Pukumauatoku and Gapitau. In addition, there is the highland shelter at Taga and the tunnel caves in Mai'i' Bay, the latter inspected by the Norwegian Expedition (Smith 1965).

In following up Stokes' observations by augering at Ha'urei village, we found no evidence of former sites, nor indeed at Area village, nor were there collections of artefacts from domestic gardens to be seen. However, the village areas are relatively substantial and small or discontinuous sites might have been missed. At Anarua, there are stone-built walls, terrace revetments of stone and piles of cobbles, but nothing immediately indicative of houses. Patches of cobbles on the shoreline showed some arrangement, possibly as fishing structures, but other patches of cobbles and gravel lacked any cultural form or content that could be observed. Augering through the dunes that lie about 100 m behind the beach produced no charcoal or any other evidence of habitation.

In the bays of Pariati, Akatamiro, Tupuaki, Akananue, Angairao, Akatanui, Angatakuri and Iri, coastal flats were augered in several places, and all existing stratigraphic exposures faced and inspected. Occasional pieces of charcoal and basalt flakes were produced, but no evidence found that was indicative of more than fleeting occupation. More intensive augering and digging of test pits over large areas of the bay headlands might locate remains of villages that eluded our initial investigation. In their apparent absence, attention concentrated on the cave sites recorded by Stokes.

Anarua Bay: Tangarutu Cave

There are two large caves on the south side of Anarua Bay. One near the point is probably 'Ogo Cave' referred to by Stokes (n.d.). It is 40 m wide, 10 m high at the entrance and extends 12 m back. However, the entrance is almost at sea level and the cave floor is piled with water-rolled cobbles and boulders. It is unlikely to contain any cultural deposits. About 300 m northeast is Tangarutu Cave (R2002-29). This is a very large shelter, opening to the north and facing across Anarua Bay and north-northwest out to sea (Figure 3.2). Reached by sea, the landing is feasible

Figure 3.2. Tangarutu Cave from the sea (top) and from the east (left). Photographs A. Anderson.

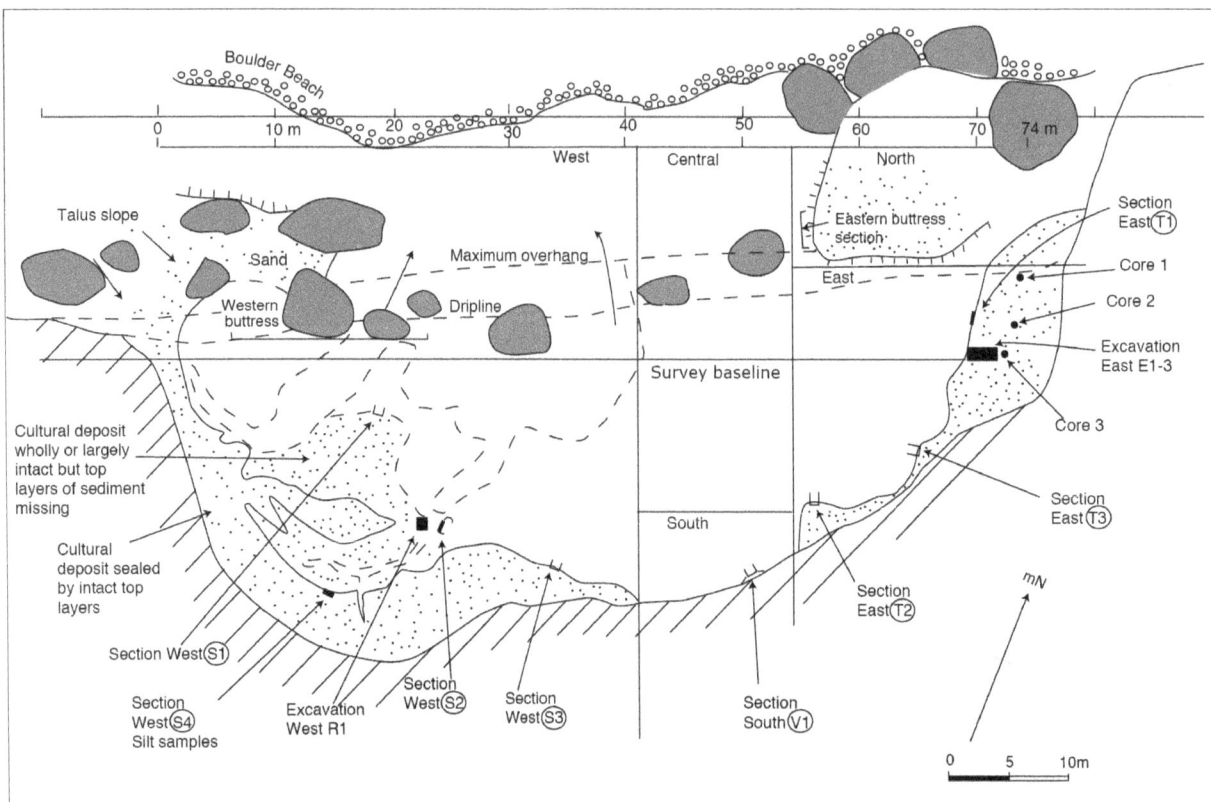

Figure 3.3. Plan of Tangarutu Cave in 2002.

in light winds from the southeast through northeast, but it is exposed to the north and west. By land, there is a steep climb from the inner bay around a bluff above cliffs. The cave is 80 m across at the dripline and it extends up to 29 m south to the back wall (Figure 3.3). The dripline is approximately 30 m from the water's edge. Within the cave is about 1450 m² of floor area to the dripline, and about 1700 m² to the maximum overhang.

In front of the cave are the remains of a sand dune, rising at the eastern edge to 5.3 m high, which sloped down seaward on to a boulder beach, and landward into the cave where, by recent times, a surface existed at up to about 4 m above mean sea level in the middle of the cave (Figure 3.4). Most of the dune is of light yellow-grey sand, which has been quarried away, leaving a sand 'buttress' at each side of the cave entrance. Sand also covers most of the floor of the cave, to a depth of 1–2 m from the original surface, the latter being mostly quarried away inside the cave but remaining around the inner sides and back (Figure 3.5). Within the remains of the dune at the mouth of the cave can be seen substantial layers of roof-fall basalt and, in the sand, some humus-stained layers, incorporating pebbles and clay, which are more strongly defined towards the top of the dune (Figure 3.6).

Excavation in 1997

The first archaeological investigations in this site were by Walczak in 1997. He dug five test pits, each 50 cm x 50 cm, in the back of the cave along a 12 m section near the southwestern wall of the cave (Walczak 2001:Figure 57). The intact face has retreated south by 2–5 m since 1997 as the result of continuing sand mining in the cave. Walczak's excavations produced a total of 36 basalt flakes, and 930 g of fish bone. The general site stratigraphy was described as three levels (Walczak 2001:298–299, Figure 56). Level 1, about 90–50 cm below the surface, contained negligible cultural material near the top of an indurated brown-black sand. This overlay a unit of brown, indurated sand finely lensed with loose white sand above a basal unit of white dune

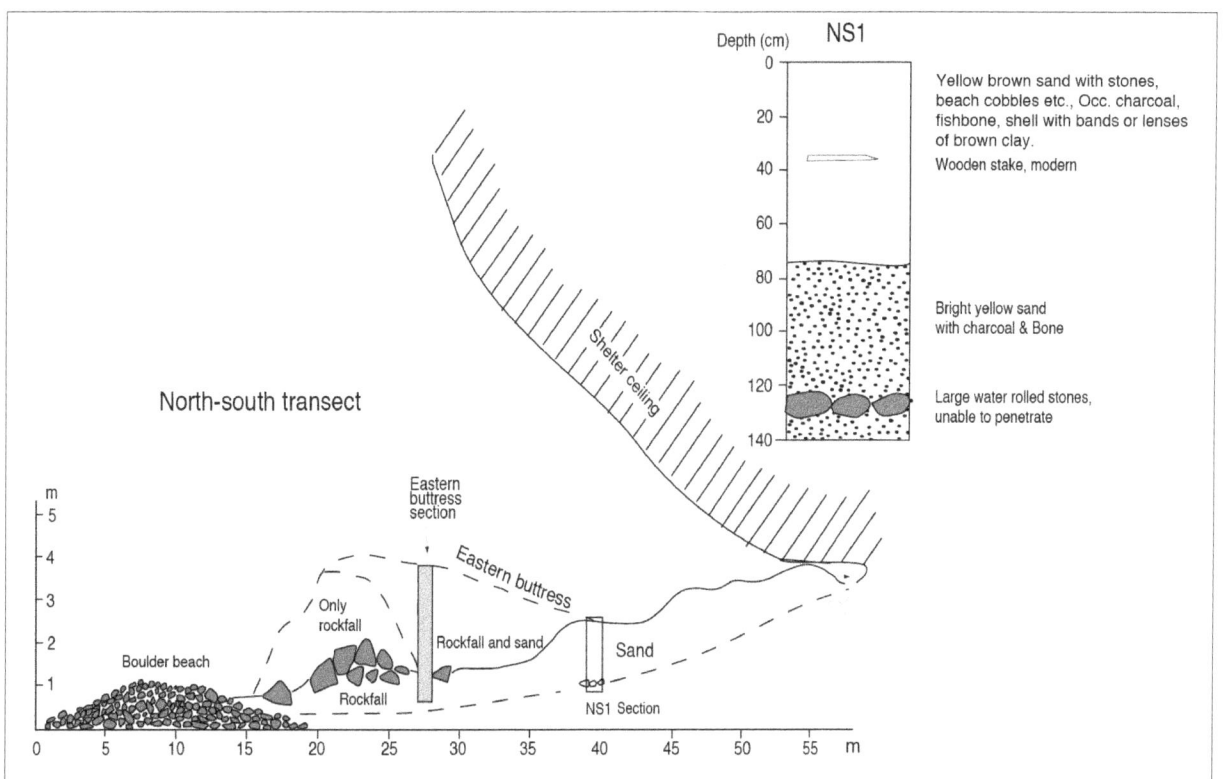

Figure 3.4. Cross-section of Tangarutu Cave, and stratigraphy of section NS1.

Figure 3.5. (above) Looking into the interior of Tangarutu Cave, showing the quarried cave floor and marginal remnants. Photograph A. Anderson.

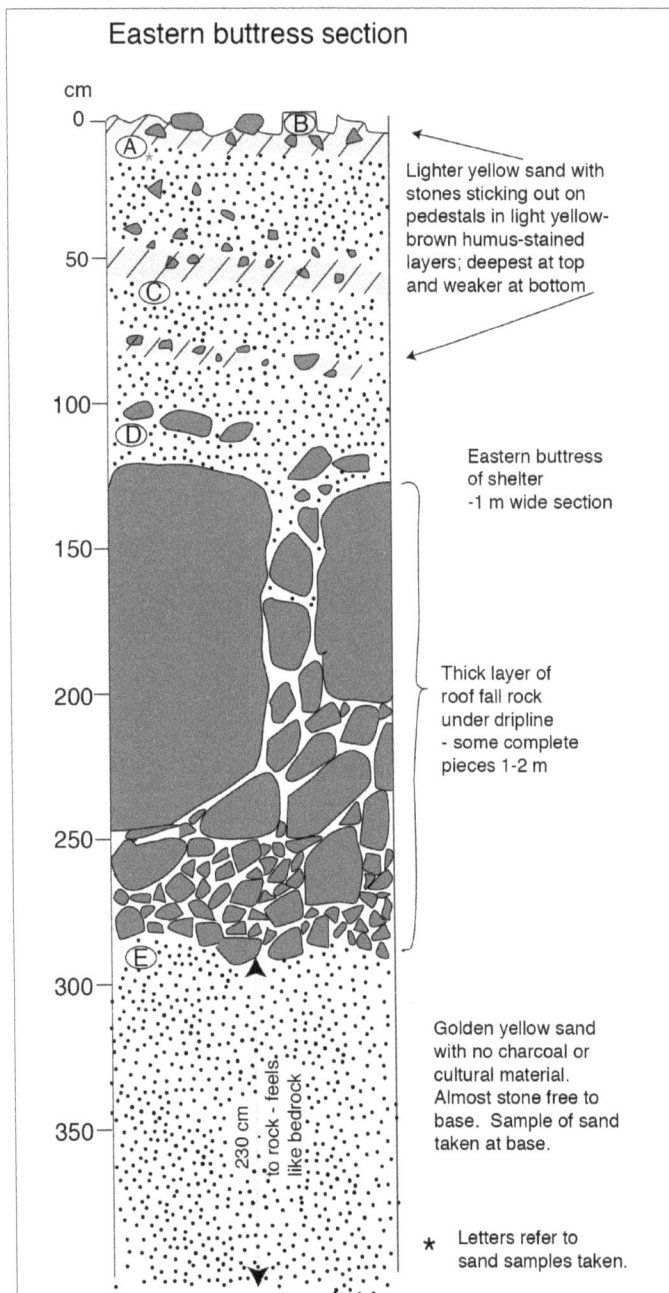

Eastern buttress section

cm

Lighter yellow sand with stones sticking out on pedestals in light yellow-brown humus-stained layers; deepest at top and weaker at bottom

Eastern buttress of shelter -1 m wide section

Thick layer of roof fall rock under dripline - some complete pieces 1-2 m

230 cm to rock - feels. like bedrock

Golden yellow sand with no charcoal or cultural material. Almost stone free to base. Sample of sand taken at base.

* Letters refer to sand samples taken.

Figure 3.6. Section at the eastern buttress of Tangarutu Cave.

sand that lay on the basalt floor of the cave. Level 2, at 50–20 cm, consisted of loose sand in which occurred shell, fish bones, bird bone, charcoal, oven stones and flakes of basalt. Level 3, at 20–0 cm, was a layer of very indurated brown sand on a base of very coarse sand or pebbles, up to 2 mm in diameter. The brown sand occurred as plates or lenses often showing whitish lines indicative of carbonate precipitation.

Walczak (2001:299–302) interpreted the stratigraphy as indicating the influence of climatic changes. His hypothesis is that as the sand dune in front of the cave increased, its back slope steepened and spilled sand into the cave. During dry periods, the transported sediment remained as loose sand, but during wetter periods, the sediments underwent some soil-forming processes which formed layers indurated by the precipitation of iron pans (alios);

> … les litages de sables bruns noirs qui nous font penser à des *alios*, c'est-à-dire a des concentrations gréseuses, indiquent que des phases un peu plus humides sont régulièrement venues ponctuées ces périodes 'sèches'. L'*alios* correspond à une dégradation superficielle du sable qui a tendance à s'oxyder sous l'impulsion d'une activité végétable ou animale. Le présence de carbonates et la consistence argileuse de ces niveeaux indurés résulte vraisemblablement de ces processus érosifs. Le niveau archéologique correspond à l'unité 2: it interviendrait donc durant une période plus sèche, qui aurait laissé plus de possibilités aux vents d'apporter du sable. (Walczak 2001:301–202)

From two of the test pits, samples of charcoal were dated, to two sigma, as follows: from Tangarutu I, 495 ± 40 bp (Ly-8577), and from Tangarutu II, 330 ± 45 bp (Ly-8578). Together with the earlier date of 370 ± 60 bp (Chapter 1), these data suggested to Walczak that the site had been occupied relatively late. He was inclined, nonetheless, to think that there must have been earlier occupation on Rapa, perhaps extending to the 12th century.

Excavation in 2002

Bad weather and rough seas caused by southeasterly gales prevented access to Tangarutu until July 18 and the field team of three people landed there had to leave after six days' work when supplies ran out. Conditions prevented returning until August 7 when a team of six began work again, but left after two days in deteriorating weather. Nevertheless, nine days on site enabled us to investigate it quite thoroughly and to obtain large samples for analysis. The cave floor and entry were mapped by tape, line-level and measuring staff, and all sections keyed for relative depth to E1 and V1 (Figure 3.7). There was no opportunity to get back to the site and survey it by total station, so our levels have an estimated error of ± 15 cm over 25 m distance.

The archaeological sections were chosen to disclose variation in the stratigraphy and each was cut down to a vertical surface 50 cm wide and generally 5–10 cm into the exposure. Augering beneath each exposed section determined whether there was lower cultural stratigraphy and defined the depth to rock. In most cases, a spade hole showed that this was the cave floor, but where rock could be reached only by auger it was uncertain whether it was *in situ* cave floor or simply rockfall. The broadly consistent level of the rock surface, however, suggested that it was indeed the floor of the cave, and the fact that in nearly all cases the rock was covered with clean sand indicates that the current basal layers of archaeological remains represent the earliest habitation in the site (Figure 3.7). Transects of auger holes and spade holes, east-west and north-south, across the disturbed central part of the site, showed a similar pattern, but disturbance by sand quarrying was evident well down in the sand, as indicated by a fresh wooden stake at 35 cm depth, among midden, in Test pit NS1. Nevertheless, there, and elsewhere in the transects, clean yellow-brown sand generally overlay rock at 1.1–1.3 m below the surface.

Inspection of the exposed stratigraphy in sections around the site margins showed that while there might have been some intermittent and incipient soil formation occurring in the sand, the overriding source of the stiff, brown, silty clays and clay-enriched sands, both often containing numerous pebble-sized and larger clasts of basalt, lies outside the cave. The thickest surface silty-clay layer, and the most frequent evidence of silty-clay lenses at depth, occured in the western half of the cave where a continuous talus slope extends westward out of the cave and into the adjacent hill slope (see Figure 3.2). The slope into the cave was marked by water channels, recent clay flows and gravel spreads. In the eastern half of the cave, silty clay was relatively infrequent, especially along the eastern margin of the cave.

The density distribution of archaeological materials was generally the inverse of the silt-clay distribution, suggesting sand was preferred as a habitation surface by the cave occupants. Consequently, the deepest surviving stratigraphy, with the most continuous and densest archaeological remains, occurred along the northeast margin of the site (Figure 3.7). Section T1 illustrates the stratigraphy of this area (Figure 3.8). It shows a cleaned-down west-facing section in sand, extending to bedrock at 2 m; cultural remains reached 1.6 m. In this northeastern quadrant of the cave, the observable sequence, confirmed by three auger holes and excavation E:1–3 (below), consisted of sterile yellow-brown sand and basalt shatter up to boulder size, deeper towards the cave entrance (e.g. in T1), overlying an upper unit of yellow-grey to grey dune sand in which there were conspicuous bands of desiccated leaf and fibre, especially higher in the section, with intermixed gravel, midden, lenses of charcoal, and burnt and broken basalt. A lower unit, below 100–110 cm in T1, had much less fibre in darker grey-brown sand, and charcoal, midden and burnt stone were sparse in the lower unit. The lower levels of the section were mostly sterile yellow sand, laminated with lenses of gravel and lines of light-brown or grey sand in which some silty clay was apparent.

In the southeastern quadrant of the site, very little of the archaeological stratigraphy remains. Section T3 (Figure 3.9) is within the distribution range of the last phase of silty-clay deposition, which preceded a terminal drift of grey-brown dune sand in which some cobbles had been

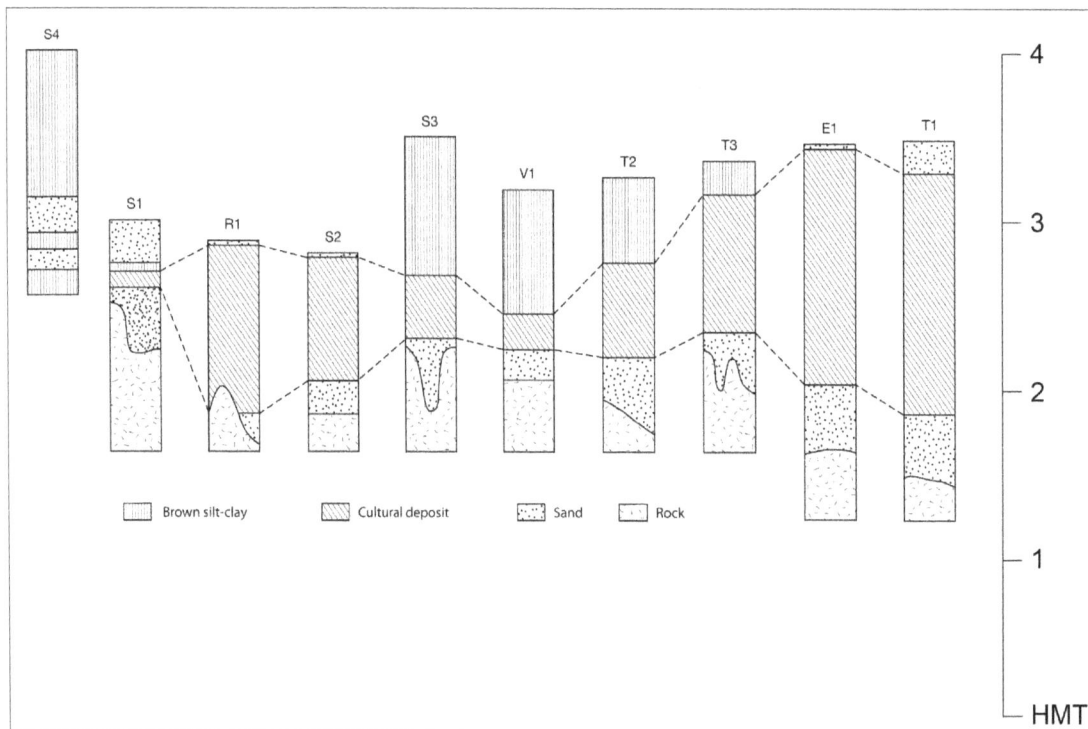

Figure 3.7. Investigated sections in Tangarutu Cave set out in order and by approximate height above sea level.

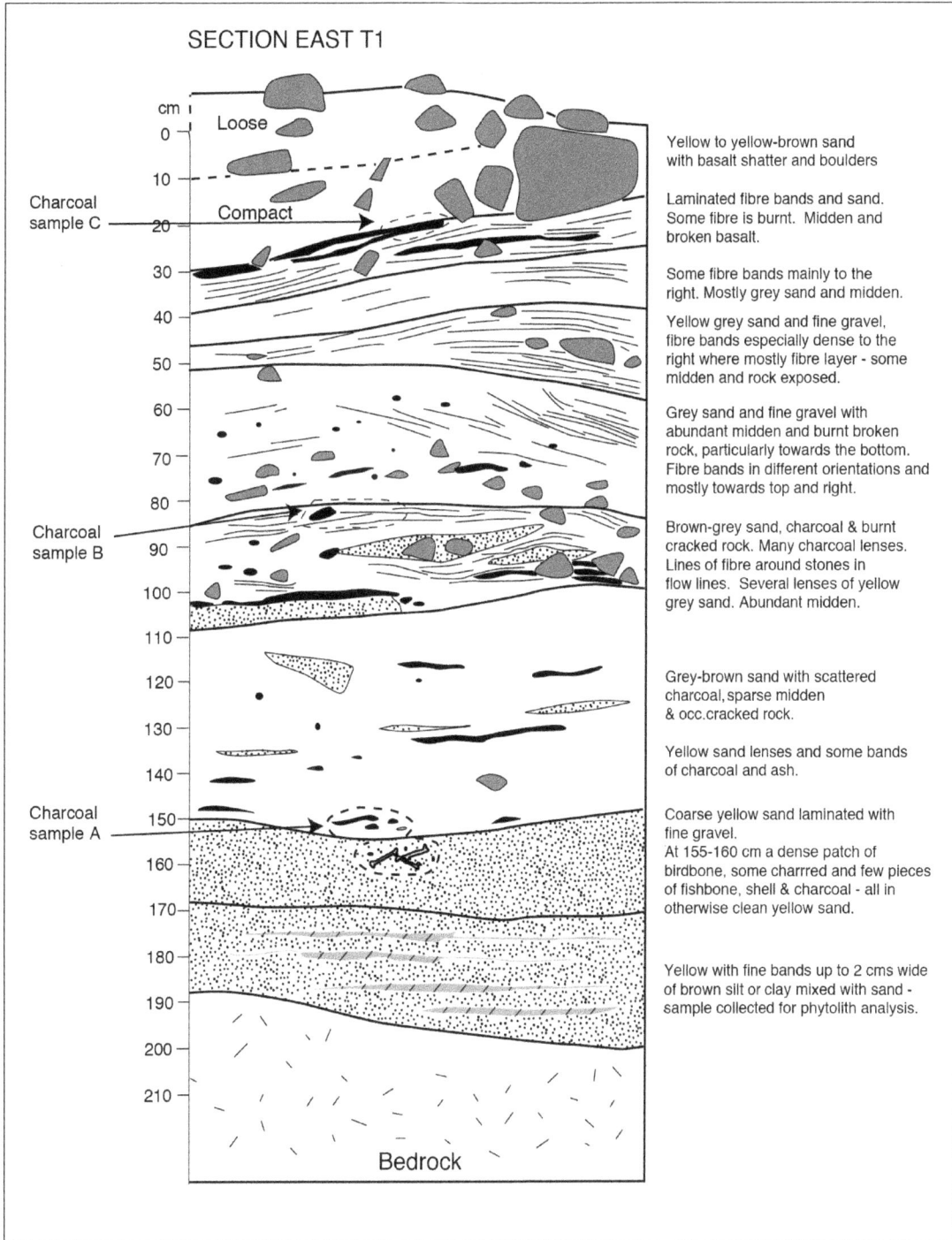

Figure 3.8. Stratigraphy at Section T1, Tangarutu Cave.

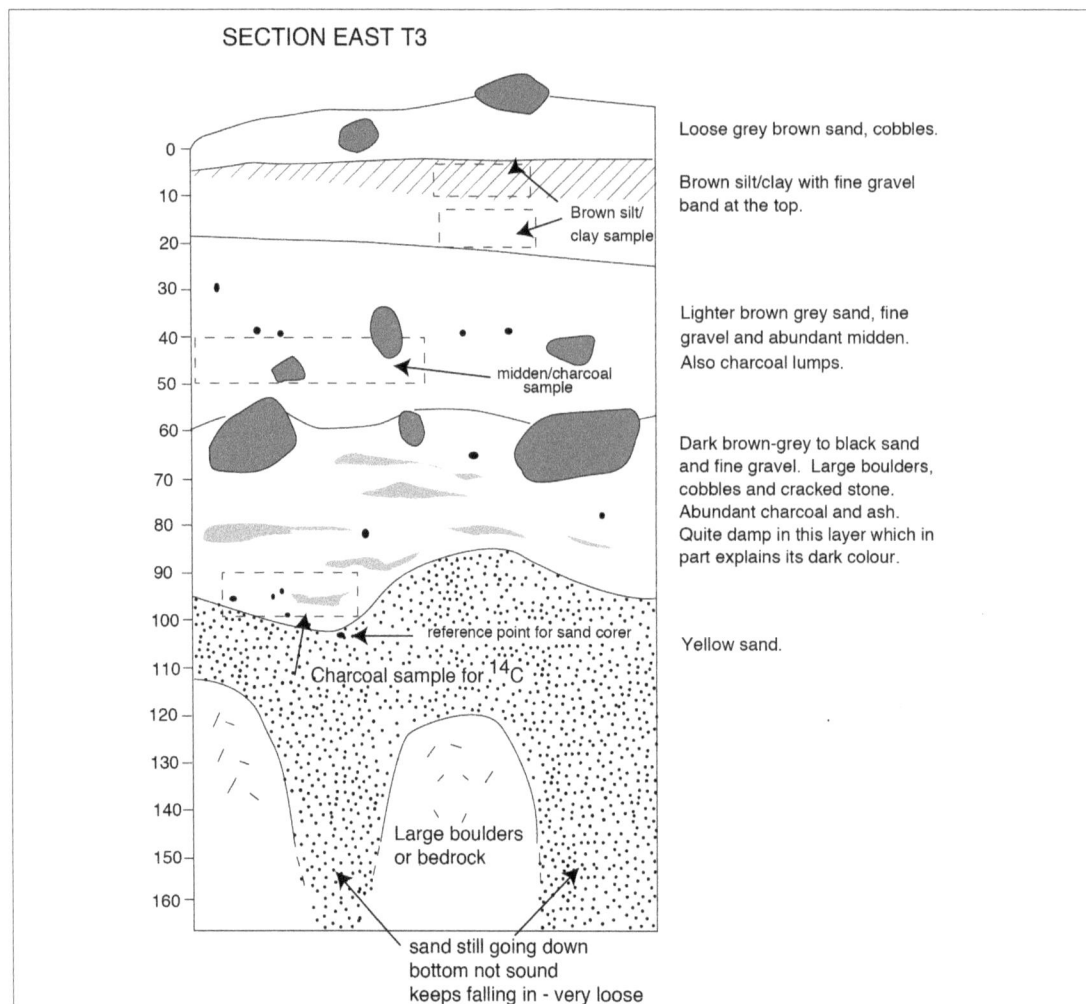

Figure 3.9. Stratigraphy at Section T3, Tangarutu Cave.

deposited. Beneath the silty clay, grey-brown sand contained abundant midden, especially of fish bone, and in the lower part of the grey-brown sand, 55–100 cm, cobbles, burnt and broken stone, charcoal and wood ash indicated the margin of an oven. Below 100 cm was clean, yellow sand. Section T2 was similar (Figure 3.10), except that the upper-silt and clay was divided into a number of fine bands separated by yellow sand, or, below 18 cm depth, by bands of fine gravel. Midden was sparse below, and near the base of the grey-brown sand were remains of a fire, with beach-rolled boulders alongside it. Section V1 (Figure 3.11) showed the same upper stratigraphy as T2, but it was thicker, at 70 cm. The grey-brown sand beneath was relatively thin, about 20 cm, but it contained abundant fish bone and lenses of charcoal.

Moving round to the western margins of the cave, it was apparent that fairly recent fluvial erosion has cut down, in a stepped fashion, through the mainly silt and clay sediments, removing the upper stratigraphy from some sections (S1, S2 and excavation R1), while retaining the upper levels at S3 and S4. There was enough overlap exposed, or dug out, to fit S4 and S3 to R1, and the latter to S1 and S2. Section S4 (Figure 3.12) was an exposure, entirely of more-or-less horizontally banded sand, gravel, silt and clay, forming the bank of a deeply incised watercourse (100 cm deep), which had run through the silty clay and associated sand into the middle of the site. The watercourse appeared quite fresh and it was very probably a consequence of sand quarrying; the removal of sediments in the centre of the site rejuvenating the erosive capability of temporary watercourses which would otherwise have dispersed across the silt-clay

SECTION EAST T2

Brown silt/clay.

Finely laminated lenses of
yellow sand and brown silt/clay.

Brown silt/clay with one fine lens of
yellow sand an two bands of fine
gravel. One small piece of charcoal.

Yellow sand with occ. pieces of charcoal.

Grey sand with bands of ash and charcoal
lens at base. Some midden.

midden sample →

Grey-brown sand; no lensing or
laminations. Occ. charcoal and midden.

Yellow sand with beach rolled
boulders and cobbles - patches of
ash and charcoal

Charcoal and midden sample

Clean yellow sand to bedrock
at 130-160 cm.

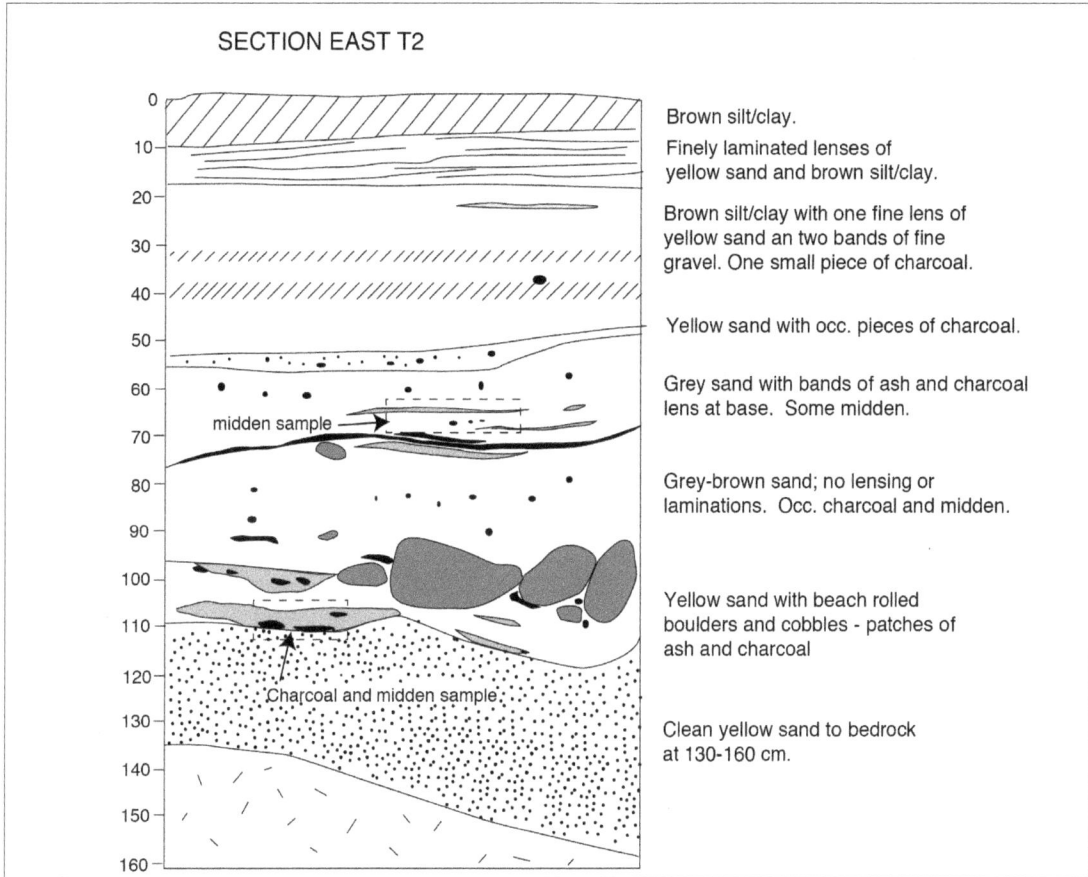

Figure 3.10. Stratigraphy at Section T2, Tangarutu Cave.

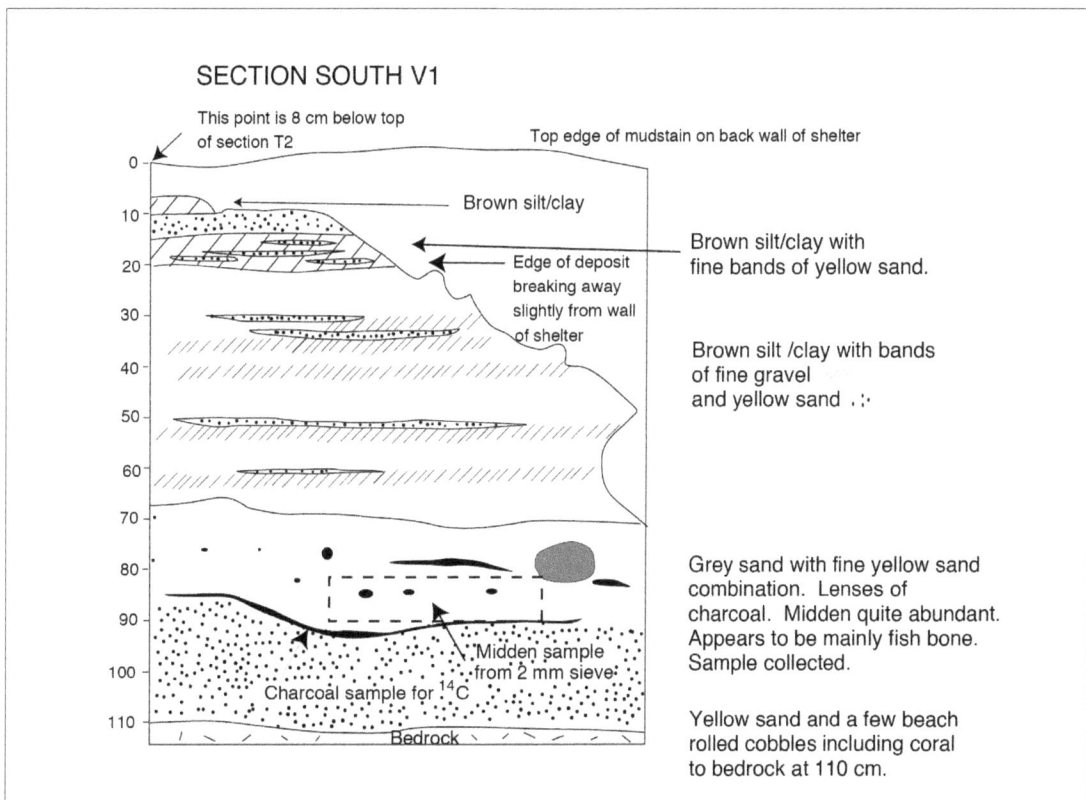

SECTION SOUTH V1

This point is 8 cm below top
of section T2

Top edge of mudstain on back wall of shelter

Brown silt/clay

Brown silt/clay with
fine bands of yellow sand.

Edge of deposit
breaking away
slightly from wall
of shelter

Brown silt /clay with bands
of fine gravel
and yellow sand

Grey sand with fine yellow sand
combination. Lenses of
charcoal. Midden quite abundant.
Appears to be mainly fish bone.
Sample collected.

Midden sample
from 2 mm sieve

Charcoal sample for ^{14}C

Bedrock

Yellow sand and a few beach
rolled cobbles including coral
to bedrock at 110 cm.

Figure 3.11. Stratigraphy at Section V1, Tangarutu Cave.

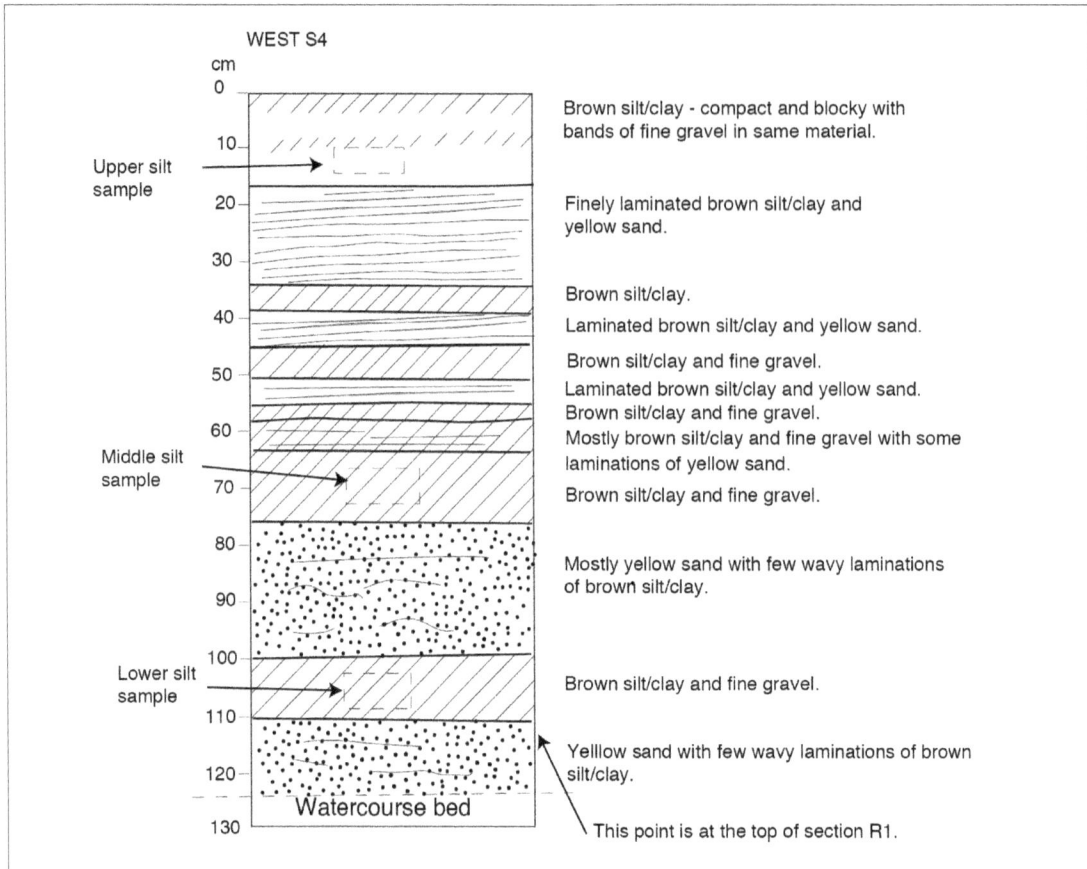

Figure 3.12. Stratigraphy at Section S4, Tangarutu Cave.

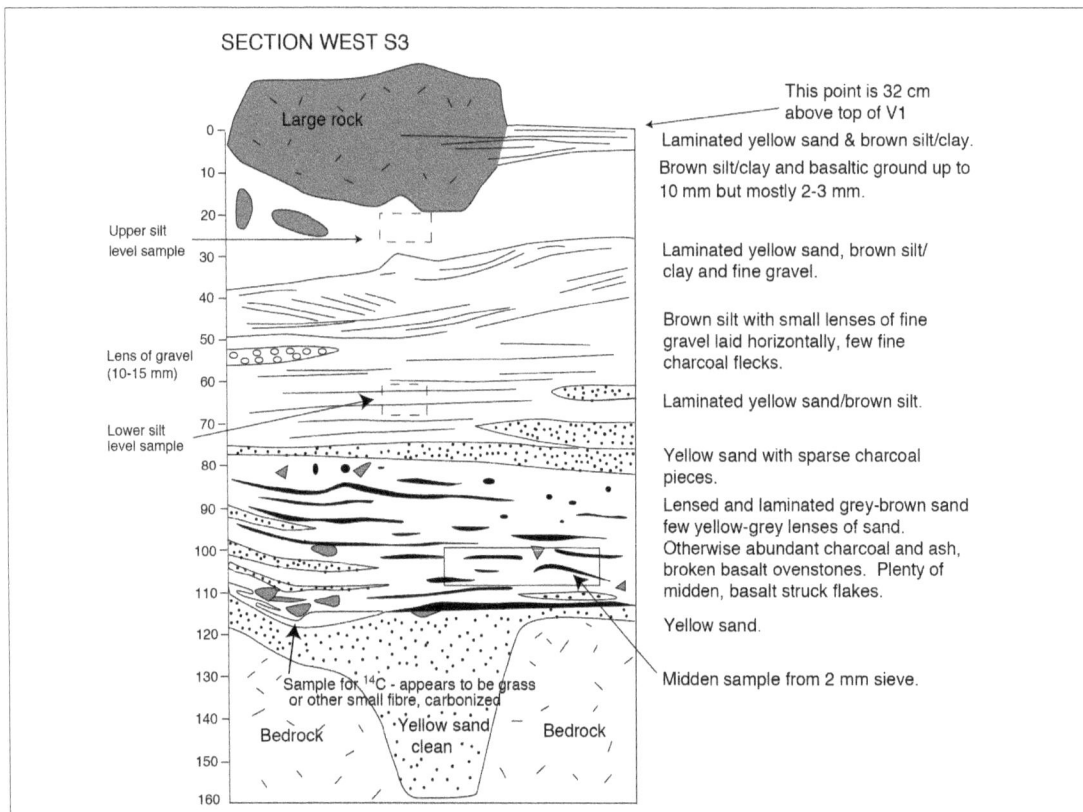

Figure 3.13. Stratigraphy at Section S3, Tangarutu Cave.

floor of the western part of the cave. The upper 80 cm of Section S3 (Figure 3.13) comprised a complexly lensed unit of brown silt-clay, finely laminated yellow sand and lenses of fine gravel, in which there were a few charcoal flecks. Grey-brown sand, 80–120 cm, was laminated with thin lenses of yellow sand and contained abundant charcoal and broken oven stones, intermixed with midden and basalt flakes.

Section S1 (Figure 3.14) begins stratigraphically at the 100 cm point in the S4 sequence. It contained similar units of sand and silty clay, but at 30 cm (1.3 m below the top of S4), there was a 10 cm band of yellow sand containing part of an adze preform and some bone midden and charcoal. Section S2 (Figure 3.15) begins stratigraphically at the 121 cm point in the Section S4 sequence. It had an upper layer of indurated grey-brown sand, silt and clay in which there was abundant charcoal and sparse midden. Beneath it was an oven with burnt, cracked stone and very abundant charcoal. A lens of brown sand through it seemed to divide successive episodes of use. The sand beneath the oven had the pinkish-brown aspect of having been burnt. The S4-S1 and S2-S4 sequences show that in the western part of the site the sediments were about as deep as in the east, 1.8 m and 2.1 m respectively to bedrock, but composed more largely of sterile sand, silt and clay. Along the south wall of the cave, the sand was shallower and bedrock was reached at 1.1 m to 1.2 m depth. The original shape of the site surface when it had been abandoned would, therefore, have been a shallow hollow, higher at each side and lower in the middle.

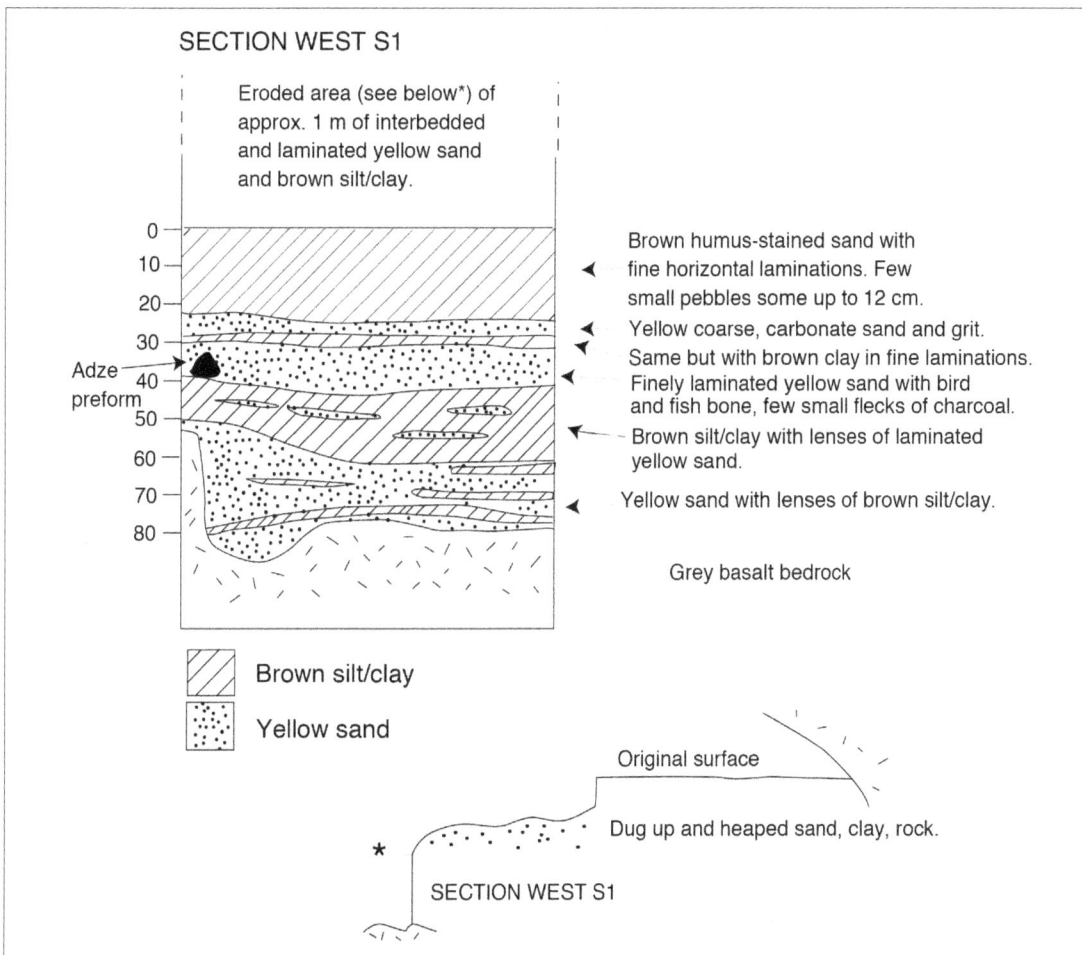

Figure 3.14. Stratigraphy at Section S1, Tangarutu Cave.

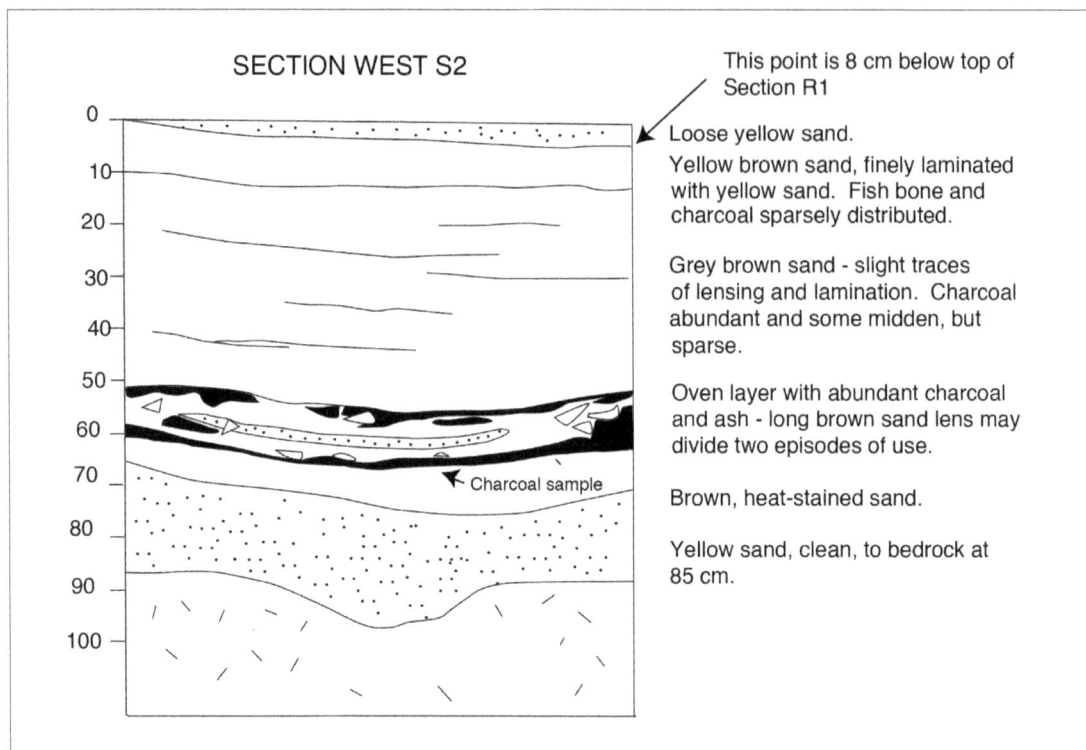

Figure 3.15. Stratigraphy at Section S2, Tangarutu Cave.

Excavation E1-3

Two small excavations were carried out at Tangarutu in 2002. In the eastern area, a 3 m x 1 m excavation area was laid out, although in the event, the excavation was so time-consuming, because of the depth and abundance of material and the time required for field sorting, that only the first two squares (E1 and E2) were excavated, a total of 1.5 m².

Square E1 was completed down to natural. In Square E2, only the adjoining or west half of the square was excavated. When the 1 m x 0.5 m excavation had reached Spit 5, bad weather was forecast, and with the boat due early the next day, the excavation was narrowed to a column 50 cm x 25 cm (Figure 3.18). It had the same stratigraphy as E1 and was excavated in 5 cm spits with 3 mm sieving down to 90 cm. With the arrival of the boat, the remaining Spits 19–25 of cultural material were taken out as whole samples. In addition to whole samples by spit, we also took out two large 'slices' in an attempt to preserve the microstratigraphy, especially the structure of the fibres, which was breaking up in sieving. These were at 10–18 cm and 45–58 cm (i.e. 8 cm and 13 cm thick respectively), each being 25 cm x 35 cm in area. They were packed into plastic boxes.

The location of Tangarutu is such that only a relatively small quantity of material could be taken out by backpack and the capacity of a small open boat was not much more, considering the persistently heavy seas. In the absence of convincing layer boundaries, excavation was by 5 cm spits in the main. The material was sieved through a 3 mm screen, except at a few points where the amount of gravel required a 4 mm screen; at those times, the residue was also sorted in a 3 mm screen. Below 70 cm, there was an abundance of broken oven stone, gravel and charcoal, but only sparse midden, mostly of large fish, and sieving switched to a 4 mm screen and 10 cm spits. A 30 cm x 18 cm plastic bag of whole sample (about 1.5 litres) was taken from each 5 cm spit and two from each 10 cm spit, for later sorting at the ANU through a 2 mm sieve. The residues were retained for future analysis.

The stratigraphy of E:1-3 (Figure 3.16) consisted of an upper unit (Level III, 0–40 cm) of slightly compact grey-brown sand and fine gravel packed with desiccated leaves, probably *Pandanus* or *Cordyline*. These often appeared as if strewn or blown into the cave, and some had become 'felted', but some also had been plaited. The leaves were very fragile and occurred as patches rather than as continuous features. Among them was abundant midden of shell, crayfish and crab exoskeleton, bone from small fish, occasional bird bone, pieces of gourd and candlenut, *Pandanus* keys and chewed fibres that were thought to be from *Cyathea* tree fern pith, along with flattened coprolites, pieces of cordage, charcoal, some basalt flakes and small fish hooks of candlenut and shell. Similar material, but much sparser, occurred at 40–70 cm (Level II), and below that (Level I, 70–150 cm) were oven remains of charcoal, oven stones and ash going down through faint grey lenses into clean yellow sand (Figure 3.17).

The material retained for analysis in this and other coastal excavations consisted of: all identifiable shell (whole shell and apertures, spires, columns etc, plus pieces of sea urchin, and crab and crayfish exoskeleton); all fish bone except for ribs and spines; fish scales; all bird, reptile and mammal bone; all wood and charcoal of >20 mm largest dimension and any pieces with potentially identifiable features; all other plant tissue (much of it candlenut, but also *Pandanus* keys and chewed pieces of possible *Cyathea* pith) and natural fibre; all woven, plaited or otherwise modified fibre; all stone flakes; and all artefacts of any other kind. In various places, samples of sand and silt were taken to enable a search for phytoliths, pollen and other microscopic components.

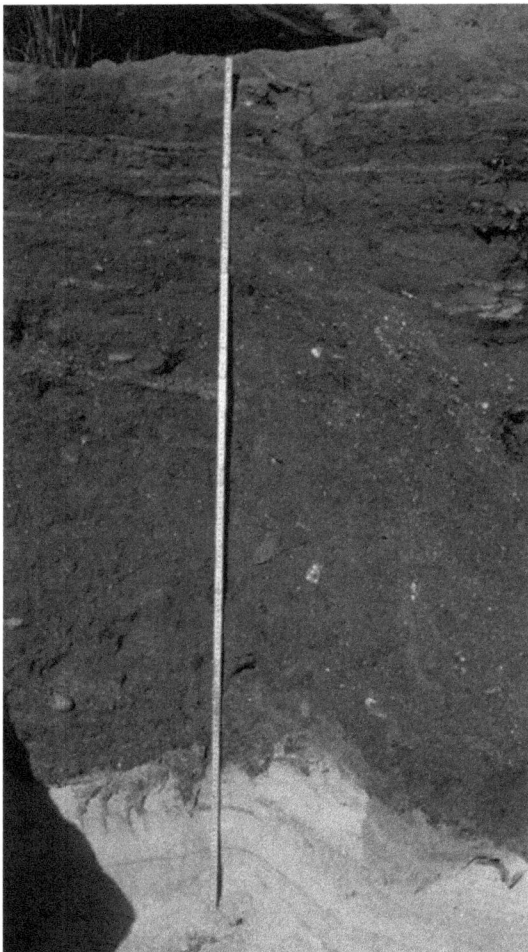

Figure 3.16. Excavated Square E1, Tangarutu Cave. Photograph A. Anderson.

EXCAVATION E1 EAST BAULK

Reference point for levelling other sections.

Loose sand, cobbles, shatter.

Compact grey brown sand and fine
gravel packed with laminated patches
of pandanus leaves.
Abundant midden, fish hooks,
basalt flakes etc. Some lenses of ash and
charred pandanus. Large amounts of charcoal.

Compact grey-brown sand and fine
gravel - below about 70 cm is dark
grey brown and more broken stone.
Fibre patches are less dense.
Abundant middent and charcoal, some
basalt flakes, bird bone (larger species)
and larger fish bone. More abundant
below 100cm. Some patches of ash
and charcoal.

Yellow sand with faint grey
patches and lines.

point of reference
for sand corer

clean yellow sand sample

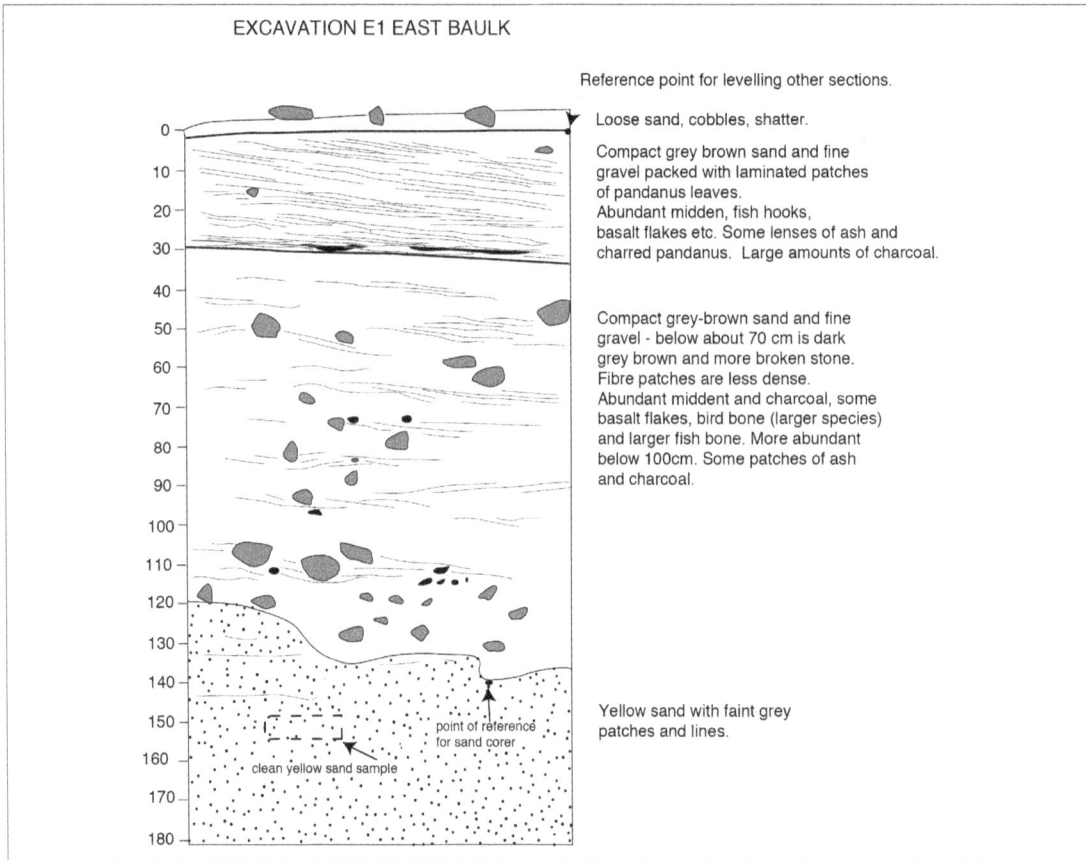

Figure 3.17. (above) Stratigraphy at Section E1, East baulk, Tangarutu Cave.

Figure 3.18. Excavation in progress at Square E2, Tangarutu Cave. Photograph A. Anderson.

Excavation R-1

A 1.0 m x 1.0 m excavation was placed in this area to sample the cultural materials in the western half of the cave (Figure 3.19). This excavation occurred at the same time as excavation of Square E2, and was constrained by the same problems with weather and transport. Excavation using the same protocols of 5 cm spits, 3 mm sieving and retention of whole samples and cultural material proceeded at R1 down to 80 cm, at which time it switched to 10 cm spits and 4 mm sieving, with two large whole samples (each about 20 litres) taken.

The cultural material, predominantly fish bone midden with scarce bird bone or shell, but abundant charcoal, was found mainly in the top 30–40 cm (designated Level III), where two units of grey sand were separated by thin lenses of yellow sand. The upper grey-sand unit was finely laminated, indicating that it had been deposited without disturbance and the sparse midden and charcoal that occurred in it had been presumably blown in. The lower grey-sand unit (ca. 20–35 cm) had abundant charcoal but very sparse midden. Similar material in brown-grey sand from 40 cm to 80 cm (Level II) contained patches of midden and charcoal. The lowest material (80–105 cm, Level I) was essentially an oven full of broken oven stone, charcoal and very sparse midden (Figure 3.20).

Figure 3.19. Excavated Square R1 at Tangarutu Cave. Photograph A. Anderson.

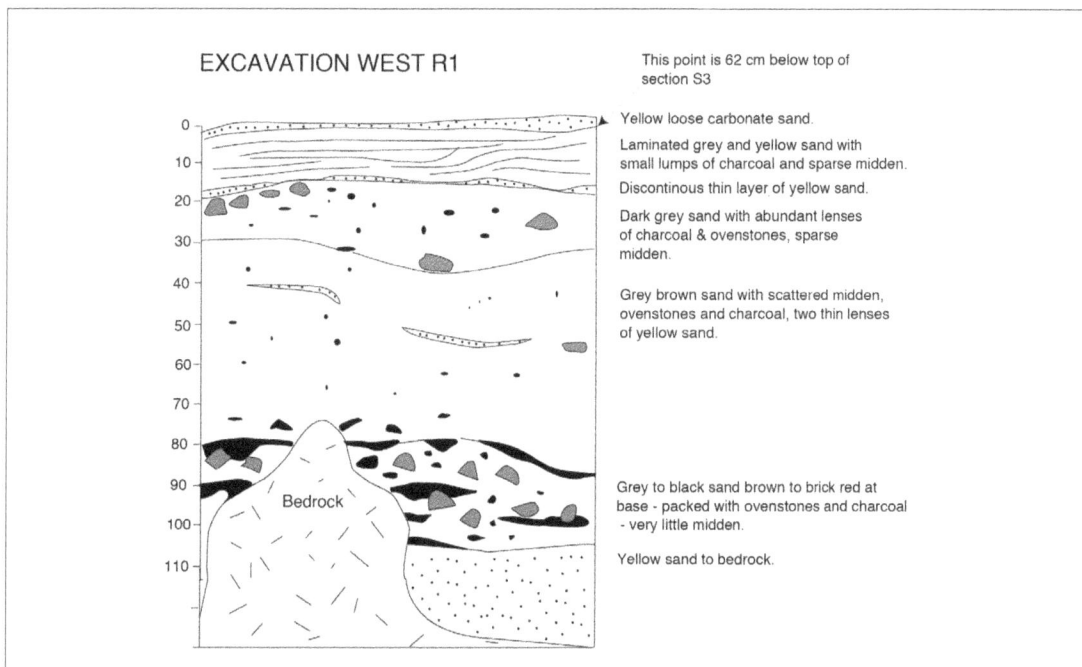

Figure 3.20. Stratigraphy at Section R1, Tangarutu Cave.

Akatanui shelters

The Akatanui shelters consist of a main site (Shelter 3) and several small shelters at the west end. Shelter 3 is a large, narrow, southeast-facing rockshelter, known ethnographically as Tikaioe (Figure 3.21). It is 102 m long and up to 12 m across to the dripline, but mostly less than 5 m wide, and it is divided by rock buttresses into five alcoves containing archaeological deposits (Figure 5.22). Most of the site is 2–2.5 m above sea level, and the shelter ceiling is 20 m high at the dripline, so the site is exposed to wind-driven rain and spray. Two small shelters are <10 m long and only one (Akatanui 1) has a cultural deposit.

Akatanui 1

A 10 cm thick deposit of midden was found over an area of 8 m^2 in this site (R2002-26). A 1 m x 1 m excavation showed the midden to contain mainly broken gastropod shell, with some fish bone, crayfish and crab shell. Among it were two shell buttons, an iron nail and a lens from a pair of spectacles, all of early 20th century form. Akatanui 2 (R2002-27) was a smaller shelter 150 m to the east. It had a very thin scatter of midden similar to that in Akatanui 1.

Akatanui 3

A series of test pits along this large shelter (R2002-28), which begins 120 m east of Akatanui 2, showed that most archaeological deposits were thin and sparse. Test-pit A1 (50 cm x 100 cm) had a 15–20 cm deep deposit of ash and charcoal, within which were some fragments of wood and fibre, and a few pieces of candlenut and gastropod shell. Test-pit B1 (50 cm x 80 cm) revealed a 4 cm thick deposit of charcoal-stained, but otherwise sterile, sand. Test-pit E1 (50 cm x 100 cm) was a sand deposit 33 cm deep, from which a very small quantity of charcoal, fish bone and gastropod shell was recovered, and Test-pit F1 (50 cm x 50 cm) was a 47 cm deep deposit of sand, gravel and basalt shatter with no archaeological material (Figure 3.22).

The main excavation was of 2 m^2 at C1 (Figure 3.23, 3.24). This part of the shelter is

Figure 3.21. Akatanui shelters looking northeast across Alcove B. Photograph A. Anderson.

lower than elsewhere, about 1.2 m above sea level, but Akatanui Bay is relatively sheltered. A broad coral reef breaks the swell offshore and a band of mangroves shelters the shoreline. The stratigraphy (Figure 3.24) disclosed by excavation comprised a single 5–15 cm thick layer of cultural deposit, which was overlain by yellow-brown carbonate sand and basalt shatter, plus some beach-rolled cobbles (Unit 1 in Figure 3.24), and underlain by gravel and sand, going down on to beach-rolled cobbles and boulders (Units 3 and 4). The cultural layer (Unit 2) was of coarse sand and gravel containing beach-rolled cobbles and boulders, abundant oven-stone fragments and charcoal, lenses of wood ash, some molluscan and crab shell, fish bone and several patches of fibre, including of *Pandanus*.

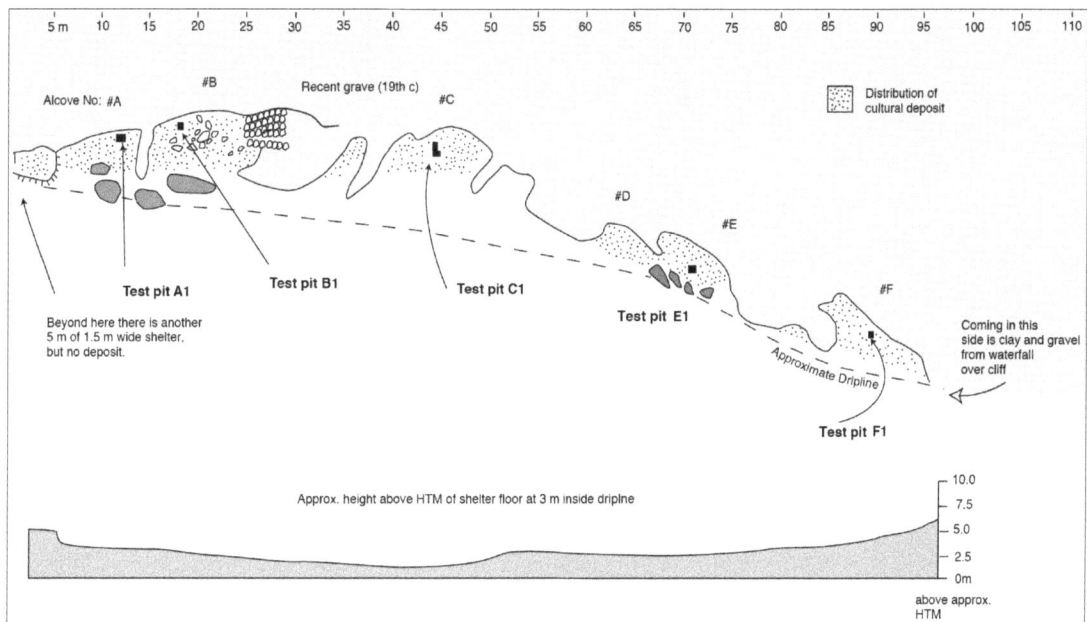

Figure 3.22. Akatanui shelters showing the alcoves and excavations, and, below, the height of the shelter floor above sea level.

Figure 3.23. Akatanui shelters showing Alcove C, and Excavation C1 in progress.
Photograph A. Anderson.

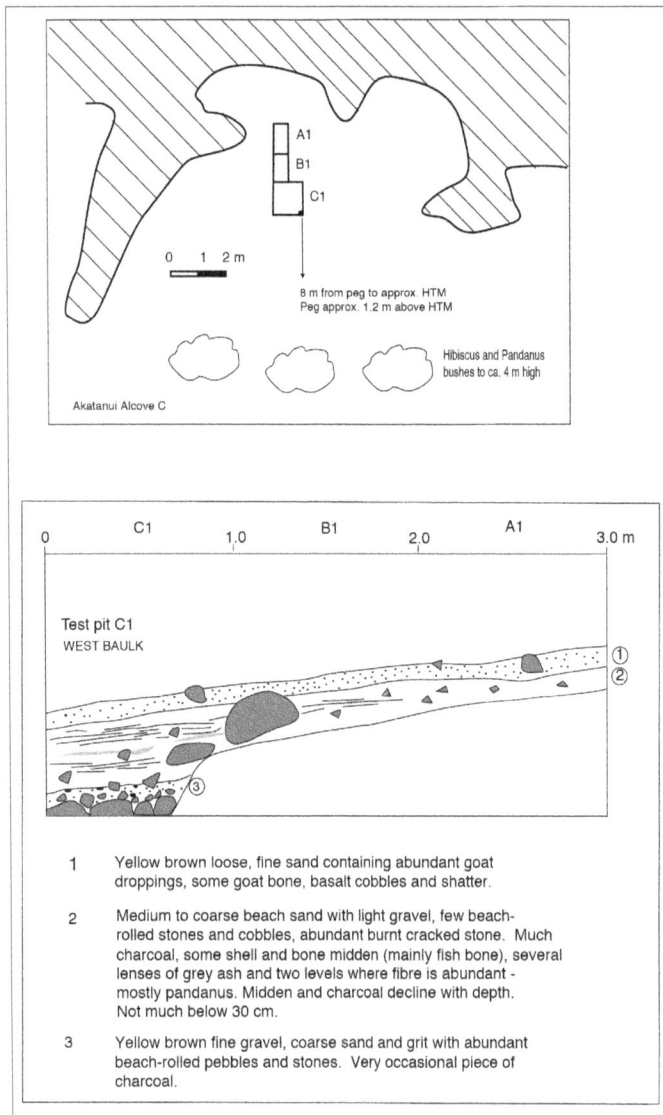

Figure 3.24. Akatanui shelters. Excavation C1 plan, above, and section, below.

Angairao shelters

On the western side of Angairao Bay, a series of rockshelters occurs along the headland running out to Point Komire, which separates Angairao from Akananue Bay (Figure 3.25). Shelters A and B proved unpromising. Shelter D (R2002-35) is 21 m long and up to 3.5 m wide and is filled with unsorted talus of clay and silt plus basalt clasts up to large boulder size. This material slopes into the shelter and, as the dripline is inside the highest point, the shelter sediments are damp. A spade pit reached 45 cm down to either bedrock or a very large boulder without disclosing any cultural material. Shelter C (R2002-34) has a silt floor behind a low piled-rock wall. A test pit (50 cm x 50 cm) disclosed an archaeological deposit of shell and bone midden with charcoal and some patches of fibre or bark near the top of it (Figure 3.25). Excavation continued down through yellow-brown silt and clay containing abundant basalt shatter to flat rocks or bedrock at about 95 cm deep.

Shelter E rock art and excavation

The main fieldwork was in Shelter E (Figure 3.26), which is an annexe to the southeastern end of Shelter D, where the talus slope falls away seaward, leaving a dry floor approximately 20 m x 5 m. On the northwest face of this shelter (R2002-36), three figures had been pecked about

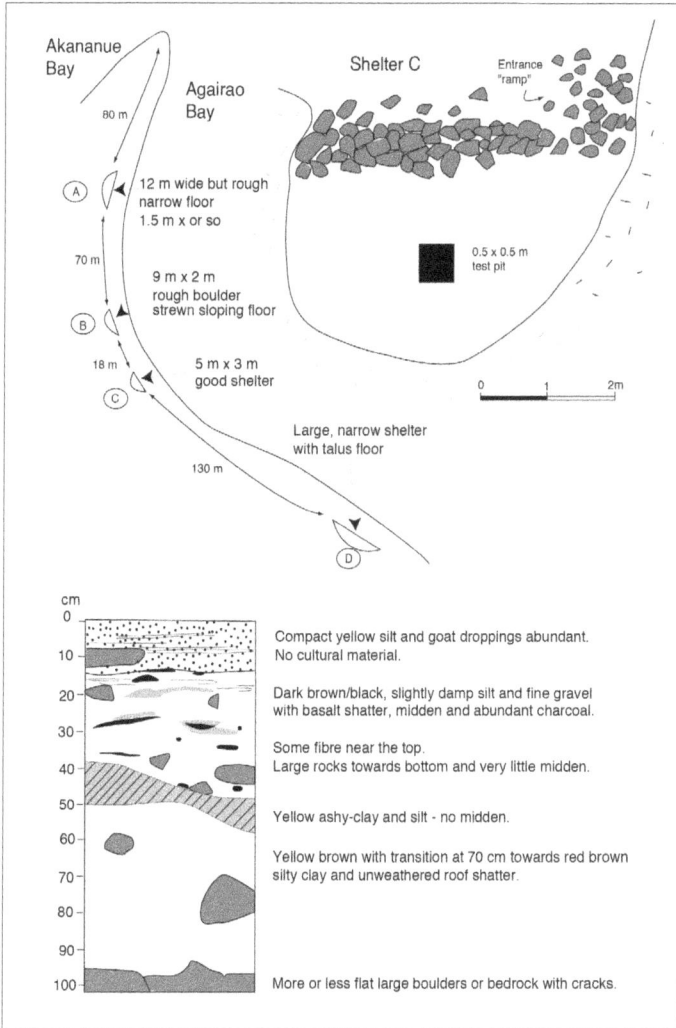

Akananue
Bay

Agairao
Bay

80 m

Shelter C

Entrance
"ramp"

(A)   12 m wide but rough
       narrow floor
       1.5 m x or so

70 m

9 m x 2 m
rough boulder
strewn sloping floor

(B)

18 m   5 m x 3 m
        good shelter

(C)

Large, narrow shelter
with talus floor

130 m

(D)

0.5 x 0.5 m
test pit

0   1   2m

cm
0

10   Compact yellow silt and goat droppings abundant.
      No cultural material.

20   Dark brown/black, slightly damp silt and fine gravel
      with basalt shatter, midden and abundant charcoal.

30

40   Some fibre near the top.
      Large rocks towards bottom and very little midden.

50   Yellow ashy-clay and silt - no midden.

60
      Yellow brown with transition at 70 cm towards red brown
70   silty clay and unweathered roof shatter.

80

90

100   More or less flat large boulders or bedrock with cracks.

Figure 3.25. Agairao Bay showing distribution of shelters and plan and section of excavation in Shelter C.

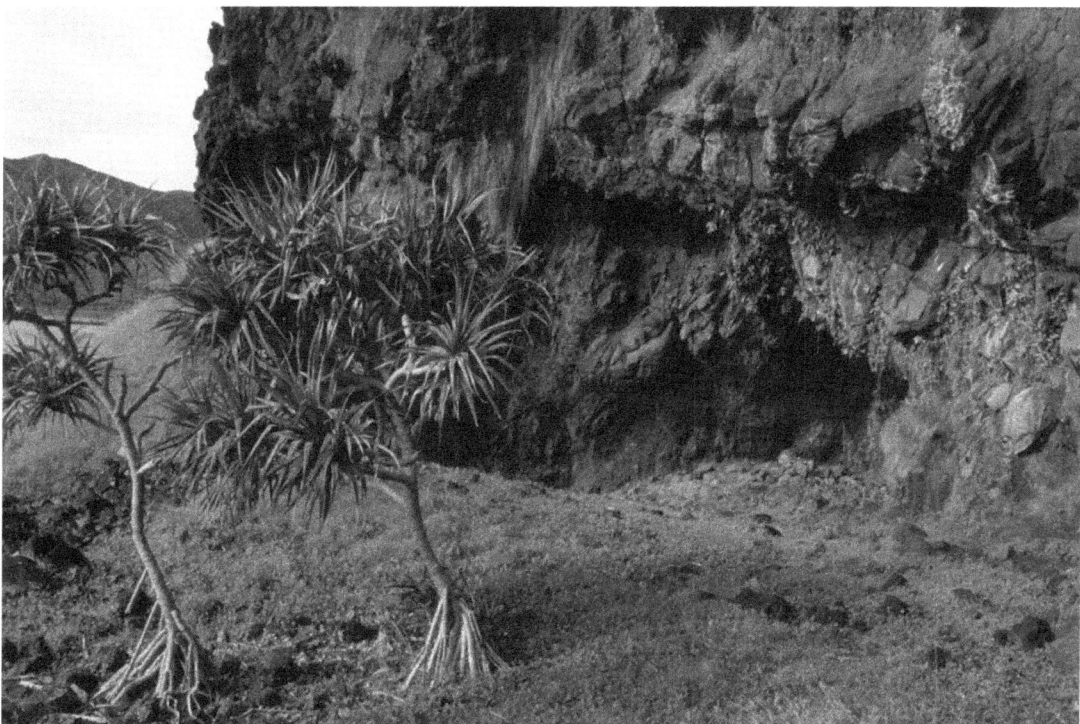

Figure 3.26. Agairao Shelter E (annexe of Shelter D). Photograph A. Anderson.

1.5 mm deep into the smooth basalt surface (Figure 3.27). These (R2002-37) were the only examples of rock art that were seen on Rapa. One figure (30 cm in height) at the bottom of the panel is rudimentary. At 33 cm above the highest incision of this begins a 61 cm tall figure representative of a bird or possibly an eel. Diagonally above that is a 25 cm human figure. The latter looked slightly fresher than the former two. Near the figures are indistinct black markings that might once have formed letters, and across them a vertical streak of red ochre. The human and the bird/fish figure are in typical prehistoric East Polynesian styles, and the possible lettering and red mark are features of rock art in New Zealand (Trotter and McCulloch 1981), and elsewhere in East Polynesia where writing partly supplanted drawing in the missionary era.

The Shelter E excavation was 1.2 m x 0.6 m and located in the back of the shelter (Figure 3.28), where the floor consisted of a 20 cm thick layer of cow dung. Beneath this the sediments were mainly of gravel and silt, plus numerous pieces of burnt stone and large pieces of basalt shatter, which were increasingly frequent with depth. Below the dung was a thin layer of fireplace remains (called 'Oven 1') overlying orange-yellow silt, probable ash and gravel. In the base of this unit was turtle bone and some fish bone midden. Below that unit was a 100 cm thick undifferentiated layer of black silt and clay with lenses of ash, abundant oven stone and charcoal. This was designated 'Oven 2'. Midden was very sparse, consisting mainly of some gastropod shell and fragments of fish bone. This unit was excavated in 10 cm spits and later divided into three levels (Level III, 60–90 cm; Level II, 90–140 cm; Level I, 140–165 cm).

Below 90 cm the deposit was damp, which probably accounts in part for the scarcity of organic remains, and below 140 cm it was wet, and charcoal was relatively scarce. At 160 cm deep there was a 3 cm thick band of grey clay without charcoal or any other cultural material. The natural layer beneath comprised red-brown, sticky clay and basalt clasts up to 40 cm in size. This was excavated for 5 cm then augered down to 186 cm below the top of the excavation, where rock was encountered all over, presumably the bedrock of the shelter.

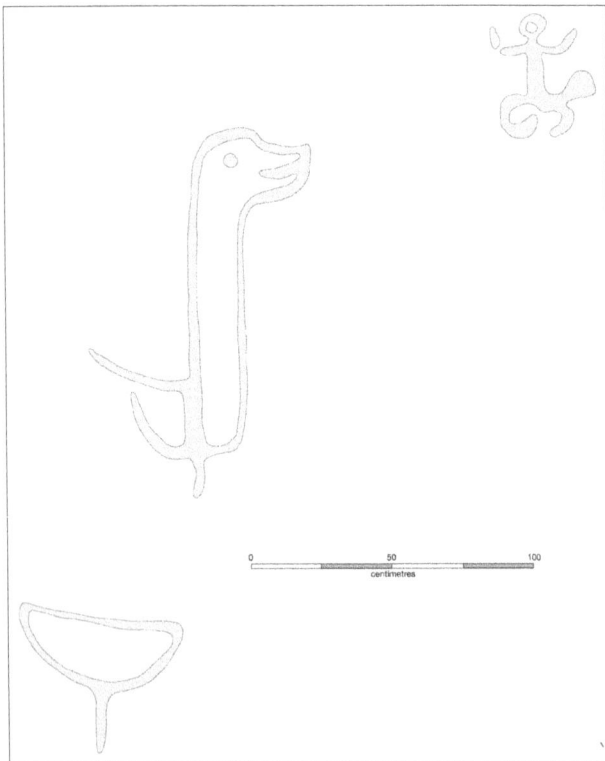

Figure 3.27. Rock engravings on the wall of Agairao Shelter E, above, and field sketch of them, left. Photograph A. Anderson.

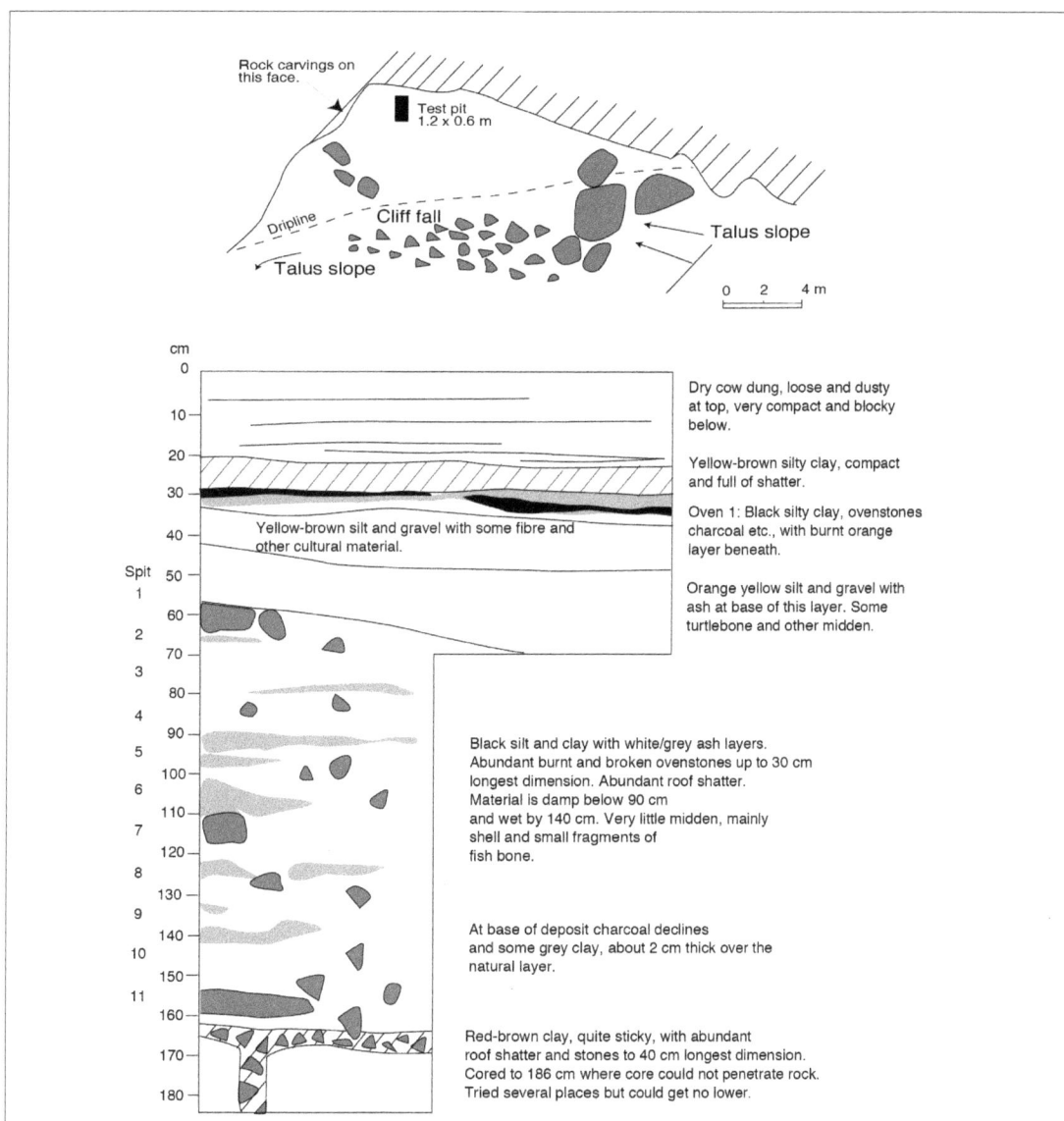

Figure 3.28. Agairao Shelter E excavation plan, above, and section, below.

Noogoriki shelter

On the eastern side of Angairao Bay, near Tematapu Point, is a large rockshelter, 25 m long and about 3.5 m wide in the middle (R2002-38). It is 5 m above sea level, but right on the shore (Figure 3.29) and exposed to westerly gales and high seas. Stokes (n.d.:360) reported that a burial platform was found inside it. A 40 cm x 40 cm excavation encountered a 60 cm thick cultural layer beneath 20 cm of modern organic material and silt (Figure 3.30). The cultural layer consisted of black silt and gravel with abundant basalt shatter and oven-stone fragments. The material was compact and damp and difficult to sieve even at 4 mm mesh. It contained very little fish bone and shell, but plenty of charcoal. A large bulk sample was taken from 70–80 cm depth.

Figure 3.29. Noogoriki Shelter in Agairao Bay. Photograph A. Anderson.

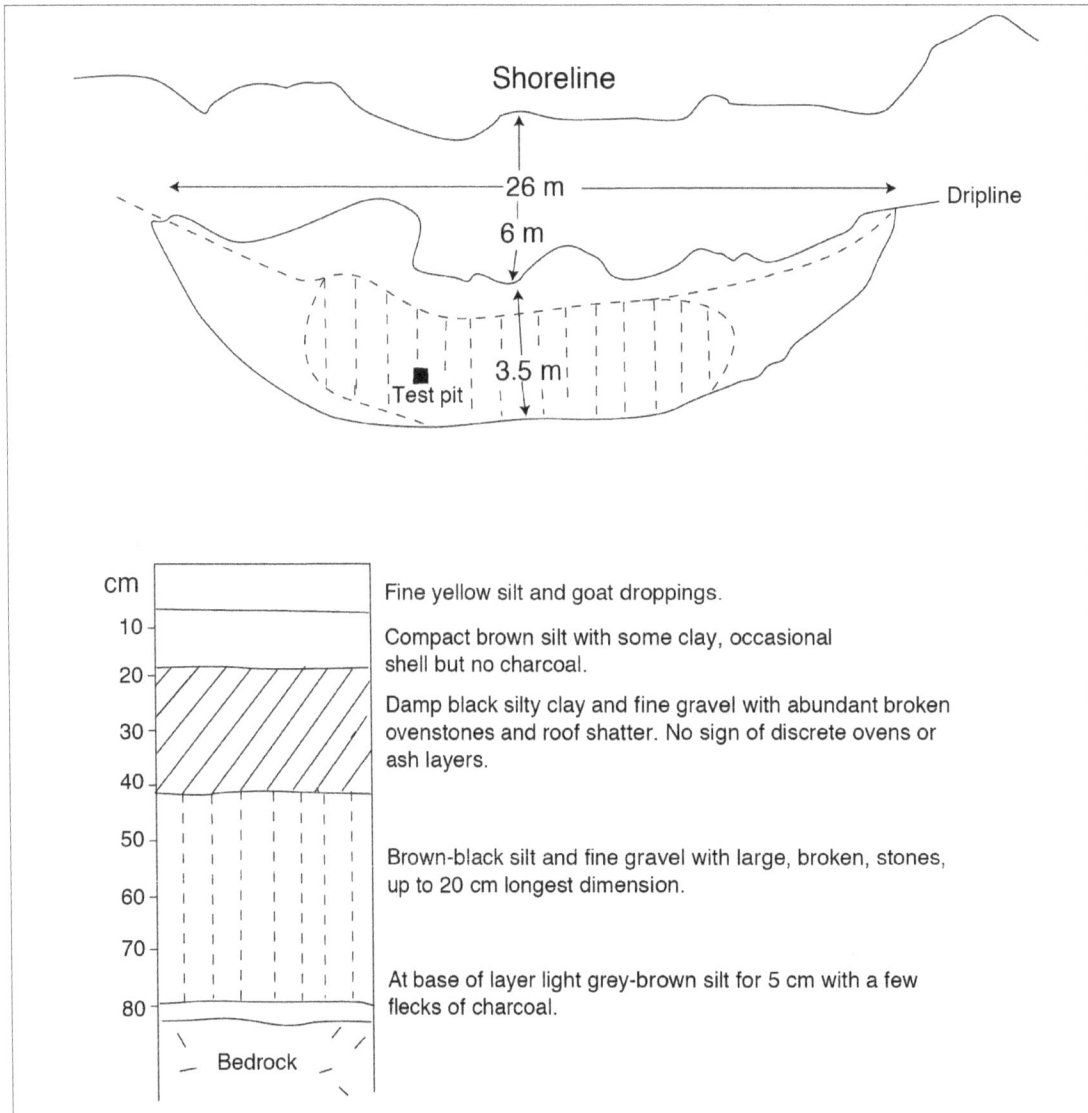

Figure 3.30. Plan and section of test pit in Noogoriki Shelter.

Additional rockshelters

Ha'urei Harbour

Near the south entrance of the harbour there is a rockshelter (R2002-30) about 12 m above sea level (Figure 3.1). It has a floor area of 10 m x 3 m behind the dripline. A 40 cm x 40 cm spade hole in the centre of the floor revealed a 12 cm layer of modern organic material overlying an 18 cm thick brown loam resting on bedrock. Within the loam were small lenses of ash and charcoal containing gastropod shell and fish bone fragments. These were sampled. At the head of the harbour is a small rockshelter (R2002-23), which contained a thin deposit of midden and charcoal.

Angatakuri Bay

Five rockshelters can be seen in the middle of the north-facing part of the southern coastline in this bay, and a further three are on the east-facing shore about 250 m northwest of the point (see Figure 3.1). All the shelters are narrow and damp and most contain no suitable sediment. Shelter A (R2002-31), about 5 m above sea level, was mostly clean down to bedrock, but contained a 16 m² area of sediment which was tested by a 40 cm x 40 cm spade pit. This showed 10–12 cm of brown sticky clay and roots over a 15 cm-deep deposit of wet, dark-grey clay containing burnt stone and charcoal, plus one flaked piece of basalt. Beneath was a thin layer of brown clay and gravel going down to bedrock. Shelter B (R2002-32) is about 8 m above sea level facing north and has a floor 17 m x 3 m to the dripline. Rainwater runs back into the floor, which has a row of taro planted in it. Two auger holes and a 40 cm x 40 cm spade pit disclosed 35 cm of sticky brown clay over a wet deposit of dark-grey clay, silt and sand, containing broken rock and charcoal, which extended to bedrock at 116–120 cm depth.

Iri Bay

The Anakere shelter (2002-33) was investigated. This is beside, and 1.5–2.0 m above, a small stream about 12 m above sea level. Most of the shelter floor is enclosed within a rectangular perimeter of placed stones, which probably had something to do with the reputed mortuary function of the site (Stokes n.d.:258). Our investigations were restricted to augering in the outer margins of the shelter (Figure 3.31). Cores 1 and 3 produced stratigraphic records. They showed that the top 35 cm consisted of reddish-brown, very compact clay. Below that there was mid-

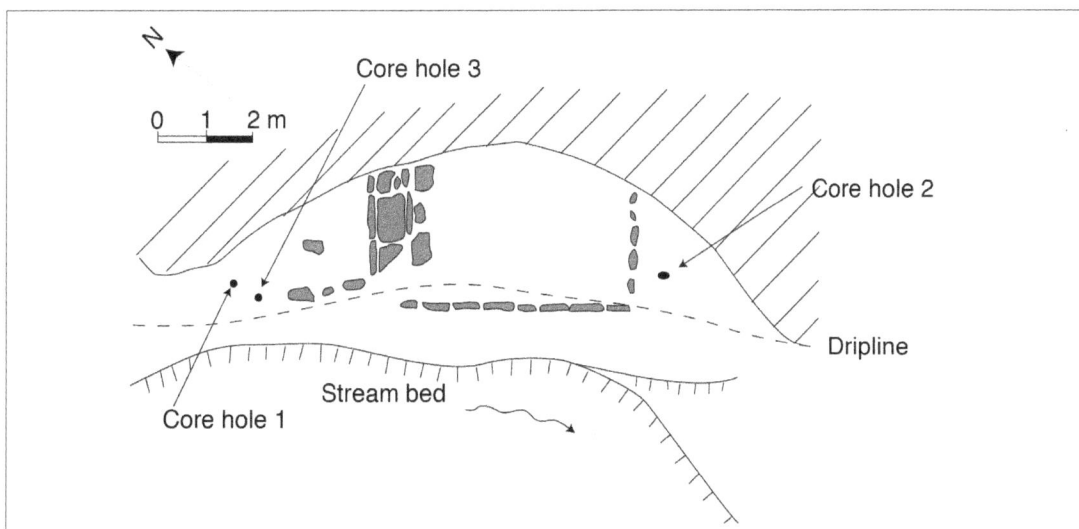

Figure 3.31. Plan of Anakere Shelter, Hiri Bay, showing location of augering.

brown clay containing water-rolled pebbles and some small pieces of charcoal down to 140 cm. The deposit beneath was sloppy brown clay and gravel, with no apparent charcoal. It could not be recovered by auger below 180 cm.

Tupuaki Bay

On the west side of this bay, in coral limestone, there are clefts and small shelters. In one of these were four human skulls, placed in secondary burial, and partly stained with red ochre. These were not touched.

Autea Bay

Near the southern point of Autea Bay, opposite Tarakoi Island is a 15 m long x 3 m deep rockshelter, facing north (R2002-46). In its larger of two alcoves a 50 cm x 50 cm test pit disclosed a 10–30 cm layer of wet black clay loam, containing charcoal, resting on the bedrock. It was overlain by 25–30 cm of damp, red-brown clay loam.

Taugatu Cave

About 200 m to the south of R2002-46, on the open coast, and about 4 m above sea level is a fairly substantial rockshelter (Figure 3.32), 20 m long by up to 4 m deep (R2002-47). A 50 cm x 70 cm test pit revealed, beneath 20 cm of modern soil and gravel, a grey-black clay loam extending below 60 cm into a grey silty clay down to 85 cm. Charcoal was found sparsely throughout and a large bulk sample was taken near the base to recover datable material. Beneath 85 cm depth was brown clay and abundant basalt shatter without charcoal (Figure 3.33).

Taga shelters

It is convenient to include the Taga shelters here (R2002-44), although they are located on high ground below the Tanga fortified site. There is a lower stone shelf, 1.5–1.8 m wide, which is very

Figure 3.32. Taugatu Shelter from the sea. Photograph A. Anderson.

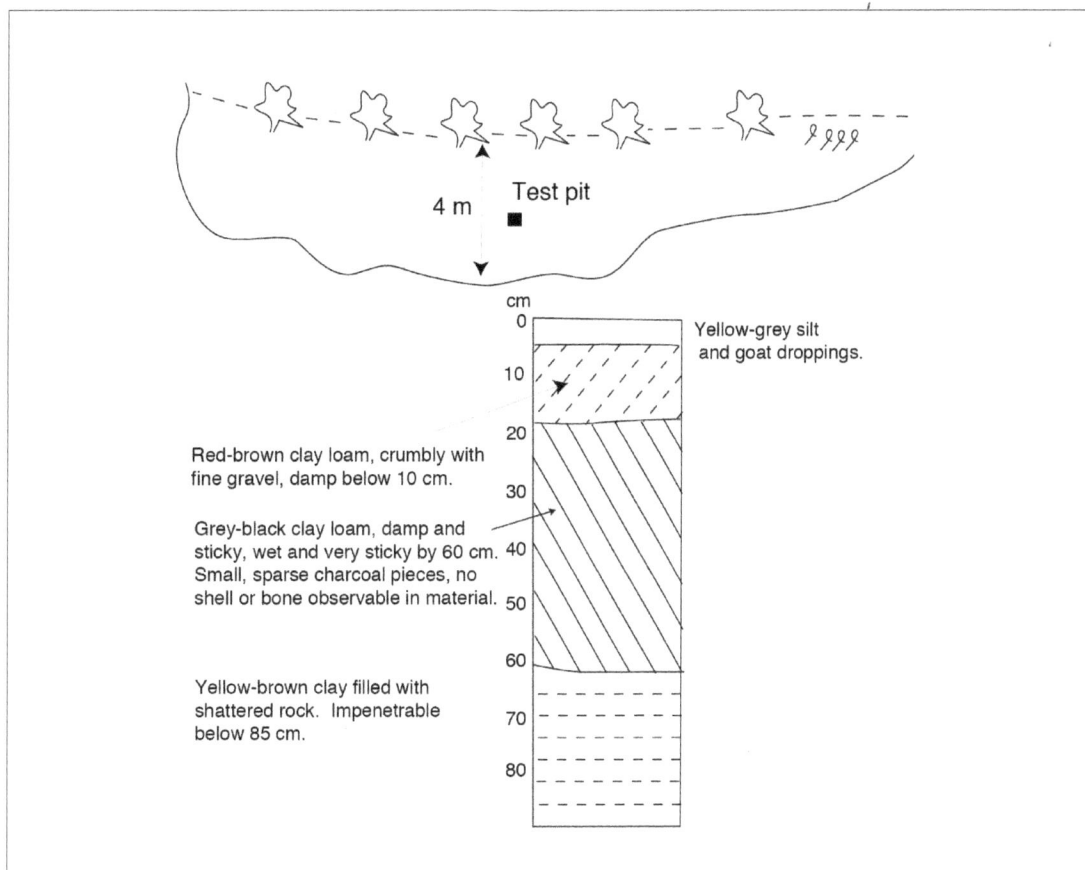

Figure 3.33. Plan and section of Taugatu Shelter test pit.

exposed and had no remaining cultural deposit and, about 2.8 m higher and to the south, an upper shelter about 30 m long in which an 8 m x 4 m area of cultural sediment was investigated (Figure 3.34). A 40 cm x 40 cm test pit (A) showed a 20 cm deep deposit of very friable silt and sand that was finely laminated in darker and lighter bands. That contained burnt stone, charcoal and some shell fragments. A second test pit of the same size (B) disclosed the remnants of an oven in section, containing abundant charcoal and burnt stone, and some fragments of marine shell and fish bone.

Coastal open sites

In Ha'urei Harbour, small ovens were seen in plan or section, sometimes occurring as clusters, in roading, stream and other erosion exposures, and basalt cores and flakes occur commonly around the shoreline (see Figure 3.1). Details of stratigraphy are omitted here, but they are available from the author. UTM coordinates for these sites are in Appendix D. In addition to work at the sites enumerated below, spade pitting and augering occurred at many places in which no cultural remains were disclosed. This was especially so to the east of Aurei village in the coastal flats at Pararaki, where ovens and stone tools had been reported. At one particular location, on the Faraire property, augering down to 2.25 m in several places showed only surface (modern) ovens and small flecks of charcoal in the higher sediments beneath. Charcoal flecks in coastal clays are common in Rapa, both in garden features and stream beds. These were sometimes sampled for palaeoenvironmental research, as in Pariati Bay, where a flight of taro terraces was systematically augered.

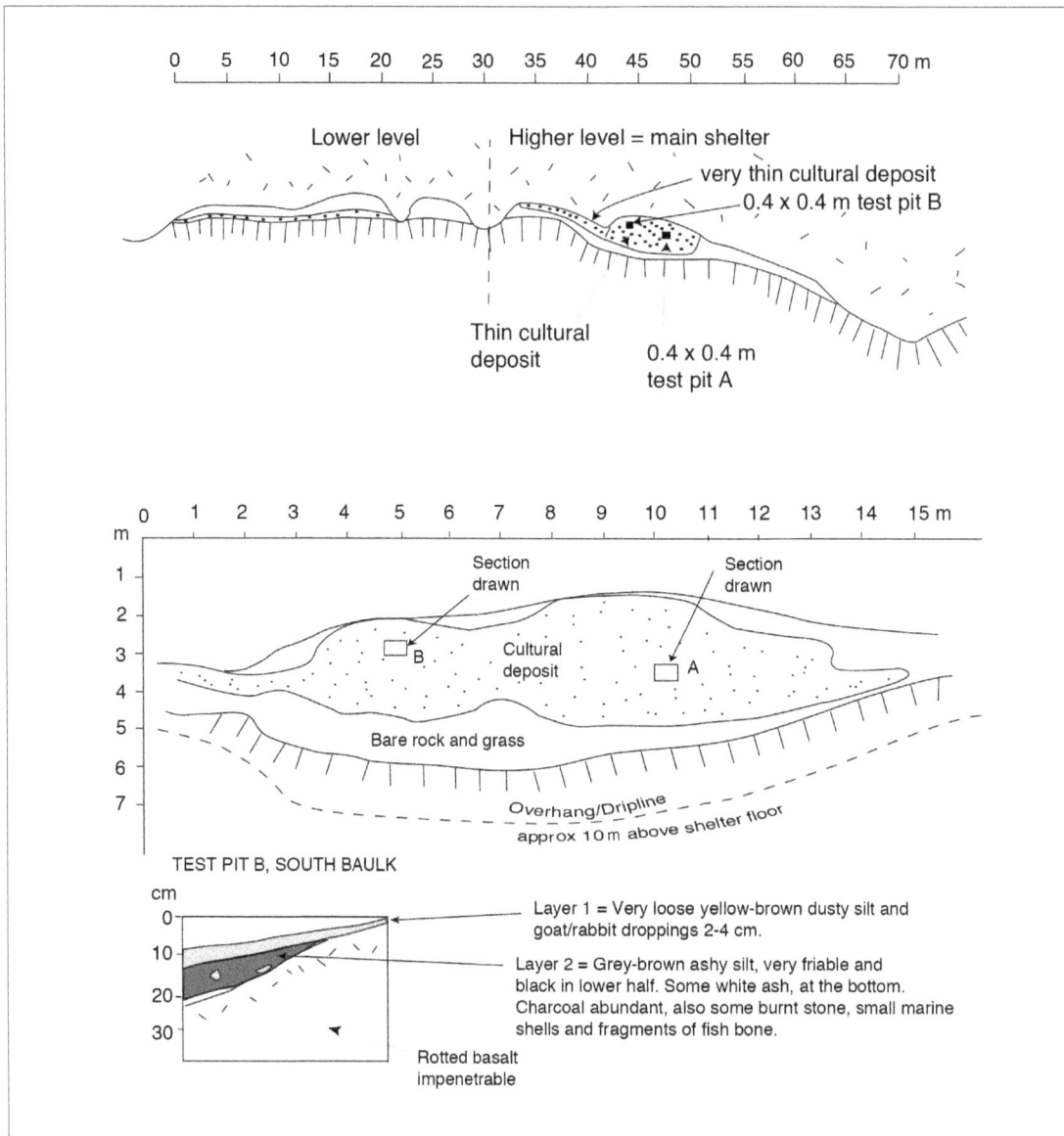

Figure 3.34. Plan, top, of Taga shelters, and plan and section, above, of Test-pit B.

Tokoroa

One main cluster of ovens was sampled along the south side of the harbour at Tokoroa, where a historical village had stood on terraces built down a broad spur. Ovens were sampled near the coastline (R2002-5), from a terrace section in which at least two events of oven use are represented (R2002-3, R2002-4), and from hillside exposures in the vicinity of the terraces (R2002-8, R2002-9). Another oven (R2002-7) was sampled in Maraia, the next small bay to the west. These ovens contained abundant charcoal but lacked oven stones and flaked stone. On the north side of the harbour, ovens were sampled in and near Aitoke (R2002-17, 18, 19, 20; of which 20 also contained some fish bone).

Tukou

In the Tukou area at the head of the harbour where there are various clay roads, more ovens were sampled in the banks or road beds. These were ovens containing both charcoal and oven stones (R2002-10, 11, 12, 13, 14, 15, 22, 24, 25; and at 11 and 12 also flaked basalt). Charcoal samples were also taken from an exposed section (R2002-16), along the edge of a knoll, beneath a stone-walled structure that formed part of a complex of features on the top of the knoll that included enclosed burials marked with slab surrounds.

The terrace site designated R-16 by Smith (1965:82) was of particular interest because it had provided a radiocarbon age of AD 1337 ± 200 (M-707). It was difficult to relocate, but after close inspection of the area we are fairly confident that it is our site R2002-45, located on the right bank of the small stream in Tukou that enters the bay near the prominent terrace site of Manga Parahurahu (Smith 1965:81). The site R2002-45 is a stone-faced terrace sectioned by stream erosion. Immediately beneath the level of the stone, facing and running back into the terrace, was a layer of friable, more-or-less stone-free, silt loam containing some pieces of charcoal, which were collected (Figure 3.35).

Conclusions

Coastal research provided several sets of data pertinent to the objectives. The site recording, though limited in scope, showed that coastal settlement patterns were probably somewhat different between Ha'urei Harbour and the outer bays. This was partly a function of the distribution of cave and rockshelter sites, which are relatively more common and usually larger in the outer bays and which had been chosen, consequently, as habitation sites. It was also, probably, a function of the relatively greater area of agricultural land in Ha'urei Harbour, especially at its head. The frequent occurrence there of possible house terraces and other structural features, plus numerous dispersed ovens, contrasts with the typical pattern in the outer bays where all suitable land has been converted into agricultural terraces and there is relatively little evidence of open habitation or ovens (although it is also the case that roads and other features in which ovens are exposed are more common in Ha'urei Harbour). One point that was widely apparent is that there has been considerably greater mobilisation of sediments since the prehistoric era. This is especially evident at Tangarutu, but in the coastal sites generally there are thick layers of hill slope and other sediments deposited on the archaeological stratigraphy, and much less often within it.

Excavations and test pits at numerous sites, and collection of many radiocarbon-dating samples provides a first overview of the chronology of the Rapan sequence. This shows that coastal locations, especially in the outer bays, were used at the beginning of the Rapan sequence, and continued to be used throughout it (Chapter 11). Tangarutu Cave, in particular, discloses a long sequence that begins with the earliest archaeological radiocarbon dates from Rapa.

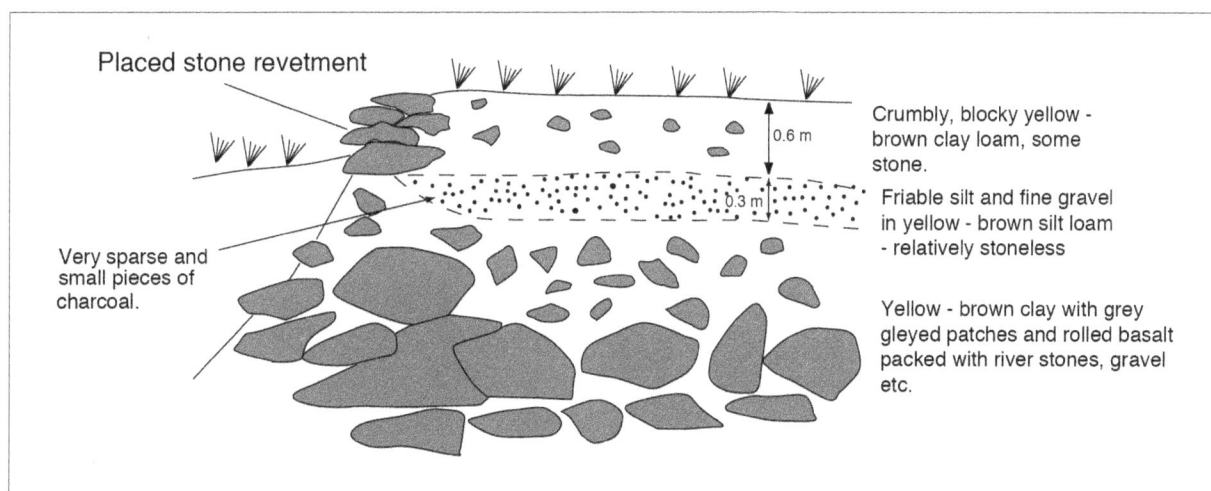

Figure 3.35. Section of R2002-45, which is probably R-16 of Smith (1965).

Analysis of excavated material (detailed in Chapters 4 to 9), most of it from the Tangarutu excavations, discloses little evidence of variation in resource use over time, despite the loss of a few bird species and the slightly greater use of larger fish taxa early on. To some extent, the variation is taphonomic, notably at Tangarutu where the survival of fibre and plant-food remains, in particular, is confined to upper levels. It is very likely that these resources were exploited at least as commonly earlier. That aside, the overriding impression is of an early and persisting focus on fishing for relatively small species and shellfishing for gastropods. Turtle was uncommon and there were no pigs, chickens or dogs before the historical era.

References

Kennett, D., Anderson, A.J., Prebble, M., Conte, E. and Southon, J. 2006. Prehistoric human impacts on Rapa, French Polynesia. *Antiquity* 80:1–15.

Smith, C.S. 1965. Report 5: Test excavations and surveys of miscellaneous sites on the island of Rapa Iti. In: Heyerdahl, T. and Ferdon, E.W. (eds), *Reports of the Norwegian Archaeological Expedition to Easter Island and the East Pacific*, Volume 2 Miscellaneous Papers. Monographs of the School of American Research and the Kon-Tiki Museum, 24 Pt. 2, pp. 77–87. Esselte AB, Stockholm.

Stokes, J.F.G. n.d. *Ethnology of Rapa Island*. Unpublished draft of B.P. Bishop Museum Bulletin of the Bayard Dominick Expedition. Five unbound volumes with multiple pagination (page numbers used here are generally the circled numbers). B.P. Bishop Museum, Honolulu.

Trotter, M.M. and McCulloch, B.A. 1981. *Prehistoric Rock Art in New Zealand.* Longman Paul, Auckland.

Walczak, J. 2001. Le peuplement de la Polynésie orientale. Une tentative d'approche historique par les exemples de Tahiti et de Rapa (Polynésie française). Unpublished PhD dissertation, University of Paris I – Pantheon Sorbonne, Paris.

Walczak, J. 2003. Presentation des données actuelles sur la préhistoire de Rapa Iti (archiple des Australes-Polynésie Française). In: Orliac, C. (ed), *Archéologie en océanie insulaire: peuplement, sociétés et paysages*, pp. 28–45. Editions Artcom, Paris.

4

The archaeobotany of Rapan rockshelter deposits

Matiu Prebble

Department of Archaeology and Natural History, Research School of Pacific and Asian Studies, The Australian
National University, and Nga Pae o te Maramatanga Trust, University of Auckland, New Zealand,
matthew.prebble@gmail.com

Atholl Anderson

Department of Archaeology and Natural History, The Australian National University

Introduction

Archaeobotanical records are becoming increasingly important in resolving several issues in the archaeology of Remote Oceania. Robust chronologies for island colonisation have been constructed for a number of islands through direct dating of plant materials with low inbuilt radiocarbon ages (e.g. Allen and Wallace 2007; Wilmshurst et al. 2011). The nature of biological introductions is better understood from abundant introduced plant remains found in archaeobotanical records (e.g. Kirch et al. 1995; Weisler 1995; Orliac and Orliac 1998; Burney et al. 2001; Allen and Wallace 2007). Increasingly, phytolith and starch grain analyses are being used as a first measure of plant use and exploitation for archaeological deposits without macrobotanical remains (e.g. Horrocks and Weisler 2007). Macrobotanical remains have been excavated from numerous sites in Remote Oceania, but surprisingly few attempts have been made to identify these plant remains.

Excavations of rockshelter deposits from Rapa (Figure 4.1) have produced abundant archaeological remains (Chapter 3). Here we describe the plant remains excavated from all the rockshelters, concentrating on the largest deposit at Tangarutu, Anarua Bay. Following the methodology of Allen and Wallace (2007), we compare radiocarbon dates obtained from young wood and seed remains as a means of excluding the potential inbuilt age effect from dating unidentified wood charcoal (e.g. Anderson 1991). We then compare the archaeobotanical data with other major excavations conducted in the Cook-Austral region. Finally, an ethnobotanical synthesis for the main plant species in the assemblages is provided. As the use of the plants identified within these deposits has changed since European colonisation, interpreting the significance of the remains is complex and is done here in reference to the ethnobotanical notes of Stokes (n.d.) gathered from Rapan informants, 1921–1922.

Vegetation history and archaeobotany

The vegetation history of Rapa has been described by Prebble (In press) and is discussed here in the context of interpreting the archaeobotanical record. Stokes (n.d.) described extensive agricultural production along some of the embayments and surrounding hill slopes and documented the abandonment of traditional land-use practices in many parts of the island due to population decrease and the increased importation of goods and services. The numerous dry-stone bund features that line many of the valley floors indicate formerly extensive *Colocasia esculenta* (Araceae) agriculture. Small pockets of tree crops introduced before European contact, such as *Aleurites moluccana* (Euphorbiaceae), *Ficus tinctoria* (Moraceae), *Musa* spp. (Musaceae) and *Cordyline fruticosa* (Laxmanniaceae), also reflect the former importance of traditional land use. The abandonment of horticulture and arboriculture complicates the interpretation of the archaeobotanical record, given the lack of vegetation available for comparing and interpreting modern and past plant use.

Environmental degradation of the island is most apparent in the valleys adjacent to the coastal rockshelter excavations at Angairao and Akatanui and the upland rockshelter at Taga. These valleys, denuded of local vegetation, show abundant signs of long-term abandonment of *Colocasia* agriculture and are overrun with feral horses, cattle and goats. Taga rockshelter lies at ca. 150 m elevation above the head of Ha'urei Bay and is surrounded by eroding embankments and entirely exotic shrub and grass vegetation sustained by feral grazing animals and regular human-lit fires. The present vegetation within each valley varies considerably, primarily as a function of differing scales of human impacts across the island.

Tangarutu rockshelter is on the south side of Anarua Bay behind a boulder beach. Indigenous trees including *Pandanus tectorius* (Pandanaceae), *Fagraea berteriana* (Loganiaceae), *Glochidion* spp. (Euphorbiaceae), *Myrsine* sp. (Myrsinaceae) and Rubiaceae species are found in small pockets along the coastline of Anarua Bay. Larger stands of indigenous plants are restricted to the ridgelines or inaccessible gulleys at the head of the valley. Agricultural activity has been abandoned in the bay and bund terrace features are now covered with exotic and invasive vegetation (e.g. *Syzygium jambos* and *Psidium gjuava* in the Myrtaceae). The dominant

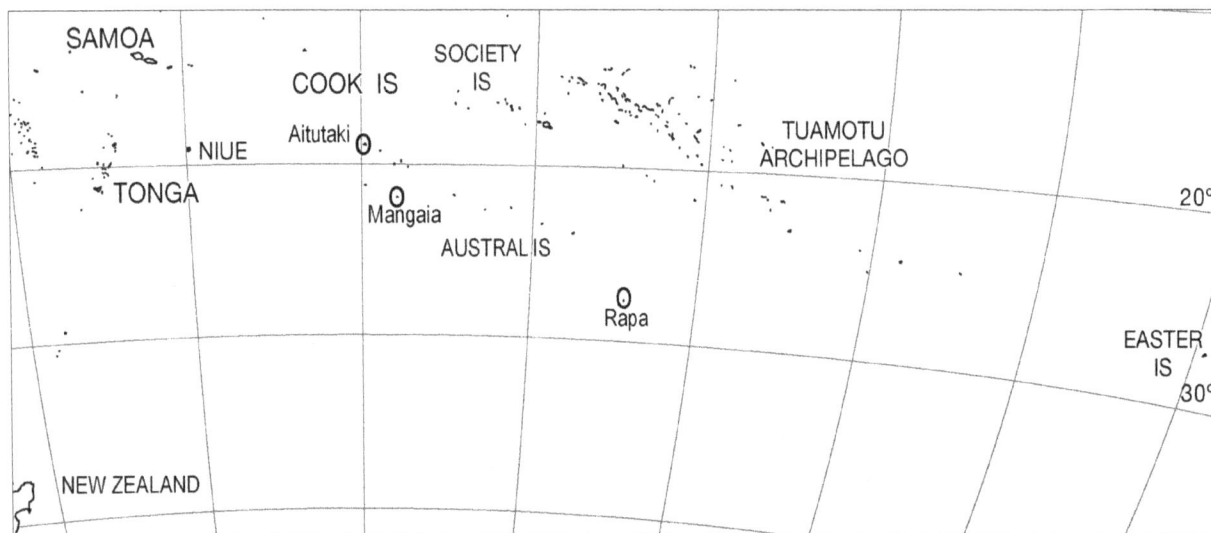

Figure 4.1. The Central Pacific, showing the location (circled) of the main islands mentioned in the text.

secondary vegetation at Anarua Bay, adjacent to Tangarutu rockshelter, is mostly of exotic tree, shrub and grass species. Driftwood lines the boulder beaches after storms and no doubt provided fuel to people inhabiting the coast.

Palaeoecological analysis of swamps in the Anarua, Akatanui, Iri and Angairao valleys provides only limited information about vegetation change during the period of human occupation, as the preservation and diversity of plant remains was limited in the swamp deposits examined. By contrast, rich swamp deposits at Tukou, in Ha'urei Bay, reveal that lowland vegetation was considerably more diverse before human colonisation and was quickly removed in the process of establishing agricultural fields for *Colocasia esculenta* (Kennett et al. 2006; Prebble In press). Based on the palaeobotanical evidence at Tukou, forest resources available to the initial colonists would have varied little across each valley. On initial colonisation, people would have encountered large *Pandanus*-dominant coastal swamp forest built up along riverbanks and behind the boulder beaches. Along the inland margins of these swamp forests were lowland forest trees and shrubs, including an extinct palm (Arecaceae), *Celtis pacifica* (Ulmaceae) and *Glochidion* spp. Sedge and rush wetlands, dominated by *Schoenoplectus subulatus* var. *subulatus* and *Eleocharis* spp. (both in Cyperaceae), would have persisted within the more permanently swampy areas, particularly along the margins of the *Pandanus* forests.

The rockshelters and preservation of plant remains

With the exception of Tangarutu, the coastal rockshelters are less than 10 m in maximum dimension and do not preserve large amounts of plant remains. The elevation of the coastal rockshelters varies from site to site, with all the shelter floors lying at least 2 m above sea level. Shelter entrances are usually behind large boulder beaches away from storm wave action or tidal surges. There is no evidence of major disturbance from coastal influences at any of the rockshelter sites. There is also no evidence to suggest that any archaeobotanical deposit is derived from beach drift, other than in material brought into the site by humans, but some remains of *Pandanus* or other plants growing near the shelter entrances might have entered the sites naturally. All shelters consist of a basaltic platform with overlying calcareous beach or dune sands, including coral pebbles and occasional boulders that have been accumulating, probably, since the mid-Holocene sea-level high stand of up to 2 m above present levels (Dickinson 2001). Most shelter floors (e.g. Tangarutu west section) show signs of recent alluvial and colluvial sedimentation, with incised channels stretching along the front of the inner face of each shelter. Reddish brown basaltic sediments associated with this channelling appear to be derived from the talus hill slope above the buttress of each shelter. The dry beach sands are partly covered by an overburden of these in-washed sediments. Despite this recent sedimentation, most deposits are dry and preserve plant materials with little evidence of diagenesis through periodic inundation and oxidation.

The excavations

Excavations on Rapa concentrated on coastal rockshelters, as they were expected to yield the best evidence of initial habitation on the island, and therefore of initial plant use. Compared with Tangarutu, excavations at Akatanui, Angairao and the upland shelters at Taga exposed shallow stratigraphy with a low abundance and diversity of cultural material and plant remains. Plant remains were recovered by hand picking during dry sieving (3 mm mesh) or as individual finds from different layers, particularly of leafy material. The base of the Angairao rockshelter stratigraphy dates to ca. AD 1350–1250 (Chapter 11), which is essentially the same as the oldest age at Akatanui, while the rockshelter at Taga suggests later occupation of this upland site. The Akatanui sequence is more indicative of continuous occupation from ca. AD 1350–1450 up to the period of European colonisation, marked by introduced materials (e.g. glass). Apart from Tangarutu, archaeobotanical remains were richest at Akatanui, with abundant wood charcoal fragments and Aleurites moluccana endocarps in cooking oven deposits. A summary of the archaeobotanical remains found at Akatanui, Angairao and Taga, including charcoal and endocarp abundance, is presented in Table 4.1, with radiocarbon ages from plant remains presented in Table 4.2.

Table 4.1. Plant materials including unidentified charcoal and *Aleurites moluccana* endocarps obtained from the Angairao rockshelter E, 2nd oven.

Spit/depth (cm)	Charcoal (g)	*Aleurites moluccana* endocarp (g)	Other (g)
Spit 3/20–30	4.18	–	23.31 (ash)
Spit 4/30–40	1.41	–	–
Spit 5/40–50	1.55	–	–
Spit 6/50–60	2.98	0.30	–
Spit 7/60–70	5.70	0.33	–
Spit 8/70–80	1.52	–	–
Spit 9/80–90	2.38	0.21	–
Spit 10/90–100	2.61	0.15	0.14 (leaf)
Spit 11/100–110	<10		

Table 4.2. List of radiocarbon dates on unidentified charcoal obtained from the Angairao Rockshelter E, 2nd Oven.

Sample/depth (cm)	Weight (g)	Lab code	C14 age (uncal.)	2 s cal. AD
E1 Spit 10/90–100	20	ANU 11851**	500+/-50	1394–1618
E1 Spit 11/100–110	<5	UCI 14767*	375+/-15	1487–1627
E1 Spit 11/100–110	<5	UCI 14766*	220+/-20	1653–1803

Presented are the sample depths, radiocarbon laboratory (UCI=University of California Irvine; ANU=The Australian National University), weight of charcoal dated/the amount of charcoal found in spit, laboratory sample codes, uncalibrated determinations (*AMS, **conventional) and calibrated ages to 2s. Dates were calibrated using the program Calib 6.0. (Stuiver et al. 2005) using the Southern Hemisphere Calibration Curve (McCormac et al. 2004).

The Tangarutu sequence

The Tangarutu rockshelter at Anarua Bay is of such a notable size (80 m x 40 m) that it is likely to have been used from the earliest period of settlement. Small test excavations on the rockshelter beach sand at the southern end of the shelter by Walczak (2001, 2003) produced calibrated radiocarbon dates between AD 1450 and 1700 (Ly-8577 and Ly-8578, see Chapter 11). Since Walczak's excavations, a large amount of archaeological material has been removed in the process of extracting sand for building projects. This may have resulted in the destruction of most of the archaeological deposit. During the 2002 expedition, the remaining undisturbed deposits towards the back of the shelter were sampled with a sand auger and about 4 m² of the deepest and richest deposits were excavated.

The east section of the shelter revealed the deepest archaeological deposit on the island, with approximately 150 cm of continuous cultural strata. It included leaf and seed fragments, abundant wood and charcoal remains of ovens, and other cultural material. A number of coprolites consisting of densely matted organic matter, often with hair and small crushed bones, were recovered during excavation. Plant remains were recovered by hand picking during dry sieving (3 mm mesh) or as individual finds from different layers, particularly of leafy material. This deposit was excavated in two 50 cm x 100 cm sections (East Section 1 and East Section 2) at 5 cm spit intervals for the first 70 cm and at 10 cm spit intervals for the remainder of the deposit. Only East Section 1 (E1) is presented here.

Analysis

Seed and fruit analysis

Seed and fruit remains were identified on the basis of comparison with reference material held at the Department of Archaeology and Natural History, ANU, macrobotanical reference collection.

Archaeological wood charcoal analysis

Charcoals were described by comparison with a wood charcoal reference collection composed by M. Prebble from collections made on Rapa, and E. Dotte (unpublished data) from a number of collections from New Caledonia. The reference collection is representative of woody taxa regarded as fuel woods which were recorded by J.F.G. Stokes and E. Stokes between 1921 and 1922. The local plant names, botanical names and uses of these taxa are listed in Table 4.3. Some taxa were not included in the reference collection due to their rarity, namely *Metatrophis margaretae* (Urticaceae), known only from a single male specimen (Timothy Motley and Jean Yves Meyer pers. comm.), and *Santalum insulare* var. *margaretae* (Santalaceae). Taxa included in Stokes' list that are known as post-European contact introductions were not included in the reference collection (*Albizia lebbeck*, *Citrus* spp., *Coffea arabica* and *Inga edulis*).

Microscopy was completed using an Olympus BH-2 epi-illumination incident compound microscope with 10x, 20x and 50x objectives. Given the low diversity of woody plant taxa on Rapa (<70) and the low number of preferred fuel woods (Table 4.3), only up to 50 charcoal pieces above 10 mm in widest dimension were randomly selected for analysis from each spit. As the basal spit (Spit 21) revealed little charcoal, additional charcoals were examined from Spit 20.

Palynological analysis

Two coprolite samples were chosen for palynological analyses to assess the potential for identifying dietary information about humans or dogs (*Canis familiaris*), the most likely producers (although dogs have not been recorded for pre-European Rapa). One cubic centimetre (cm^3) volume sub-samples were taken from each coprolite. Pollen analysis of the coprolite samples was conducted using the standard preparation techniques. Microscopic charcoal fragments were also counted for each sample using the point count method. Pollen and spore identification was assisted by reference material collected in the field and regional reference collections held in the Department of Archaeology and Natural History, ANU.

Results

Archaeobotanical assemblages

The stratigraphic profile of the East Section 1 excavation is shown in Chapter 3. Associated weights for each type of plant material identified from each excavation spit are presented in stratigraphic order in Figure 4.2. The deposit can be divided into three units – beach sand with almost no cultural remains, and basal and upper cultural units. In the basal cultural unit of

Table 4.3. List of pre-European contact fuel woods used on Rapa, based on a botanical collection and ethnobotanical survey conducted by Margaret and John Stokes between 1920 and 1921. ANU reference wood charcoals are also listed.

Rapa vernacular	Stokes identification	Family: botanical name	Other uses apart from fuel wood	Reference charcoal
Aï	Tree (sandalwood)	Santalaceae: *Santalum insulare* var. *margaretae*	–	*Santalum neocaledonicum**
Aito	Tree (*Weinmannia rapensis*)	Cunoniaceae: *Weinmannia rapensis*	Boat building	*Weinmannia rapensis*
Aki	Tree fern	Cyatheaceae: *Cyathea* spp.	Food, graters for oil	*Cyathea medularis*
Anei	Tree (Compositae)	Asteraceae: *Fitchia rapensis*	House posts	*Fitchia rapensis*
Ariki	Bush (*Homolanthus* sp.)	Euphorbiaceae: *Homolanthus stokesii*, *H. nutans*	–	–
Gaio/Ngaio	Tree (*Myoporum* sp.)	Myoporaceae: *Myoporum rapensis*	Boat building, medicinal	*Myoporum rapensis*
Gatae/Ngatae/Patai	Introduced tree (*Erythrina indica*) or possible *Inga edulis*	Fabaceae: *Erythrina variegata*	Canoes	*Erythrina variegata*
Kaeka	Tree (*Eugenia* sp.), probably introduced	Myrtaceae: *Syzygium malaccense*	Food	*Syzygium malaccense**
Kaema /Kaima	Tree (*Glochidion longfieldiae*)	Euphorbiaceae: *Glochidion longfieldiae*	–	–
Kai'ara	Tree (*Pandanus* sp.) natives state 'indigenous' and 'introduced'	Pandanaceae: Pandanus tectorius	Food, medicinal, house thatch (recent), stringing, candles etc	*Pandanus tectorius*
Kakatua	Shrub (*Piper* spp.)	Piperaceae: *Macropiper* sp., *Peperomia* spp.	Medicinal	*Macropiper puberulum*
Karaka	Tree (Sapotaceae/*Nesoluma polynesicum*)	Sapotaceae: *Nesoluma* spp.	–	*Pouteria cinerea*
Koe	Shrub/bamboo	Poaceae: *Schizostachyum glaucifolium*	–	–
Kofe	Tree	Araliaceae: *Meryta pauciflora*	–	*Schefflera* spp.
Koi'ivai	Shrub (Rubiaceae/*Coprosma rapensis*)	Rubiaceae: *Coprosma* spp.	–	–
Maiage	Tree (*Sesbania* sp./*Sophora tetraptera*)	Fabaceae: *Sophora tomentose*	House posts, modern tool handles	*Sophora tomentosa**
Mairirakau	Shrub (*Alyxia stellata*)	Apocynaceae: *Alyxia stellata*	–	*Alyxia stellata*
Maroro	Bush (*Metatrophis margaretae*)	Urticaceae: *Metatrophis margaretae*	–	–
Mati	Introduced tree (*Ficus tinctoria*)	Moraceae: *Ficus tinctoria*	Cordage	*Ficus tinctoria*
Pakora/Nioi	Shrub (*Plectronia kakenua* var. *obiculata* or possibly the tree *Cyclophyllum barbartum*	Rubiaceae: *Plectronia* sp./*Cyclophyllum barbartum*	–	*Cyclophyllum barbartum**
Po'oto	Tree (*Eurya rapensis*)	Theaceae: *Eurya japonica* var. *Nitida*	–	*Eurya japonica* var. *nitida*
Purau	Introduced tree (*Hibiscus* sp.)	Malvaceae: *Hibiscus tiliaceus* syn *Talipariti tiliaceum*	House posts, canoes, paddles, boats, cordage, sandals, medicinal	*Hibiscus tiliaceus* syn. *Talipariti tiliaceum*
Pua	Tree (*Fagraea berteriana*)	Loganiaceae: *Fagraea berteriana*	Houses, canoes, medicinal, adornment	*Fagraea berteriana*
Pūru/Purum	Tree or shrub (*Sida rhombifolia*)	Euphorbiaceae: *Claoxylon collenettei***	Perfume	–
Rakau papa'a	Introduced tree (*Albizia lebbech*)	Fabaceae: *Albizia lebbeck*	–	–
Raupata	Tree (two forms of Compositae)	Asteraceae	–	–
Rautea ***	Tree	*Corokia collenettei* and *C. serrata*	–	–
Tiairi or tuitui	Introduced tree (*Aleurites triloba*)	Euphorbiaceae: *Aleurites moluccana*	Canoes, lights, oil,	*Aleurites moluccana*
Tireuei	Tree (*Melastoma* sp./*Celtis paniculata* var. *rapensis*	Ulmaceae: *Celtis pacifica*	–	*Celtis pacifica, C. hypoleuca*

*From Emilie Dotte (unpublished reference collection); all other woods are from Rapa and other islands of the Austral archipelago.

**Pūru* given for *Claoxylon collenettei* by Papaafatu (pers. comm.), Rapa.

****Rautea/lautea* recorded by Tim Motley (unpublished data).

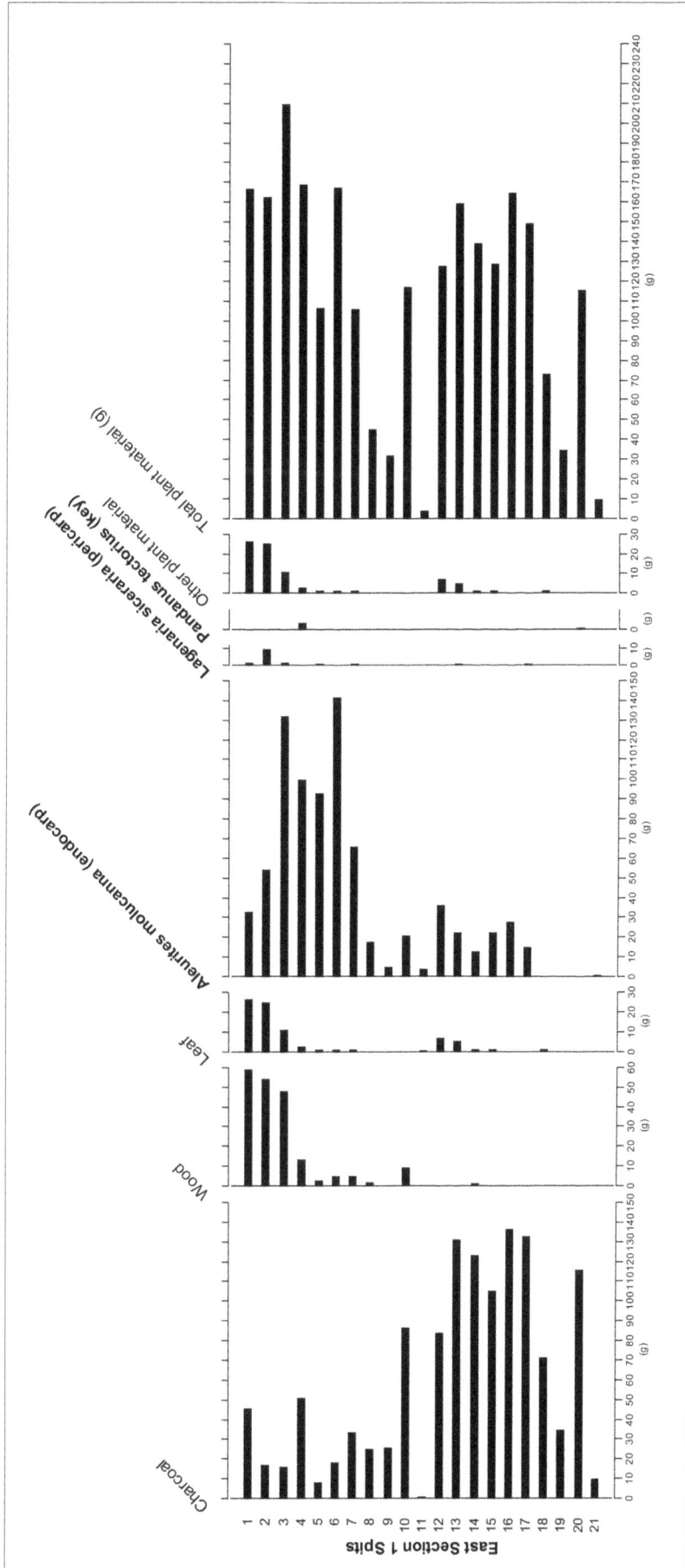

Figure 4.2. The material weights per excavated spit (the top 10 spits were excavated to a depth of 5 cm, with the lower seven spits to a depth of 10 cm) for the Tangarutu rockshelter from the E1 section. The deposit is divided into three units, a sterile basal sand layer underlying a charcoal-rich oven feature with oven stones within a sandy matrix (basal cultural unit). From Spit 7 (35–40 cm) to the surface, *Aleurites moluccana* and pieces of uncharred wood dominate a sandy matrix overlying a leafy layer at between 35 cm and 30 cm in depth (upper cultural unit). Introduced taxa labelled in **bold** text.

the deposit, from 140 cm to 35 cm in depth, we found fragments of charcoal associated with rounded basaltic stones indicative of an oven feature. Small amounts of *Aleurites moluccana* (10–35 g per spit; see Figure 4.2) were located in the upper part of this unit from 120 cm to 40 cm. The archaeological charcoal from 110–130 cm (spits 20 and 21) and 15–20 cm (Spit 4) is presented in Figure 4.3 and reveals distinct changes in fuel use. The basal spits are dominated by introduced cf. *Hibiscus tiliaceus* syn. *Talipariti tiliaceum* (Malvaceae) and cf. *Cordyline fruticosa*, but this changes in the uppermost spit to predominantly indigenous fuel and timber woods. The upper spit is dominated by the endemic species cf. *Myoporum rapensis* (Myoporaceae) and cf. *Fitchia rapensis* (Asteraceae), now restricted to small coastal populations and upland populations respectively (Figure 4.4 shows modern reference and archaeological charcoals).

Above 35 cm, a 5–10 cm thick layer of leafy remains distinguishes the upper unit, and upon sieving it produced pieces of *Hibiscus tiliaceus* syn. *Talipariti tiliaceum* cordage and fragments of plaited *Pandanus* and *Freycinetia* (Pandanaceae) baskets (Chapter 5). The amount of *A. moluccana* in each spit increased to weights between 70 g and 140 g per spit. Also in this unit the amount of unburnt wood remains increased, whereas the amount of charcoal and oven stones decreased. Fragments of the bottle gourd *Lagenaria siceraria* (Cucurbitaceae; Figure 4.4) and *Pandanus* keys (individual drupes of syncarpous fruits) were also identified within this unit. Other plant remains, including the abundant uncharred wood, have yet to be identified.

Two small, consolidated organic parcels located from the upper unit of E1, thought to be coprolite samples on the basis of the presence of hairs and crushed bone, were processed for pollen as a further means of identifying the presence of plant species in the Tangarutu deposit. Percentage pollen diagrams of these samples are presented in Figure 4.5. The uppermost sample found in Spit 1 (5 cm in depth) produced a range of pollen and spores, most known as wind-dispersed palynomorphs. The presence of *Freycinetia* and Euphorbiaceae pollen in these samples suggests that material from these plants may have been brought into the site. In the lower sample, found in Spit 2 (10 cm in depth), 75% of the palynomorphs identified are from *Freycinetia* (*F. arborea* or *F. rapensis*). Other pollen types probably introduced rather than wind blown into the site include Rubiaceae, cf. Liliaceae type and a high percentage of Cyperaceae pollen (ca. 18%). The high percentage of *Freycinetia* pollen is indicative of the probable introduction of these large flowers into the site, either brought in with leaves used for weaving and cordage, or with fruits for consumption.

Chronology

The archaeological material yielding the oldest radiocarbon ages at Tangarutu consisted of wood charcoal, unidentified to taxa at the time, immediately after excavation, when no means of identification was available (the formation of a Rapan identified wood collection being one of the objectives of the project, which took some time to reach fruition). Radiocarbon dates on charcoal samples, unidentified to taxa, indicate that the base of Tangarutu dates to at least AD 1300, with the upper deposits beginning about AD 1600 and extending up to immediately before European arrival (Chapter 11).

Later, three radiocarbon ages were taken from fruit and nut remains from East Section 1 (see Table 4.4), one from *Aleurites moluccana* endocarp, one from *Lagenaria siceraria* pericarp and one from a *Pandanus* cf. *tectorius* key. Unlike unidentified charcoal, the inbuilt age of fruit and nut remains is expected to be merely a year or so. Radiocarbon dates from *A. moluccana* endocarp provide the most reliable chronology, because of their inherently low inbuilt age and their availability through almost all of the stratigraphic units. The earliest date from *A. moluccana* endocarp has an age range of AD 1049–1628 (ANU 12102), which brackets the age range

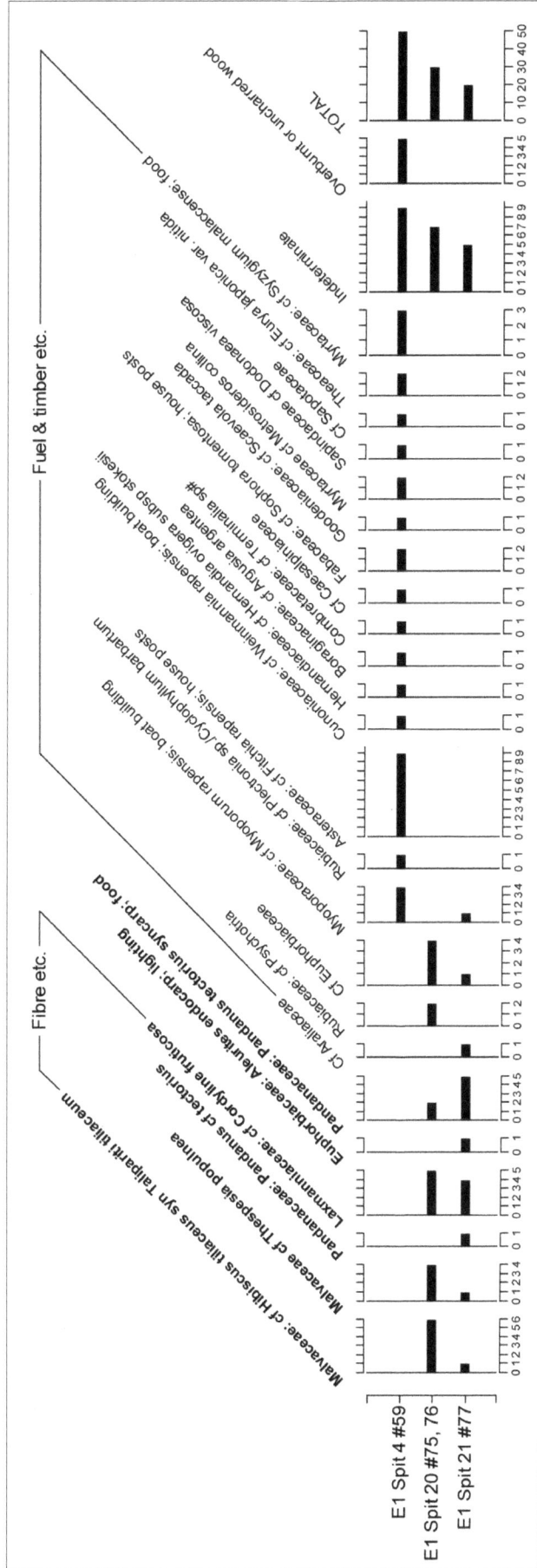

Figure 4.3. The archaeological charcoal count data (by tentative family and species determinations) for the Tangarutu rockshelter from three spits of the E1 section. The basal spits (E1 spits 21 and 20) are from the base of a charcoal-rich oven feature with oven stones within a sandy matrix and represent the (basal cultural unit of the E1 section). The upper spit (E1 Spit 4) is from a leaf (*Freycinetia* and *Pandanus*), candlenut (*Aleurites moluccana* endocarp) charcoal and wood-rich unit. Taxa are arranged firstly by first appearance, then by use (e.g. fibre etc.). Introduced taxa labelled in **bold** text.

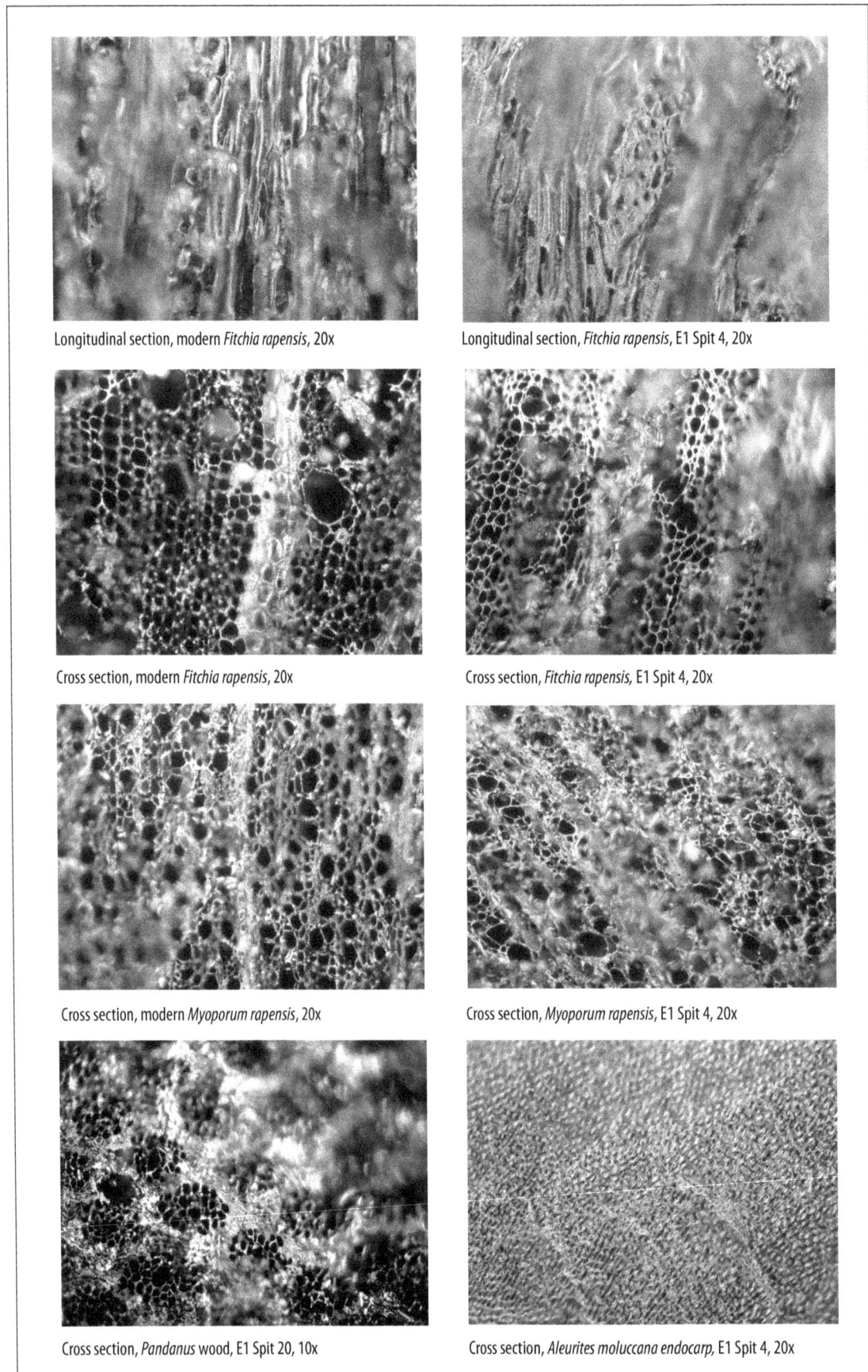

Longitudinal section, modern *Fitchia rapensis*, 20x

Longitudinal section, *Fitchia rapensis*, E1 Spit 4, 20x

Cross section, modern *Fitchia rapensis*, 20x

Cross section, *Fitchia rapensis*, E1 Spit 4, 20x

Cross section, modern *Myoporum rapensis*, 20x

Cross section, *Myoporum rapensis*, E1 Spit 4, 20x

Cross section, *Pandanus* wood, E1 Spit 20, 10x

Cross section, *Aleurites moluccana endocarp*, E1 Spit 4, 20x

Figure 4.4. Digital images of modern reference and archaeological charcoals, *Fitchia rapensis, Myoporum rapensis, Pandanus* and *Aleurites moluccana* endocarp.

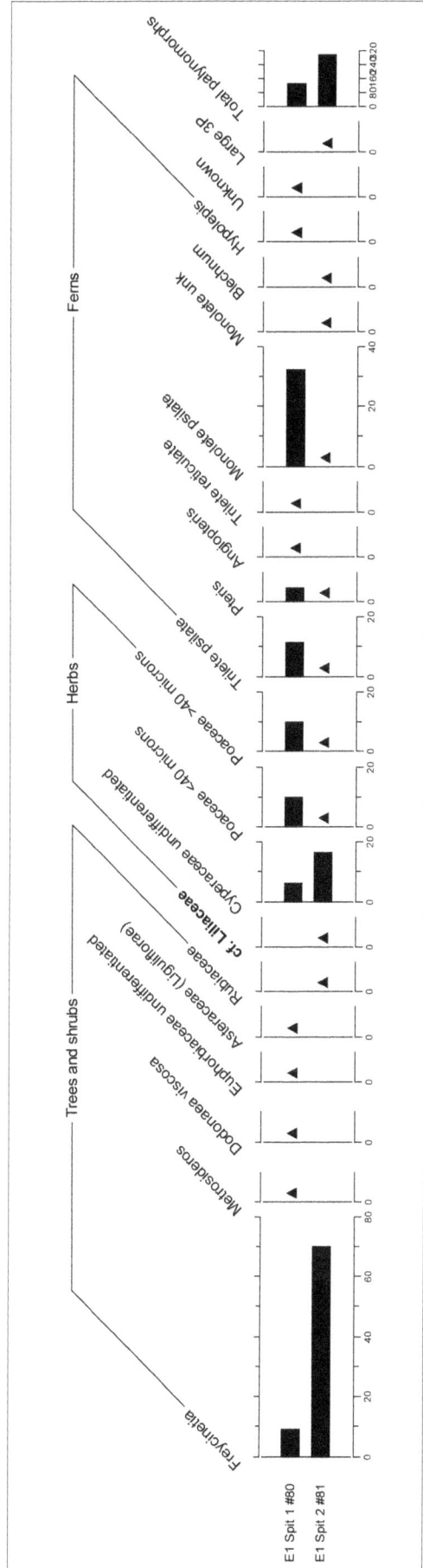

Figure 4.5. Percentage diagram of pollen and spore assemblages from two consolidated organic samples from the East Section 1 excavation (spits 1 and 2), Tangarutu rockshelter. Taxa with >5% of total palynomorph sum are presented as bars; samples with proportions <5% are presented as triangle symbols; and total palynomorph counts. Introduced taxa labelled in **bold** text.

Table 4.4. List of radiocarbon dates obtained from the Tangarutu rockshelter East section Square E1 and for comparison E2.

Sample/depth (cm)	Material dated	Weight (g)/amount in spit (g)	Lab code	C14 age (uncal.)	2 s cal. AD
E1 Spit 4/20–25	*Lagenaria siceraria* pericarp	<2/6	UCI 14763*	320+/-15	1510–1648
E1 Spit 4/20–25	*Aleurites moluccana* endocarp	12/100	ANU 12101**	410+/-60	1442–1638
E1 Spit 11/55–60	*Aleurites moluccana* endocarp	5/5	UCI 14772*	345+/-20	1501–1642
E2 Spit 18/100–110	*Aleurites moluccana* endocarp	12/n.d.	ANU 12100	380+/-60	1449–1648
E1 Spit 19/110–120	*Pandanus cf. tectorius* key	2.55/20	ANU 12102*	660+/-150	1049–1628
E2 Spit 23–25/130–150	Unidentified charcoal	10/10	ANU 11848**	710+/-70	1228–1407
East Section T1/150	Unidentified charcoal	<10/20	UCI 14769**	905+/-20	1152–1222

Presented are the sample depths, radiocarbon laboratory (UCI=University of California Irvine; ANU=The Australian National University), material dated, weight of material dated/the amount of material found in spit, laboratory sample codes, uncalibrated determinations (*AMS, **conventional) and calibrated ages to 2s. Dates were calibrated using the program Calib 6.0. (Stuiver et al. 2005) using the Southern Hemisphere Calibration Curve (McCormac et al. 2004).

from a piece of unidentified charcoal from the lowest unit of the excavation, AD 1128–1407 (ANU 11848). Unfortunately, the basal *Pandanus* key produced a large uncalibrated error due to inadequate carbon concentration.

Archaeobotanical research in the Austral and Cook islands

Tangarutu rockshelter is notable for having well-preserved plant remains found in very high concentrations that are comparable to other excavations from tropical and subtropical Remote Oceania (e.g. Kirch et al. 1995; Weisler 1995; Burney et al. 2001; Allen and Wallace 2007). Aside from charcoal, the recovery of identified plant remains from archaeological sites in the Cook and Austral islands has been minimal. In tables 4.5 and 4.6, indigenous and introduced plant remains excavated from Tangarutu are compared with those from excavations at Ureia, Aitutaki (Allen and Wallace 2007), and Tangatatau, Mangaia (Kirch et al. 1995) in the Cook Islands. Wood charcoal (unidentified to species) and endocarps of *Aleurites moluccana* are the most common archaeobotanical remains found at each site.

Indigenous plant remains

Charred and uncharred keys and some wood charcoals of *Pandanus* cf. *tectorius* (Figure 4.4) represent the indigenous food plant identified at Tangarutu, Tangatatau and Ureia (Table 4.3). Apart from *Pandanus, Hibiscus tiliaceus* syn. *Talipariti tiliaceum* is the only wood found at Ureia and Tangarutu, where it was probably used for both fibre and fuel (Table 4.3). All the remaining taxa identified at Tangarutu are, from the ethnobotanical notes of Stokes (n.d.), primarily fuel woods and mostly endemics, including species of *Myoporum, Fitchia* and *Hernandia* (Figure 4.3).

Pandanus tectorius Parkinson

It is possible that remains of *Pandanus* represent indigenous species other than *P. tectorius*, but this cannot be established from the macrobotanical remains alone. Whistler (1991) has questioned the status of *Pandanus tectorius* as an introduced species to Remote Oceania. He suggested that *P. tectorius* of both Tonga and Samoa is represented by both indigenous and introduced populations, but queried the indigenous status of *Pandanus tectorius* in the Cook, Austral, Society, Marquesas and Hawaiian islands. *Pandanus* pollen has been identified from pre-human Holocene sediments on Rapa, Rimatara (Prebble and Wilmshurst 2009) and Mangaia.

Table 4.5. Comparison of indigenous plants identified from Ureia, Aitutaki (Allen and Wallace 2007), Tangatatau, Mangaia (Kirch et al. 1995), and Tangarutu archaeobotanical deposits.

Indigenous taxa	Ureia	Tangatatau	Tangarutu
Argusia argentea syn. *Tournefortia* (Boraginaceae) wood	+	?	n
Caesalpinia major (Fabaceae) seed	?	+	n
Freycinetia sp. (Pandanaceae) leaf	n	n	+leaf, pollen
Guettarda speciosa (Rubiaceae) wood	+	?	n
Hernandia sp. (Hernandiaceae) seed		+	-
Hibiscus spp. cf. *tiliaceus*[1] (Malvaceae) fibre, bark	+	?	+ fibre, charcoal?
Pandanus sp. (Pandanaceae) leaf, keys	+keys	+keys, leaf	+keys, leaf, charcoal
Pemphis acidula (Lythraceae) wood	+	?	n
Pouteria grayana syn. *Plachonella* (Sapotaceae) seed	+	?	n
Palmae (Arecaceae) wood	+	?	?
Terminalia (Combretaceae) wood	+	?	n
Thespesia populnea[2] (Malvaceae) wood	+	?	n

+= identified in the deposit; ?= found on the island but has yet to be identified in the deposit; n=is currently not located on the island.

1 The indigenous or exotic status of *Hibiscus* cf. *tiliaceus* syn. *Talipariti tiliaceum* on the Cook and Austral islands is uncertain (Whistler 1991; Florence 2004).

2 The indigenous status of *Thespesia populnea* on Rapa is uncertain (Florence 2004).

Table 4.6. Comparison of introduced plants identified from Ureia, Aitutaki (Allen and Wallace 2007), Tangatatau, Mangaia (Kirch et al. 1995), and Tangarutu archaeobotanical deposits.

Introduced taxa	Ureia	Tangatatau	Tangarutu
Aleurites moluccana (Euphorbiaceae) endocarp	+	+	+endocarp (Figure 4.4)
Artocarpus altilis (Moraceae) wood, fruit	+	?	?
Calophyllum inophyllum (Clusiaceae) wood	+	?	n
Cocos nucifera[1] (Arecaceae) endocarp, husk, leaf, bracts, wood charcoal	+	+	?
Colocasia esculenta (Araceae) corm	?	+	+
Cordia subcordata[2] (Boraginaceae) seed	+	?	n
Cordyline fruticosa (Laxmanniaceae) stem, leaf, charcoal	+	+	+leaf, charcoal?
Cyrtosperma merkusii (Araceae) corm	?	+	n
Ipomoea batatas (Convovulaceae)	?	+	?
Inocarpus fagifera (Fabaceae) wood charcoal	?	+	n
Lagenaria siceraria (Cucurbitaceae) pericarp	?	+	+
Musa sp. (Musaceae) leaf	?	+	?
Saccharum officinarum (Poaceae) stem	?	+	?
Schizostachyum glaucophylum (Poaceae) stem	?	+	?

+= identified in the deposit; ?= found on the island but has yet to be identified in the deposit; n=is not located on the island and is unlikely to be found in the deposit.

1 Considered to be indigenous to the Cook and Austral islands, except on Rapa but has been repeatedly introduced by Polynesians, contributing to the expansion of its natural range on islands (Athens 1997).

2 Considered to be introduced to the Cook Islands (Bill Sykes pers. comm. 2007).

Ellison (1994) establishes the indigenous status of *Pandanus* on these islands and presumably the other Cook and Austral islands. Further support for the indigenous status of *Pandanus* in Remote Oceania comes from an unpublished report (in Athens 1997) of Pleistocene macrofossil remains of *Pandanus* on the Hawaiian Islands, where it has a minimum age of 500,000 years.

The botanist Archibald Menzies (Shineberg 1986) on the initial European visit to Rapa in 1791 mentioned *Dracaena* leaves, which probably refers to *Pandanus*, in reference to a girdle suspended around the waists of the local Polynesians. Indications from the pollen records from Rapa suggest that these trees were probably common at first European contact. Whether the *Pandanus* population had natural as well as cultural origins is unknown.

Pandanus is a dioecious genus with extreme morphological diversity that can be influenced by cultivation practices. This has resulted in a number of inconsistent taxonomic determinations of members of this genus (see Stone 1976, 1988; and St. John 1976, 1979). From his Pacific Island plant collections from the 1920s, St. John (Fosberg and St. John 1934) identified 13 endemic species of *Pandanus* on Rapa alone. Most of these species have subsequently been grouped into *Pandanus tectorius*, and one other species has yet to be described (Tim Motley and Jacques Florence pers. comm. 2004). The morphological diversity in the genus *Pandanus* that St. John identified on Rapa may be a result of genetic or environmental processes, but may also reflect the introduction of cultivated varieties by Polynesians both pre- and post-European contact.

The ethnobotanical importance of *Pandanus* on Rapa is confusing. One of Stokes' (n.d. Box 7.1) main informants, Teraau, noted the indigenous status of *kai'aral fara* (*Pandanus*) and *magu* (*Freycinetia* spp.), but asserted that there was no mat-making, which is unlikely and contradicted by abundant ethnographic evidence (Chapter 2) and some archaeological remains (Chapter 5).

Hibiscus L. and *Thespesia populnea (L.)* Solander ex Correa

The lack of early ethnographic evidence for fibre production involving the Polynesian *miro* (*Thespesia populnea*) and *purau* (*Hibiscus* spp.) is intriguing. The indigenous status of *T. populnea* on Rapa is uncertain and it is more often considered a Polynesian introduction (Florence 2004). The few specimens that now remain on Rapa appear to survive only by cultivation, but the overwhelming effect of feral grazing animals precludes any reasonable test of whether they could survive otherwise. The most reliable and earliest radiocarbon age obtained directly from archaeobotanical material in the Cook and Austral islands material comes from cf. *T. populnea* wood at the Ureia site, Aitutaki, dated to AD 1240–1405 (Wk-18408; Allen and Wallace 2007). No pre-human remains of *T. populnea*, pollen, wood or charcoals have been identified from the Cook or Austral islands. The status of *Hibiscus* is more confusing given that Florence (2004) has described two species (*H. australensis* and *H. tiliaceus*) and one subspecies (*H. tiliaceus* subsp. *tiliaceus*). Like *Thespesia*, no pre-human remains of *Hibiscus* have been identified from the Cook or Austral islands, and for this reason these genera should be considered Polynesian introductions to Rapa and perhaps to the most southern islands of the Cook and Austral islands.

Introduced plants

Introduced taxa make up the greatest proportion of plant remains identified from the base of the main E1 sequence. The basal cultural unit outlined is indicative of an oven and an associated midden, initially used 1300–1400 AD. The dominance of remains from tropical and introduced fibre plants (*Cordyline fruticosa*, *Hibiscus tiliaceus* syn. *Talipariti tiliaceum* and *Thespesia populnea* and candlenut *Aleurites moluccana*) suggests that the early economic activity on this sub-tropical island centred on processing plants imported from the tropics. Fibre plants used for cordage and basketry are essential components of Polynesian material culture for clothing, binding for boats and weapons, fishing equipment, lashing for building construction and numerous other tasks. Apart from *Pandanus tectorius* and *Freycinetia* spp., there are few indigenous plants that could provide fibre essential for sustaining Polynesian material culture.

In his ethnography of Rapa, Stokes (n.d. box 7.1) doubted the claims from his informants that all the main fibre plants aside from *Pandanus* and *Freycinetia* – *purau*, *orā*, *aute* and *mati* (See Table 4.3) – are indigenous. Even if these plants were not indigenous to Rapa, as on other islands, they remain prime candidates for early introduction given their economic importance to Polynesians. Almost all the plants identified in the assemblage, indigenous or introduced, are now rare or absent from the vicinity of the rockshelter and from Anarua Bay.

Aleurites moluccana (L.) Willdenow (Euphorbiaceae)

Of the introduced plant taxa represented in rockshelter deposits on Rapa, *A. moluccana* endocarps make up a large proportion of the archaeobotanical material identified, especially in the case of the Tangarutu excavation. Kirch et al. (1995) did not present data on the amount of endocarp identified from the Tangatatau excavation, but suggest it is abundant. In the Tangatatau and Tangarutu excavations, *A. moluccana* endocarps are represented throughout each deposit. Endocarps of *A. moluccana* are only represented in the basal Zone E deposit of Ureia (Allen and Wallace 2007).

In Remote Oceania, endocarps of *A. moluccana* have been identified from several archaeological sites in the Hawaiian Islands (e.g. Māhā'ulepū, Kaua'i, Burney et al. 2001; Mauna Kea, Hawai'i, Allen 1981), Mangareva (Weisler 1995; Conte and Kirch 2005), Henderson Island (Weisler 1995), Pitcairn Island (Weisler 1996), and more recently, New Caledonia (Emilie Dotte pers. comm.). Athens and Ward (1997) located *A. moluccana* endocarp and wood from Maunawili (Core 1) at 86–94 cm below the swamp surface, and provided an interpolated age from a charcoal date of 688–655 BP (Beta-5490). The pre-European contact distribution and introduction of *A. moluccana* may have extended as far as Raoul Island in the Kermadec Group (New Zealand), although this could represent a historic introduction (Sykes and West 1996).

Despite the abundance of preserved *A. moluccana* endocarps in the archaeological record from Rapa, this tree was not listed in any early accounts of the island until Jacques Moerenhout (1837) visited in 1834. Stokes (n.d.) noted the use of *A. moluccana* wood for construction of canoes and nuts for lighting. From visits to the island between the 1920s and 1930s, both Stokes (n.d.) and Fosberg (in Mueller-Dombois and Fosberg 1998:403 respectively) considered *A. moluccana* to be a major component of moist forests on Rapa. Despite its importance only 50 years ago, few trees currently exist on the island. Some trees are located precariously on the margins of coastal plains or in a few localities around the major settlements of Ha'urei and Area, where the nuts provide fodder for pigs.

Fosberg (1991:18) has questioned whether the tree has been introduced to Remote Oceania, as the nuts of this tree are commonly found as beach-drift throughout the Pacific:

> The theory that it is an introduction is favoured and, indeed, suggested by the unlikelihood of its having climbed the steep mountain slopes [of the Hawaiian Islands] up to its present habitat without human assistance. If it was brought by humans and carried up the hills by them, it spread to dominate a whole zone on many islands, forming pure stands and shading out almost all other plants, and made an important change. On some islands kukui forest occupies roughly the rainfall belt (between 1500 and 2250 mm of rainfall a year), with tongues of this forest running some distance down moist ravines to lower elevations. The landscape was modified conspicuously by the introduction of *A. moluccana*, whether by the hand of humans or dispersed naturally.

Lagenaria siceraria (Mol.) Standlicher (Cucurbitaceae)

The most recent analyses of the distribution and ethnobotany of *L. siceraria* in Remote Oceania come from Decker-Walters et al. (2001), Smith (2005) and Clarke et al. (2006). Archaeological remains suggest that the domestication of *L. siceraria* may have been independently developed in the Americas by 7000 BC (Smith 2005), South East Asia between 8000 and 4000 BC, and Africa between 3000 and 2000 BC (Heiser 1979). Bellwood (1997) has observed that *L. siceraria* was present in Taiwan at the time of the Austronesian expansion out of this area about 3000 BC, and Decker-Walters et al. (2001) assessed the diversity of landraces of *L. siceraria* from each of the above areas, including New Guinea, using random amplified polymorphic DNA. They found that the landraces of New Guinea could be distinguished from American specimens.

Based on linguistic and limited archaeobotanical evidence, Green (2000, following Ross 1996) suggests that *L. siceraria* was absent from Near Oceania at the time the closest islands in Remote Oceania were first settled around 1500 BC to 1000 BC. Green supports this claim by noting the absence of *L. siceraria* in the rich archaeobotanical assemblages from the waterlogged sites at Dongan in the lower Ramu, Papua New Guinea (Swadling et al. 1991). Green (2000) also cites the earliest interpolated date in Near Oceania for *L. siceraria* at 1230–1960 BC (ANU-43) from the Manton site at Warrawau, upper Wahgi Valley, Central Highlands, Papua New Guinea (Golson et al. 1967). Golson (2002), however, has now revised the Manton gourd rind determination, and has tentatively assigned it to the wax gourd *Benincasa hispida* on the basis of recent finds of this rind in an archaeological site at Kana (dated to 1005 BC to 20 AD; ANU-9487), at a slightly higher altitude to Manton, also in the Wahgi Valley.

Fragments of *L. siceraria* pericarp have been identified from a number of archaeological sites in the Hawaiian Islands, including the Ewa Plain and Kawainui Valley (Allen-Wheeler 1981) on O'ahu, as well as Maha'ulepu Caves, Kaua'i (Burney et al. 2001). Horrocks et al. (2000) identified *L. siceraria* pollen in an exposed section of two archaeological stone garden mounds at Pouerua, Northland, New Zealand. *L. siceraria* has an entomophilous flowering biology in which pollen is only deposited in the direct vicinity of the parent plant. This effect would be intensified given the low stature of *L. siceraria*. Horrocks et al. (2002) have identified *L. siceraria* pollen from dog or human coprolites of around AD 1300–1600 (NZA-12591) buried in a beach dune on Great Barrier Island in the Hauraki Gulf, New Zealand. These data suggest direct consumption of flowers, but might also reflect consumption of residues on young *L. siceraria*, or even inadvertent ingestion during hand pollination (Horrocks 2004).

The introduction of *L. siceraria* on Rapa contradicts Green's (2005) argument that *L. siceraria* was brought with *I. batatas* after European contact. The 16th century age for bottle gourd on Rapa suggests it was introduced pre-contact. However, the lack of evidence for *I. batatas* from any excavation on Rapa and the late appearance of *L. siceraria* in the Tangarutu E1 sequence imply that neither plant was introduced during initial Polynesian colonisation.

Further support for the Polynesian introduction of *L. siceraria* to Rapa comes from the description of 'dried pumpkin' by Faddei Von Bellingshausen, although this might otherwise describe *Ipomoea batatas* tubers (Barratt 1988). Ethnographic information collected by Stokes (n.d.) and others on Rapa suggests that *L. siceraria* was one of the few actively cultivated plants on Rapa in the early 1900s, other than *Colocasia esculenta*, *Dioscorea* spp. and *Ipomoea batatas*. Stokes (n.d. Group 2 Box 7.1) found that 'Seeds of the gourd (koali) are set in the ground with little preparation, and the plants are left to look after themselves'. Fosberg and St. John (1934) only identified *L. siceraria* cultivations at Akatanui Bay, a site now largely abandoned for cultivation.

Conclusion

The Tangarutu assemblage is exceptional in both the abundance and preservation quality of plant materials. *Aleurites moluccana* endocarps, *Lagenaria siceraria* pericarp (bottle-gourd) and leaf fibres of *Pandanus* spp. and *Freycinetia* spp. are well preserved. Archaeological charcoals in the basal part of this deposit are derived primarily from introduced economic taxa, including cf. *Hibiscus tiliaceus* syn. *Talipariti tiliaceum*, cf. *Thespesia populnea* and cf. *Cordyline fruticosa*, suggesting that the establishment of introduced plants was rapid and an important part of island colonisation strategy. Radiocarbon ages obtained from fruit and seed remains excavated from the Tangarutu sequence are discussed in reference to the settlement sequence of Rapa. The earliest ages obtained from *A. moluccana* endocarp and *Cordyline* wood, produced from introduced and cultivated trees, are slightly later than the Bayesian-modelled age estimate for initial colonisation of the island.

References

Allen, M.S. 1981. *An analysis of the Mauna Kea adze quarry archaeobotanical assemblage.* Unpublished MA thesis, University of Hawaii.

Allen, M.S. and Wallace, R. 2007. New evidence from the East Polynesian gateway: substantive and methodological results from Aitutaki, Southern Cook Islands. *Radiocarbon* 49:1163–1179.

Allen-Wheeler, J. 1981. Archaeological excavations in Kawainui Marsh, island of O'ahu. Report prepared for Department of Planning and Economic Development. Department of Anthropology, B.P. Bishop Museum, Honolulu.

Anderson, A. 1991. The chronology of colonization in New Zealand. *Antiquity* 65:767–795.

Athens, J.S. 1997. Hawaiian native lowland vegetation in Prehistory. In: Kirch, P.V. and Hunt, T.L. (eds), *Historical ecology in the Pacific Islands: prehistoric environmental and landscape change.* Yale University Press, New Haven, pp. 248–270.

Athens, J.S. and Ward, J.V. 1997. The Maunawili core: prehistoric inland expansion of settlement and agriculture, O'ahu, Hawai'i. *Hawaiian Archaeology* 6:37–51.

Barratt, G. 1988. *Southern and Eastern Polynesia, Russia and the South Pacific, 1696–1840.* University of British Columbia Press, Vancouver.

Bellwood, P. 1978. *Archaeological Research in the Cook Islands.* Pacific Anthropological Records 27, B.P. Bishop Museum, Honolulu.

Bellwood, P.S. 1997. *Prehistory of the Indo-Malaysian Archipelago.* University of Hawai'i Press, Honolulu, Hawaii.

Burney, D.A., James, H.F., Burney, L.P., Olson, S.L., Kikuchi, W., Wagner, W.L., Burney, M., McCloskey, D., Kikuchi, D., Grady, F.V., Gage, R. II and Nishek, R. 2001. Fossil evidence for a diverse biota from Kaua'i and its transformation since human arrival. *Ecological Monographs* 71:615–641.

Clarke, A.C., Burtenshaw, M.K., McLenachan, P.A., Erickson, D.L. and Penny, D. 2006. Reconstructing the origins and dispersal of the Polynesian bottle gourd (*Lagenaria siceraria*). *Molecular Biology and Evolution* 23:893–900.

Conte, E. and Kirch, P.V. 2005. *Archaeological investigations in the Mangareva Islands (Gambier Archipelago) French Polynesia.* Archaeological Research Facility, University of California, Berkeley.

Decker-Walters, D., Staub, J., Lopez-Sese, A. and Nakata, E. 2001. Diversity in landraces and cultivars of bottle gourd (*Lagenaria siceraria*; Cucurbitaceae) as assessed by random amplified polymorphic DNA. *Genetic Resources and Crop Evolution* 48:369–380.

Dickinson, W.R. 2001. Paleoshoreline record of relative Holocene sea levels on Pacific islands. *Earth-Science Reviews* 55:191–234.

Ellison, J. 1994. Paleo-lake and swamp stratigraphic records of Holocene vegetation and sea-level changes, Mangaia, Cook Islands. *Pacific Science* 48:1–15.

Florence, J. 2004. *Flore de la Polynésie française Volume II*. IRD Éditions, Paris.

Fosberg, F.R. 1991. Polynesian plant environments. In: Cox, P.A. and Banack, S.A. (eds), *Islands, plants, and Polynesians*. Dioscorides Press, Portland, pp.11–23.

Fosberg, F.R. and St. John, H. 1934. Check list and field notebook of the plants of Southeastern Polynesia: Society Islands, Tuamotus, Austral Islands, Rapa. B.P. Bishop Museum Herbarium Archive, Honolulu.

Golson, J., Lampert, R.J., Wheeler, J.M. and Ambrose, W.R. 1967. A Note on Carbon Dates for Horticulture in the New Guinea Highlands. *Journal of the Polynesian Society*. 76:369–371.

Golson, J. 2002. Gourds in New Guinea, Asia and the Pacific. In: Bedford, S., Sand, C. and Burley, D. (eds), *Fifty years in the field: essays in honour and celebration of Richard Shutler Jr's archaeological career*. New Zealand Archaeological Association, Auckland, pp. 69–78.

Green, R.C. 2000. A range of disciplines support a dual origin for the bottle gourd in the Pacific. *Journal of the Polynesian Society* 109:191–197.

Green, R.C. 2005. Sweet potato transfers in Polynesian prehistory. In: Ballard, C., Brown, P., Bourke, R.M. and Harwood, T. (eds), *The sweet potato in Oceania: a reappraisal*. Oceania Monograph. Pandanus Books, Canberra, pp. 43–62.

Heiser, C.B. 1979. *The gourd book*. University of Oklahoma Press, Norman, Oklahoma.

Horrocks, M. 2004. Polynesian plant subsistence in prehistoric New Zealand: a summary of the microfossil evidence. *New Zealand Journal of Botany* 42:321–334.

Horrocks, M. and Weisler, M.I. 2006. Analysis of Plant Microfossils in Archaeological Deposits from Two Remote Archipelagos: The Marshall Islands, Eastern Micronesia, and the Pitcairn Group, Southeast Polynesia. *Pacific Science* 60:261–280.

Horrocks, M., Jones, M.D., Carter J.A. and Sutton, D.G. 2000. Pollen and phytoliths in stone mounds at Pouerua, Northland, New Zealand: implications for the study of Polynesian farming. *Antiquity* 74: 863–872.

Horrocks, M., Jones, M.D., Beever, R.E. and Sutton, D.G. 2002. Analysis of plant microfossils in prehistoric coprolites from Harataonga Bay, Great Barrier Island, New Zealand. *Journal of the Royal Society of New Zealand* 32:617–628.

Kennett, D., Anderson, A., Prebble, M., Conte, E. and Southon, J. 2006. Prehistoric human impacts on Rapa, French Polynesia. *Antiquity* 80:340–354.

Kirch, P.V., Steadman, D.W., Butler, V.L., Hather, J. and Weisler, M.I. 1995. Prehistory and human ecology in Eastern Polynesia: Excavations at Tangatatau Rockshelter, Mangaia, Cook Islands. *Archaeology in Oceania* 30:47–65.

McCormac, F.G., Hogg, A.G., Blackwell, P.G., Buck, C.E., Higham, T.F.G. and Reimer, P.J. 2004. SHCal04 Southern Hemisphere Calibration 0–11.0 cal kyr BP. *Radiocarbon* 46:1087–1092.

Moerenhaut, J.A. 1837. *Voyages aux iles du Grand Ocean*. Paris.

Mueller-Dombois, D. and Fosberg, F.R. 1998. *Vegetation of the tropical Pacific islands*. Springer, New York.

Orliac, C. and Orliac, M. 1998. The disappearance of Easter Island's forest: overexploitation or climatic catastrophe? In: Stevenson, C.M., Lee, G. and Morin, F.J. (eds), *Easter Island in Pacific context, South Seas Symposium. Proceedings of the Fourth International Conference on Easter Island and East Polynesia*. Easter Island Foundation, Los Osos, pp. 129–134.

Prebble, M. In press. The palaeobotanical record of Rapa (French Polynesia): phytogeographic implications for the Austral Archipelago. In: Meyer, J-Y. (ed), *Biodiversity of the Austral Islands*.

Prebble, M. and Wilmshurst, J. 2009. Detecting the initial impact of humans and introduced species on island environments in Remote Oceania using palaeoecology. *Biological Invasions* 11:1529–1556.

Ross, M. 1996. Reconstructing food plant terms and associated terminologies in Proto Oceanic. In: Lynch, J. and Fa'afo, P. (eds), Oceanic studies: proceedings of the First International Conference on Oceanic Linguistics. *Pacific Linguistics* Series C no. 133. The Australian National University Canberra, Australia, pp. 163–221.

Shineberg, D. 1986. Archibald Menzies' account of the visit of the *Discovery* to Rapa and Tahiti, 22 December 1791–25 January 1792. *Pacific Studies* 9:59–102.

Smith, B.D. 2005. Reassessing Coxcatlan Cave and the early history of domesticated plants in Mesoamerica. *Proceedings of the National Academy of Science, USA* 102:9438–9445.

St. John, H. 1976. Revision of the Genus Pandanus Stickman. Part 40. The Fijian species of the section Pandanus. *Pacific Science* 30:249–315.

St. John, H. 1979. Revision of the Genus Pandanus Stickman. Part 42 *Pandanus tectorius* Parkins. ex Z and *Pandanus odoratissimus* L.f. *Pacific Science* 33:395–401.

Stokes, J.F.G. n.d. *Ethnology of Rapa.* Bernice P. Bishop Museum Archives, Honolulu.

Stone, B.C. 1976. The Pandanaceae of the New Hebrides, with an essay in intraspecific variation in *Pandanus tectorius*. *Kew Bulletin* 31:47–70.

Stone, B.C. 1988. Notes on the genus Pandanus (Pandanaceae) in Tahiti. *Botanical Journal of the Linnean Society* 97:33–48.

Stuiver, M., Reimer, P.J. and Reimer, R.W. 2005. CALIB 5.0. [WWW program and documentation].

Swadling, P., Araho, N. and Ivuyo, B. 1991. Settlements associated with the inland Sepik-Ramu sea. *Bulletin of the Indo-Pacific Prehistory Association* 2:92–112.

Sykes, W.R. and West, C.J. 1996. New records and other information on the vascular flora of the Kermadec Islands. *New Zealand Journal of Botany* 34:447–462.

Tuggle, H.D. and Spriggs, M. 2001. The age of the Bellows Dune site O18, O'ahu, Hawai'i, and the antiquity of Hawaiian colonization. *Asian Perspectives* 39:165–188.

Walczak, J. 2001. *Le peuplement de la Polynésie orientale: Une tentative d'approche historique par les exemples de Tahiti et de Rapa (Polynésie française).* Unpublished PhD thesis.

Walczak, J. 2003. Présentation des données actuelles sur la préhistoire de Rapa Iti (archiple des Australes-Polynésie Française). In: Orliac, C. (ed), *Archéologie en océanie insulaire: peuplement, sociétés et paysages.* Éditions Artcom, Paris, pp. 28–45.

Weisler, M.I. 1995. Henderson Island prehistory: colonization and extinction on a remote Polynesian island. *Biological Journal of the Linnean Society* 56:377–404.

Weisler, M.I. 1996. Taking the mystery out of the Polynesian 'mystery islands': a case study from Mangareva and the Pitcairn Group. In: Davidson, J.M., Irwin, G., Leach, B.F., Pawley, A. and Brown, D. (ed), *Oceanic culture history: essays in honour of Roger Green.* New Zealand Journal of Archaeology Special Publication, Dunedin, pp. 615–629.

Whistler, W.A. 1991. Polynesian plant introductions. In: Cox, P.A. and Banack, S.A. (eds), *Islands, plants, and Polynesians.* Dioscorides Press, Portland, pp. 41–66.

Wilmshurst, J.M., Hunt, T.L, Lipo, C.P. and Anderson, A.J. 2011. High-precision radiocarbon dating shows recent and rapid initial human colonization of East Polynesia. *Proceedings of the National Academy of Science, USA* 108:1815–1820.

5

Cordage from Rapan archaeological sites

Judith Cameron

Department of Archaeology and Natural History, The Australian National University, Canberra, Australia,
judith.cameron@anu.edu.au

Introduction

More than 80 per cent of the items of material culture produced by traditional Polynesian groups were made from plant fibres (Kirch and Green 2001:164–165), yet very little is known about prehistoric fibre artefacts in French Polynesia. The first Europeans to discover Rapa in 1791 (Chapter 2) exchanged iron for Rapan artefacts, some of fibre. Among them was a fishing line from the Vancouver Collection of the British Museum (Chapter 2). During his fieldwork on Rapa (1920–21), Stokes (n.d.) found several fragments of archaeological cordage on Rapa, but they were all surface finds of unknown age. An assemblage of securely provenanced fibre artefacts was recovered during the 2002 excavations on Rapa. Here, the species of plants used are identified, functional attributes of the specimens in the assemblage are described, function is inferred, and the artefacts are compared with examples from other parts of Polynesia.

The assemblage

Although dampness and humidity destroy archaeological textiles (a generic term for cordage, matting, basketry, textiles), the Rapan fragments were well-preserved for two reasons: relatively cooler and drier conditions than occur in tropical Polynesian islands, and stratigraphic contexts in dry sand, notably at Tangarutu. The assemblage consists of 19 fragments of worked fibres (Figure 5.1), 17 from Tangarutu and two from Akatanui. The functional attributes of the fragments (Table 5.1) include form, material composition, number and width of individual elements, length and width of grouped elements, numbers and angles of crossing. The number of crossings per 100 mm was documented as a measure of tightness and strength.

Form of cordage

The simplest cordage has two strands of the same material composition, diameter and twist. Elaborations are generated by increasing the number of strands, varying the direction of the twists (S and Z), employing elements of unequal diameter or altering the construction process by including knots, loops, or other elements (Hurley 1979). The cordage in the Rapan assemblage is of three different types: twisted, braided and knotted. Both twisting and braiding are techniques that increase the tensile strength and durability of fibres, whereas knotting

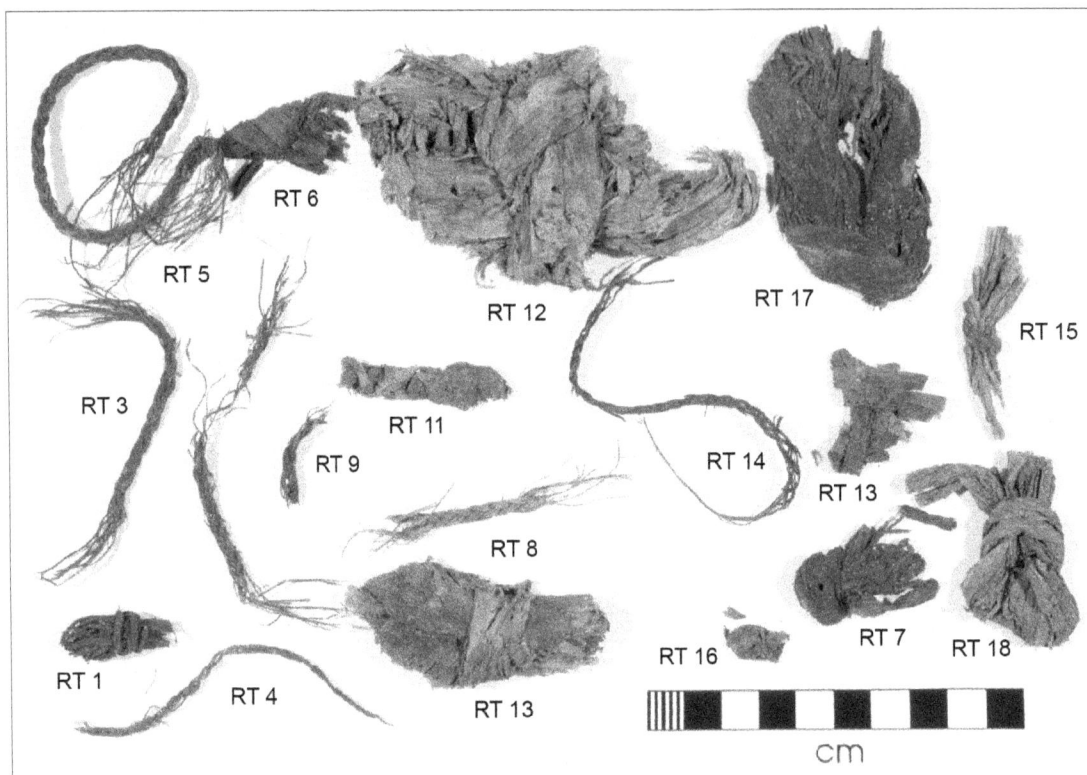

Figure 5.1. Assemblage of fibre artefacts from Tangarutu and Akatanui. See Table 5.1 for information about each item.

Table 5.1. Functional attributes of fibre artefacts from Tangarutu (RT) and Akatanui (RA).

Number	Location	Form	Material composition	Length (mm)	Width (mm)	Width of single element (mm)	Number of elements	Number of crossings	Crossings per 100 mm	Angle of crossing
RT 1	E1 Spit 1	twisted cordage	*Hibiscus sp.*	50	6	1.2	4	n/a	n/a	50
RT 2	E1 Spit 2	braided cordage	*Freycinetia sp.*	230	4	1.2	3	n/a	n/a	60
RT 3	E1 Spit 2	braided cordage	*Freycinetia sp.*	110	4	1.1	3	6	5	60
RT 4	E1 Spit 2	braided cordage	*Freycinetia sp.*	95	3	1.0	3	11	12	65
RT 5	E1 Spit 2	braided cordage	*Freycinetia sp.*	140	3	1.0	3	15	11	60
RT 6	E1 Spit 2	braided cordage	*Freycinetia sp.*	41	2	6.0		1	0.5	n/a
RT 7	E2 Spit 3	braided cordage	*Freycinetia sp.*	170	8	8.0	3	?	n/a	n/a
RT 8	E2 Spit 3	knotted fibre	*B. papyrifera*	70	19	19.0	1	2	3	n/a
RT 9	E2 Spit 3	braided cordage	*Freycinetia sp.*	25	4	1.1	3	3	12	65
RT11	E1 Spit 2	twisted cordage	*Hibiscus sp.*	44	9	4.0	3	2	4	50
RT 12	E1 Spit 1	knotted cordage	*B. papyrifera*	115	4	1.1	3	1	n/a	n/a
RT 13	E1 Spit 1	knotted cordage	*B. papyrifera*	14	10	4.5	2	1	n/a	60
RT14	E2 Spit 2	braided cordage	*Freycinetia sp.*	115	4	1.2	3	7	6	65
RA 15	C1 Spit 3	knotted fibre	*B. papyrifera*	35	20	6.0	?	n/a	n/a	n/a
RA 16	C1 Spit 2	knotted fibre	*B. papyrifera*	48	5	5.0	1	2	4	n/a
RT 17	E1 Spit 3	knotted fibre	*B. papyrifera*	35	20			4	12	n/a
RT 18	E1 Spit 3	knotted fibre	*B. papyrifera*	95	9	4.0	2	3	3	n/a
RT 19	E2 Spit 1	braided cordage	*Freycinetia sp.*	110	3	1.2	3	5	5	65
RT 20	E2 Spit 1	braided cordage	*Freycinetia sp.*	85	4	1.2	3	3	4	65

*Note: RT10 is not included. Microscopic analysis revealed it was actually an unworked piece of gourd. RT 19 and RT 20 are not shown in Figure 5.1.

generally increases length. All specimens are small and fragmentary with no use-wear patterns, dyes, or stains discernible.

The two twisted fragments (RT1 and RT11) consist of more than two strands of hard, outer fibres. Although RT11 is defined as twisted cordage, strictly speaking it is simply wrapped. The core element of RT11 is rigid, with untwisted fibre wrapped around the core, a twig. The single elements of this three-stranded cordage measured 4 mm in diameter. The cord is not wrapped at right angles, but in a helix spiralling from the lower left to the upper right, at regular intervals. The cord would first have been attached to the twig, then wrapped continuously in an oblique way until reaching the end of the twig, then reversed and wrapped in the opposite direction, crisscrossing and overlapping the first layer cord six times, with greater density at one end. The function of RT11 is not indicated by context, but this technique was often used in west Polynesian coiled basketry. Coiling is a basketry technique where active, flexible elements are wound around passive, stationary elements called the foundation. Successive circuits of the foundation are bound together by wrapping. The same technique was also used to make other artefacts such as the cordage used in the fishing device from the Vancouver Collection (Chapter 2) and some small fish hooks from Rapa that may also be from the Vancouver Collection (Figure 5.2), although that is not certain.

RT1 is the end piece of a fibre artefact showing an elaboration of the twisting technique evidenced in RT11. RT1 was worked using four individual strands, each single element measuring 1.2 mm in diameter. As with RT11, a stick forms the base, but instead of using a single unspun, untwisted element for spiral wrapping, a number of semi-rigid fibre strands are wrapped around the stick over the end, with four strands used to bind the cordage.

Ten of the fragments (RT2, RT3, RT4, RT5, RT6, RT7, RT9, RT14, RT19, RT20) in the assemblage were flat, constructed by braiding. In the early contact literature, the term *sennit* or *sinnet* was often used for braided coconut cordage and warp-woven tapes. Braiding is a process derived from diagonal plaiting which produces cordage (and textiles) that is invariably greater in length than width. Braiding can be either two-dimensional with odd or even sets of strands, or three-dimensional forms (tubular and compact), including looped, interlooped, interlinked and knotted structures (Emery 1980:60).

None of the individual elements of the braided cordage in the assemblage had been previously twisted or spun. The commencement point of cordage is generally culturally determined, but this feature could not be ascertained, as the archaeological pieces were fragmentary. The absence of wooden stick fixtures at the site suggests that the braided cordage was probably worked with loose ends. All fragments were worked from flexible fibres and shared the same basic configuration. Six of the fragments were constructed using three strands, called three-ply braiding; one is four-ply. The three-ply braids were plaited by passing the elements in the right-hand strand over those in the middle strand, then by reversing the process. During construction, the terminal elements were folded back on themselves at angles ranging from 60° to 65° and replaited into the body of each band. The angle of crossing shows a high degree of standardisation. The number of crossings per 100 mm indicates the tightness of the cordage: the greater the number of twists, the stronger the cordage. Most of the braided cordage in the assemblage was tightly worked, with measurements ranging from >10 crossings per 100 mm, with a few examples of loosely plaited forms of <5 per 100 mm. Some fragments exhibit 2/1/2 and 2/4/2 shifts.

Seven fragments (RT8, RT12, RT13, RA15, RA16, RT17 and RT18) in the assemblage were knotted. The knot in RT17 is a basic overhand knot, formed by pulling one end through a simple loop. As the fragment is incomplete, its function is unclear. The longest knotted fragments (RT16, RT18), measuring 4.4 cm in length, were found at Akatanui (Table 5.1). Other types

Figure 5.2. Fishing hooks collected from Rapa Island. In the British Museum (Beasley 1928:Plate LXIII; 037 BM). It is not clear whether these were in the Vancouver Collection. All appear to have wood or candlenut shanks, fully bound, but the example at lower left seems to have a shell or bone tip inserted into the shank.

of knotted cordage in the assemblage are more complex and give better insights into function. RT16 is an example of a slightly more complicated knot, the sheet bend, which is still widely used for fishing nets throughout Polynesia.

Material composition

Identifications by M. Prebble (pers. comm.) indicate that the knotted cordage was made from *Broussonetia papyrifera* (paper mulberry), the braided cordage appears to have been worked from the roots of *Freycinetia* spp. (*kiekie* vine) and the twisted cordage was worked from *Hibiscus* spp. (purau or hau). While *Cocos nucifera* (coconut) fibre is not in the archaeological assemblage, Stokes (n.d.) identified coconut fibre cordage, but this might have been from material of 19th century origin, or identified wrongly. Altogether, 37 per cent of the cordage in the Rapan assemblage was made from *Broussonetia papyrifera,* a fibre introduced by early Polynesians primarily for *tapa*. The bast would have been removed from the outer bark and dried in the sun before being cut into workable strips. All the *B. papyrifera* fibres were knotted, with individual strips ranging from 1.1 mm to 20 mm in diameter. The largest was made from a single strip of the plant; most were multiple strips of one to three strands. In the Rapan assemblage, 10 per cent of the cordage was made from *Hibiscus* spp. In the Society Islands, *hau* is the term for the bast and *more* for the cordage from hibiscus. The beach hibiscus is pantropic in distribution, deposited originally by seawater-dispersed seeds (Whistler 1991:65). More than half, 52 per cent, of the cordage in the Rapan assemblage appears to be made of roots from *Freycinetia* spp. (kiekie). All worked examples of this fibre were braided.

Archaeological comparisons

All of the cordage types in the Rapan assemblage have been recovered also in surface deposits in caves or from stratified sequences in Hawaii (Kirch 1979; Burney and Kikuchi 2006) and New Zealand (Goulding 1971; Lawrence 1989; Anderson et al. 1991; McAra 2004). The most common cordage in the Pacific archaeological record is *aha (Cocos nucifera)*. It comprises 49% of the cordage in the B.P. Bishop Museum's archaeological collections (Summers 1990). Of the 98 examples of twisted *aha* cordage in the Bishop Museum collection, 87 are two-ply of remarkably uniform diameter (0.8–1.5 mm). Throughout Hawaii, the primary function of twisted *aha* cordage was for nets (Summers 1990).

Braid is the dominant cordage type in the Bishop Museum's archaeological collection. On Rapa and other Polynesian islands, men were responsible for braiding to produce cordage, whereas women were responsible for twisting cordage and for making bark cloth. Most Hawaiian braid was untwisted and three-ply, but five-ply and seven-ply braided cords (B.P. Bishop Museum:4755, 4756, 4749, 6870) were used to lash canoe hulls to outrigger booms *('iako)*. The width of the cordage in the Bishop Museum ranged from 4.8 mm to 5.4 mm, whereas the three-ply cordage from Rapa measured between 3.0 mm and 4.0 mm. Four of the seven hafted adzes in Cook expedition collections are lashed with braided three-ply *aha* cordage (Kaeppler in Summers 1990:88).

On Rapa, Stokes (n.d.:294) found several pieces of *nape kiekie (Freycinetia* spp.), with a piece of coir cordage attached to canoe boards in a burial cave at Akatanui. Stokes observed that *ka'a*, the original Rapan name for this type of cordage, was slowly being replaced by *nape*, the Tahitian term for braid. According to Stokes, *nape* from *kiekie* was said to be fairly durable but did not last as long as coir cordage. Braid was also a component of the close-meshed *kiekie* fishing baskets (*inaki*) woven on Rapa using the twining technique (Plate 8442). *Kiekie* baskets from Rapa were in demand in Tahiti and Mangareva. Stokes (n.d.) also recorded wide-meshed war nets, woven, probably, from *kiekie*.

Precisely the same technique was used to work a fragment of tightly braided three-ply *uki uki* (*Dianella* sp.) cordage recovered from a burial site (designated 1985.669.013) in Kohala, Hawaii (Summers 1990). Stokes (n.d.:Plates 8550, 8551) found decayed woven fragments (Plates 8550 and 8551), identified as mortuary cloaks, in some Rapan rockshelters. His descriptions of cloaks indicate that warps were made of rigid fibres from the giant rush, *Scirpus* spp., placed in parallel rows manipulated by the weaver's feet. The soft, pliable wefts, made from twisted bast fibres, such as *more* from *Hibiscus tiliaceus*, or *raupo* from *Typhus* spp., were worked at right angles. The wefts created a soft pile regarded by Rapans as good for cold weather. (Stokes n.d.). The closed-twining technique was also used for *ti* (*Cordyline* spp.) kilts. While twined fish baskets were widespread throughout Polynesia (Burrows 1970:26), twined kilts did not occur in western Polynesia, being confined to the Tuamotus and Rapa. Short lengths of braided *Freycinetia* spp. cordage were attached to cloaks and mortuary robes for fastening. Stokes compared Rapan cloaks with New Zealand equivalents and found Rapan forms to be similar, but less refined. Cloaks held considerable social and ritual significance throughout Polynesia and Ellis' informant,

Teraau, explained the colour symbolism of Rapan cloaks. Royal cloaks incorporated dark blue feathers from *kotokoto* birds (species unknown, but possibly the Tuamotuan kingfisher, *Halcyon gambieri* (SOPF 1999:41), the feathers of which were probably imported in the European era), whereas those intended for commoners were made from black and white petrel feathers.

New Zealand excavations have also produced fragments of mortuary cloaks and cordage. Lawrence (1989) recovered cordage during excavations of a historical site in the Waitakere Ranges, and Lander (1992) similar material from Raupa. Anderson et al. (1991) found numerous fragments of *harakeke* (*Phormium tenax*) cordage during excavations at Fiordland, and also a piece of a woven *harakeke* and bird-feather cloak. *Harakeke* netting and cordage fragments were also reported from waterlogged contexts at the late Maori village of Kohika (McAra in Irwin 2004) and from a cave on the Banks Peninsula (McAra in Irwin 2004).

Conclusions

The main sources of cordage on Rapa were the fibrous roots and vines of native *kiekie* and the introduced paper mulberry, with a small proportion of samples from hibiscus. While some coconut-fibre artefacts might have been collected by Stokes, no coconut fibre occurs in the excavated samples, and this is consistent with the probable absence of coconut until the historical era.

Given the multiple uses of cordage, it is difficult to determine the function of examples in the Rapan assemblage. However, as most of the material came from Tangarutu cave, which had functioned very largely as a fishing station, it is most likely that the fibre artefacts were associated with that activity. The cord-wrapped stick from Tangarutu could either be the handle of a fishing basket or part of a fishing line, with the softer bast elements wrapped around the rigid elements to protect the user's hands. The knotted *aute* cordage compares favourably with archaeological *aute* from Hawaii identified as carrying bags and nets. The absence of twisting suggests the Rapan samples are probably the remains of nets. The braided cordage in the assemblage seems most likely to have been the remains of a longer length of cordage used for fishing lines or nets.

References

Anderson, A., Goulding, J. and White, M. 1991. Bark and fibre artefacts. In: Anderson, A.J. and McGovern-Wilson, R. (eds), *Beech Forest Hunters: the archaeology of Maori rockshelter sites on Lee Island, Lake Te Anau, in southern New Zealand*, pp. 43–55. New Zealand Archaeological Association, Auckland.

Beasley, H.G. 1928. Pacific Island Records: *Fish Hooks*. Seeley Service, London.

Burney, D. and Kikuchi, W.P. 2006. A Millennium of human activity at Makauwahi Cave, Maha'ulepu, Kaua'i. *Human Ecology* 34:219–247.

Burrows, E.C. 1970. *Western Polynesia: a study of cultural differentiation*. University Book Shop, Dunedin.

Emery, I. 1980. *The Primary Structures of Fabrics*. The Textile Museum, Washington.

Goulding, J. 1971. Identification of archaeological and ethnographical specimens of fibre-plant material used by the Maori. *Records of the Auckland Institute and Museum* 8:57–101.

Hurley, W.M. 1979. *Prehistoric Cordage: identification of impressions on pottery*. Taraxacum, Washington.

Irwin, G. 2004. *Kohika: The Archaeology of a late Maori lake village in the Ngati Awa rohe, Bay of Plenty, New Zealand*. Auckland University Press, Auckland.

Kirch, P. 1979. *Marine Exploitation in Prehistoric Hawaii*. Pacific Anthropological Record 29. Bernice P. Bishop Museum, Honolulu, Hawaii.

Kirch, P. and Green, R. 2001. *Hawaiki: Ancestral Polynesia: An Essay in Historical Anthropology*. Cambridge University Press, Cambridge.

Lander, M. 1992. Fibre fragments from the Raupa site, Hauraki Plains. *Records of the Auckland Institute and Museum* 29:7–23.

Lawrence, J. 1989. The Archaeology of the Waikakere Ranges. Unpublished MA thesis, University of Auckland.

McAra, S. 2004. Kohika fibrework. In: Irwin, G. (ed), *Kohika: The Archaeology of a late Maori lake village in the Ngati Awa rohe, Bay of Plenty, New Zealand*, pp. 149–159. Auckland University Press, Auckland.

Stokes, J.F. n.d. *Ethnography of Rapa*. Manuscript in the Bernice P. Bishop Museum Collection, Honolulu, Hawaii.

Summers, C. 1990. *Hawaiian Cordage*. Bernice P. Bishop Museum, Honolulu, Hawaii.

Whistler, W.A. 1991. Polynesian plant introductions. In: Cox, P.A. and Banack, S.A. (eds), *Islands, Plants and Polynesians: an introduction to Polynesian ethnobotany*, pp. 41–66. Dioscorides Press, Portland, Oregon.

6

Bird, reptile and mammal remains from archaeological sites on Rapa Island

Alan J. D. Tennyson

Museum of New Zealand Te Papa Tongarewa, Wellington, New Zealand, AlanT@tepapa.govt.nz

Atholl Anderson

Department of Archaeology and Natural History, The Australian National University

Introduction

Rapa Island, French Polynesia, has a land vertebrate fauna typical of an isolated oceanic South Pacific Island. Birds dominate the fauna and there are no native mammals or terrestrial reptiles. Together with its smaller offshore islands, Rapa has a small, poorly known but important bird fauna. Bird species recorded breeding or as migrant residents are: Christmas shearwater *Puffinus nativitatis*, little shearwater *Puffinus assimilis myrtae*, Kermadec petrel *Pterodroma neglecta neglecta*, Murphy's petrel *Pterodroma ultima*, black-winged petrel *Pterodroma nigripennis*, white-bellied storm petrel *Fregetta grallaria titan*, Polynesian storm petrel *Nesofregetta fuliginosa*, red-tailed tropicbird *Phaethon rubricauda*, grey duck *Anas superciliosa*, spotless crake *Porzana tabuensis*, golden plover *Pluvialis fulva*, wandering tattler *Tringa incana*, brown noddy *Anous stolidus*, grey noddy *Procelsterna cerulea*, white tern *Gygis alba*, Rapa fruit dove *Ptilinopus huttoni* and long-tailed cuckoo *Eudynamys taitensis* (Pratt et al. 1987; Thibault and Varney 1991b). The fruit dove and the subspecies of little shearwater and white-bellied storm petrel are endemic to the island group.

The history of introduced mammals on Rapa is sketchy but Pacific rats (*Rattus exulans*) arrived in prehistoric times and, apparently, are still the only rat species present today (Thibault and Varney 1991a, 1991b). At times, rats have been 'very numerous' (Hall 1869). There is no historical evidence suggesting the pre-European introduction of dogs (*Canis familiaris*), pigs (*Sus scrofa*) or chickens (*Gallus gallus*). These were introduced in the 19th century, along with sheep (*Ovis aries*), which 'did not seem to thrive' (Hall 1869:80), cattle (*Bos taurus*) and goats (*Capra hircus*). The latter are now in large numbers and the vegetation and integrity of upland soils is suffering considerably as a result. Cats (*Felis catus*) were introduced at an unknown date but were established by 1921 (Holyoak and Thibault 1984).

Vertebrate remains recovered by archaeological excavations in the coastal sites were mainly of fish, but bird and rat bones were also quite common. Here, we report the identification and quantification of bird, reptile and mammal bone.

Methods

Comparative collections in the Museum of New Zealand Te Papa Tongarewa (NMNZ) were used by Tennyson to identify faunal remains. Specimens of closely related taxa were used when comparative skeletons of species known from Rapa were not available. Numbers of individual birds given represent only the minimum number of individuals based on the fragmentary remains collected. When calculating minimum numbers of individuals, identifications to a probable species were lumped with certain identifications of that species.

List of main comparative skeletons used (NMNZ unless otherwise noted)

Pink-footed shearwater *Puffinus creatopus* OR.27754; flesh-footed shearwater *Puffinus carneipes* S.771, OR.26448; wedge-tailed shearwater *Puffinus pacificus* OR.16209, OR.27270, OR.27271; Christmas shearwater OR.24682; little shearwater OR.23972, OR.24230; Audubon's shearwater *Puffinus lherminieri* OR.27467, OR.27551; black-winged petrel OR.24226; Kermadec petrel OR.11423, OR.25216; Murphy's petrel OR.24403; white-bellied storm petrel OR.16071, OR.27781; Polynesian storm petrel OR.27482, OR.27504; white-tailed tropicbird OR.27835; red-tailed tropicbird OR.16056; red-footed booby *Sula sula* OR.24594; brown booby *Sula leucogaster* OR.16058; domestic chicken *Gallus gallus* OR.16485; banded rail *Gallirallus philippensis* OR.22842; spotless crake OR.26455, OR.27985a; golden plover OR.22509; wandering tattler OR.26437; sooty tern *Sterna fuscata* OR.22945; brown noddy OR.25348; black noddy *Anous minutus* OR.23958; grey noddy OR.24377; white tern OR.23699; Cook Islands fruit dove *Ptilinopus rarotongensis* OR.22463; extinct Fijian pigeon *Ducula lakeba* S.39286; collared lory *Phigys solitarius* Fiji Museum 22; Horned parakeet *Cyanoramphus cornutus* OR.25730; long-tailed cuckoo OR.18339; hawksbill turtle *Eretmochelys imbricata* RE.5307; Norway rat *Rattus norvegicus* LM.1274; dog LM.1412; cat LM.807, LM.808, LM.1413, LM.1414; pig LM.1410, Canterbury Museum FMa 4086; goat LM.539, ex D.S.I.R. collection no.4494.

Identification of taxa

Spits within excavations are shown in brackets for identified taxa. S-numbers are NMNZ accession codes. All rat remains were assumed to be Pacific rat, based on their small size.

Abbreviations. cf. = similar to and probably, juv = juvenile, prox = proximal, dist = distal, L = left, R = right, pt = part, frag = fragment, cra = cranium, pmx = premaxilla, mand = mandible, quad = quadrate, vert = vertebra, cor = coracoid, scap = scapula, ster = sternum, hum = humerus, uln = ulna, rad = radius, cmc = carpometacarpus, alphal = alar phalange, pel = pelvis, fem = femur, tbt = tibiotarsus, fib = fibula, tmt = tarsometatarsus, phal = phalanx.

Tangarutu Cave

Location T1

Location T1 in loose sand at base of main exposure directly below eroding pocket of bones exposed at 155–160 cm depth. The loose bones were:

Kermadec petrel: 4 L 1 juv R 1 R hum, 3 R uln, 1 L rad, 2 R cmc; S.44406.

red-tailed tropicbird: 1 ster; S.44407.

Unidentified remains: S.44408.

Additional material excavated from the face of T1 at 155–160 cm depth:

flesh-footed/pink-footed shearwater: 1 skull, 1 mand, 1 L 1 R hum, 1 L 1 R uln, 1 rad, 1 pel, 1 R fem, 1 R tbt, 1 toe; S.44391.

little shearwater: 1 dist R hum, 1 R uln, 1 R rad; S.44403.

Kermadec petrel: 1 frag mand, 1 furcula, 2 R cor, 7 dist L 6 dist R hum, 9 L 5 R uln, 7 L 7 R rad, 6 L 6 R cmc, 6 L 3 R manus, 4 alphal; S.44404.

Unidentified remains: S.44405, S.44409.

Excavation E1

little shearwater: 1 shaft uln (1), 1 prox rad (1), 1 R cmc (14); S.44416, S.44451.

black-winged petrel: 1 pt cra (1), 1 mand (10), 2 R scap (14), 1 pt L 1 pt R 1 R cor (16), 2 pt L 1 R hum (17), 1 L uln (18), 1 dist rad (19), 1 R cmc 2 (19), manus (19), 1 pel (16), 1 dist L 2 L 1 R fem (16), 1 prox L 1 dist L 1 shaft L 1 prox R 1 dist R 1 R tbt (18), 2 R tmt (21); S.44417, S.44434–35, S.44450, S.44459, S.44467, S.44475–76, S.44487, S.44489, S.44541, S.44544, S.44553, S.44558.

Kermadec petrel: 3 pt mand (1), 2 R quad (7), 2 pt furcula (10), 2 L scap (13), 1 L 3 pt R cor (14), 1 R scap (14), 1 frag ster (14), 1 prox L 1 L 2 prox R 1 frag R 2 R hum (16), 3 dist L 2 L 2 dist R 1 R uln (17), 2 dist R 1 prox R rad (18), 2 dist L 2 prox R 1 dist R 1 R cmc (18), 1 manus (19), 3 alphal (14), 1 pt pel (14), 1 R fem (15), 2 prox L 2 dist L 4 dist R tbt (16), 1 fib (17), 3 pt L 2 R tmt (16), 5 toes (16); S.44412, 44429, S.44433, S.44445, S.44449, S.44458, S.44466, S.44474, S.44484, S.44486, S.44491, S.44536, S.44539, S.44543, S.44547, S.44552.

red-tailed tropicbird: 1 pt mand (1), 1 prox L hum (14), 1 dist L hum 1 (14), shaft cmc (21); S.44413, S.44452, S.44492, S.44537.

spotless crake: 1 dist L tbt (11); S.44596.

brown noddy: 1 R scap (3), 1 R rad (3), 1 dist R cmc (17), 2 dist R tbt (18), 1 dist R tmt (16); S.44422, S.44468, S.44477, S.44545.

grey noddy: 1 cor (13); S.44446.

white tern: 1 pt pmx (11), 2 pt mand (15), 2 L cor (17), 1 L scap (18), 2 dist L hum (17), 1 L cmc (17), 1 manus (17); S.44439, S.44456, S.44469, S.44478, S.44548, S.44556.

Rapa fruit dove: 1 pt L cor (13), 1 R cmc (18); S.44447, S.44480.

pigeon (cf. *Ducula*): 1 prox L fem (14), 1 toe (16); S.44453, S.44461.

parrot (cf. *Cyanoramphus*): 1 dist L tbt (18); S.44481.

Unidentified bird feathers: S.44418, S.44420, S.44423, S.44426–27.

rat: 1 cra, 9 mand, 2 teeth, 5 vert, 2 hum, 1 pt pel, 2 fem; S.44436, S.44438, S.44441, S.44443, S.44460, S.44464, S.44470, S.44482, S.44528, S.44534, S.44538, S.44549.

cf. Goat: 1 pel; S.44415.

Unidentified mammal fur: S.44424.

turtle: 1 ?uln, 1 piece of plastron; S.44414, S.44483.

Unidentified remains: S.44419, S.44421, S.44425, S.44428, S.44430–31, S.44437, S.44440, S.44442, S.44444, S.44448, S.44454–55, S.44457, S.44462–63, S.44465, S.44471–73, S.44479, S.44485, S.44488, S.44490, S.44493, S.44529–33, S.44535, S.44540, S.44542, S.44546, S.44550–51, S.44554–55, S.44557, S.44559.

Excavation E2

black-winged petrel: 1 dist R hum (10–13); S.44515.

Kermadec petrel: 1 pt L scap (4), 1 shaft L 1 L 1 R cor (8–9), 1 prox L 1 pt R hum (10–13), 1 dist R uln (14), 1 pt pel (16–17), 1 dist L tmt (23–25); S.44504, S.44510–11, S.44514,

S.44518, S.44520–21, S.44564.

1 red-tailed tropicbird: 1 vert (9), 1 alphal (22), 1 pt pel (23–25); S.44512, S.44562, S.44565.

parrot (cf. *Cyanoramphus*): 1 prox R uln (10–13), 1 R rad (14); S.44516, S.44560.

Unidentified bird toes: S.44500, S.44526.

Unidentified feathers: S.44392–93, S.44494, S.44497, S.44501.

rat: 2 mand (1), 1 tooth (1), 2 pt pel (18), 1 tibia (14); S.44495, S.44498, S.44523, S.44561.

Unidentified remains: S.44496, S.44499, S.44502–03, S.44505–09, S.44513, S.44517, S.44519, S.44522, S.44524–25, S.44563, S.44566.

Excavation R1

little shearwater: 1 L fem (4), 1 prox R fem (7); S.44574, S.44578.

black-winged petrel: 1 L cor (3), 1 dist L hum (4), 1 dist R hum (8); S.44571, S.44573, S.44580.

Kermadec petrel: 1 quad (1), 2 L 1 R cor (3), 1 L scap (4), 1 dist L 1 frag R hum (6), 1 dist rad (7), 1 pel (8), 1 dist R fem (8), 1 toe (8); S.44567, S.44570, S.44572, S.44575, S.44577, S.44579, S.44582.

Unidentified remains: S.44410–11, S.44568, S.44569, S.44576, S.44581.

Excavation S1

little shearwater: 1 ster (3); S.44362.

black-winged petrel: 1 L scap, 1 ster, 1 pel (all 3); S.44396.

Kermadec petrel: 3 frag cra, 1 L scap, 3 ster, 1 dist L uln, 1 dist L rad, 3 L cmc, 1 prox L tmt toe (all 3); S.44395.

white-bellied storm petrel: 1 L cor (3); S.44397.

red-tailed tropicbird: 1 L cor (3); S.44398.

rail (cf. *Gallirallus*): 1 L tmt (3); S.44399.

pigeon: 1 frag ster (3); S.44400.

rat: 1 dist fem (3); S.44401.

Unidentified remains: S.44402.

Akatanui shelters

Shelter 1

white-bellied storm petrel: 1 dist hum (2); S.43679.

?chicken: 2 toes (2); S.43680.

rat: 2 teeth, 1 pel, 2 tibia (1); S.43676–77, S.43685.

cat: 1 pt maxilla (1); S.43674.

Unidentified mammal: 1 rib, 1 phal; S.43682.

Unidentified remains: S.43675, S.43678, S.43681, S.43683–84, S.43686.

Shelter 3 Square A1

rat: 1 tooth (1), 1 scap (1), 2 hum (1), 2 pel (2), 3 fem (2), 1 tibia (2); S.43688, S.43690, S.43692, S.43694.

Unidentified bird feathers: S.43687, S.43691.

Unidentified remains: S.43689, S.43693, S.43695.

Shelter 3 Square B1

grey noddy: 1 dist hum (1); S.43696.

Unidentified bird feathers: S.43697, S.43703.

rat: 3 mand (1), 1 tooth (1), 1 vert (1), 1 pel (2), 2 fem (2), 1 tibia (2); S.43699, S.43701, S.43705, S.43708.

Unidentified mammal: 1 juv vert, fur; S.43704, S.43706.

Unidentified remains: S.43698, S.43700, S.43702, S.43707.

Shelter 3 Square C1

white-bellied storm petrel: 1 prox tmt (2); S.43713.

grey noddy: 1 prox L hum (1); S.43709.

rat: 1 skull (1), 1 mand (1), 3 scap (2), 1 hum (2), 2 fem (2), 3 tibia (3); S.43710, S.43715, S.43719–20.

?pig: 1 tooth (1); S.43712.

Unidentified mammal: 1 juv hum, fur; S.43714, S.43716.

Unidentified remains: S.43711, S.43717–18, S.43721.

Shelter 3, Test-pit E1

little shearwater: 1 R fem (1); S.43723.

Kermadec petrel: 1 dist R cmc (2); S.43728.

red-tailed tropicbird: 1 shaft R uln (1); S.43724.

rat: 2 mand, 1 tooth, 1 prox fem, 1 dist tibia (all 1); S.43722, S.43726.

cf. goat: 2 vert, 2 rib (both 1); S.43725.

Unidentified remains: S.43727, S.43729.

Angairao Bay shelters

Shelter C

little shearwater: 1 pt cra, 1 dist L rad (both 2); S.44366, S.44368.

black-winged petrel: 1 dist L 1 dist R tbt (3); S.44372.

white-bellied storm petrel: 1 dist tbt (2); S.44367.

rat: 2 pt cra (2), 2 mand (2), 3 teeth (2), 4 vert (2), 1 hum (2), 1 pel (2), 3 fem (3), 4 tibia (3); S.44364, S.44370, S.44373.

cf. goat: 1 vert (2); S.44375.

Unidentified remains: S.44365, S.44369, S.44371, S.44374.

Shelter E

rat: 1 vert (9); S.44386.

cf. goat (juv) (4); S.44376, S.44379.

turtle: 1 piece of plastron (4); S.44380.

Unidentified remains: S.44377–78, S.44381–85.

Noogoriki

little shearwater: 1 cmc (1); S.44388.

Unidentified bird feather: S.44389.

Unidentified remains: S.44387, S.44390.

Taugatu Shelter

Unidentified remains: S.44527.

Discussion and conclusions

It is not certain that all of the bird bones recovered from the Rapa sites had been deposited as midden rather than by natural accumulation. No bones showed clear signs of charring or human butchery and elements from all skeletal components were preserved. However, the clear cultural context of the sites and the presence of introduced mammal remains, particularly of rat (cf. *Rattus exulans*), throughout the stratigraphy show that the deposits were at least laid down after human settlement. Of domestic animals, the chicken was identified tentatively by two toe bones recovered at a shallow depth (10–20 cm) in Akatanui Shelter 1, where there was also material from the European era, including a spectacle lens, iron nails and a button. A cat maxilla was also found (0–10 cm) at this site. A probable pig tooth occurred in the surface spit (0–10 cm) at Akatanui Shelter 3. Goat bones were the most common of introduced faunal material, occurring in surface deposits at Akatanui, Test-pit E1, at Tangarutu E1 in surface sand and at Angairao Shelter E, where the remains were at 30–40 cm depth below an oven. No dog bone was recovered and the ethnographic evidence that Rapa had no introduced mammals other than the Pacific rat before European arrival is sustained by the archaeological data. No seal bone was recorded.

The reptile remains were exclusively from marine turtle. Plastron at Angairao Shelter E occurred in conjunction with goat bone (above), but at Tangarutu excavation E1 it was recovered from near the base of the site, in Spit 18. Turtles are not common around Rapa, but still the scarcity of their remains in the sites is surprising.

Fifteen species of birds, represented by a total of 118 individuals, were identified by remains from all sites combined (Table 6.1). Most bones identified were of species currently breeding at Rapa (Pratt et al. 1987; Thibault and Varney 1991b), and most (90%) of the bird remains identified were seabirds. The dominant species was Kermadec petrel, comprising almost half of all avian remains. As this petrel is one of the more common seabirds breeding on Rapa today (Thibault and Varney 1991b), its prevalence in the deposits is not surprising.

The little shearwater bones are presumed to be from the race endemic to Rapa. This is a poorly known bird that currently only breeds on a few small islets off the main island (Thibault and Varney 1991b). Black-winged petrels breed on some of the islets offshore from Rapa today (Thibault and Varney 1991b). The species is undergoing a rapid expansion in its breeding range (e.g. Jenkins and Cheshire 1982; Tennyson 1991), but the remains identified in this study demonstrate that the Rapa population has been long-standing and therefore is not a new colonisation, contrary to the conclusions of Thibault and Varney (1991b). Red-tailed tropic birds, grey noddies, brown noddies and white terns are also common seabirds currently breeding on Rapa (Thibault and Varney 1991b).

The four storm petrel bones identified are larger than the bones of the white-bellied storm petrel subspecies breeding at the Kermadec and Juan Fernandez islands and smaller than bones of the Polynesian storm petrel, so they are consistent with the large endemic white-bellied subspecies breeding on islets off Rapa (Murphy and Snyder 1952; Thibault and Varney 1991b). However, the flesh-footed or pink-footed shearwater specimen is a surprising find. Rapa is thousands of kilometres outside the normal range of both these species, which breed to the west and east of Rapa respectively (Marchant and Higgins 1990). Both species are migrants – perhaps their migration route takes them nearer Rapa than previously realised. If so, the Rapa specimen may be a vagrant. Alternatively, Rapa might be a former breeding location of one or other species.

Two rail bones were identified. The tarsometatarsus is similar to but smaller than that of a banded rail. Therefore, it seems likely that an endemic form, in the widespread genus *Gallirallus*, was once resident on Rapa. Estimates of the number of extinct rails in Oceania range from 200 to 3000 (Steadman 1995; Tennyson and Martinson 2006), so an extinct form on Rapa is to be expected. The only rail known from Rapa today is the much smaller spotless crake (Pratt et al. 1987), which was represented by one distal tibiotarsus.

The smaller pigeon bones were assigned, on the basis of size alone, to the sole extant dove on Rapa. In addition, at least one other larger species of pigeon, similar to a large *Ducula* species, once occurred. Large *Ducula* species have been eliminated from several of the Pacific Islands (e.g. Worthy 2001), so an extinct species on Rapa might be expected. The fragmentary pigeon sternum of unknown relationships (S.44400 from Spit 3 of excavation S1 at Tangarutu) has a low, rounded keel, indicating that this species may have had reduced powers of flight.

The three parrot bones are the first evidence that any parrots once lived in the Austral Island group. Few parrot species occur in Eastern Polynesia and those that do (or did) belong to the genera *Vini* (lorikeets) and *Cyanoramphus* (parakeets) (Pratt et al. 1987). The Rapa bones fit *Cyanoramphus* well, so they probably represent an extinct endemic species and extend the range of this genus further east than previously known. Both *Cyanoramphus* species recorded from tropical Eastern Polynesia (*C. zealandicus* from Tahiti and *C. ulietanus* from Raiatea) are also extinct (Pratt et al. 1987).

Overall, remarkably few of the resident bird species on Rapa today were missing from the archaeological samples (the missing taxa are: Christmas shearwater, Murphy's petrel, Polynesian storm petrel, grey duck, golden plover, wandering tattler and long-tailed cuckoo). The small size of the collection is likely to explain the absence of most of these species but they might also have been relatively uncommon on Rapa. As the remains of large birds are more commonly preserved in such deposits, the absence of some large taxa that are otherwise widespread in the South Pacific (e.g. wedge-tailed shearwaters, boobies and frigatebirds) could suggest that these may not have been present on Rapa.

It seems likely that further excavations will reveal more lost Rapa bird taxa because at least three extinct species were detected in this small study. The remains of the fruit dove and local subspecies of the little shearwater and white-bellied storm petrel are the first skeletal material of these taxa to be collected. They provide a basis for future reference and taxonomic work. Further work is required to determine the identity of the parrot, flesh-footed/pink-footed shearwater, *Gallirallus*-type rail and large pigeon. It is highly likely that the bird extinctions detected were the result of human impact and that seabird species now confined to nesting on small offshore islands previously bred on main Rapa.

Table 6.1. Distribution by site and excavation unit of identified bird bone.

	Flesh-footed/ Pink-footed shearwater	Little shearwater	Black-winged petrel	Kermadec petrel	White-bellied storm petrel	Red-tailed tropic bird	Rail	Spotless crake	White tern	Grey noddy	Brown noddy	Large pigeon	Rapa fruit dove	Parrot	Chicken
Tangarutu															
Location T1	1	1		14		1									
Excavation E1															
Spit 1		1	1	3		1									
Spit 3											1				
Spit 7				2											
Spit 10			2	2											
Spit 11								1	1						
Spit 13				2						1			1		
Spit 14		1	2	3		1						1			
Spit 15				1						2					
Spit 16			1	3							1	1			
Spit 17			1	2						2	2				
Spit18			1	3						1			1	1	
Spit 19			1	2											
Spit 21			2	1		1									
MNI Total	**1**	**3**	**11**	**38**		**4**			**6**	**1**	**4**	**2**	**2**	**1**	
Excavation E2															
Spit 4				1											
Spits 8-9				1		1									
Spits 10-13			1	1										1	
Spit 14				1										1	
Spits 16-17				1											
Spit 22						1									
Spits 23-25				1		1									
MNI Total			**1**	**6**		**3**								**2**	
Excavation R1															
Spit 1				1											
Spit 3			1	2											
Spit 4		1	1	1											
Spit 6				1											
Spit 7		1		1											
Spit 8			1	1											
MNI Total		**2**	**3**	**7**											

Continued on next page

Table 6.1. *continued*

	Flesh-footed/Pink-footed shearwater	Little shearwater	Black-winged petrel	Kermadec petrel	White-bellied storm petrel	Red-tailedtropic bird	Rail	Spotless crake	White tern	Grey noddy	Brown noddy	Large pigeon	Rapa fruit dove	Parrot	Chicken
Excavation S1															
Spit 3		1	1	3	1	1	1					1			
TOTAL	**1**	**6**	**16**	**54**	**1**	**8**	**1**	**1**	**6**	**1**	**4**	**3**	**2**	**3**	
Akatanui															
Shelter 1															
Spit 2				1											1
Shelter 3															
Spit 1		1			1					1					
Spit 2					1	1									
TOTAL		**1**		**1**	**2**	**1**				**1**					**1**
Angairao															
Shelter C															
Spit 2		1			1										
Spit 3			1												
Noogoriki		1													
TOTAL		**2**	**1**		**1**										
ALL SITES															
TOTAL MNI	**1**	**9**	**17**	**55**	**4**	**9**	**1**	**1**	**6**	**2**	**4**	**3**	**2**	**3**	**1**
Per cent	**0.8**	**7.6**	**14.4**	**46.6**	**3.4**	**7.6**	**0.8**	**0.8**	**5.1**	**1.7**	**3.4**	**2.5**	**1.7**	**2.5**	**0.8**

Acknowledgements

Thanks to Sunita Mahat for assistance with registration and databasing, Jean-Claude Stahl for help with translating Holyoak and Thibault (1984) and Trevor Worthy for commenting on the manuscript.

References

Hall, J.V. 1869. On the island of Rapa. *Transactions and Proceedings of the New Zealand Institute* 1:128–134.

Holyoak, D.T. and Thibault, J-C. 1984. Contribution à L'étude des oiseaux de Polynésie Orientale. *Mémoires du Muséum National D'Histoire Naturelle Série A, Zoologie*, 127:1–209.

Jenkins, J.A.F. and Cheshire, N.G. 1982. The black-winged petrel (*Pterodroma nigripennis*) in the south-west Pacific and the Tasman Sea. *Notornis* 29:293–310.

Marchant, S. and Higgins, P.J. 1990 (co-ordinators). *Handbook of Australian, New Zealand and Antarctic Birds, Volume 1, Ratites to Ducks*. Oxford University Press, Melbourne.

Murphy, R.C. and Snyder, J.P. 1952. The "*Pealea*" phenomenon and other notes on storm petrels. *American Museum Novitates* 1596:1–16.

Pratt, H.D., Bruner, P.L. and Berrett, D.G. 1987. *A Field Guide to the Birds of Hawaii and the Tropical Pacific*. Princeton University Press, New Jersey.

Steadman, D.W. 1995. Prehistoric extinctions of Pacific Island birds: biodiversity meets zooarchaeology. *Science* 267:1123–1131.

Tennyson, A.J.D. 1991. The black-winged petrel on Mangere Island, Chatham Islands. *Notornis* 38:111–116.

Tennyson, A.J.D. and Martinson, P. 2006. *Extinct Birds of New Zealand*. Te Papa Press, Wellington.

Thibault, J-C. and Varney, A. 1991a. Numbers and habitat of the Rapa fruit-dove *Ptilinopus huttoni*. *Bird Conservation International* 1:75–81.

Thibault, J-C. and Varney, A. 1991b. Breeding seabirds of Rapa (Polynesia): numbers and changes during the 20th century. *Bulletin of the British Ornithologists' Club*, 111(2):70–77.

Worthy, T.H. 2001. A giant flightless pigeon gen. et sp. nov. and a new species of *Ducula* (Aves: Columbidae), from Quaternary deposits in Fiji. *Journal of the Royal Society of New Zealand* 31:763–794.

7

Prehistoric fishing on Rapa Island

Yolanda Vogel

Department of Anthropology, University of Otago, Dunedin, New Zealand,
bones.stones@gmail.com

Atholl Anderson

Department of Archaeology and Natural History, The Australian National University

Introduction

This chapter presents the results of analysing fish-bone assemblages from Rapa, while Chapter 9 will discuss some points of interpretation. The material was recovered from a number of rockshelter sites around Rapa (see Chapter 3, Figure 3.1 for site locations). Most of the fish bone comes from the Tangarutu rockshelter, with another large assemblage from the Akatanui 3 rockshelter. Four other rockshelters (Akatanui 1, Angairao C, Angairao E and Noogoriki) provided only small amounts of fish bone. The material was dry sieved in the field using 3 mm sieves, and bulk samples were also retained at most sites. Primary sorting occurred in The Australian National University archaeological laboratory (Department of Archaeology and Natural History), where bulk samples were sieved to 2 mm. Residues were retained. The fish-bone component was sent to the Otago Archaeology Laboratory (OAL), in the Anthropology Department, University of Otago, for further analysis by Vogel.

Methods

The fish bone is in a very good state of preservation. It was identified using the OAL Pacific fish-bone reference collection, which contains 108 specimens in 33 families and 49 genera, with seven specimens having no information below family level (see Appendix A for the full list).

Many studies of prehistoric Pacific fishing practices have relied on the protocol devised by Anderson (1973, 1979) and Leach (1979, 1986), which involved identification of five paired mouth bones (dentary, premaxilla, articular, maxilla and quadrate), plus various 'special' bones. However, recent work in Pacific fish-bone analysis at the OAL and other laboratories has shown that different identification and quantification methods significantly influence measures of relative abundance and the number of taxa represented, thereby affecting interpretations (Weisler 1993; Walter 1998; Vogel 2005). During the rebuilding of the OAL Pacific fish-bone collection in the early 1990s, it was decided to include a wider range of elements beyond the five paired mouth bones and 'special' bones, in order to address a greater range of issues in

Pacific ichthyoarchaeology (Walter et al. 1996). Currently, the collection allows for the routine identification of 17 elements from the cranium, pectoral girdle and pelvic girdle, plus otoliths and some 'special' elements, and it is these that were used in this study.

Identification of the fish bone involved two steps – to element and to taxon. As much as possible of the assemblage was identified to element, using reference specimens and diagrams (e.g. Cannon 1987; Wheeler and Jones 1989; Rojo 1991). The remaining material consisted of fragments with no landmark features, plus material that was unable to be identified to element at this stage. Seventeen elements, plus dorsal spines for Acanthuridae and Balistidae, dermal spines for Diodontidae, teeth and vertebra for Elasmobranchii, and fourth epibranchials for Scaridae, were then identified to family (see Table 7.1). Where a family match did not exist in the OAL reference collection, the element was recorded as Not in Collection (NIC), followed by a number to distinguish between elements obviously from different families. Otoliths were absent from the assemblages. It is possible they did not survive, but this does not seem likely, given that otoliths have been shown to survive when other elements have not (Weisler 1993; Weisler et al. 1998), and given the overall excellent preservation of the fish remains. Another possibility, given the overall very small size of the fish represented in the assemblages, is that even with the use of 3 mm sieves, the otoliths were so small they were not retained. Bulk sample residues were retained, and microscopic investigation of these in the future may reveal the presence of otoliths.

Considerable debate exists within archaeology about the best method of quantification (Grayson 1984), and Pacific ichthyoarchaeology is no exception to this (Butler 1988; Walter 1998). Issues surrounding the use of NISP (Number of Identified Specimens) pertain to the fragmentation level of the material analysed, differing numbers of elements identified for different taxa, and taxa identified by 'special' bones, of which there are multiple numbers per individual. The main issue with the use of MNI (Minimum Number of Individuals) has to do with the units of aggregation used. In order to alleviate some of the problems inherent in the different quantification methods, both NISP and MNI are reported here, along with the raw data on which they are based, thus providing a much fuller account of the archaeological assemblage than would be provided by MNI counts alone. The use of the two quantification methods also allows for greater comparability between the Rapan assemblages and those from other islands in the Pacific, as many reports contain results using only one or the other method.

Table 7.1. Elements identified to taxonomic level.

Elements	
Vomer	Epihyal
Parasphenoid	Inferior pharyngeal cluster
Post temporal	Superior pharyngeal cluster
Articular	Cleithrum
Dentary	Scapula
Maxilla	Palatine
Premaxilla	Dorsal spine (Acanthuridae and Balistidae only)
Quadrate	Dermal spine (Diodontidae only)
Opercular	Tooth (Elasmobranchii only)
Preopercular	Vertebra (Elasmobranchii only)
Hyomandibular	4th epibranchial (Scaridae only)
Ceratohyal	

NISP is given for all material, whereas MNIs were calculated using the 17 elements targeted for family-level identification (see Tables 7.2, 7.3). MNI was calculated by taking the most frequent sided element (or straight element count in the case of unpaired bones) for each family. No attempts were made to account for size matching.

Results

Twenty-one families, one subclass (Elasmobranchii) and one order (Anguilliformes) were identified in the assemblage, while at least six additional families represented in the archaeological record were not in the OAL collection (elements designated as NIC). This latter number was calculated based on the presence of six distinctive sets of hyomandibular bones throughout the assemblages. The NIC material has been excluded from the remainder of this paper because MNIs cannot be generated accurately; full details for the elements represented in this category are given in Appendix A.

The top-ranked taxa are Scaridae (parrotfish), Muraenidae (moray eels), Chaetodontidae (butterflyfish), Labridae (wrasses), Serranidae (grouper), Pomacentridae (damselfish) and Congridae (conger eels). The presence of Muraenidae, Congridae, Chaetodontidae and Pomacentridae in the highest-ranked taxa is somewhat anomalous, and will be discussed further later. The remaining three taxa, Scaridae, Serranidae and Labridae, commonly rank highly in tropical East Polynesian fish-bone assemblages. The following families were represented only in small numbers: Lethrinidae, Acanthuridae, Mullidae, cf. Aulostomidae, Belonidae, Exocoetidae, Holocentridae, Kyphosidae, Mugilidae, Siganidae, Bothidae, Carangidae, Diodontidae, Elasmobranchii, Monacanthidae and Anguilliformes, and a number of specimens not in the reference collection. The results for each site are presented below.

Tangarutu Cave

The material from Tangarutu forms the largest assemblage, with a total of 14,419 bones, and it is made up of material from a number of sampling stations within the site (Appendix A). Each of these will be considered as separate units, as the stratigraphic association between them, although broadly apparent (Chapter 3), is uncertain in detail. The bulk of the material comes from the E1 and E2 contiguous units, considered here as a single unit, and the R1 unit.

Excavation E1/E2

This was an excavation of approximately 1.5 m², although, as explained in Chapter 3, only part of the E2 area was taken down to natural. The stratigraphy was divided into three levels (I (oldest) to III, details in Chapter 3) and results of bone identification are grouped into these and shown in Figures 7.1–7.3. A total of 21 families were identified to taxa, although the exact number and composition varies between levels. The assemblage from this excavation consists of 11,417 pieces of fish bone.

In the lowest level, the top five taxa, all representing more than 5% of the assemblage each, make up 87% of the assemblage. The remaining 11 taxa in this layer all comprise less than 2% of the assemblage each. Figure 7.1 shows a clear dominance by Scaridae, comprising 40% of the assemblage. The other taxa in the top five, in order of abundance, are Muraenidae, Labridae, Chaetodontidae and Serranidae.

The pattern seen in Level I changes in Level II (Figure 7.2). Scaridae drops to 17% of the assemblage, and Muraenidae becomes the top-ranking taxon. Chaetodontidae also increases to 16%, Labridae increases slightly to 12%, while a second eel family, Congridae, takes the place of Serranidae as fifth-ranked taxon. Serranidae drops to sixth in terms of rank order, representing

Table 7.2. MNI for all sites.

Site	Area	Level	Acanthuridae	Aulostomidae	Belonidae	Bothidae	Carangidae	Chaetodontidae	Congridae	Diodontidae	Elasmobranchii	Exocoetidae	Holocentridae	Kyphosidae	Labridae	Lethrinidae	Monocanthidae	Mugilidae	Mullidae	Muraenidae	Pomacentridae	Scaridae	Serranidae	Siganidae	Total
Tangarutu	E1/E2	III	1	2	1			15	5	1	1	1	1	1	12	5			1	24	7	21	16		**115**
		II	1		2			11	5	1			1	1	8	2				19	1	12	4	1	**69**
		I	1		1		1	8	2	1				1	8		1	2	1	13	1	33	7	1	**82**
	R1	III	1					13	5	1	1		1		8				1	19	1	6	5		**62**
	R1	II		1				1	3					1	1	1			1	9		7	2		**27**
	R1	I																		1					**1**
	T1												1										1		**2**
	T3																								
Akatanui 3	C1		1	1		1	1	2	8	1	1	1	1	1	8				1	9	23	26	7		**93**
	E1		1																			3	2		**6**
	A1																					1	1		**2**
Akatanui 1			1					1			1				1							5	3		**12**
Angairao C															2						1	1		1	**5**
Angairao E		III												1	1						1	5	2		**10**
		II	1						1						1						1		1		**5**
		I									1				1				1	2		1	1		**7**
Noogoriki							1													1		4	1		**7**
Total			**8**	**4**	**4**	**1**	**3**	**50**	**30**	**5**	**5**	**2**	**5**	**6**	**51**	**8**	**1**	**2**	**6**	**100**	**33**	**125**	**53**	**3**	

Table 7.3. NISP for all elements identified to taxa.

Site	Area	Level	Acanthuridae	Aulostomidae	Belonidae	Bothidae	Carangidae	Chaetodontidae	Congridae	Diodontidae	Elasmobranchii	Exocoetidae	Holocentridae	Kyphosidae	Labridae	Lethrinidae	Monocanthidae	Mugilidae	Mullidae	Muraenidae	Pomacentridae	Scaridae	Serranidae	Siganidae	Total
Tangarutu	E1/E2	III	6	7	4			56	28	4	6	3	6	2	52	11			5	97	15	180	230		**712**
		II	1		3			43	22	1			1	4	56	3				67	3	75	57	1	**337**
		I	6		5		1	26	8	3			1		27		1	2	2	52	4	303	57	7	**505**
	R1	III	1					24	31	2	1		1		42				3	56	2	73	55		**291**
	R1	II		1				2	6					1	5	1			2	26		32	13		**89**
	R1	I																		1					**1**
	T1												1										1		**2**
	T3																								**0**
Akatanui 3	C1		1	1		2	2	5	33	1	13	2	2	3	31				4	31	75	166	75		**447**
	E1		2																			15	3		**20**
	A1																					4	2		**6**
Akatanui 1			1					1			2				1							28	14		**47**
Angairao C															2						2	1		1	**6**
Angairao E		III												1	1						3	19	5		**29**
		II	1						1						1						2		1		**6**
		I									1				1				1	3		5	1		**12**
Noogoriki							1													1		6	4		**12**
Total			**19**	**9**	**12**	**2**	**4**	**156**	**130**	**11**	**23**	**5**	**11**	**12**	**219**	**15**	**1**	**2**	**17**	**341**	**99**	**907**	**518**	**9**	

6% of the assemblage. A further eight taxa comprise 3% or less of the assemblage each.

There are also notable changes in rank order in Level III (Figure 7.3). Serranidae increases to 14% of the assemblage, and is ranked third. Pomacentridae now represents 6% of the assemblage, up from 1%. Muraenidae remains the top-ranked taxon, but falls in terms of percentage of the assemblage.

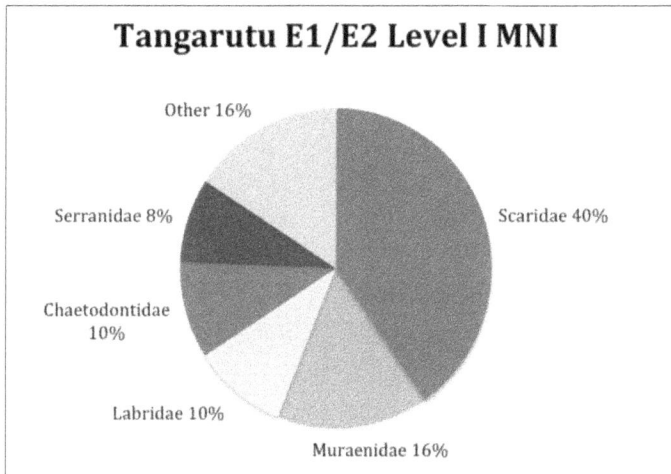

Figure 7.1. Relative abundance (MNI) of taxa for Tangarutu E1/E2 Level I.

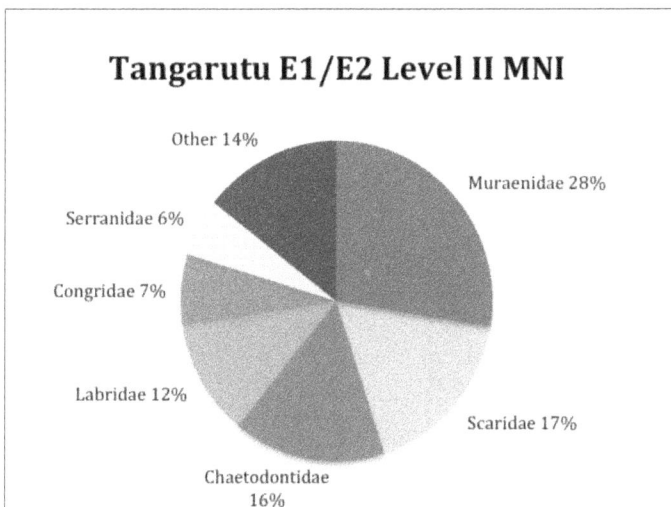

Figure 7.2. Relative abundance (MNI) of taxa for Tangarutu E1/E2 Level II.

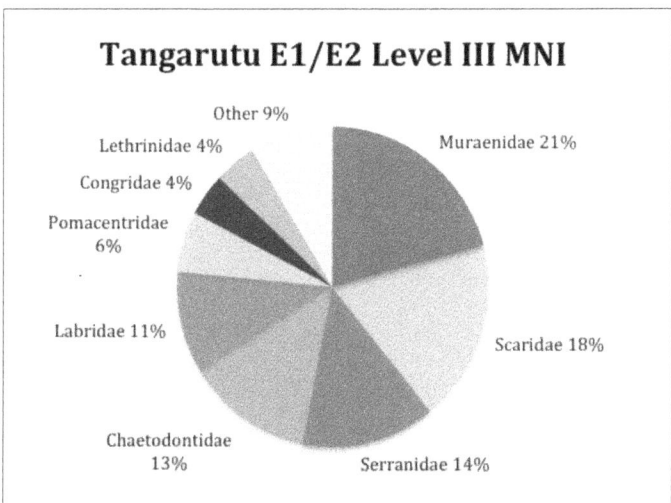

Figure 7.3. Relative abundance (MNI) of taxa for Tangarutu E1/E2 Level III.

Excavation R1

This material comes from a 1 m² square excavation and the assemblage consists of 2845 pieces of fish bone, representing 14 families able to be identified to taxa. Overall, the top-ranking taxa are the same as those seen in the E1/E2 area, although there are some differences in rank order (Figures 7.4–7.5).

The lowest level of the R1 area contained very little fish bone (NISP=22), with only one bone able to be identified to taxon. This belonged to the family Muraenidae. In Level II, the top four taxa make up 78% of the assemblage, with a further six taxa contributing the remaining 22%. Taxa in this latter group all have an MNI of one. Figure 7.4 shows a dominance by Muraenidae, comprising 33% of the assemblage, followed by Scaridae, Congridae and Serranidae in order of abundance. Together, Muraenidae and Scaridae make up more than half the Level II assemblage.

Level III shows a dramatic change in the pattern from that in Level II (Figure 7.5). Muraenidae remains the top-ranking taxon, but there is a considerable increase in the number of Chaetodontidae represented, increasing to 21% of the assemblage (Chaetodontidae is present in Level II, but with an MNI of only one, falls into the category of 'other'). Concurrently, there is a marked decrease in Scaridae, now representing only 10% of the assemblage. Labridae numbers also increase in Level III, contributing 13%, while Congridae falls slightly in terms of percentage and Serranidae remains stable. Six taxa, each with an MNI of one, make up the remaining 10% of the assemblage.

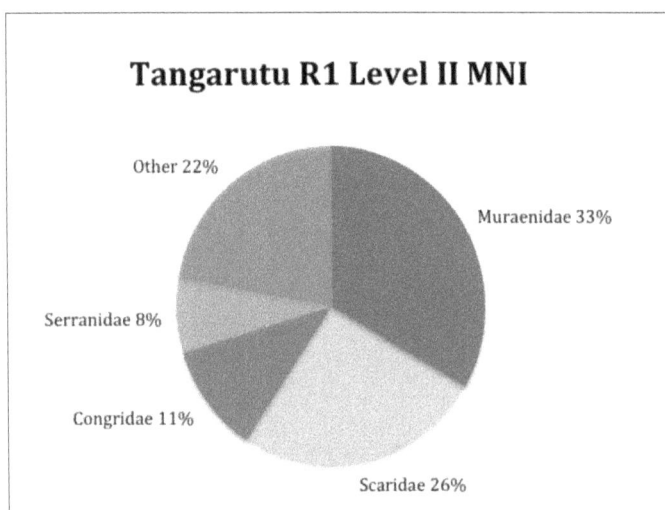

Figure 7.4. Relative abundance (MNI) of taxa for Tangarutu R1 Level II.

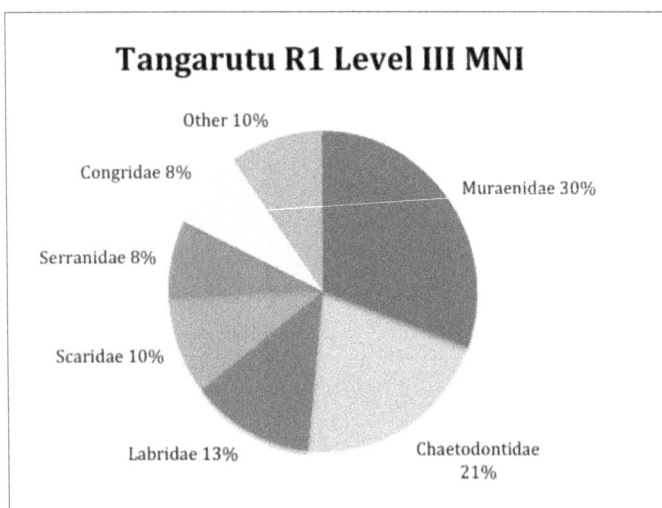

Figure 7.5. Relative abundance (MNI) of taxa for Tangarutu R1 Level III.

In light of the results for the R1 area, it was decided to re-examine the E1/E2 data for Level II, to see whether the decrease in Scaridae and increase in Chaetodontidae could be pinpointed more accurately. This revealed that Scaridae is still the dominant taxon at the base of Level II (Figure 7.6), falling to fourth rank in the middle of Level II, where it comprises 13% of the assemblage (Figure 7.7), and falling further to fifth rank and only 6% of the assemblage at the top of Level II (Figure 7.8). Chaetodontidae represents only 7% of the assemblage at the base of Level II, although it ranks third, but it increases significantly in the middle of Level II to become the dominant taxa. At the top of Level II, Chaetodontidae and Muraenidae rank first equal. Thus, the initial analysis of Level II masks some quite significant changes in the assemblage, and the increasing importance of Chaetodontidae.

The E1/E2 data for Level III were also reanalysed, to see whether the changes in that level were also more abrupt than the initial results suggest, particularly in terms of the Scaridae, which clearly increase in numbers again from the low seen at the top of Level II. The data for Level III were split into two subsets representing spits 1–4 and spits 5–8. The decision about where to make the split was chiefly based on the appearance of fish hooks in this level (see below). Muraenidae maintains its dominance in the bottom half of Level III (Figure 7.9), but Chaetodontidae numbers drop off considerably, falling to third rank and only 12% of the assemblage. In contrast, Serranidae numbers increase significantly, to 17%. Scaridae increases to 12% of the assemblage, placing it fourth equal with Chaetodontidae, while Labridae and Congridae both drop in numbers and rank.

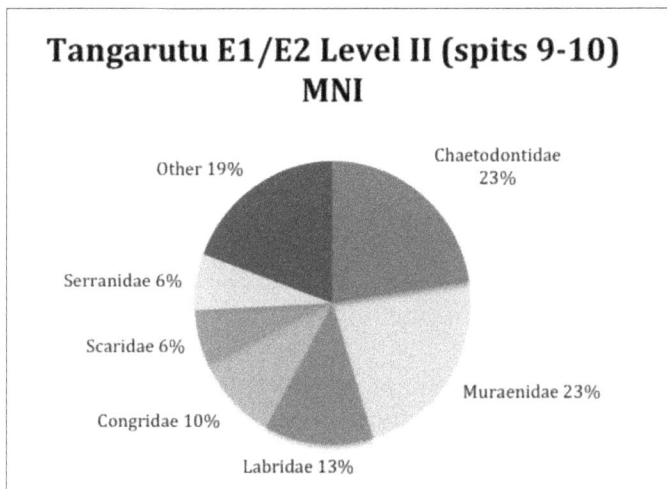

Figure 7.6. Relative abundance (MNI) of taxa for Tangarutu E1/E2 Level II spits 9–10.

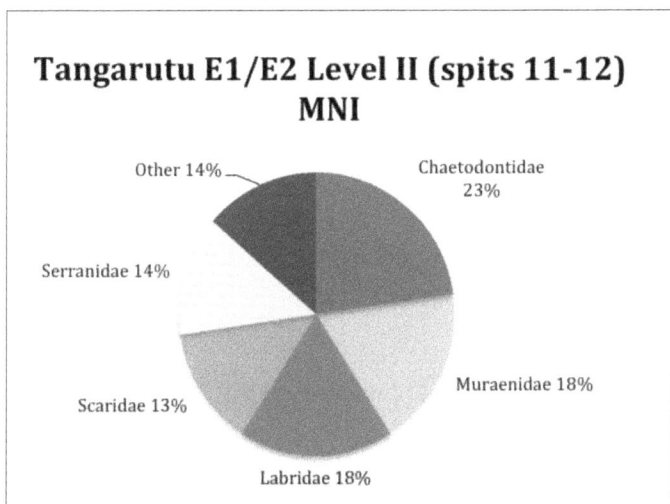

Figure 7.7. Relative abundance (MNI) of taxa for Tangarutu E1/E2 Level II spits 11–12.

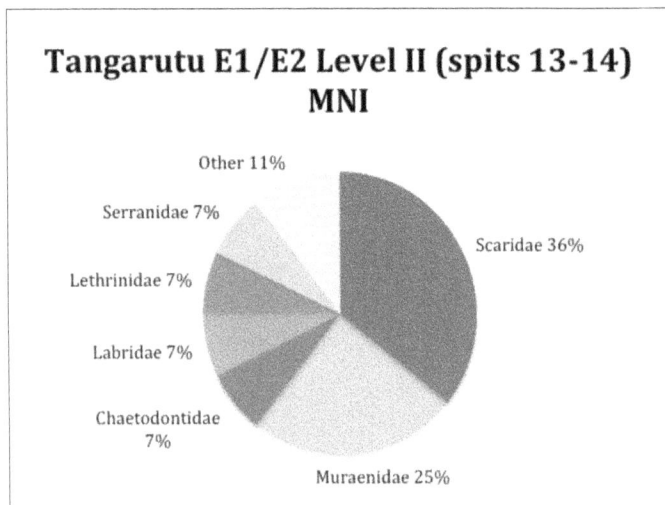

Figure 7.8. Relative abundance (MNI) of taxa for Tangarutu E1/E2 Level II spits 13–14.

In the top half of Level III, Scaridae becomes the dominant taxon once again, representing 20% of the assemblage (Figure 7.10). Muraenidae numbers drop, along with its fall to second rank, as does Serranidae, slipping back to fourth rank and 13% of the assemblage. Chaetodontidae remains fairly stable. It is in this upper part of Level III that Pomacentridae increases in numbers also, now representing 8% of the assemblage. As with Level II, the initial analysis of Level III masked some interesting changes in terms of taxa representation and rank order abundance.

Additional Tangarutu assemblages

Tangarutu T1 and T3 are both very small assemblages resulting from facing of sections (i.e. cutting straight sections down exposed faces to inspect stratigraphy and content). The T1 area yielded 49 pieces of fish bone, of which two could be identified to taxa, while another two belonged to a taxon not represented in the OAL collection. This resulted in an MNI of one for Serranidae and Holocentridae, and an MNI of two for the unknown taxon. The T3 area yielded 108 pieces of fish bone, of which none were identifiable to taxa. The majority of this assemblage was made up of scales, with a NISP of 72.

Akatanui shelters

The Akatanui Bay assemblages come from two separate rockshelters: Akatanui 1 and Akatanui 3 (Appendix A). The Akatanui 3 excavations resulted in material from three areas: C1, which was an excavation of 2 m², and test pits at E1 and A1.

Akatanui 3 C1 excavation

This area yielded the greatest amount of fish bone for this shelter, with a total of 2490 pieces recovered. The results of the taxonomic identification, based on MNI, are shown in Figure 7.11. The taxa exploited are essentially the same as those at Tangarutu, but the rank ordering is quite different. Scaridae and Pomacentridae together make up more than half of the assemblage. While both eel families are still represented in the top six taxa, their contribution is far less than at Tangarutu, particularly in the case of Muraenidae. Interestingly, Chaetodontidae, one of the top-ranking taxa at Tangarutu, makes very little contribution to this assemblage.

Additional Akatanui assemblages

Akatanui E1 and A1 are both very small assemblages. The E1 material consists of 122 pieces of bone. Three taxa were identified: Scaridae (MNI=3), Serranidae (MNI=2) and Acanthuridae (MNI=1). The A1 assemblage contains only nine pieces of bone, but six of these were identified

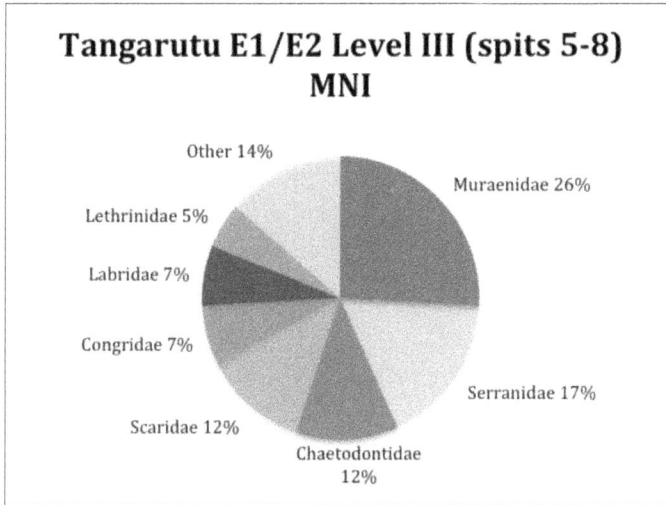

Figure 7.9. Relative abundance (MNI) of taxa for Tangarutu E1/E2 Level III spits 5–8.

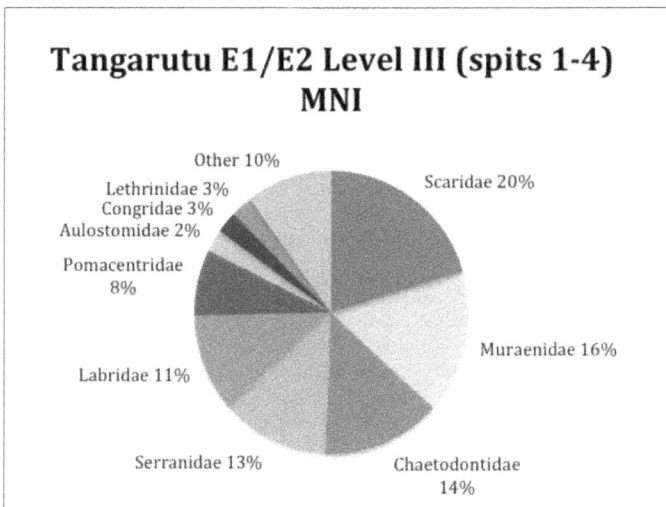

Figure 7.10. Relative abundance (MNI) of taxa for Tangarutu E1/E2 Level III spits 1–4.

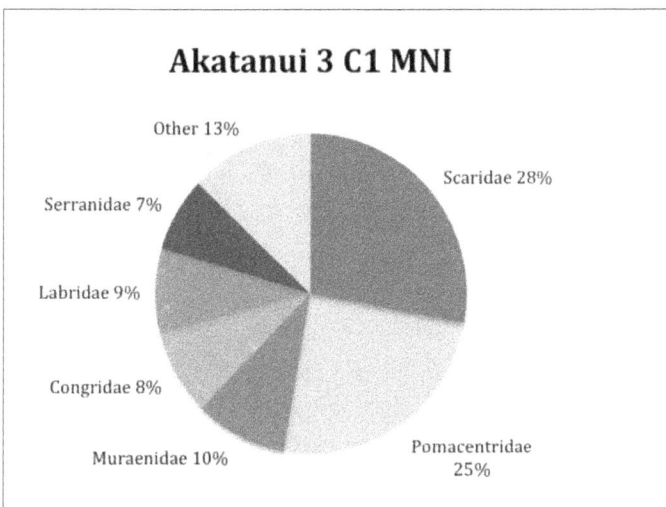

Figure 7.11. Relative abundance (MNI) of taxa for Akatanui 3 C1.

to taxa, resulting in an MNI of one each for Scaridae and Serranidae. Akatanui 1 yielded a very small assemblage, consisting of 338 pieces of fish bone. Six taxa were identified: Scaridae (MNI=5), Serranidae (MNI=3), Acanthuridae (MNI=1), Congridae (MNI=1), Elasmobranchii (MNI=1) and Labridae (MNI=1).

Angairao Bay shelters

The material from Angairao Bay comes from three provenances (Appendix A). The most productive of these was the excavation at Angairao E.

Angairao E excavation

This was a 1.2 m x 0.6 m excavation down to 70 cm and then 0.5 m x 0.6 m below that (Chapter 3). In the top 70 cm, there were remains of an oven, but with no associated midden. The midden was in an underlying unit ('Oven 2'), at 70–165 cm depth, which was divided into three levels (Chapter 5) for bone analysis.

The Angairao E assemblage yielded a total of 269 pieces of fish bone. While nine taxa were identified in the assemblage, only three are present in all levels: Serranidae, Labridae and Muraenidae. Scaridae, however, has the highest overall MNI. The MNI and NISP by level can be seen in Tables 7.2 and 7.3.

Additional Angairao assemblages

The Angairao C assemblage consisted of 30 pieces of fish bone, from which four taxa were identified: Labridae (MNI=2), Scaridae (MNI=1), Muraenidae (MNI=1) and Siganidae (MNI=1). The Noogoriki assemblage, from the opposite side of Angairao Bay (Chapter 3), consisted of 27 pieces of fish bone, with four taxa able to be identified: Scaridae (MNI=4), Muraenidae (MNI=1), Serranidae (MNI=1) and Carangidae (MNI=1).

Discussion

The reconstruction of past fishing practices requires more than just archaeological faunal data. Information on local ecology, ethnographic accounts of fishing, and information on material culture relating to fishing (Walter and Weisler 2002) are also useful sources. Ethnographic information on fishing for Rapa is discussed in Chapters 2 and 9, and these data can be combined with analogies from other Pacific islands to provide a more rounded interpretation than afforded by the faunal data alone.

Fishing strategies can also be reconstructed to some extent by considering the preferred habitats and feeding behaviours of the taxa represented in the faunal assemblage (Butler 1994; Walter 1998; Allen et al. 2001; Weisler 2001). This method is not without its problems, as species within some families can inhabit different ecological zones (e.g. Serranidae). Using feeding behaviour to infer capture techniques is also problematic, because some taxa can be caught using a number of techniques, and feeding behaviour and capture techniques can also vary between species within a family. Nevertheless, such data can help to delimit the possibilities of fishing strategy.

Table 7.4 has been constructed by taking a broader view of tropical Polynesian ethnographic information on fishing techniques and ecological variation. Walter (1998) divides the marine exploitation zones into five categories (offshore pelagic, inshore pelagic, inshore benthic, reef edge and reef flat), and Allen et al. (2001) include lagoon as one of their zones. Rapa differs from many Pacific islands in that it has lagoon of any extent only in Ha'urei Harbour, while around the open sea perimeter there is almost no intertidally exposed fringing reef. In this respect, a better analogy in terms of marine environment may be provided by Easter Island. Rapa is surrounded by a gently sloping platform, on which coral communities grow in the sheltered bays, perhaps providing a zone similar to the reef flats of other islands. With this in mind, the marine zones have been broken into only three categories: inshore, benthic and pelagic.

Another factor likely to be important to reconstructions of past fishing behaviour is the dichotomy between the marine environment within the many bays and that outside the bays. The bays are noted as being relatively calm, although Ha'urei Harbour is often choppy and turbid, especially towards the head. The remaining coastline is characterised by steep cliffs and, frequently, rough waters. While there are areas of rocky shore outside the bays, the predominance of cliffs rising almost directly from the water's edge ensured fishing outside the bays was usually from a canoe.

Putting the information in Table 7.4 together with the results of fish-bone analysis, it is possible to draw some conclusions about the nature of fishing at the various sites around Rapa.

Tangarutu

Fishing from this site seems to have concentrated almost exclusively on the inshore zone. The few taxa that are associated more often with offshore zones rank very low, and they are probably best interpreted as opportunistic or unintentional catches of fish that came into the bay and

Table 7.4. The ecology of taxa identified in the Rapan assemblages and possible methods of capture.

Family	Habitat/Zone	Activity	Feeding	Capture technique
Acanthuridae	Inshore benthic, reef edge, reef flat	Diurnal	Herbivore	Netting, trapping, spearing, angling
Aulostomidae	Outer reef, reef flat		Piscivore	
Belonidae	Inshore			Trolling
Bothidae	Inshore			Netting
Carangidae	Reef flat, passes, outer reef	Various	Piscivore	Angling, netting, spearing
Chaetodontidae	Inshore	Diurnal	Invertebrates	Netting
Congridae	Reef	Nocturnal	Carnivore	
Diodontidae	Reef flat, outer reef	Nocturnal	Invertebrates	Angling, trapping, netting
Elasmobranchii	Outer reef, pelagic		Omnivore/benthic carnivore	Angling, spearing, netting
Exocoetidae	Pelagic	Various	Omnivore	Netting
Holocentridae	Reef flat, outer reef	Nocturnal	Invertebrates	Angling, netting
Kyphosidae	Reef flat, outer reef	Diurnal	Herbivore	
Labridae	Reef flat, outer reef	Diurnal	Invertebrates	Angling, netting, trapping
Lethrinidae	Reef flat, outer reef	Nocturnal	Invertebrates	Angling, netting
Monocanthidae	Inshore		Omnivore	
Mugilidae				
Mullidae	Reef flat		Omnivore	Netting, angling
Muraenidae	Reef flat	Nocturnal	Carnivore	Spearing, poisoning, trapping, snaring, netting
Pomacentridae	Inshore	Diurnal	Omnivore	Angling, netting, trapping
Scaridae	Inshore	Diurnal	Herbivore	Netting, spearing, trapping
Serranidae	Inshore		Piscivore	Angling, netting, trapping, spearing, poison
Siganidae	Inshore			Netting, trapping

closer to shore than usual. This pattern is fairly typical of Pacific marine exploitation systems (Anderson 1986:ix).

The oldest level in the E1/E2 area at Tangarutu shows a clear dominance of Scaridae, but this gives way to a dominance by Chaetodontidae and Muraenidae in the middle level and Muraenidae in the upper level. Interestingly, Scaridae numbers increase again in the upper level. While the presence of Muraenidae in the assemblage is not unusual in itself, these eels usually rank very low in terms of relative abundance at other sites throughout the Pacific.

Another interesting observation about this assemblage is the high incidence of Chaetodontidae, particularly in Level II. This represents the first positive identification of Chaetodontidae in an assemblage from the Pacific. This is probably related to the methodology used for identification. However, it cannot be assumed that Chaetodontidae has merely been overlooked in all other Pacific assemblages, nor that it would occur in such high numbers were it to be identified in other assemblages. Given the dominance by Muraenidae in much of the Tangarutu assemblage, it is safe to say that this assemblage differs considerably from many others in the region in terms of some of the favoured, or available, taxa, and the presence of Chaetodontidae is probably evidence of this.

Occupation at Tangarutu spanned about 500 years, and there is obvious change through time in the assemblage. The first of these changes is an apparent decrease in Scaridae. One possible explanation for this is simply differential survivability. Scaridae has some elements that are particularly robust, and thus has an increased likelihood of survival through time (Bilton 2001). In this scenario, numbers of identifiable elements for other taxa are fewer in older layers due to taphonomic factors, while Scaridae elements remain intact, but in younger layers greater survival of elements from other taxa reduces the proportional representation of Scaridae. When considering the percentage of unidentified fragments in each level, the amount for the oldest level is significantly higher than for the other layers (32.5% in the oldest, versus 22% for the middle level and 18.5% for the youngest), which does lend weight to this argument, although no data were collected on the size of the fragments, so it might be only that the unidentified fragments in the lowest layer are more fragmented. If so, that was not obvious during excavation; indeed, the contrary seemed more apparent.

However, as the assemblage as a whole shows excellent preservation, it is unlikely that differential survivability has skewed the numbers in favour of Scaridae to any great extent, and therefore it cannot explain the marked change in abundance between the lowest and middle levels. Also, Labridae is subject to the same positive bias as Scaridae in terms of survivability (Bilton 2001), yet its relative abundance between the oldest and middle levels remains fairly constant. Another possible explanation is that the earliest occupants focused their attention heavily on Scaridae, thereby depleting the standing stock, which may have already been low in comparison to other islands in the region due to Rapa's subtropical location. Breeding rates may have been lower for the same reason. However such an explanation is very difficult to substantiate without further data on fish numbers, breeding rates and so on for the island. Environmental changes may also provide an explanation for the changes in relative abundance of taxa evident at Tangarutu, and the following chapter returns to this topic.

The other major temporal change that occurs in this assemblage is between the middle level and the upper level. Here, Serranidae increases from 6% to 17% of the assemblage and moves from sixth-ranked taxa in terms of relative abundance, to second in the bottom half of the level, although its numbers drop off again slightly in the upper half. The upper level also sees Pomacentridae enter the top-ranking taxa for the first time, comprising 8% of the assemblage in the upper half of the level, and Lethrinidae also increases in numbers.

The data for the R1 area at Tangarutu are similar to those from the E1/E2 area in terms of taxa composition. There are, however, some differences in relative abundance. There is a general stratigraphic connection between the two areas (Chapter 3), but it is not certain that the levels at R1 occupy the same periods as those at E1/E2.

The lowest level in the R1 area does not contain sufficient fish bone to make any statements about it. In Level II, Muraenidae dominates, with Scaridae making a significant contribution also. This changes significantly in Level III, where Chaetodontidae numbers increase substantially, while Scaridae numbers drop. This level shows considerable similarity to the upper two-thirds of the middle level in the eastern area, again indicating a predominance of netting or basket trapping. Of particular note is the fact that the rapid decrease in the number of Scaridae is evident in both areas.

Akatanui

The assemblage from Akatanui 3 shows some interesting differences from those at Tangarutu. While three areas were excavated at Akatanui 3, only one of these provided sufficient fish bone to make any meaningful comment on fishing strategies. Radiocarbon dates suggest that occupation at this shelter began later than at Tangarutu, but that occupation at the two locations overlaps. Akatanui is located on the eastern, and windward, side of the island, and although the shelters investigated are located further into the bay than Tangarutu on the leeward side of the island, the differences in ecology and environment may be expected to have had some impact on fishing in terms of accessibility to some families of fish.

While the same species as in the Tangarutu assemblage are seen at Akatanui 3, there are differences in ranking and relative abundances. The most startling of these is the large proportion of Pomacentridae present, making up 25% of the assemblage and almost equal to the proportion of Scaridae. Pomacentridae is rarely identified in Pacific fish-bone assemblages, and when it is, it ranks very low. While this is probably due at least in part to the methodology used for identification, the large number present in this assemblage is surprising. It is interesting to note that Chaetodontidae ranks very low in the Akatanui 3 assemblage. The question of the significance of both Pomacentridae and Chaetodontidae in the Rapan assemblages is taken up below.

Eels continue to be important at Akatanui 3, as at Tangarutu, but in lower numbers. Labridae and Serranidae also contribute to the top-ranking families, with roughly the same numbers as Muraenidae and Congridae.

The differences seen between the Tangarutu assemblages and Akatanui 3 are probably related to ecology, perhaps due to the leeward/windward distinction, rather than a choice to focus on different fish at each site.

Unusual taxa

Returning to the large numbers of Chaetodontidae and Pomacentridae in the Rapan assemblages, ethnographic data suggest that these fish should also be present in other Pacific Island fish-bone assemblages, and that their absence in other assemblages is therefore due, at least in part, to methodological issues. Akimichi (1986), Goto (1986, 1990), Kirch and Dye (1979) and Masse (1986, 1989), in particular, note the presence of both these families in fish catches recorded ethnographically for Satawal, Hawaii, Niuatoputapu and Palau respectively. Ayres (1986) also reports Chaetodontidae and Pomacentridae as families known or suspected to have been exploited on Easter Island, and provides a schematic drawing showing the zones in which they were probably caught. Both Hawaii and Easter Island share similarities with Rapa in terms of environment and marine ecology, with the cooler climates of these islands inhibiting coral growth and their remoteness resulting in an impoverished range of marine taxa (Anderson 2001). The coastal characteristics of Easter Island are analogous to those of Rapa in terms of the lack of a fringing reef and the presence of deep embayments (Ayres 1986; Anderson 2001). Particularly for the small number of Pacific Island assemblages that have yielded Pomacentridae mouth parts, a reanalysis using the methodology used for Rapa may provide some very interesting results, given that not a single bone from the standard five paired mouth bones normally used in analyses of Pacific fish bone was identified in the Rapan assemblages.

The large number of marine eels present in the Rapan assemblages, particularly those from Tangarutu, is also somewhat anomalous. This is unlikely to be due to methodology, as MNIs for these were based on the five paired mouth parts for both Congridae and Muraenidae. Rather, it seems likely that the environmental conditions on Rapa resulted in eels being more easily accessible, or perhaps more plentiful, than those families usually more favoured by Polynesians.

Fish size

A final observation about the Rapan assemblages is the very small size of the remains. While no quantitative data on element size was collected (although it could be in another project on the bone assemblages), casual inspection suggests the bones are much smaller than is typical for tropical fish-bone assemblages. This is true for all families represented in the assemblage, although the occasional large example does exist. In this respect, while Pomacentridae and Chaetodontidae could possibly be considered of little economic importance in many fish catches due to their size, for Rapa they are probably within the average size of the catch, although, of course, this cannot be substantiated without quantitative data.

While Rapa may appear anomalous in terms of fish size, there are several other sites throughout the Pacific where the archaeological fish-bone remains have been particularly small, including Nan Madol, Leluh on Kosrae, Palau, and Cikobia in Fiji, and sites in New Caledonia and the Loyalty Islands (Davidson et al. 2002). Leach et al. (1996) proposed various explanations for the small size of the fish from Nan Madol: fishing was concentrated in areas where small fish congregated (i.e. the canals formed by the artificial islets that make up Nan Madol); the fish harvest was distributed according to rank (resulting in all the small-fish remains ending up in one area); the selection of small specimens for ritual purposes; ecological impact (i.e. decreasing size through time due to over-harvesting); the use of small mesh nets; and the use of fish poison. Some of these explanations may be applicable to Rapa, although others can be ruled out.

Fishing in confined areas where small fish congregated seems an unlikely explanation for Rapa, as areas such as those characteristic of Nan Madol were not present. It should be noted, however, that stone-walled fish weirs were used historically and can be seen in some of the bays around the island, especially in the main harbour. Over-harvesting also seems unlikely, given that Level I in Tangarutu is thought to represent initial, or very early occupation of the island (Kennett et al. 2006), and the fish remains are small throughout the entire span of occupation. Distribution of fish according to rank also seems unlikely, given that the fish bone from all excavated areas, in some cases several areas within one site, is equally small, and ritual uses can be ruled out for the same reason. Of the possibilities listed by Leach et al. (above), this leaves small meshed nets, the use of fish poison, and environmental constraints as the most likely explanations for the small size of fish remains from Rapa.

A case has already been made for the use of netting to account for many of the top-ranking fish families seen in the Rapan assemblages, and Masse (1986) discusses the use of fine-meshed nets (*derek*) for capturing Chaetodontidae in Palau. However, this does not account for the small size of the fish likely to have been caught using other methods, such as the Serranids and eels.

Davidson et al. (2002) propose an argument for fish poisoning at Nan Madol, but these waterways are especially slow moving. Poisoning is a possible explanation, although it was unknown ethnographically (Stokes n.d.). The presence of fish hooks at Tangarutu testifies to the use of angling, and the very small size of some of them suggests that quite small fish were being targeted by angling. It seems likely, therefore, that the small size of the fish in the Rapan assemblages is best attributed to environmental factors relating to climate and accessibility. The cooler waters surrounding Rapa might have resulted in slower growth rates and smaller mature sizes for families better suited to tropical waters. Alternatively, as even in modern times fishing is mostly confined to the calmer waters of the bays (Hanson 1970), larger-bodied offshore fish might have been caught rather seldom.

Pacific comparisons

How does the archaeological evidence of Rapan fishing compare with that from other islands in the Pacific? The analysis of archaeological fish bone from the Pacific has revealed an emphasis on inshore exploitation, focused mainly on the reef but also including the benthic zone, with the dominant families caught including Scaridae, Serranidae, Lethrinidae, Labridae, Diodontidae, Holocentridae, Acanthuridae, Balistidae, Carangidae and marine eels (Butler 1988, 1994; Masse 1989; Allen 1992, 2002; Nagaoka 1993; Anderson 1997; Walter 1998; Leach and Davidson 2000; Allen et al. 2001; Weisler 2001; Walter and Anderson 2002). Exceptions are known; some families that usually rank fairly low in assemblages dominate in a few cases, especially where offshore fishing is more prominent, or it has been focussed on one family (Butler 1994; Leach et al. 1997; Fraser 1988, 2001; Rolett 1998; Davidson et al. 1999; Leach and Davidson 2000; Walter and Anderson 2001). In terms of captured species, Pacific fish remains from archaeological sites generally represent a wide range of species drawn from a limited number of families.

In both the tropical Pacific and New Zealand selective predation of a particular family of fish is suggested (Leach and Boocock 1993; Anderson 1997 (but see Weisler et al. 1998); Leach et al. 1997; Fraser 1998, 2001; Walter and Anderson 2001). Scombridae (tuna) remains are generally scarce or absent in Pacific fish-bone assemblages, but it appears that tuna fishing was more common in some periods in the Marquesas and Society Islands during prehistory (Leach et al. 1997; Fraser 1998, 2001; Rolett 1998; Davidson et al. 1999; Leach and Davidson 2000). Walter and Anderson (2001) observed that Lethrinidae, a family of benthic-dwelling carnivores, provided the dominant catch at Emily Bay, Norfolk Island, suggesting that temperate waters resulted in a fishing strategy more akin to that of New Zealand than that of tropical Polynesia. In New Zealand, fish-bone analysis implies an emphasis on barracouta (*Thyrsites atun*) in the southern South Island, although there are exceptions, as at Kakanui. Whether these are formed by different targeting or different analytical methodology remains open to debate (Weisler et al. 1998; Anderson and Smith 1999; Weisler 1999).

The Pacific fishing industry, derived from the Lapita cultural complex (Walter 1989), displays a great deal of homogeneity across the region in terms of basic fishing strategies. But there are important differences at both the intra- and inter-island levels. Butler (1994) reviewed the evidence for Lapita fishing strategies and found that, contrary to earlier assertions, angling was used by the Lapita peoples, as evidenced by the presence of carnivorous fish remains at some sites. It was also found that eastern sites were dominated by herbivorous/omnivorous species, while sites in western Melanesia tended to contain more carnivorous fish, implying a regional difference in fishing strategies.

While the strategies employed across the region are much the same, the species targeted show variations in relative abundance. Specialisations, such as in tuna fishing, are an extreme example of this. The tuna fishing industry seems to be an example of cultural choice, but in some sites the differences appear to be related to local ecology. Scaridae was a favoured fish family during prehistory, yet its remains are scarce in the fish-bone assemblages from Ma'uke and Mangaia. Walter (1998) attributes this to the inaccessibility of the outer reef face on these two islands, highlighting the need for a knowledge of local fishing grounds, ecology and accessibility when analysing fish remains.

While Rapa seems to fit the mould of an emphasis on inshore exploitation in general terms, it has already been noted that the Rapan assemblages differ on a number of points, specifically the high number of marine eels present, the presence of Chaetodontidae and Pomacentridae, and the small size of the fish. But are there other islands where a similar pattern can be seen?

Comparisons between assemblages are difficult due to differences in identification and quantification methodologies. Many early reports relied on a limited number of elements for identification, and few have used more than the standard five paired mouth bones. Furthermore, some researchers report only NISP values, while others give only MNI. NISP values may be inflated for some families due to the use of a wider range of elements for identification (e.g. Scaridae) or the use of elements for which each individual has multiple elements (e.g. Diodontidae). The present study is obviously skewed in comparison with others by the use of a wider range of elements for identification purposes. However, if these factors are taken into account, some observations are able to be made.

Eels are generally considered unusual in prehistoric middens, yet they show up in a number of middens throughout the region (e.g. Kirch and Yen 1982; Allen 1992; Nagaoka 1993; Leach et al. 1996; Walter 1998; Butler 2001; Walter and Anderson 2001; Davidson et al. 2002; Walter and Anderson 2002), although only occasionally in high-ranking positions. However, only on one other island is the dominance as clear as at Rapa, and that is on Easter Island, with the other dominant family in these sites being Labridae (Ayres 1986). The similarities between Rapa and Easter Island in terms of ecology and geomorphology have already been discussed, and it is not surprising to see similarities between the two in terms of fishing strategies. So, do the fish-bone assemblages from Rapa and Easter Island represent what could be considered a subtropical fishing strategy?

Only a small number of subtropical islands have been investigated archaeologically, and reports on fishing are pending for some. Norfolk Island displays a fishing strategy more like that of New Zealand, focusing on a single family (Walter and Anderson 2001) rather than the more generalised strategy common throughout the tropical zone. However, Norfolk is further outside the tropical zone than Rapa and Easter Island, and coral formation is extremely limited. Norfolk Island also lacks the bays characteristic of both Rapa and Easter Island, which no doubt affected accessibility to fishing grounds. This suggests that the pattern seen at Rapa and Easter Island is just one way in which prehistoric Polynesians adapted to subtropical islands, and that as in the tropical zone proper, local ecology played a large part in shaping fishing strategies.

The Rapan fish-bone assemblages show a strategy closely aligned to tropical Polynesia, with some interesting adaptations to local ecology and its constraints. A generalised strategy focused on several families is evident, dominated by inshore taxa. The large numbers of Pomacentridae and Chaetodontidae in the assemblages are at this stage unique to Rapa, but the use of more elements for the identification of assemblages from other localities should reveal whether or not this is an anomaly. In particular, it is interesting that the scarcity or absence of these families from archaeological assemblages in Hawaii and Easter Island has been queried, as both places have some similarities with Rapa in terms of coastal geomorphology and ecology. The dominance of marine eels, in particular Muraenidae, is paralleled in other parts of the Pacific, particularly in Easter Island. What at first appears to be a strange set of assemblages may yet turn out to be not so strange after all.

References

Akimichi, T. 1986. Conservation of the sea: Satawal, Micronesia. In: Anderson, A. (ed), *Traditional Fishing in the Pacific*. Pacific Anthropological Records 37:15–33.

Allen, M. 1992. Dynamic Landscapes and Human Subsistence: archaeological investigations on Aitutaki island, southern Cook Islands. PhD thesis, University of Washington.

Allen, M. 2002. Resolving long-term change in Polynesian marine fisheries. *Asian Perspectives* 41(2):195–212.

Allen, M, Ladefoged, T. and Wall, J. 2001. Traditional Rotuman fishing in temporal and regional context. *International Journal of Osteoarchaeology* 11:56–71.

Anderson, A.J. 1973. Archaeology and Behaviour: prehistoric subsistence behaviour at Black Rocks peninsula, Palliser Bay. MA thesis, Anthropology Department, University of Otago.

Anderson, A.J. 1979. Prehistoric exploitation of marine resources at Black Rocks Point, Palliser Bay. In: Leach, B.F and H.M. (eds), Prehistoric Man in Palliser Bay. *National Museum of New Zealand Bulletin* 21:49–63.

Anderson, A.J. 1986. Introduction. In: Anderson, A. (ed), *Traditional Fishing in the Pacific*. Pacific Anthropological Records 37:ix–xi.

Anderson, A.J. 1997. Uniformity and regional variation in marine fish catches from prehistoric New Zealand. *Asian Perspectives* 36(1):1–26.

Anderson, A.J. 2001. No meat on that beautiful shore: The prehistoric abandonment of subtropical Polynesian islands. *International Journal of Osteoarchaeology* 11:14–23.

Anderson, A.J. and Smith, I.W.G. 1999. Letter to the Editor. *Archaeology in New Zealand* 42:182–184.

Ayres, W.S. 1986. Easter Island subsistence. *Journal de la Société des Ocieanistes* 80:103–124.

Bilton, M. 2001. *Taphonomic Bias in Pacific Ichthyoarchaeological Assemblages: A Marshall Islands Example*. Unpublished MA thesis, Department of Anthropology, University of Otago.

Butler, V.L. 1988. Lapita fishing strategies: The faunal evidence. In: Kirch, P.V. and Hunt, T.L. (eds), *The Archaeology of the Lapita Cultural Complex: A Critical Review*. Thomas Burke Memorial Washington State Museum Research Report, No. 5, pp. 99–116, Seattle.

Butler, V.L. 1994. Fish feeding behaviour and fish capture: The case for variation in Lapita fishing strategies. *Archaeology in Oceania* 29:81–90.

Butler, V.L. 2001. Changing fish use on Mangaia, Southern Cook Islands: Resource depression and the prey choice model. *International Journal of Osteoarchaeology* 11:88–100.

Cannon, D.Y. 1987. *Marine Fish Osteology: A Manual for Archaeologists*. Simon Fraser University Publication 18, Department of Archaeology.

Davidson, J., Fraser, K., Leach, B.F. and Sinoto, Y.H. 1999. Prehistoric fishing at Hane, Ua Huka, Marquesas Islands, French Polynesia. *New Zealand Journal of Archaeology* 21:5–28.

Davidson, J., Leach, F. and Sand, C. 2002. Three thousand years of fishing in New Caledonia and the Loyalty Islands. In: Bedford, S., Sand, C. and Burley, D. (eds), *Fifty Years in the Field: Essays in Honour and Celebration of Richard Shutler Jr's Archaeological Career*. New Zealand Archaeological Association Monograph 25:153–164.

Fraser, K. 1988. *Fishing for Tuna in Pacific Prehistory*. Unpublished MA thesis, Department of Anthropology, University of Otago.

Fraser, K. 2001. Variation in tuna fish catches in Pacific prehistory. *International Journal of Osteoarchaeology* 11:127–135.

Goto, A. 1986. Prehistoric Ecology and Economy of Fishing in Hawai'i: An Ethnoarchaeological Approach. Unpublished PhD thesis, University of Hawai'i.

Goto, A. 1990. Prehistoric Hawaiian fishing lore: An integrated approach. *Man and Culture in Oceania* 6:1–34.

Grayson, D.K. 1984. *Quantitative Zooarchaeology: Topics in the Analysis of Archaeological Faunas.* Academic Press, San Diego.

Hanson, F.A. 1970. *Rapan Lifeways: Society and History on a Polynesian Island.* Little, Brown and Company Ltd, Boston.

Kennett, D., Anderson, A., Prebble, M., Conte, E. and Southon, J. 2006. Prehistoric human impacts on Rapa, French Polynesia. *Antiquity* 80:340–354.

Kirch, P.V. and Dye, T. 1979. Ethnoarchaeology and the development of Polynesian fishing strategies. *Journal of the Polynesian Society* 88(1):53–76.

Kirch, P.V. and Yen, D.E. 1982. *Tikopia: The prehistory and ecology of a Polynesian outlier.* Bernice P. Bishop Museum Bulletin 238, Honolulu.

Leach, B.F. 1979. Excavations in the Washpool Valley, Palliser Bay. In: Leach, B.F. and H.M. (eds), Prehistoric Man in Palliser Bay. *National Museum of New Zealand Bulletin* 21:67–136.

Leach, B.F. 1986. A method for the analysis of Pacific island fish bone assemblages and an associated database management system. *Journal of Archaeological Science* 13:147–159.

Leach, B.F. and Boocock, A. 1993. *Prehistoric Fish Catches in New Zealand.* Oxford: British Archaeological Reports, International Series 584.

Leach, B.F., Davidson, J. and Athens, J.S. 1996. Mass harvesting of fish in the waterways on Nan Madol, Pohnpei, Micronesia. In: Davidson, J., Irwin, G., Leach, F., Pawley, A. and Brown, D. (eds), *Oceanic Culture History: Essays in Honour of Roger Green*, pp. 319–341. New Zealand Journal of Archaeology Special Publication, Wellington.

Leach, B.F., Davidson, J., Horwood, M. and Ottino, P. 1997. The fishermen of Anapua Rock Shelter, Ua Pou, Marquesas Islands. *Asian Perspectives* 36(1):51–66.

Leach, B.F. and Davidson, J. 2000. Fishing: A neglected aspect of Oceanic economy. In: Anderson, A. and Murray, T. (eds), *Australian Archaeologist: collected papers in honour of Jim Allen*, pp. 412–426. Coombs Academic Publishing, The Australian National University, Canberra.

Masse, W.B. 1986. A millennium of fishing in the Palau Islands, Micronesia. In: Anderson, A. (ed), *Traditional Fishing in the Pacific: Ethnographical and Archaeological Papers from the 15th Pacific Science Congress.* Pacific Anthropological Records, No. 37, pp. 85–119. Department of Anthropology, Bernice P. Bishop Museum, Honolulu.

Masse, W.B. 1989. *The Archaeology and Ecology of Fishing in the Belau Islands.* Unpublished PhD thesis, University of Southern Illinois.

Nagaoka, L. 1993. Faunal assemblages from the To'aga site. In: Kirch, P.V. and Hunt, T.L. (eds), *The To'aga Site: Three Millennia of Polynesian Occupation in the Manu'a Islands, American Samoa.* Contributions of the University of California Archaeological Research Facility No. 51, pp. 189–216. Berkley, California.

Rojo, A.L. 1991. *A Dictionary of Evolutionary Fish Osteology.* CRC Press, Boca Raton.

Rolett, B. 1998. Fishing strategies: Ethnographic observations and analysis of the excavated fish remains. In: Rolett, B. *Hanamiai: Prehistoric Colonisation and Cultural Change in the Marquesas Islands (East Polynesia)*, vol. 81, pp. 118–146. Department of Anthropology and the Peabody Museum, Yale University, New Haven, Connecticut.

Stokes, John F.G. n.d. Ethnology of Rapa. Manuscript on file. Bernice P. Bishop Museum, Honolulu.

Vogel, Y. 2005. *Ika.* Unpublished MA thesis, Department of Anthropology, University of Otago.

Walter, R. 1998. Fish and fishing. In: Walter, R. (ed), *Anai'o: The Archaeology of a Fourteenth Century*

Polynesian Community in the Cook Islands. New Zealand Archaeological Association Monograph 22, pp. 64–73.

Walter, R. 1989. Lapita fishing strategies: A review of the archaeological and linguistic evidence. *Pacific Studies* 13:127–149.

Walter, R. and Anderson, A. 2001. Fishbone from the Emily Bay settlement site, Norfolk Island. In: Anderson, A. and White, P. (eds), *The Prehistoric Archaeology of Norfolk Island, Southwest Pacific.* Records of the Australian Museum, Supplement 27, pp. 101–108. Australian Museum, Sydney.

Walter, R. and Anderson, A. 2002. Marine fishbone. In: Walter, R. and Anderson, A. (eds), *The Archaeology of Niue Island, West Polynesia.* Bishop Museum Bulletin in Anthropology 10, pp. 94–102. Bishop Museum Press, Honolulu.

Walter, R. and Weisler, M. 2002. Late prehistoric fishing adaptations at Kawakiu Nui, Moloka'i. *Hawaiian Archaeology* 8:42–61.

Walter, R., Weisler, M. and Smith, I. 1996. The Pacific fish bone reference collection at the University of Otago. *Archaeology in New Zealand* 39:200–212.

Weisler, M. 1993. The importance of fish otoliths in Pacific Island archaeofaunal analysis. *New Zealand Journal of Archaeology* 15:131–159.

Weisler, M. 1999. Letter to the Editor. *Archaeology in New Zealand* 42:184–186.

Weisler, M. 2001. *On the Margins of Sustainability: Prehistoric Settlement of Utrok Atoll, Northern Marshall Islands.* British Archaeological Reports International Series 967, Oxford.

Weisler, M., Lalas, C. and Rivett, P. 1998. New fish records from an Archaic midden, South Island. *Archaeology in New Zealand* 42:37–43.

Wheeler, A. and Jones, A.K.G. 1989. *Fishes.* Cambridge University Press, Cambridge.

8

The Tangarutu invertebrate fauna

Katherine Szabó

Centre for Archaeological Science, University of Wollongong; Department of Archaeology and Natural History, The Australian National University, Canberra, Australia, Kat.Szabo1@gmail.com

Atholl Anderson

Department of Archaeology and Natural History, The Australian National University

Introduction

The island of Rapa presents an interesting lens through which to investigate human decision-making and resource-use patterns in a marginal environment. In addition to being small and isolated, Rapa is climatically marginal, being positioned on the southern fringe of the tropical Indo–West Pacific marine province. Most obviously, this geographical situation translates to restricted species diversity, with a great many common tropical taxa not able to survive the conditions. However, as pointed out by Preece (1995:345), it would be a mistake to see the marine fauna of marginal Polynesian islands as simply an impoverished subset of the tropical Indo–West Pacific community. Indeed, Paulay and Spencer (1988, in Irving 1995:321) suggest that there is a belt of islands in the central-eastern Pacific (including Easter Island, the Pitcairn Islands, Kermadecs, Rapa and Lord Howe) that have a littoral fauna specifically adapted to cooler conditions. Such species include a number of endemics, as well as species restricted solely to the islands listed above. The dominant mollusc within the Tangarutu assemblage – *Nerita morio* – is one such species (see below for discussion).

While this distinctive intermediate fauna may suggest a reasonable degree of faunal stability through time, studies done at other islands within this zone (notably the Pitcairn Group) have demonstrated otherwise. A comparison of Pleistocene subfossil assemblages and extant littoral communities on Henderson Island showed considerable turnover (Paulay and Spencer in Irving 1995:321). Such turnovers can be explained in different ways, including by relatively small population sizes, species existing at the limits of their environmental tolerances, and isolation limiting recruitment of individuals from other islands. While only providing a small slice of Rapa's history, the Tangarutu marine invertebrate assemblage presents an opportunity to assess human subsistence practices in an environment that is therefore not only impoverished, but dynamic in its constituents.

The Tangarutu site is adjacent to Anarua Bay, which contains a variety of littoral invertebrate-bearing habitats. With tall cliffs at the northern and southern ends, the bay is west-facing and thus usually sheltered from the prevailing southeasterlies. The prevailing winter winds in Rapa are westerlies (Irving 1995:321), meaning Anarua Bay would see high wave action for a period each year. Within the bay itself are rocky intertidal platforms, sandy patches and basalt gravel zones, providing a variety of niches for infaunal (within the substrate) and epifaunal (atop the substrate) littoral marine life. The archaeological deposits excavated from Tangarutu contained small but consistent quantities of invertebrate remains, representing a varied mix of mollusc, crustacean and echinoid species. This chapter presents the results of analysis, and considerations of subsistence, palaeoenvironment and gathering strategies.

Methodology

All shell, crustacean and echinoderm remains from the E1 and E2 squares of Tangarutu were analysed, with all molluscan remains identified to the lowest possible taxonomic level – generally species. Molluscan taxonomy follows Dharma (2005), with up-to-date taxonomy drawn from the OBIS online database (http://clade.ansp.org/obis/). Crustacean remains included crab exoskeleton fragments, as well as 'goose barnacle' (*Lepas anatifera*) plates. All crab remains were quantified as a single taxonomic category without any attempt at identification, while *Lepas anatifera* remains were quantified separately. Echinoderms were represented by teeth, spines and test fragments of a single taxon, identified as *Diadema* cf. *setosum* (but see discussion of urchin identification below).

Remains were highly fragmented at all levels, although otherwise very well preserved. While both MNI and NISP values, along with weights, were recorded, the NISP values will be reported here. This is not only due to the small sample sizes and consistent levels of breakage across taxa, but also because the calculation of MNI values relies on detailed stratigraphic understanding (Grayson 1984). As reported in Chapter 3, excavation at Tangarutu proceeded in 10 cm spits, and while stratigraphic layers were also recorded, the excavators noted complexity that went beyond the three recorded cultural layers (Vogel 2005:24). Given this, it was decided to report the results using the recorded spits rather than layers.

Results

Forty molluscan taxa were identified, supplemented by crustacean remains in the form of *Lepas anatifera* plates and abundant crab exoskeleton fragments. These classes of remains will be discussed individually below, together with a discussion of spatial and temporal patterning within the studied sample, insights into local ecology and gathering strategies, and the role of various marine invertebrates within the overall Tangarutu assemblage.

Despite being adjoining squares, there are distinct differences between squares E1 and E2. Firstly, there is a difference in gross sample size, with the E1 total (NISP) for molluscan remains being 1280, and E2 874 (i.e. excluding crab, urchin, barnacle etc, shown in Table 8.1). However, differences in species representation do not simply relate to the effect of variable sample sizes. A number of species are more strongly represented in the smaller E2 sample, including the most common mollusc *Nerita morio* (E1 n=376; E2 n=398), as well as *Clypeomorus batillariaeformis* (E1 n=106; E2 n=123), and less common taxa such as *Drupa morum* (E1 n=0; E2 n=5). There are also species clustered in E1 that are correspondingly underrepresented in E2, including the limpet *Cellana tahitensis*[1] (E1 n=169; E2 n=54), polyplacophoran (chiton) plates (E1 n=91; E2 n=24), and *Trochus* cf. *radiatus* (E1 n=81; E2 n=26). Taxa represented by 10 or more fragments in E1 and E2 are graphed in figures 8.1 and 8.2 respectively. Table 8.1 shows overall NISP values for all identified marine invertebrate fauna for both squares E1 and E2.

What these clusters of different taxa appear to represent are episodes of dumping from a specific series of gathering and/or processing events. Figure 8.3 clearly shows that these species-specific dumps are not directly correlated with vertical stratigraphy. For example, *Nerita morio* fragments are entirely restricted to Square A2 in Spit 1, while there are much higher numbers of *Clypeomorus batillariaeformis* within Square A2 over spits 5, 6 and 7. The complexity of the Tangarutu stratigraphy has been commented on in Chapter 3, and these few examples from the distributions of molluscan taxa amply demonstrate intricate horizontal as well as vertical patterning.

Although the Tangarutu marine invertebrate sample was collected in arbitrary spits rather than stratigraphic layers, considerable vertical patterning is evident. Most obviously, this patterning can be seen in gross overall quantities of molluscan, crustacean and urchin remains. While the pattern is slightly skewed by the conflation of spits 10–13, it can still be seen that the collection of molluscs dominates over crustacean or urchin exploitation in the lower three spits. Furthermore, this dumping of molluscan remains (see Figure 8.4) is restricted for the

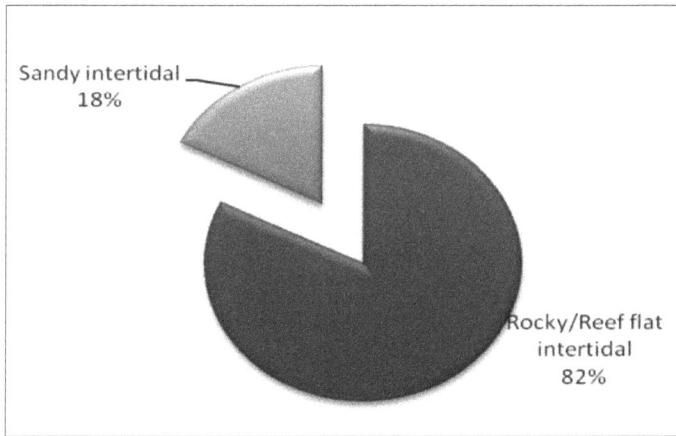

Figure 8.1. Invertebrate taxa represented by 10 or more fragments (NISP) in Square E1, Tangarutu.

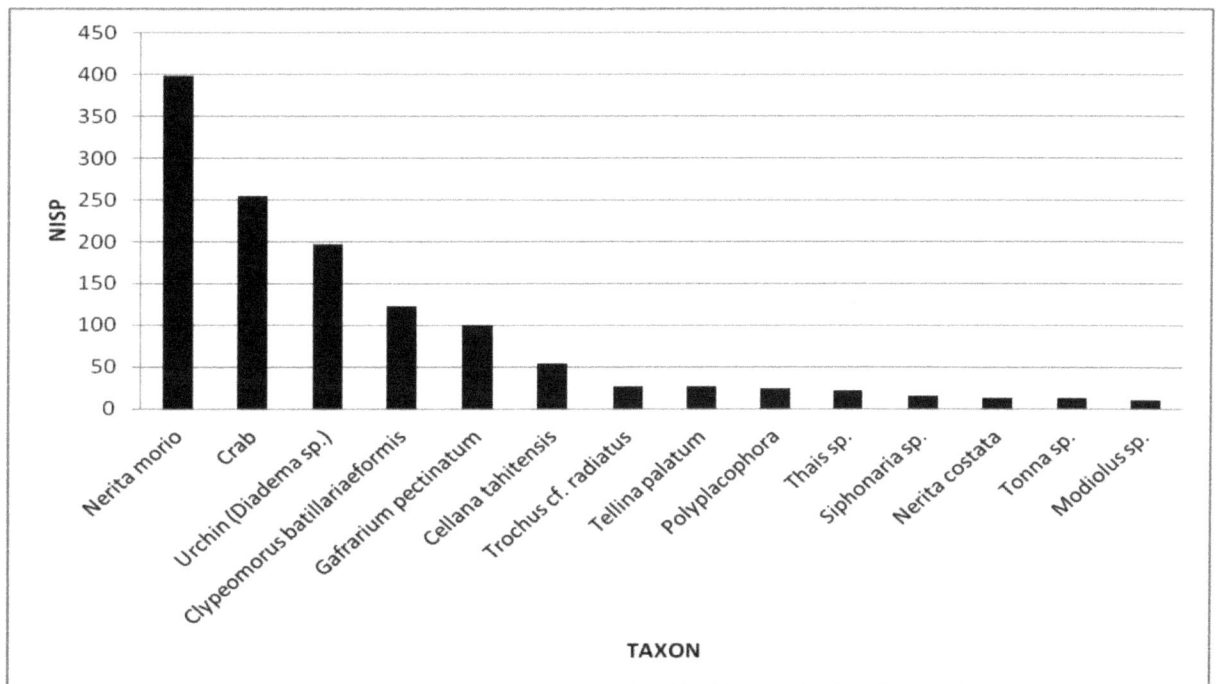

Figure 8.2. Invertebrate taxa represented by 10 or more fragments (NISP) in Square E2, Tangarutu.

Table 8.1. Invertebrate taxa identified within the E1 and E2 samples from Tangarutu. NISP values given represent the total number of fragments identified for each square. ∧Indicates absence.

Taxon	E1	E2	Habitat
Crab	658	255	variable
Nerita morio	376	398	intertidal rocks
Urchin (Diadema sp.)	363	197	inter/sub-tidal
Cellana tahitensis	169	54	intertidal rocks
Gafrarium pectinatum	169	100	sandy intertidal
Clypeomorus batillariaeformis	106	123	intertidal rocks
Polyplacophora ("Chiton")	91	24	intertidal rocks
Trochus cf. radiatus	81	26	intertidal rocks
Tellina palatum	38	26	sandy intertidal
Thais sp.	37	21	intertidal rocks
Cypraea caputserpentis	35	7	intertidal rocks
Cypraea spp.	33	4	variable
Modiolus sp.	21	10	intertidal rocks
Nerita spp. Opercula	18	15	variable
Patella flexuosa	15	2	intertidal rocks
Drupa spp.	15	7	intertidal rocks
Lepas anatifera	13	4	pelagic
Chama pacifica	12	1	inter/sub-tidal rocks
Tonna sp.	10	13	sandy inter/sub-tidal
Conus spp.	9	∧	variable
Nerita plicata	8	1	upper intertidal rocks
Drupa ricinus	5	∧	intertidal rocks
Pyrene sp.	5	∧	intertidal sand/rubble
Drupa morum	∧	5	intertidal rocks
Cardita variegata	4	1	intertidal rocks
Tellina scobinata	3	∧	sandy intertidal
Antigona (Periglypta) reticulata	3	∧	sandy intertidal
Drupa rubisidaea	∧	3	intertidal rocks
Astraea rhodostoma	2	∧	intertidal rocks
Phos sp.	2	2	intertidal rocks
Nassarius sp.	2	∧	variable
Pinctada margaritifera	2	∧	sub-tidal
Astraea sp.	1	∧	intertidal rocks
Nerita costata	1	13	upper intertidal rocks
Planaxis sulcatus	1	∧	upper intertidal rocks
Cypraea cribraria	1	∧	sandy intertidal
Strombus sp.	1	∧	sandy intertidal
Siphonaria sp.	1	15	intertidal rocks
Corbula sp.	1	∧	sandy intertidal
Saccostrea cucullata	1	∧	intertidal rocks
Codakia tigerina	1	∧	sandy intertidal
Turbo cinereus	∧	1	intertidal rocks
Hipponix conicus	∧	1	on other shells
Fragum sp.	∧	1	sandy intertidal
TOTAL	**2335**	**1342**	

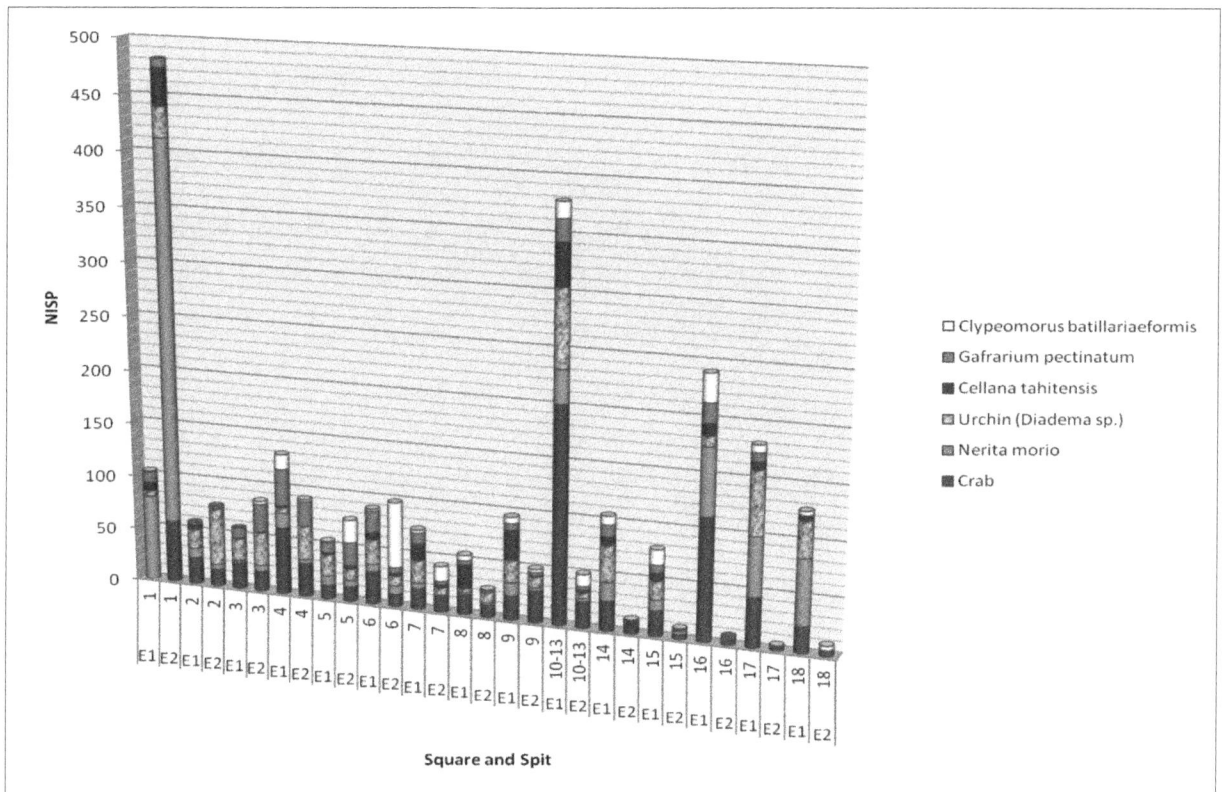

Figure 8.3. The six highest-ranking (NISP) invertebrate taxa graphed by square and spit.

most part to Square E1. Indeed Spit 1 and Spit 6 represent the only two time brackets where molluscan remains are primarily dumped in Square E2. Low levels of *Diadema* cf. *setosum* urchin remains are present throughout the sequence, but urchin only predominates over molluscan and crustacean remains in Spit 2, where it is strongly represented in both squares E1 and E2. There are also notable levels of urchin remains in Spit 17, Square E1. Crustacean remains appear in highly variable numbers, but are well represented towards the lower part of the sequence (spits 16 and 17, E1), in the mid-sequence (spits 10–13), and towards the upper part of the sequence (Spit 4 in Square E1 and Spit 1 in Square E2).

Within the molluscan sample, the most obvious stratigraphic difference in species representation can be seen in the large dump of *Nerita morio* in Spit 1 (largely Square E2) (see Figure 8.3). *Nerita morio* is present in low levels throughout the sequence, but has a notably strong presence in spits 16–18 (Square E1) at the lowest part of the Tangarutu sequence. Conversely, the soft-shore bivalve *Gafrarium pectinatum* is represented most strongly in spits 3–6 where representation of *Nerita morio* is fairly weak. While this could feasibly be construed as a shift away from a focus on the hard shore to the soft shore, the occurrence of other soft-shore species is scattered and diffuse, with a range of species contributing only a few individuals (e.g. *Tellina palatum, Antigona reticulata*). As such, any pattern across soft-shore taxa is difficult to pin down (see further discussion in Chapter 9).

Within the hard-shore intertidal category, there is clearly a number of complex relationships between taxa, with both the limpet *Cellana tahitensis* and the horn shell *Clypeomorus batillariaeformis* showing different patterns of occurrence to *Nerita morio*. Although virtually restricted to Square E1, *Cellana tahitensis* is the dominant mollusc from Spit 7 to Spit 9, with strong occurrences also in spits 10–13. Apart from a small accumulation in Spit 2 (Square E2), *Cellana tahitensis* numbers are otherwise negligible. The small gastropod *Clypeomorus*

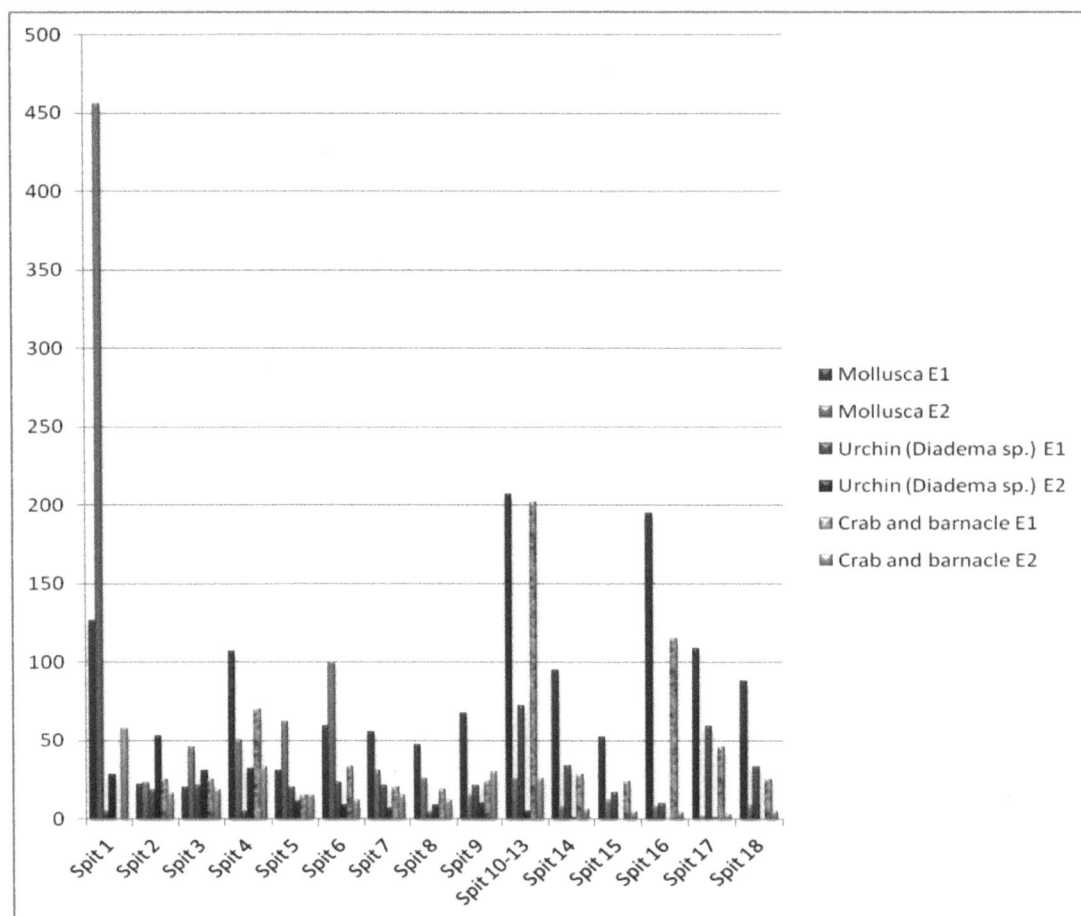

Figure 8.4. Occurrences of molluscan, crustacean and urchin remains throughout the Tangarutu sequence (NISP values).

batillariaeformis has two patches of fairly strong occurrence in the mid-sequence; the first in spits 4–7 (largely in Square E2), and the second lower down, in spits 10–16, oscillating in concentration between squares E1 and E2.

A gross environmental breakdown shows that molluscan taxa derive from two environmental zones: the rocky/reef-flat intertidal niche and the sandy intertidal zone (see figures 8.5 and 8.6). However, the foregoing discussion makes it clear that there are more complex environmental and/or gathering issues at play than simply a focus on either hard- or soft-shore resources.

Nerita morio dominates the Tangarutu molluscan sample as a whole, but as mentioned above, its importance within the overall invertebrate sample fluctuates markedly through time. *Nerita morio* is one of a group of black nerites that inhabits the temperate and sub-tropical fringes of the Indo–West Pacific, joined by the Australian *Nerita atramentosa*, the Australian, Lord Howe, Kermadecs, Pitcairn Islands and northern New Zealand *Nerita melanotragus*, and the Easter Island endemic *Nerita lirellata* (Spencer et al. 2007). *Nerita morio* can be found on Easter and Pitcairn islands, as well as the Australs, and is fairly abundant within its restricted geographical range (T. Eichhorst pers. comm.). An algal grazer, it lives under rocks and in tidal pools of the intertidal zone (T. Eichhorst pers. comm.).

Little information is available on the limpet *Cellana tahitensis*, but it likely shares many features with other species in this wide-ranging genus. *Cellana* spp. limpets are algal grazers, and nearly all eschew limestone, being found primarily on intertidal basalt surfaces (Preece 1995:346). *Clypeomorus batillariaeformis*[2] tends to inhabit the upper mid-littoral zone among

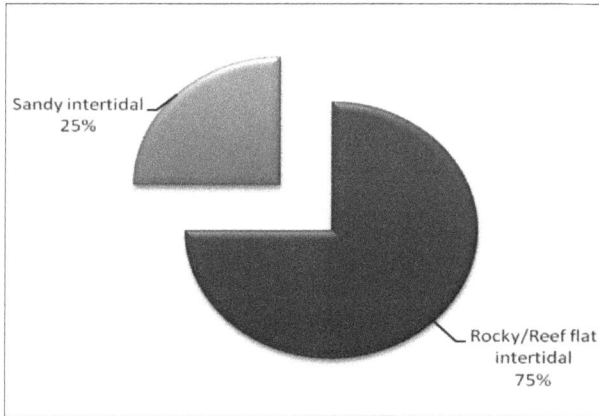

Figure 8.5. Graph to show the broad ecological niches from which the E1 molluscan samples derive.

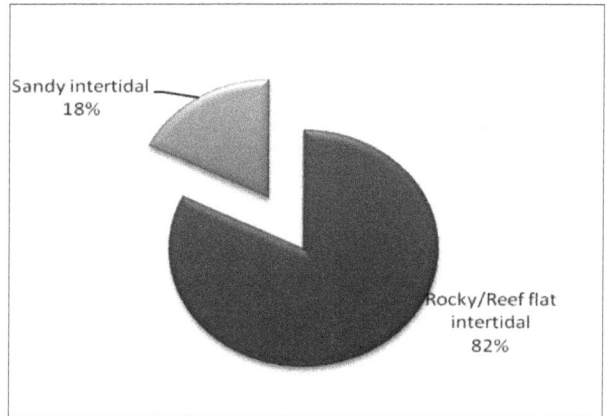

Figure 8.6. Graph to show the broad ecological niches from which the E2 molluscan samples derive.

rocks or in crevices, being most active during nocturnal low tides (Ayal and Safriel 1983:40). *C. batillariaeformis* can tolerate some degree of wave action and sand movement (Ayal and Safriel 1983:40), but personal observations of this species on Guam suggest its preference for calmer waters (KS pers. obs. 2007–2008, Tapa'chang Beach, Guam).

The dominance of gastropods over bivalves in the Tangarutu sample is to be expected given the isolation and ecology of Rapa. As Preece (1995:343) points out, insular marine molluscan assemblages tend to be dominated by gastropods, and small islands appear to skew faunal compositions even further in this direction. The presumed reason for this is the frequent paucity of soft littoral substrates on small islands, as opposed the variety of hard-shore habitats that accommodate a diversity of gastropods (Preece 1995:343). Dispersal mechanisms and food availability may also play a part in this (Vermeij in Preece 1995:344).

All urchin remains recovered from the Tangarutu deposits were identified as belonging to the species *Diadema* cf. *setosum*. The closely related *Diadema savignyi* has been identified for Pitcairn Island (Paulay 1989), although greater caution in species attribution for Pitcairn is shown by Irving (1995:314). It is possible that the Tangarutu specimens could belong to either species, or indeed a mix of the two sympatric *Diadema* taxa. Identification keys are based on discrete colour and anatomical differences (Muthiga 2003), neither of which could be utilised in the analysis of the Tangarutu assemblage.

Diadema spp. urchins have a very fragile test, with long, hollow black spines (Miskelly 2002:22), but one of the most notable features of the Tangarutu *Diadema* spp. remains is the low numbers of spine and test fragments (Figure 8.4). Instead, urchins were dominantly represented by 'teeth' or other components of the feeding apparatus known as the 'Aristotle's lantern'. This pattern would suggest that primary processing of urchin remains did not happen at the rockshelter itself, but at or near the point of collection. Given the length of *Diadema* spp. primary spines (up to 30cm), which are capable of causing a painful injury (Miskelly 2002:22), there is good reason to remove the spines before transport. Thus, the Tangarutu urchin remains would indicate that, generally, the flesh and mouthparts alone were transported back to the site.

Diadema setosum is an algal grazer, which prefers a substrate of coarse sand to rubble and little in the way of macrophytes such as *Sargassum* spp. (Dumas et al. 2007:96). It has been found to avoid finer sediments, such as fine sand or mud, and tends to shun more architecturally intricate substrates such as areas of complex or branching coral cover (Dumas et al. 2007:96). Observations by KS of *Diadema setosum* in eastern Indonesia (Pulau Kanawa, western Flores), suggest that its gregarious nature combined with its occurrence in shallow, coarse sand and rubble areas makes it a highly visible target. Despite its nocturnal feeding patterns, KS has also seen high levels of activity in the late afternoon. The clear abundance of this species in close proximity to the site, coupled with the abundance of algal-grazing molluscs, indicates extensive algal-bearing habitats in Anarua Bay.

A small number of *Lepas anatifera* barnacle plates were identified within both the E1 and E2 samples. Goose barnacles attach themselves to floating objects such as driftwood by a flexible stalk (Gunson 1983:44; Debelius 2001:310) and, as such, are only found in the intertidal zone or on beaches when washed up with ocean debris. Thus, rather than representing a food source, they indicate the presence of driftwood introduced to the site. While numbers are too small to make any statistically meaningful statements, it is interesting to note that in both squares E1 and E2, occurrences of *Lepas anatifera* plates stratigraphically match spikes in the abundance of *Clypeomorus batillariaeformis*. This may indicate periods of slightly greater exposure at Anarua Bay or the introduction of material collected in the winter months.

Tangarutu invertebrate remains in context

When dealing with a culturally accumulated faunal assemblage, it is difficult to determine whether patterning is due to human agency, the nature of available resources, or a complex mixture of the two. This issue is surely compounded on Rapa, where already sensitive and unstable ecological communities had to incorporate a new member – human colonists. Teasing apart the direct and indirect effects of human intervention in an environment that is apparently so precariously balanced *without* humans is unlikely to move past reasoned speculation.

That said, arguments for human impact through over-predation have been made for other zones of marginal East Polynesia. Fluctuating frequencies of various molluscan taxa were also detected by Weisler (1995) for Henderson Island in the Pitcairn Group.[3] At Site HEN-10, Weisler (1995:397, 399) noted that cerithid gastropods (identified mainly as *Cerithium tuberculiferum*) completely disappear from the record after a period of heavy exploitation. Although Weisler (1995:397, 399) cites this as an example of human over-predation, we would be reluctant to apply such an interpretation to the fluctuating representations of various taxa at Tangarutu, given the ecological complexities.

There can be little doubt that human predation impacted on the local littoral fauna on Rapa, but whether humans directly caused the local extinction or extirpation of particular species at Anarua Bay is more difficult to establish. In addition, while species such as *Clypeomorus batillariaeformis* are completely absent from the uppermost spits of Tangarutu, other gastropods such as *Nassarius* sp. and *Tonna* sp. are completely absent from the lower sections of the stratigraphy. On present evidence, such patterns are just as likely to represent a littoral community in flux as human gathering patterns and/or associated over-predation.

One of the major differences between Weisler's (1995) Henderson Island sites and the Tangarutu sample is the contribution made by urchins and crabs at the latter and their complete absence within the former. Paulay (1989:4) observed in his 1987 survey of Henderson Island invertebrate resources that *Diadema* sp. urchins occurred 'spine-to-spine'. In his assessment of coral reef biotopes on Henderson Island, Irving (1995:317) cites urchins as 'the most conspicuous invertebrates'. He goes on to state that molluscs and crustaceans were difficult to locate on Henderson's reefs, 'with the presence of many only being revealed by their dry remains on the strandline' (Irving 1995:317). Whether urchins were as abundant around Henderson Island in the past, or whether the archaeological pattern provides evidence of avoidance, is a question that remains unanswered. Urchin exploitation was clearly important to the inhabitants of Tangarutu, and although the level of exploitation fluctuated, it was clearly never heavy enough to wipe out local populations. It is more difficult to be categorical about the status of crab, as this category represents a mixture of different species that may show different temporal patterning with further analysis. Nevertheless, it is clear that decapod crustaceans were exploited at steady levels throughout the utilisation of the Tangarutu shelter.

Looking at the overall faunal exploitation patterns in the Henderson Island and Tangarutu assemblages, the differences appear greater than the similarities. Fishing is undoubtedly important in both locales, and it was supplemented by consistent levels of mollusc exploitation. However, there is greater variety of invertebrate exploitation at Tangarutu, with urchins and crabs making a solid contribution to the overall subsistence picture through time. It is possible that this diversification in littoral exploitation on Rapa was a response to the lack of pig and turtle, which evidently were present on Henderson Island. A greater reliance on native resources can also be seen in the use of *Aleurites moluccana* endocarp and human bone for fishhook manufacture on Rapa (see Chapter 9), while more traditional shell resources were available (or acquired) for fishhook (*Pinctada* sp.) and adze (*Tridacna* sp.) manufacture on Henderson Island.

There are obvious difficulties associated with living on small, isolated, impoverished and climatically marginal islands. Given this, it is instructive to note the differences in littoral exploitation patterns between Rapa and Henderson, islands which are so often grouped together for the purposes of ecological discussion (e.g. Paulay 1989:12 and references therein). Both the differences between human subsistence behaviour on the two islands and the fluctuating importance of various marine invertebrate resources within the Tangarutu sample suggest that flexibility and the ability to resource-switch are important factors for survival. Indeed, there can be no 'one-size-fits-all' strategy in a fluid environment. The fact that domesticated animals were not introduced to Rapa in prehistory and the fact that the prehistoric inhabitants of Henderson Island were not capitalising on crustacean and echinoderm resources amply demonstrate that even when resources are scarce, choices exist. A longer-range view of marine invertebrate populations on Rapa, including palaeontological information and modern survey data, may shed more light on fluctuations in community structure and bring into clearer focus the impact of human predation on Rapa's coastal resources.

Notes

1. *Cellana tahitensis* is the current valid name for *Cellana* (=*Patella*) taitensis more commonly seen in regional literature (OBIS database, record 35389).
2. Ayal and Safriel refer to this species by its junior synonym *Clypeomorus moniliferum*. Another junior synonym commonly seen in the literature is *Clypeomorus moniliferus.*
3. It would appear from the molluscan species list that Henderson and Rapa are not directly comparable, with Henderson having some 'classic' Indo–West Pacific taxa such as *Turbo* spp. and *Tridacna* sp. which are largely absent from Rapa. The diminutive *Turbo cinereus* is the only species of *Turbo* recorded for the Tangarutu sample.

Acknowledgements

Thank you to Tom Eichhorst for (once again) so generously sharing his vast knowledge of neritids, and to Yolanda Vogel for unpublished information and discussion.

References

Ayal, Y. and Safriel, Y.N. 1983. Does a suitable habitat guarantee successful colonisation? *Journal of Biogeography* 10:37–46.

Debelius, H. 2001. *Crustacea Guide of the World*. Conchbooks, Hackenheim.

Dharma, B. 2005. *Recent and Fossil Indonesian Shells*. Conchbooks, Hackenheim.

Dumas, P., Kulbicki, M., Chifflet, S., Fichez, R. and Ferraris, J. 2007. Environmental factors influencing urchin spatial distributions on disturbed coral reefs (New Caledonia, South Pacific). *Journal of Experimental Marine Biology and Ecology* 344:88–100.

Grayson, D.K. 1984. *Quantitative Zooarchaeology – Topics in the analysis of archaeological faunas*. Academic Press, Orlando, Fl, and London.

Gunson, D. 1983. *Collins Guide to the New Zealand Seashore*. Collins, Auckland.

Irving, R.A. 1995. Near-shore bathymetry and reef biotopes of Henderson Island, Pitcairn Group. *Biological Journal of the Linnean Society* 56:309–324.

Miskelly, A. 2002. *Sea Urchins of Australia and the Indo-Pacific*. Capricornia Publications, Lindfield, NSW.

Muthiga, N.A. 2003. Coexistence and reproductive isolation of the sympatric echinoids *Diadema savignyi* Michelin and *Diadema setosum* (Leske) on Kenyan coral reefs. *Marine Biology* 143:669–677.

OBIS Indo-Pacific Molluscan Database. 2006. *Cellana tahitensis* species listing. URL: http://clade.ansp.org/obis/search.php/35389 Accessed 14 June 2008.

Paulay, G. 1989. Marine invertebrates of the Pitcairn Islands: species composition and biogeography of corals, molluscs and echinoderms. *Atoll Research Bulletin* 326:1–28.

Preece, R.C. 1995. The composition and relationships of the marine molluscan fauna of the Pitcairn Islands. *Biological Journal of the Linnean Society* 56:339–358.

Spencer, H.G., Waters, J.M. and Eichhorst, T.E. 2007. Taxonomy and nomenclature of black nerites (Gastropoda: Neritimorpha: *Nerita*) from the South Pacific. *Invertebrate Systematics* 21:229–237.

Vogel, Y. 2005. Ika. Unpublished MA thesis, University of Otago, Dunedin.

Weisler, M.I. 1995. Henderson Island prehistory: colonisation and extinction on a remote Polynesian island. *Biological Journal of the Linnean Society* 56:377–404.

9

Marine resource exploitation on Rapa Island

Archaeology, material culture and ethnography

Katherine Szabó
Centre for Archaeological Science, University of Wollongong, NSW, Australia, Kat.Szabo1@gmail.com

Yolanda Vogel
Department of Anthropology, University of Otago

Atholl Anderson
Archaeology and Natural History, The Australian National University

Introduction

As Rapa lacked the usual suite of Polynesian domesticated animals, it is not surprising that evidence for marine fishing and marine exploitation in general is strong. However, the discussion of fishing techniques and broader aquatic resource exploitation must be placed within the unique environmental context of the island; no straightforward transference of traditions or interpretations in other parts of Polynesia will suffice to explain the patterns seen here. The cultural adaptations that formed on Rapa are exemplified by a remarkable assemblage of very small fish hooks produced in candlenut endocarp that was recovered from Tangarutu. In the absence of tropical coral reef littoral environments, species of shell so important elsewhere for fish-hook manufacture, such as the pearl oyster *Pinctada margaritifera*, were not locally available on Rapa[1] and creative new solutions had to be found. What follows here, then, is an investigation into Rapan flexibility in modifying cultural techniques and practices to the limitations and idiosyncrasies of the environment in which they lived.

After a description of the remarkably preserved Tangarutu fish hooks, the assemblage will be considered within the context of both Rapan environments and generic Polynesian fishing traditions. The Rapan fish hooks are argued to represent, among other things, the creative confluence of traditional practice and material constraint. Neither cultural mores nor environmental context is seen as a determining factor in its own right. Rather, both are seen to inform each other in generating an inventive solution and, with it, a new trajectory in Polynesian fishing technologies.

The fish-hook assemblage

The fish-hook assemblage from Tangarutu consists of 15 complete hooks and hook fragments. Ten of these have been manufactured from the tough endocarp of the candlenut (*Aleurites moluccana*), with the remaining five produced in bone. Within the candlenut fish-hook assemblage, three specimens are unfinished, thereby allowing additional insights into manufacturing procedures. The candlenut fish hooks also preserve evidence of the *Pandanus* carrier(s) in which they were wrapped, as well as the line fibres lashed below the protruding knobs at the heads of the hooks. The candlenut and bone fish hooks will be discussed in turn.

Candlenut fish hooks

Candlenut seems an unlikely raw material in which to fashion fish hooks, although the use of coconut (*Cocos nucifera*) endocarp is widespread (e.g. see Anell 1955:94–5, 98, 102). The coconut palm grows poorly on Rapa, and perhaps grew not at all in the prehistoric past, while *Aleurites moluccana* is common. The use of candlenut endocarp, however, restricts manufacture to very small fish hooks. The average size of the finished hooks at Tangarutu, measuring from the head to the bend, is 10.04 mm long, with a standard deviation of 0.43 mm. Full measurements are given in Table 9.1. There is a standardised plan to the hook morphology, despite some variation (see Figure 9.1), with all hooks, bar the one broken example, showing an incurving point leg, a thickened bend area, and a protruding knob at the head to keep the line in place. All candlenut hooks can be classified as 'rotating'; largely by virtue of the abrupt incurve of the terminal end of the point leg – similar to the *fong* hooks of Tobi described by Johannes (1981:117–118). This hook morphology helps to keep the fish on the hook and/or hold the bait on the hook (Johannes 1981:117).

Table 9.1. Maximum dimensions and provenance of all Tangarutu complete and fragmented fish hooks.

Fishhook description		Length (mm)	Width (mm)	Provenance
finished candlenut hook	1	10.04	7.25	E1, Spit 4
	2	10.31	9.20	E1, Spit 4
	3	9.21	6.85 (broken)	E2, Spit 2
	4	9.98	7.55	E1, Spit 4
	5	10.50	7.67	East E1, Spit 4
	6	10.37	7.68	East E1, Spit 4
	7	9.87	7.12	East E1, Spit 14
candlenut hook preform	1	10.08	7.65	E1, Spit 3
	2	13.17	9.09	East E2, Spit 1
	3	6.39 (broken)	8.94	East E1, Spit 1
bone hook*				
shank only	1	29.67	7.28	West R1, Spit 4
shank and bend	2	29.07	3.65	Unstratified
point leg	3	8.78	2.27	East E1, Spit 5
bend	4	22.05	7.07	E2, Spit 2
shank/partial bend	5	33.44	7.70	E1, Spit 4

*None of the bone hooks are complete, so these values represent maximum fragment dimensions. Maximum widths represent maximum fragment widths rather than hook widths.

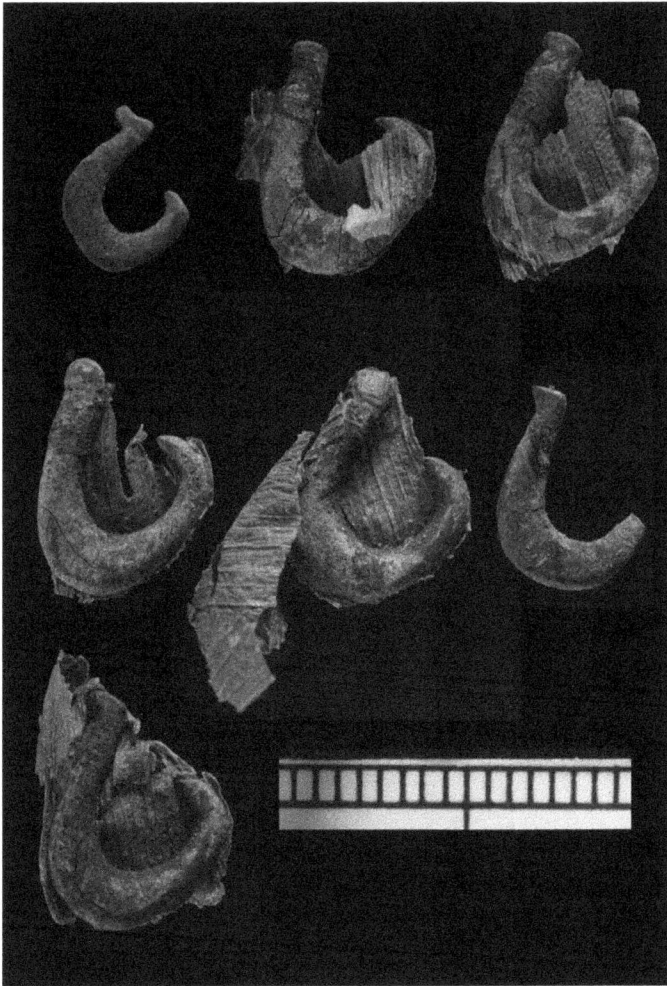

Figure 9.1. The Tangarutu candlenut finished fish-hook assemblage. Scale in mm. Photograph D. Boyd.

The presence of the three preforms (see Figure 9.2) allows insight into how these hooks were produced. The blank was obtained by cutting a number of straight edges to generate the general outer form of the hook. A hole was then drilled through the blank to initiate the formation of the inner shank, bend and point surfaces (seen most clearly in Figure 9.2c). This hole was then widened through abrasion, and the outer periphery of the fish hook was abraded to the desired finished shape. There are clear parallels here with the production of fish hooks in other materials – most notably shell and bone – and this will be discussed further below. The preforms indicate that the head was one of the last pieces of the hook to be shaped. The general abrasion of finished hook surfaces, as well as the presence of the remnants of line lashing on all but one finished specimen (see Figure 9.3), indicate that the hooks were used. Fragments of a woven *Pandanus* case also adhere to all but one of the finished specimens, and while the hooks could have been wrapped individually, it is conceivable they could have been wrapped together in a woven fish-hook 'kit', as seen in Tahiti (see Anell 1955:Plate 3). In this respect, it is notable that the one candlenut fish hook that does not have evidence of lashing or an outer wrapping was recovered from Spit 14 of the Tangarutu excavations, whereas the other finished examples were all recovered in close proximity to one another (refer to Table 9.1).

Bone fish hooks

All the bone fish hooks were manufactured from terrestrial mammal cortical bone, and given the size, density and visibly homogenous texture, as well as the lack of domesticated mammals on Rapa, it is most likely that they were produced from human bone (see Figure 9.4). There are no

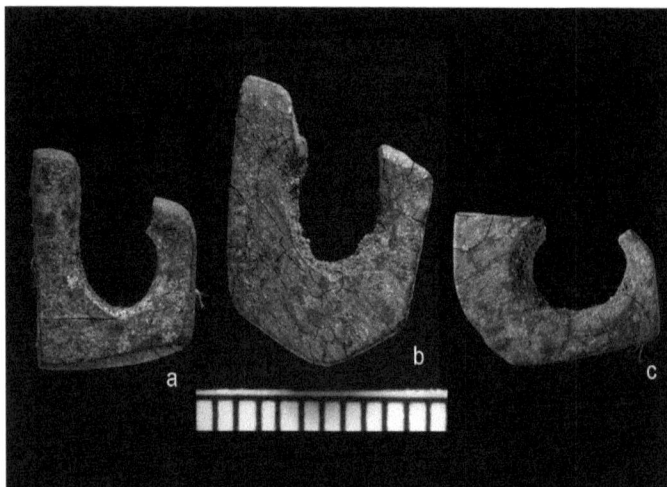

Figure 9.2. The Tangarutu candlenut fish-hook preforms. Scale in mm. Photograph D. Boyd.

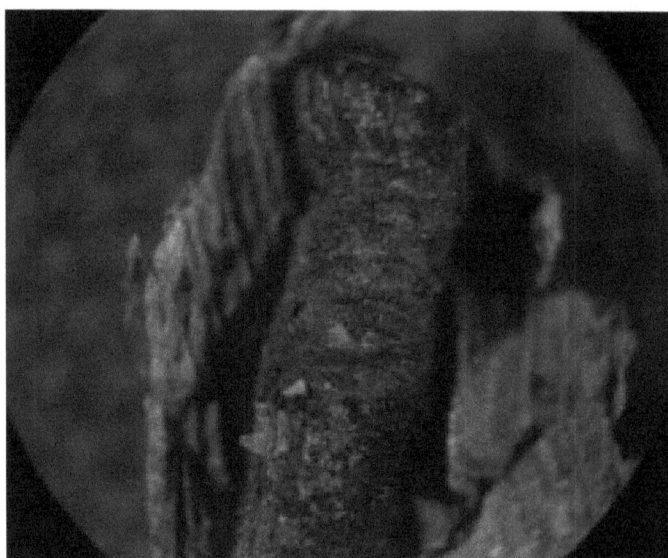

Figure 9.3. Finished candlenut fish-hook head and upper shank showing remnants of cordage line attachment lashing; 20x magnification. Photograph P. Piper.

complete examples and thus it cannot be determined whether the bone fish hooks were rotating or jabbing types. Where detectable, features such as an incurving point leg and a projecting-knob form of line attachment match those seen in the candlenut fish hooks. No remnants of either lashing or casing are evident.

Discussion

The stratigraphic placement of the candlenut fish hooks indicates that these were deposited, and probably made, late in the sequence represented at Tangarutu (ca. 1450–1600 AD, based on associated, calibrated radiocarbon dates published in Kennett et al. 2006). This places their manufacture considerably earlier than the first European contact with Rapans in 1792. There is, however, evidence that they continued in production until after European contact.

The unpublished manuscript of Stokes (n.d.), produced in 1920–21, makes mention of small fish hooks produced in candlenut (*tuitui*), although the discussion of them is based on the memory of four older men, none of whom had actually seen such hooks being made. Two forms of candlenut hook were stated as having been manufactured in the past, one from the median section of the endocarp, and one cut 'from the side of the nut shell' (Stokes n.d.). The examples recorded from Tangarutu fall into the latter category. Stokes further points out that the hook produced from the side of the endocarp would have been much stronger than the 'flimsy' version produced from the cross-section (Stokes n.d.).

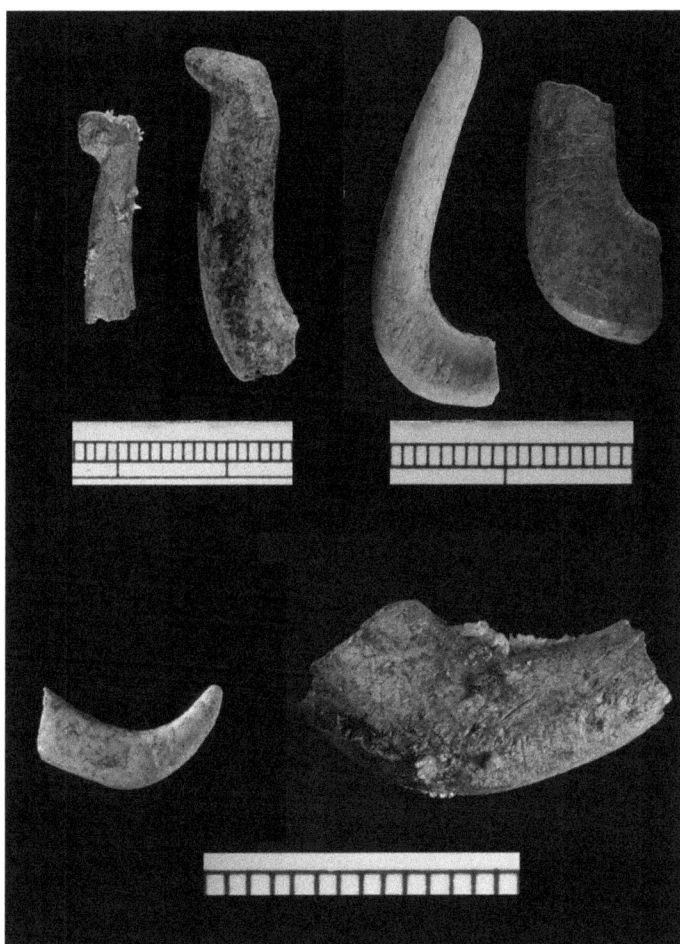

Figure 9.4. The Tangarutu bone fish-hook assemblage. Scale in mm. Photograph D. Boyd.

Stokes' discussion of candlenut fish hooks demonstrates that this technological innovation evidenced at Tangarutu was not simply a matter of shortlived experimentation, but a distinctively Rapan solution that continued in use for some centuries. As pointed out by Stokes (n.d.), the use of candlenut endocarp as a raw material for fish-hook manufacture is not recorded elsewhere in Polynesia. However, the evidence contained in the preforms sheds light on how this solution might have come about. The cutting of a blank out of a convex surface, the drilling and subsequent filing of the inner hook form, the abrasion of the outer perimeter and the formation of a knob-shaped head have clear parallels in fish-hook production in bone and shell across Polynesia.

While shell fish-hook blanks were often chipped and filed into shape, rather than sawn (e.g. Kirch and Yen 1982:239; Szabó 2007), bone fish-hook blanks were more commonly generated through sawing (Emory, Bonk and Sinoto 1968:Plate 5). Modification of the inner surfaces of shell fish hooks was initiated through either the drilling of a hole or the creation and enlargement of a notch (Szabó 2007; Kirch and Yen 1982), while the drilling of a central hole in the tab appears to be more standard in bone fish-hook production (e.g. see Emory, Bonk and Sinoto 1968:Plates 4 and 5). Thus, while the use of candlenut endocarp as a raw material can be seen as a technological innovation, the techniques applied are firmly rooted in other Polynesian (and arguably Micronesian) fish-hook manufacturing traditions.

It is also noteworthy that the only other raw material used for the production of the Tangarutu fish hooks is bone. There is no record of any of the standard Polynesian domesticates (pig, dog or chicken) on Rapa, either within the archaeology or ethnographically (Buck 1954:181, 320) and the bone hooks from Tangarutu are probably manufactured from human bone. Where identifiable, longbone has been used, rather than cranial pieces (see Skinner 1942:217). While the use of human bone for fish-hook production has precedents across Polynesia, its use is commonly bound up in symbolic aspects of war and revenge (e.g. see Best 1929:36), rather than in serving a purely practical need. In the case of Rapa, it is unclear whether the use of human bone for fish hooks had another level of meaning beyond a matter-of-fact answer to a shortage of traditional raw materials. Stokes (n.d.), at least, does not record symbolic meanings beyond practical application. He does, however, posit that materials such as turtle shell and sperm-whale teeth would have been used in the past, despite local assertions to the contrary. The Tangarutu fish-hook assemblage reinforces his Rapan informants' views that candlenut endocarp and human bone were the dominant materials used in the production of hooks (Stokes n.d.).

By virtue of their size and morphology, the candlenut hooks must have been produced to target particular sorts of fish. In particular, these are likely to have been small-mouthed fish capable of being taken effectively with a rotating hook. Stokes (n.d.) cites an informant who stated that both forms of candlenut hook were used for catching 'komokomo'. The informant had been shown how to use the ring-section hooks to catch komokomo as a child, explaining that three such hooks were attached to the line, with the hooks holding fish in place until all three hooks were filled (Stokes n.d.). Stokes further notes that the candlenut hooks described to him corresponded closely, in terms of form, to metal hooks used for catching komokomo at the time of his observations (Stokes n.d.). Fishbase (2007) recognises the Rapan komokomo as being *Leptoscarus vaigiensis* within the Scaridae. Stokes does not specify which species of fish we should associate with komokomo in his unpublished manuscript, and later he (Stokes 1955:334) translates komokomo simply as 'a fish'. Randall and Sinoto (1978), however, state that komokomo is *L. vaigiensis*, an algal and sea-grass grazer that inhabits sheltered bays, harbours and lagoons. While it seems unlikely that such a fish would take a hook, both the Stokes reference and information provided by a local fisherman to AA in 2002 confirm that the seagrass parrotfish is indeed captured with a small candlenut hook, especially in the month of March. Stokes further records that the *tuitui* fish hooks were also used to catch the damselfish *Stegastes fasciolatus* (Pomacentridae). *S. fasciolatus* is an 'algal farmer' in shallow waters, and as such can be highly territorial of a small patch on the reef (Cardona and Clayton 1999).

In the context of the Rapan assemblages, the appearance of these small fish hooks coincides neatly with the increase in Scaridae and Pomacentridae in the latter half of the upper level of the E1/E2 area. While serranid numbers, which could potentially be associated with angling technologies, do increase in Level III, the increase occurs in the bottom half of the level, with numbers dropping off somewhat in the upper half of the level, and thus does not directly coincide with the appearance of the candlenut fish hooks. The combination of the ethnographic data with those from the fishbone analysis suggests that the occupants of Tangarutu were indeed using candlenut fish hooks to catch komokomo/*L. vaigiensis* and nganga/*S. fasciolatus*.

The uniqueness of the Tangarutu candlenut hooks makes direct analogy impossible, but extremely small hooks are reported both archaeologically and ethnographically from other locales in Polynesia and Micronesia. In his observations of fishing practices and archaeological fishing gear from the southern Cook Island of Ma'uke, Walter (1988) reported the use of small shell hooks in association with *titomo* fishing (see also Walter 1991). As described by Walter (1988:222), the hooks were used on a short line for catching a type of mackerel known as *koperu*. Unripe coconut is spread on the water's surface to draw the fish, and after their arrival, the fishermen enter the water and place their baited hooks in the group of feeding fish. Fish are quickly jerked into the boat when caught. While archaeological examples of the hooks used for this specialised form of fishing, identified for the archaeological site of Anai'o on Ma'uke

(Walter 1988), are roughly the same size as those in the Tangarutu assemblage, the *titomo* hooks are jabbing hooks, whereas all those from Tangarutu are rotating.

The ethnographic fishing study undertaken by Johannes (1981) on the Micronesian island of Tobi also discusses the specialised use of small hooks, and in particular, the small *fong*-type rotating fish hook called *haufong*. This is used by Tobians to target triggerfish, which are notorious 'bait-stealers', only nipping at bait unless the hook is small enough for the fish to take it in whole (Johannes 1981:117). Johannes (1981:118) comments that hooks similar to the *haufong* were used in various locales across Oceania, but that in other examples the *fong* (i.e. the recurved point) was longer and thicker, and generally served to hold the bait in place rather than the fish on the hook. While such a generalised distinction is perhaps debatable, what is clear is that the highly standardised though unique Tangarutu fish hooks were produced to a definite format to serve a clear purpose. It should be noted that triggerfish (Balistidae) are altogether absent from the Rapan fishbone assemblages.

Ethnoarchaeology and Rapan marine exploitation

The unpublished manuscript on Rapan lifeways by John F.G. Stokes (n.d.) provides a firsthand account of Rapan fishing, as well as providing some details on the types of littoral invertebrate fauna consumed. There are some clear disparities between Stokes' information and the evidence from the archaeological record, but the ethnographic window provided by his manuscript also provides useful insights into how a living was made in this unique environment. Here, we consider the information provided by Stokes' unpublished manuscript, as well as his published article 'Language in Rapa' (1955), supplemented by Randall and Sinoto (1978) and information on fishing collected by AA during the course of the Rapan excavation season, and assess its potential to inform the archaeological record. Detailed descriptions of fish-capture techniques provide an opportunity to push beyond broad correlations between fish families and capture technologies, and Stokes' notations regarding invertebrate processing methods offer a possible explanation for fragmentation patterns noted archaeologically. Perhaps most significantly, the ethnographic record contains clear statements about cultural ideas surrounding 'edibility' and which marine foods were or were not taken. This information allows us to assess change through time in cultural attitudes towards aquatic food sources, both within the archaeology itself, and with the archaeological and ethnographic records juxtaposed.

Fishing – the ethnographic record

Stokes' (n.d.) manuscript provides ethnographic data on fishing and fishing technology, including hook and line angling, the use of various forms of nets and basket traps, and snares for eeling, as well as Rapan names for the fish commonly caught using each method. The names of fish provided by Stokes (n.d.) and their capture techniques have been matched with the species names given by Randall and Sinoto (1978), and this information is provided in Table 9.2.

Line fishing

The small candlenut hooks used for the capture of *komokomo* and *nganga* have been discussed above, however Stokes (n.d.) also provides information on the use of hook and line for the capture of other fish species. Fishing from canoes with hook and line produced, primarily, the *rari* (a large-mouthed red fish like a rock cod, with large anal spines, possibly the flagtail grouper, *Cephalopholis urodeta* (Lieske and Myers 1994:25). Rensch (1988:237) and Randall and Sinoto (1978:298) also have *rari* as *Epinephelus fasciatus*, the blacktip grouper, which is another red fish of similar form. While relatively small, around 27 cm in average length, it has the reputation

Table 9.2. Aquatic vertebrate and invertebrate fauna covered in Stokes (n.d.) with local names and details of capture techniques where specified.

Family	Species	Rapan name	Capture method (from Stokes n.d.)	Present in assemblage?
Pisces				
Muraenidae (moray eels)			snare	yes
Congridae (conger eels)			snare	yes
Atherinidae (silversides)	*Pranesus insularum*	kiamu/kiamo	ngake (hand net)	no
Serranidae (groupers/basses)	*Cephalopholis urodelus*	tumutumuraupoo	hook and line	yes
	Epinephelus fasciatus	rari	hook and line	
Carangidae (jacks)	*Pseudocaranx cheilio*	matu	rau, hook and line	yes
	Serioloa lalandi	ma'aki	rau, hook and line	
Mullidae (goatfish)	*Parupeneus fraterculus*	kature/katuri	'inaki ika (basket trap)	yes
Chaetodontidae (butterflyfishes)	*Chaetodon* spp.	amuamu	'inaki ika	yes
	Chaetondon smithi	vaiti	'inaki ika	
Pomacentridae (damselfishes)	*Stegastes fasciolatus*	nganga	candlenut hook	yes
Labridae (wrasses)	*Gomphosus varius*	pokou	'inaki ika	yes
	Hologymnous sp.	pokou	'inaki ika	
	Pseudolabrus inscriptus	kariva	'inaki ika	
	Thalassoma lutescens	pokou	'inaki ika	
Scaridae (parrotfishes)	*Leptoscarus vaigiensis*	komokomo	spearing	yes
	Scarus chlorodon	pahoro	candlenut hook, toto (oval dip net)	
	Scarus ghobban	para	'inaki ika	
	Scarus globiceps	pahoro	'inaki ika	
			'inaki ika	
Acanthuridae (surgeonfishes)	*Acanthurus leucopareius*	mama/ma'a ma'a	toto	yes
Echinoidea				
Echinidae	'*Echinus* sp.'	vana		No
Crustacea[1]				
Palinuridae (marine crayfish)	probably *Panulirus ascuensis*	koura	'inaki ika (basket trap)	not noted
Atyidae (river shrimps)	probably *Caridina rapaensis*	koura kotae		not noted
Bathysquillidae	*Bathysquilla microps* (Stokes: *Squilla* sp.)	pongaponga		not noted
Grapsidae	probably *Leptograpsis variegatus* (Stokes: 'rock crab found at base of cliffs')	karami		yes
Carpiliidae	? *Carpilius convexus* (Stokes: 'rock crab – common form')	papaa		yes
Ocypodidae	*Uca tetragonon* (Stokes: 'small mud crab with large red claw')	tararoa		possibly
Portunidae (swimming crabs)	*Thalamita cerasma* (Stokes: 'swimming crab')	tumomi		possibly
?	species unknown (Stokes: 'small crab found under stones')	kōrao		?
?	species unknown – recently moulted crab? (Stokes: 'small rock crab with a soft shell')	pakapakaraumia		?
Mollusca				
Nacellidae	'a limpet' – probably *Cellana tahitensis*	pangi		yes
Trochidae	*Trochus radiatus* (observed by Stokes in midden deposits)	name unknown		yes
Neritidae	*Nerita morio*	'ī		yes
Cerithiidae	*Clypeomorus batillariaeformis* (observed by Stokes in midden deposits)	name unknown		yes
Ranellidae?	'*Triton* sp.'	pu		no
Arcidae	*Anadara* (= *Arca*) sp.	akaikai		no
Mytilidae	*Modiolus* sp.	piuu		yes
Isognomonidae	*Melina* sp.	kotakota		no
Chamidae	*Chama* sp.	pa'ua		yes
Spondylidae	*Spondylus* sp.	pa'ua		no
Psammobiidae	*Asaphis violascens*	ka'i		no
Tellinidae	*Tellina rugosa*	pipi		yes
	Tellina sp. ('small')			
	Tellina scobinata	tupere		yes
Veneridae	*Gafrarium pectinatum*	mitata		yes
	Periglypta reticulata	tupere		yes
	'*Venus* sp.'	tupere		?

in Tahiti of never being poisonous (Bagnis et al. 1974:106), unlike many snappers and coral trout. Two carangids (*matu*, *maaki*) were also caught by hook and line. Randall and Sinoto (1978:299) equate these with *Pseudocaranx cheilio* and *Seriola lalandi* respectively. The tough wood of the *mairari* shrub (*Dodonea viscosa*) was used to make large and medium-sized bait hooks by training the branches to grow in the required shape. A hook of *mairari* wood with a *tuitui* point was used to catch albacore (*ahi*). Temporary hooks were tipped with *rari* anal spines (Stokes n.d.:259–262). Pearl shell was absent at Rapa, but turtle shell and whale bone may have been used in earlier days.

Rau (leaf sweeps)

Stokes (n.d.) describes the occasional use of large leaf sweeps (*rau*) for fishing. These consisted of two wings (*rau*) of stiff rope with suspended *ti* leaves attached to a central *pohue*, or pound, and they were used to drive fish, as in using a seine net. Stokes (n.d.) observed one catch, which included *matu* (*Pseudocaranx cheilio*) and *maaki* (*Serioloa lalandi*) and a large quantity of unnamed smaller fish. Although deployed infrequently in modern times, the leaf sweep is said to have been an ancient form of fishing on Rapa.

Netting

Stokes (n.d.) states that net fishing had been largely abandoned at the time of his visit, however '… in former days [it] was of the greatest importance'. Nets (*kupenga*) used included seines, hand nets and dip nets. Seine nets were used either in shallow water or from canoes further out, but no details of fish catches are provided. Seines were also used for the capture of turtles. Hand nets (*ngake*) attached to two sticks were used to capture a small fish called *kiamo*, which Randall and Sinoto (1978) identify as the silverside *Pranesus insularum*. Dip nets (*toto*) were said to have been used for the capture of *mama* (*Acanthurus leucopareius*) and *komokomo* (*Leptoscarus vagiensis*). These were oval in shape with a single handle and could be operated either by a single person or with others driving the fish.

Basket traps

Baskets traps ('*inaki ika*), generally made from *kiekie*, were also used for fishing and crayfishing. These traps are used in the month of November to capture *kature*, which Randall and Sinoto (1978) name as the goatfish *Parupeneus fraterculus*. In addition to the seasonal capture of *kature*, '*inaki ika* are also used to take *pahoro* (*Scarus chlorodon*, *Scarus globiceps*), *para* (*Scarus ghobban*), *keikei* (taxon unknown), *amuamu* (*Chaetodon* spp.), *vaiti* (*Chaetodon smithi*), *poko* (*Gomphosus varius*, *Hologymnous* sp., *Thalassoma lutescens*) and *kariva* (*Pseudolabrus inscriptus*) (Randall and Sinoto 1978; Stokes n.d.).

Eel snaring

Marine eels were snared in the reef shallows by women (Stokes n.d.). The eel snare (*ngati*) consisted of two sticks, one of which held a bait, and the other a slip noose. Following snaring, the eel was dashed against the rocks to kill it.

Spearing

Fish were caught in shallow water by casting or stabbing a wooden spear. This was generally done from shore or when wading, and spears were also carried in canoes. Fish caught by this method were parrotfish and 'other shore feeders', with crayfish also taken using spears from canoes (Stokes n.d.).

Stone weirs

Stone fish traps (*pa ika*), regarded as of ancient origin, can be seen along the margins of east coast bays, although by the 1920s it seems they were no longer used. Stokes (n.d.) notes the use of one form that consisted of stone-built leaders and a *ngake* for the capture of *kiamo* (*Pranesus insularum*), and also that spearing was used for taking fish from weirs.

Other ethnographic data on fishing

Enquiries of an experienced fisherman on Rapa in 2002 (Mr Teraura Oitokaia, interviewed by his daughter, Roti Oitokaia) elicited the information that *rari* was still a popular fish, especially when it was fattest, from March to May. *Komokomo* (above), apparently known also as *tapio,* is taken by hook in March and by diving from December to January. *Nanue* and similar fish called *pakavai* and *karamami* are caught from April to September. According to Bagnis et al. (1974), *nanue* is herbivorous, a seaweed feeder, and a popular subtropical food fish. Randall and Sinoto (1978) equate all three names with varying sizes of the rudderfish *Kyphosus bigibbus*. It is caught by driving schools towards the shore, using seines of coconut fronds. If there were fish remains from middens along the harbourside, these might well contain *nanue*. Other species caught today include flying fish or *marara* (*Cypselurus* sp.), which are in best condition in April, and the *parapo'atu*, which arrives at Rapa in March to eat the *maamanga* (identified by Stokes (n.d.) as a type of seaweed). Randall and Sinoto (1978) identify *parapo'atu* as the rabbitfish *Siganus argenteus*. Perhaps the most interesting aspect of this evidence is the well-defined seasonality of Rapan fishing.

Gathering of aquatic invertebrates – the ethnographic record

Stokes (n.d. 1955) provides much less information about invertebrate collection and consumption than he does about fish and fishing. Exploited crustaceans are listed and given their Rapan names, and although virtually no information on capture is provided, Stokes does state whether aquatic invertebrates were normally consumed cooked or raw. Similar information is provided for urchins. For molluscs, Stokes (n.d.) generally provides both local and scientific names for taxa gathered and consumed, as well as information about whether the animals were eaten cooked or raw, with occasional information about processing techniques. Of particular interest with regard to molluscs, Stokes (n.d.) casually investigated eroding shell-midden deposits in various locations around Rapa. He recorded the major taxa present and reports this information, together with the then-current 'edibility' status of these species as provided by contemporary informants. Both the archaeological and ethnographic elements of this survey provide revealing points of comparison with the Tangarutu record.

Stokes (n.d.) lists a variety of medium-large crustaceans consumed as food on Rapa at the time of his fieldwork. The marine crayfish, or *koura* (probably the locally common *Panulirus pascuensis*), is at the top of the list, and also listed as prominent among exchange items with early European voyagers in Rapan waters (Barratt 1988:201). In a section of the Stokes manuscript detailing fishing technologies, he mentions that crayfish were taken in basket traps (Stokes n.d.). Stokes (n.d.) also names the river shrimp, *koura kotae* (probably *Caridina rapaensis* in the Atyidae family), and a species of stomatopod termed *pongaponga* (probably *Bathysquilla microps*) among species of exploited Crustacea. All were apparently consumed cooked. None of these species were obviously recognisable within the archaeological samples from Tangarutu,[2] but a lack of reference specimens means that less-diagnostic fragments might have been overlooked. Even so, the majority of the Tangarutu crustacean remains clearly derives from species of brachyuran crab.

Stokes (n.d.) lists seven types of crab, named only by local names, accompanied by descriptions of varying usefulness. The *tararoa*, described as 'a small mud crab with a red claw', is clearly *Uca tetragonan*, although an identification for the *kōlao* – 'a small crab found under stones' – is more elusive. All named taxa bar the unidentified *kōlao* and *pakapakaraumia* (a crab with a 'soft shell', perhaps a general term for newly moulted crabs) can be assigned to a species with relative confidence with the aid of distributional checklists and databases cataloguing French Polynesian crustaceans (Poupin 1996, 1998; also http://decapoda.free.fr/).

Of the crab taxa listed by Stokes (n.d.), *karami* (*Leptograpsis variegatus*) and *papaa* (*Carpilius convexus*) are certainly represented in the Tangarutu assemblage, with possible additional occurrences of *tararoa* (*Uca tetragonan*) and *tumomi* (*Thalamita cerasma*). Levels of fragmentation within the assemblage are such that reference specimens would be required for full identification and quantification. Nevertheless, with these provisional identifications in hand, it is clear that relatively large and sometimes aggressive and very mobile crabs were being taken as food both archaeologically and ethnographically.

Although Stokes (n.d.) gives no information on crab capture, it is possible that some crabs were caught in basket traps that were laid for the capture of various fish and possibly also crayfish (see above). Some information on crab capture on Rapa was provided to AA by Teraura Oitokaia. Apparently, crabs are caught all year round and are captured by pressing down on the carapace, flipping them over, and piercing the eyes with the thumb. Sticks are used to catch those secreted in holes. The species, or perhaps group of species, captured in these ways is not specified.

Urchins are mentioned only briefly by Stokes (n.d.), who provides the local name *vana* for a species of *Echinus*. It is likely that the attribution to *Echinus* is incorrect and was simply a shorthand reference to 'urchins' using a well-known European/Atlantic genus, in much the same way as '*Chiton* sp.' is sometimes used to refer to polyplacophorans generally rather than those in the genus *Chiton* or family Chitonidae per se. There is no description given to guide scientific identification, but clearly from Stokes' (n.d.) record, urchins were collected, and he states they were eaten raw. The collection of urchins for food was also mentioned by Teraura Oitokaia in information passed on to AA. The species being discussed is unclear, but Mr Oitokaia indicated a preference for collection before spawning.

Certainly if the urchin in question was *Diadema setosum*, hand collection is unlikely, given the length and toxicity of the spines. This implies that some sort of tool-assisted capture method was in use, and as with crabs it is possible that urchins were caught on occasion in basket traps. As detailed in Chapter 8, the relatively low levels of spine and test fragments present in the Tangarutu deposits relative to the number of mouth parts suggest that preliminary urchin processing took place away from Tangarutu shelter.

With regard to molluscs, information about cephalopods, gastropods and bivalves is provided by Stokes (n.d.). Three species of cephalopod (two octopuses and a squid) are mentioned as being taken and eaten either cooked or raw, with the archaeology having, necessarily, nothing to add to this information. Stokes (n.d.) goes on to list bivalves and gastropods eaten or known to be edible to contemporary informants, and those he observed in eroding midden deposits. Although he states that shelled molluscs were not widely collected or eaten on Rapa during his stay, save by children, a fairly wide range of molluscs is listed, along with local names and occasional additional information.

Stokes' (n.d.) list of mollusc species named as food sources by local informants leans heavily towards bivalves, with only a few gastropods named. Hard-shore taxa include *Chama* sp., *Spondylus* sp., *Modiulus* sp. mussels and *Isognomon* (=*Melina*) sp., while soft-shore species include *Gafrarium pectinatum,* various species within the Tellinidae, *Asaphis violascens, Anadara* (=*Arca*) sp. and *Periglypta reticulata*. Stokes (n.d.) observed the colonial soft-shore bivalve *Gafrarium pectinatum* to be the most commonly consumed mollusc, eaten either raw or cooked. Only three gastropods are included in Stokes' (n.d.) list, including a limpet identified as *Patella* (but more likely *Cellana*, which was until recently placed in the Patellidae), the endemic *Nerita morio*, and a 'triton' species. A subset of those molluscs listed by Stokes (n.d.) was named by Mr Oitokaia. He mentions only one gastropod, the *pangi'i* limpet. Mussels, *Isognomon* sp. and *Gafrarium pectinatum* are the most regularly taken of the bivalves, with *Tellina rugosa* and *T. scobinata* now stated as rare on the island.

In Stokes' wanderings around the island, he came across shells deposited on ridgelines, which he took – doubtless correctly – to represent midden refuse. He notes the presence in a number of locations of *Chama* sp. and *Spondylus* sp., with the former being common enough for Stokes to consider it one of the major molluscan foods of past times. Also noted as being present on the hillslopes were pieces of the unidentified *pu* whelk and *Trochus* sp. Of the latter, Stokes (n.d.) states that there was no local name at the time of his investigations. It is likely, based on the Tangarutu results, that this was *Trochus radiatus*. Of particular interest is Stokes' discussion of the diminutive horn snail *Clypeomorus batillariaeformis*. In a casual investigation of the remnants of a hearth within a 'cliff shelter', he notes the presence of crabs' claws and a number of shells, including 165 *Gafrarium pectinatum* valves and 550 *Clypeomorus batillariaeformis* – nearly all of which were broken. Although Stokes' informants knew of no local name for *C. batillariaeformis* and did not consider it a food source, Stokes says it was the most common shell in the 'backwaters of the harbour' and surmised that it was probably an 'article of diet' in the past. This conclusion is confirmed by the presence of *C. batillariaeformis* in the Tangarutu midden.

Ethnographic information and the archaeological record

The early 20th century observations of Stokes, together with information provided to Anderson by Mr Oitokaia, allow us to pinpoint changing subsistence practices through time relating to both environmental changes and shifts in cultural frameworks.

The information on fishing techniques and the taxa exploited provided by Stokes (n.d.) generally provides a good fit with the archaeological fishbone assemblages from Rapa. Although identification of the archaeological material was only undertaken to family level, many of the species discussed by Stokes are represented, generally strongly, within families present in the assemblages.

Both the archaeological analysis and ethnographic data suggest that netting and the use of basket traps are likely to have been important throughout the sequence at Tangarutu, with angling likely increasing in importance in the latter stage of occupation. Stokes (n.d.) lists species in the Scaridae, Chaetodontidae and Labridae as being caught using basket traps (Table 9.2), and these taxa featuring prominently throughout the Tangarutu sequence. Eels can be caught using a number of techniques, including netting, but the fact that they are nocturnal while the other taxa present are diurnal suggests that perhaps another method was employed, unless nets were left set overnight. Several authors report the use of basket traps to capture eels ethnographically throughout the Pacific (Masse 1986; Goto 1990; Davidson et al. 2002), although Stokes (n.d.) does not list eels among the taxa captured using this method. The fact that eel snaring is documented for Rapa (Stokes n.d.) means that this also must be considered a possible method of capture at Tangarutu. The data from Tangarutu suggests an increase in angling late in the sequence, as evidenced by the concurrent increase in Scaridae and Pomacentridae stated by Stokes to be taken with *tuitui* hooks, and the appearance of candlenut fish hooks as discussed above. Species in the Serranidae and Lethrinidae, most commonly caught with a hook and line, also increase in the upper portion of the site.

While the Stokes data and the information obtained in 2002 provide a good fit with the high-ranking taxa from Tangarutu, there are several taxa mentioned in these accounts that are either absent or rank very low in the assemblages. The first of these are the small silversides, *kiamo/Pranesus insularum*. These are either wholly absent, or accounted for by some of the bones that were not in the reference collection. Silversides are very small, slender fish, growing to an average length of around 10 cm (Randall 2005), so their absence may be due to taphonomic factors. The goatfish, *kature/Parupeneus fraterculus*, while present, is scarce at Tangarutu. Mullids have very fragile bones (Bilton 2001), so there may again be a taphonomic explanation for this. However, Stokes (n.d.) notes that these fish are caught seasonally in November, so it is also possible that their absence reflects seasonality or sampling issues. Other fish mentioned in the ethnographic records that do not feature prominently, but are present in the Rapa assemblages, are the carangids *matu/Pseudocaranx cheilio* and *maaki/Serioloa lalandi*, the acanthurid *mama/Acanthurus leucopareius*, the kyphosids *Nanue, pakavai* and *karamami* (*K. bigibbus*), the exocoetid *marara/Cypselurus* sp., and the siganid *parapo'atu/Siganus argenteus*. Taphonomic factors may account for the low numbers of exocoetids and siganids, and the seasonal nature of fishing on Rapa may also provide an explanation for the low occurrence of many of these taxa in the archaeological record. There are also several low-ranking taxa in the assemblages that are not mentioned in the ethnographic information (see Table 9.3).

Stokes spends considerably less time discussing marine invertebrates, but comparison of his information with the midden record from Tangarutu is revealing nevertheless. The species of molluscs listed by Stokes (n.d.) are virtually all present in the Tangarutu midden sample, outwardly signalling some sort of constancy through time. However, the relative importance of various taxa seems to alter dramatically. At the most general level, there seems to be a clear swing away from gastropods as the most frequently collected and consumed class of mollusc to a reliance on bivalves by the time of Stokes' observations. While most of the bivalve species that Stokes lists *are* present in the Tangarutu sample, numbers are very low, with only occasional, and sometimes solitary, specimens. Viewed another way, this shift from gastropods to bivalves can equally be seen as a shift from hard-shore to soft-shore species. This may reflect changing coastal conditions, with increased progradation in modern times, but more data would be required to fully assess that possibility.

That things may have been more complex than a straightforward transition from rockier to more sediment-rich littoral zones is suggested by the pattern seen in *Chama* and *Spondylus*. Both of these genera cement the lower valve to a hard substrate, and as such are associated with

Table 9.3. Fish taxa not mentioned by Stokes (n.d.).

Family	Common/Rapan name if known
Belonidae	needlefishes
Exocoetidae	flyingfishes
Holocentridae	squirrelfishes
Aulostomidae	trumpetfishes
Lethrinidae	emperorfishes
Kyphosidae	rudderfishes
Mugilidae	mullets
Siganidae (*Siganus argentus*)	rabbitfishes (parapuata – small/moroa – large)
Bothidae	lefteye flounders
Monocanthidae	filefishes
Diodontidae	porcupinefishes

hard shores. However, the numbers of *Chama* are low in the Tangarutu sample – despite a preponderance of hard-shore taxa – and according to Stokes were important at the time of his data collection. *Chama pacifica* is represented by only 12 fragments in E1 and a single fragment in E2. Of these 13 fragments, three are heavily worn and cannot have entered the site with a live mollusc inside. There are no *Spondylus* sp. remains in the Tangarutu sample at all.

At present, the same comparisons between Stokes' information and the results of midden analysis cannot be extended to the crustaceans or echinoderms. Species-level data would be required on both sides. It is apparent that brachyuran crabs and urchins have been a fairly stable part of the diet through time on Rapa, although the midden data at least would suggest that their importance has fluctuated.

Dynamic environments and culture through time

Drawing together the archaeological and ethnographic data on marine exploitation on Rapa, there is clear evidence of change through time, as on other East Polynesian islands, such as Aitutaki (Allen 2002). Some of these changes are quite specific, such as those seen in fishing technologies, whereas others concern the broad nature of marine resource use. Environmental change is surely playing a part, and a palaeoecological investigation of the marine-derived faunas through time demonstrates the subtlety of the dynamics of Anarua Bay. Following a discussion of clear trajectories of change in the exploitation of marine resources, we assess, as a whole, the various lines of evidence from both fish and invertebrate fauna to look at shifts in the nature of Anarua Bay and human interaction with it through time.

Elements of change

The rising importance of angling

The archaeological data from Tangarutu point to a fishing strategy focused mainly on the use of nets and basket traps, however the ethnographic data provided by Stokes (n.d.) indicates that the use of hook and line had overtaken these methods in more modern times. While Stokes' information does provide details of netting and basket trapping, he points out that these methods have either fallen into disuse, or are seldom practised. Indeed, he speaks of their occasional use as a 'fad'. The ethnographic data collected by Anderson in 2002 also emphasises hook and line fishing. This would appear to be a continuation of the changes that can be seen in the latter stage of occupation at Tangarutu, where a rise in angling is clearly evident and fish hooks appear in the archaeological record.

The rise in importance of soft-shore niches

As detailed above, the rocky/hard-shore-dominated molluscan assemblage from Tangarutu contrasts with the information on molluscan foods supplied by Stokes (n.d.). Stokes (n.d.) does mention hard-shore species, and soft-shore bivalves are present in the Tangarutu assemblage, so nothing as dramatic as a faunal turnover is evidenced. Even so, the transition from a hard-shore gastropod-dominated focus to a soft-shore bivalve one speaks to a change in the nature of littoral habitats and with it, approaches to the gathering of shellfish. Such shifts in species availability are apparently not uncommon in the context of Anarua Bay, and will be discussed further below.

Shifts in the composition of fish catches

While there is a considerable amount of stability in the taxa commonly exploited at Tangarutu, the changes in relative abundance of these taxa throughout the archaeological sequence are quite pronounced. The implications of these changes in terms of ecology and fishing strategies will be considered below. The archaeological data show a reliance on Scaridae at initial occupation, lasting throughout Level I and extending into the base of Level II, although giving way somewhat to Muraenidae at this stage. Above Spit 13, in the mid section of Level II, there is a dramatic increase in the occurrence of Chaetodontidae, rising from 7% of the assemblage at the base of that level to 23%, with Scaridae numbers dropping to only 6% of the assemblage. Muraenidae ranks second in terms of relative abundance throughout Level II. The uppermost level of the site sees further change, with Chaetodontidae numbers decreasing and an increase in Serranidae in the bottom half of the level. This changes again in the top half of the level, with Scaridae returning to the position of top-ranking taxon.

<u>Shifts in the composition of molluscan assemblages beyond hard/soft shore</u>

While the hard-shore/soft-shore dichotomy between the archaeological and ethnographic records is distinctive, a number of more subtle changes can be detected within hard-shore assemblages of the Tangarutu sample. Figure 9.5 shows the relative proportions of the four major mollusc species, spit by spit, for squares E1 and E2. There are clear spatial differences in deposition between E1 and E2, despite broadly similar changes. However, the strong stratigraphic patterning in the deposits also validates interpretations of change through time.

Although sample sizes differ widely between spits, this percentage-based view of composition still highlights some noteworthy patterns. *Nerita morio* is clearly dominant in the uppermost spits, with *Gafrarium pectinatum* and then *Clypeomorus batillariaeformis* taking over in relative importance from spits 3–6 in E1, and 3–7 in E2. The limpet *Cellana tahitensis* makes the strongest contribution from spits 7 to 13 in E1, and in Spit 14 in E2. Below this, *Nerita morio* is again the most important species in E1, with *Clypeomorus batillariaeformis* dominating the much smaller samples towards the base of E2.

These differences in relative abundance of molluscan taxa in the Tangarutu midden hint at environmental transformations considerably more subtle than swings between hard-shore and soft-shore environments. *Nerita morio*, *Cellana tahitensis* and *Clypeomorus batillariaeformis* are all microphagous algal grazers on hard surfaces. Indeed, *Gafrarium pectinatum* is the only major mollusc species represented in the Tangarutu assemblage that is not an algal grazer. This hints that the changes in community structure and composition may be related to shifts in the nature and coverage of algae in Anarua Bay. Overlying the urchin and fish data adds increasing weight to this argument.

<u>Algae: The impact of putative changes in the lowest trophic level at Anarua Bay</u>

The shell data from Tangarutu clearly show shifts in the local abundance and availability of algal-grazing taxa through time. However, algae feeders also characterise the urchin sample and a notable proportion of the fish assemblage from Tangarutu. As with the Tangarutu shell, changes in the availability and exploitation of various taxa through time are conspicuous (see Figure 9.6).

The urchin *Diadema setosum* grazes on non-crustose filamentous algal turfs within and below the intertidal zone. Studies have shown that *Diadema* spp. is one of the major grazers and bioeroders in inshore contexts, with herbivorous fish, such as those in the Scaridae, Acanthuridae and Pomacentridae, playing a relatively minor role in overall algae removal in habitats conducive to urchins (Foster 1987). Indeed, following a mass die-off of the Caribbean *Diadema antillarum*, algal cover in Jamaican inshore habitats increased markedly to a mean of 95% coverage of recorded substrates (Hughes et al. 1987; see also Liddell and Ohlhorst 1986). *Diadema* density in inshore habitats appears to be influenced by a number of features. In terms of the physical nature of preferred habitats, *Diadema* prefers coarser sediments, shunning muddy or silty substrates, dislikes complex reef architecture, and avoids high-wave-energy areas (Foster 1987; Dumas et al. 2007). *Diadema* further prefers micro- over macroalgae, avoiding *Sargassum*

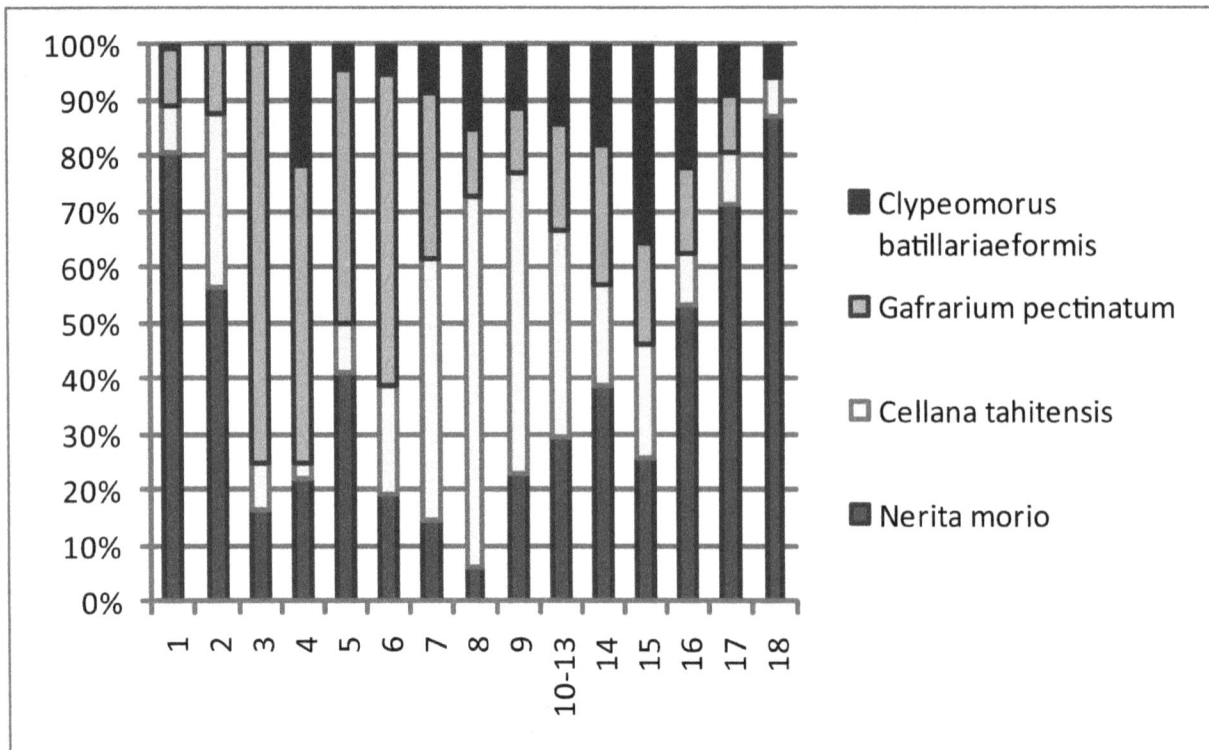

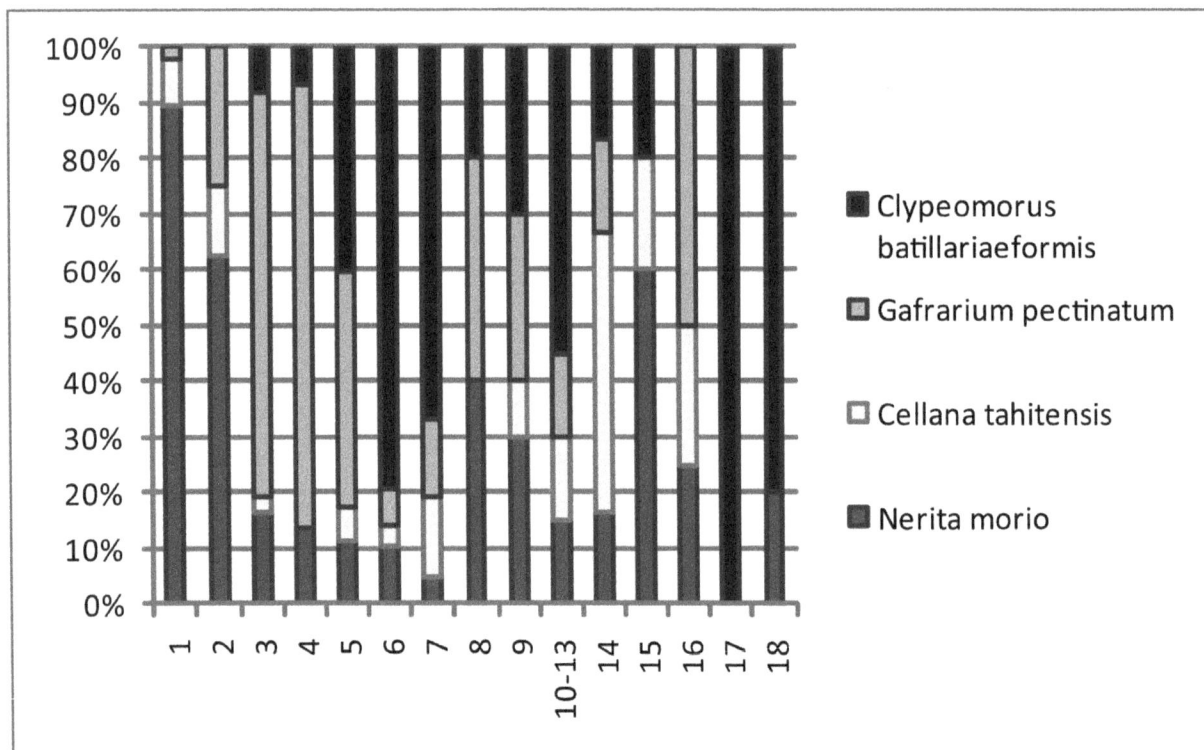

Figure 9.5. Percentage graphs of the four major shell species in squares E1 (above) and E2 (below). Note that the E2 sample is generally smaller and below spits 10–13 is negligible.

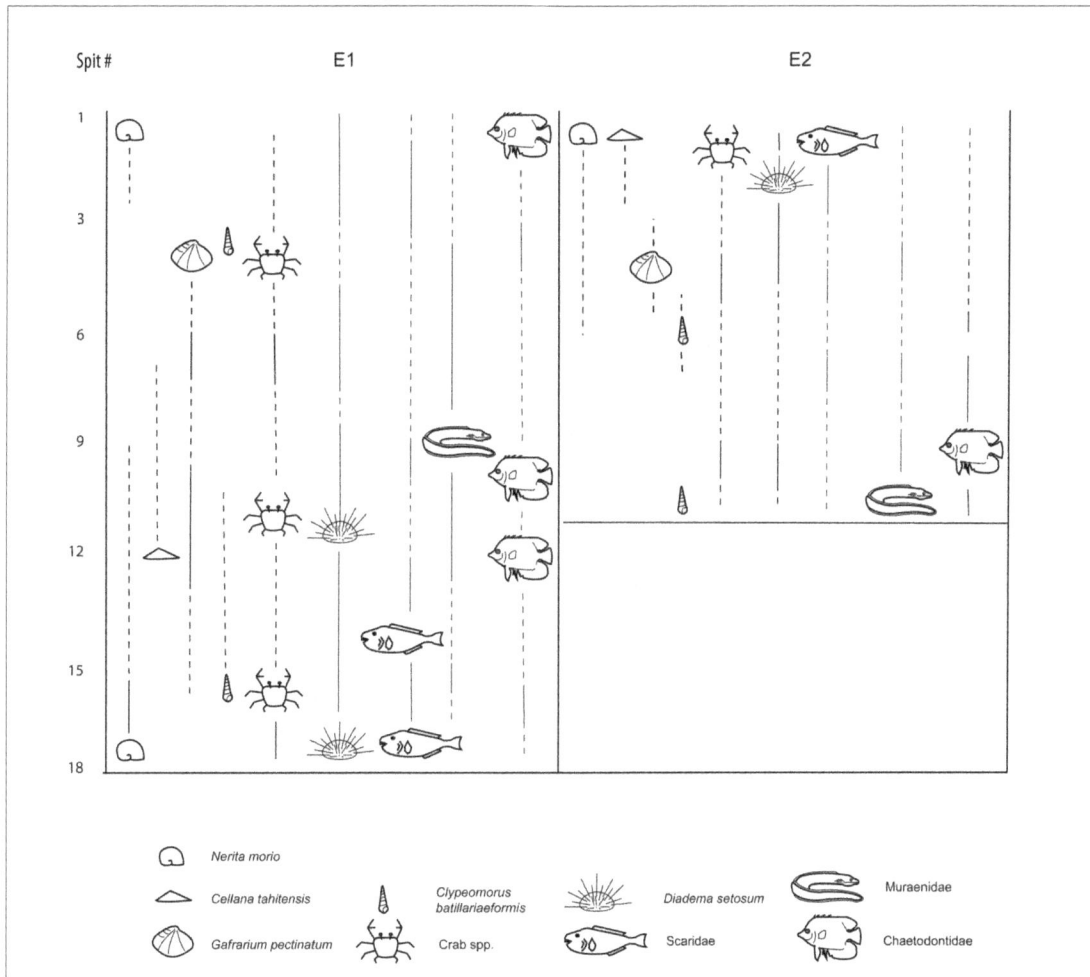

Figure 9.6. Schematic representation of abundances of major marine taxa represented in Tangarutu squares E1 and E2 by depth. Taxon picture placements indicate a high level of occurrence at that depth, with solid lines indicating a sustained presence and dotted lines indicating lower levels of occurrence.

in particular (Shunula and Ndibalema 1986; Dumas et al. 2007). A number of studies have also demonstrated that *Diadema* densities are considerably higher in impacted/fished inshore habitats than in protected, unfished areas (McClanahan et al. 1994; Carreiro-Silva and McClanahan 2001). Indeed, *Diadema setosum* is one of the most conspicuous inhabitants of heavily altered dynamite-fished coral-reef habitats (KS pers. obs.).

Diadema remains are present throughout most of the Tangarutu sequence, although there are marked changes in frequency through time. In terms of the invertebrate record, the lowest urchin densities in squares E1 and E2 coincide with the dominance of the bivalve *Gafrarium tumidum* (see Figure 9.6), suggesting that Anarua Bay at these times hosted greater expanses of fine-grained soft sediments than was ordinarily the case. The highest densities of *Diadema* remains tend to occur with high levels of *Nerita morio* and/or *Cellana tahitensis* (see Figure 9.6), all affirming the presence and productiveness of micro-algal turfs in Anarua Bay through many parts of the early, middle and later Tangarutu sequence.

The strong showing of invertebrate taxa favouring algal environments is also reflected in the fish taxa present. Given the low numbers of identified fish relative to invertebrates, the small sample of fish taxa cannot be taken to present a comprehensive picture of inshore stocks or habitats. Nevertheless, a presence-absence approach to the occurrence of certain taxa at different depths, such as butterflyfishes and damselfishes, allows us to draw some conclusions regarding the nature of inshore niches at particular times in Anarua Bay. Algal-grazing fish taxa dominate the Tangarutu assemblage, with grazing taxa including scarids, pomacentrids and chaetodontids, supplemented by the fluctuating presence of serranids and the more consistent presence of eels in the Muraenidae and Congridae. While there are 13 species in the Chaetodontidae known from Rapa, the only species-level identification provided by Randall and Sinoto (1978) is *vaiti/C. smithi*, which is known to aggregate in areas of algae-covered rocky reefs (Lieske and Myers 1994). As previously discussed, both *komokomo/L. vaigiensis* and *nganga/S. fasciolatus*, associated ethnographically with the candlenut fish hooks, also inhabit areas of abundant algal growth.

Collectively, the fish, urchin and shell data from Tangarutu suggest that Anarua Bay supported extensive hard-substrate habitats, which in turn supported substantial non-crustose micro-algal turfs. However, the oscillations in the frequencies of different algal-grazing mollusc taxa, grazing *Diadema* urchins and fish taxa hint that parallel changes may have occurred in the structure and extent of these local algal turfs. A closer look at the ecological literature on tropical marine algal-grazing communities offers some insights into how community structure can be altered in the face of rather subtle changes or disturbances – including by fishing.

As might be expected, various of these algivorous creatures compete with each other – sometimes aggressively. *Stegastes* spp. are known collectively as 'farmer damselfish', as they carefully maintain and 'weed' patches of non-crustose algae in a territory that they defend vigorously (Russ 1987). While microalgal-grazing molluscs may be tolerated in *Stegastes* territories, *Diadema* urchins are not (Lieberman et al. 1984; Klumpp and Polunin 1989). Similarly, *Stegastes* may patch-share with acanthurids, which are poorly represented in the Tangarutu sample, but will ward off scarids. Given that in some zones of the Tangarutu deposits quantities of *Diadema* and pomacentrid remains occupy the same stratigraphic position (e.g. the upper spits of E1), it would appear that distinct, non-overlapping zones of the rocky reef are being exploited by the local residents. But the ecological literature suggests that such discrete zones are likely to change in extent and community composition through time.

Grazing strongly effects the distribution of algal species (Lieberman et al. 1984; McClanahan et al. 1994). This is especially the case where grazers selectively target algal taxa that do not dominate in biomass terms (Hatcher and Larkum 1983). Pomacentrids will selectively remove non-favoured algae from their territories, thus increasing the biomass of favoured species (Klumpp and Polunin 1989), while intensive urchin grazing promotes algal growth, keeping the standing crop trimmed, thereby decreasing 'self-shading' (Klumpp and McKinnon 1989). It stands to reason that the removal of algal grazers in any numbers, whether urchins, fish or even numbers of grazing molluscs, will impact on the growth rate and taxonomic composition of algal communities, and indeed such effects have been demonstrated.

The above discussion stresses natural processes and indirect human impacts that may be contributing to changes in exploited marine resources through time at Tangarutu. However, we also know that the forms of human impacts themselves were changing. The late-stratigraphic association of the candlenut fish hooks demonstrates tangibly that fishing technologies transformed through time, and this might be expected to have had an impact on the landed assemblage.

The subtle oscillations through time in the community structure and balance of algal-grazing herbivorous marine taxa, both vertebrate and invertebrate, suggest that environmental and habitat parameters were also constantly shifting. Some of this variability may relate to strictly environmental factors such as variations in storm frequency, wave intensity and cycles of erosion and progradation. However, the marine ecology literature would suggest that high levels of occurrence of the urchin *Diadema setosum* are likely to be the product of at least moderate human fishing pressure on marine communities within Anarua Bay (see McClanahan et al. 1994; Carreiro-Silva and McClanahan 2001). Although it is presumed that the rise in *Diadema* densities in tandem with fishing pressure was largely due to the removal of urchin predators in the system (e.g. McClanahan 1998), it is also likely that the greater availability of food following the removal of herbivorous algal-grazing fish, particularly within the Scaridae, Acanthuridae and Pomacentridae (Foster 1987), promoted growth in urchin populations.

In a similar vein to the relationship between fish and urchin population structure and abundance, the relationship between levels of crayfish (*Panulirus pascuensis*) exploitation and urchin abundance may turn out to be linked. A link between heavy exploitation of the urchin predator *Panulirus* and a rise in urchin numbers has been established (Tegner and Levin 1983). At present, this relationship cannot be assessed from the Tangarutu sample; species-level identification of the crustacean remains would be required.

High levels of *Diadema* urchin grazing have been found to alter significantly the composition of organisms that compete with algae (Sammarco 1980, 1982). Not only is coral recruitment hindered by urchin grazing, but the diversity of fleshy algae, polychaete worms, encrusting coralline algae, filamentous greens and foraminifers is reduced, with some groups being virtually excluded (Sammarco 1980). This scenario has flow-on implications for the structure and composition of herbivorous vertebrate and invertebrate communities, as well as for those creatures that prey on them.

The consistent presence, and even more so the sporadically high abundance, of *Diadema setosum* remains within the Tangarutu deposit indicates that Anarua Bay was not only subject to fishing pressure, but that the various trophic levels and competing species within them were constantly adjusting to intra-community and environmental pressures. The respective roles of grazing gastropods, urchins, crustaceans, eels and various species of herbivorous and predatory fish in the Anarua system varied as different species and classes jostled for survival and dominance.

Humans and marine resources at Anarua Bay

The archaeological and ethnographic records offer some insights into how humans impacted this dynamic ecosystem through time. The relationship between densities of *Diadema* urchins and fishing pressure has been discussed above, but an argument for depletion of the standing stocks of Scaridae due to overfishing in the early part of the sequence could perhaps be advanced. This family is present throughout the sequence, though it is probable that the species targeted changed through time. The ethnographic data for differing capture methods for different species of scarid provided by Stokes (n.d.) and the increase in Scaridae at the end of the sequence, concurrent with the appearance of the candlenut fish hooks, would tend to support this.

Overall, the picture of marine resource use by the occupants of Tangarutu shelter through time is one of flexibility. Resource-switching is frequent, probably reflecting concomitant changes in inshore habitats and resources. Strategies employed for food capture seem to be general enough that a wide range of taxa is accessible at any given time, yet flexible enough to allow such resource-switching if local marine conditions and communities change. Both these facets of subsistence behaviour are also in evidence in the ethnographic record. The fish and eel capture technologies described by Stokes, as well as the roster of captured species, show that a balance was maintained between more generalist capture strategies, such as the use of weirs, nets and basket traps, and very targeted strategies, such as the use of candlenut hooks, to capture *Leptoscarus vaigiensis*.

A closer comparison of the archaeological and ethnographic records also reveals that resource-switching in a Rapan context was not always simply a matter of economic expediency – at least it is not always explained as such. As noted by Stokes, many of the species of mollusc seen by locals as 'inedible' were abundant in midden deposits. Eels feature prominently in the assemblage from Tangarutu throughout the sequence, and are also present in the assemblage from Akatanui 3. Sharks, while low ranking in terms of relative abundance, are also present in both assemblages. The capture of both eels and sharks was still in evidence during the time Stokes (n.d.) collected his ethnographic data. However, the information collected by AA during the 2002 field season indicates that neither sharks nor eels are taken today. Rapans consider shark repugnant and eels tapu. Thus, shifts in resource procurement and consumption also appear to have a cultural dimension, with ideas about food sources changing markedly through time.

Conclusion

In the two-way traffic of human-environmental interactions seen at Anarua Bay there occurred active modifications in traditional Polynesian ways of life. Many of the resources so important elsewhere in Polynesia were not available to Rapans, and new strategies and solutions had to be consciously developed. Such creative problem solving is clearly evidenced in the Tangarutu fish-hook assemblage, where traditional working techniques are applied to novel materials. A further potential way of solving the problem of the lack of availability of traditional raw materials would have been to import them – a solution seen elsewhere in Polynesia (Weisler 1993). There is no evidence that such action was ever pursued by Rapans.

Cultural innovation can typically be understood as a creative reconfiguration of traditional practice; ideas do not emerge from nowhere, but from the knowledge base already present in a given society (e.g. see Bijker 1987; Hickman 1995). As such, innovation often represents incremental change rather than a complete disjuncture (Kroeber 1948:360). Thus, while the candlenut fish hooks recovered from Tangarutu appear as a cultural novelty, they have strong technological parallels with traditional Polynesian fish-hook manufacture in other materials.

Technological innovations do not follow trajectories, but rather *create* them (Bijker and Law 1992; Szabó 2005:93), and given the late provenance of the Tangarutu hooks it appears that developing solutions to living in a Rapan environmental context was an ongoing and reciprocal process between population and environment (Kennett et al. 2006) throughout prehistory.

Notes

1. Juvenile specimens of *Pinctada margaritifera*, with a maximum width of ca.12 mm, have been recorded in the Tangarutu shell midden, but there is no indication that specimens of the size and robusticity required for fish-hook manufacture were locally available.
2. Several crayfish mandibles were seen during excavation at E1 and E2, Tangarutu, but they were not identified in the retained samples.

References

Allen, M. 2002. Resolving Long-Term Change in Polynesian Marine Fisheries. *Asian Perspectives* 41(2):195–212.

Anell, B. 1955. *A Contribution to the History of Fishing in the Southern Seas*. Studia Ethnographica Upsaliensia IX, Uppsala.

Bagnis, R., Mazellier, P., Bennett, J. and Christian, E. 1974. *Fishes of Polynesia*. Landsdowne Press, Melbourne.

Barratt, G. 1988. *Southern and Eastern Polynesia*. Volume 2 of *Russia and the South Pacific 1696–1840*. University of British Columbia Press, Vancouver.

Best, E. 1929. *Fishing Methods and Devices of the Maori*. Dominion Museum Bulletin 12, Wellington.

Bijker, W.E. 1987. The Social Construction of Bakelite: Toward a theory of invention. In: Bijker, W.E., Hughes, T.P. and Pinch, T.J. (eds), *The Social Construction of Technological Systems*, pp. 159–187. MIT Press, Cambridge MA and London.

Bijker, W.E. and Law, J. 1992. Do Technologies Have Trajectories? In: Bijker, W.E. and Law, J. (eds), *Shaping Technology/Building Society: Studies in Sociotechnical Change*, pp. 17–19. MIT Press, Cambridge MA and London.

Bilton, M. 2001. *Taphonomic Bias in Pacific Ichthyoarchaeological Assemblages: A Marshall Islands Example*. Unpublished MA thesis, Department of Anthropology, University of Otago.

Buck, P. 1954. *Vikings of the Sunrise*. Whitcombe and Tombs, Christchurch.

Cardona, M. and Clayton, W. 1999. The Algal Community of the Farmer Damselfish, *Stegastes fasciolatus*, at Three Sites in Fiji and the Kingdom of Tonga. *Bios* 70(2):71–75.

Carreiro-Silva, M. and McClanahan, T.R. 2001. Echinoid bioerosion and herbivory on Kenyan coral reefs: the role of protection from fishing. *Journal of Experimental Marine Biology and Ecology* 262:133–153.

Davidson, J., Leach, F. and Sand, C. 2002. Three thousand years of fishing in New Caledonia and the Loyalty Islands. In: Bedford, S., Sand, C. and Burley, D. (eds), *Fifty Years in the Field: Essays in Honour and Celebration of Richard Shutler Jr's Archaeological Career*. New Zealand Archaeological Association Monograph 25:153–164.

Dumas, P., Kulbicki, M., Chifflet, S., Fichez, R. and Ferraris, J. 2007. Environmental factors influencing urchin spatial distributions on disturbed coral reefs (New Caledonia, South Pacific). *Journal of Experimental Marine Biology and Ecology* 344:88–100.

Emory, K.P., Bonk, W.J. and Sinoto, Y.H. 1968. *Fishhooks*. Bernice P. Bishop Museum Special Publication 47, Honolulu.

Fishbase 2007. *Leptoscarus vaigiensis*. http://filaman.ifmgeomar.de/Summary/SpeciesSummary. php? ID =4360 &genusname =Leptoscarus&speciesname=vaigiensis

Foster, S.A. 1987. The relative impacts of grazing by Caribbean coral reef fishes and *Diadema*: effects of habitat and surge. *Journal of Experimental Marine Biology and Ecology* 105:1–20.

Goto, A. 1990. Prehistoric Hawaiian fishing lore: An integrated approach. *Man and Culture in Oceania* 6:1–34.

Hatcher, B.G. and Larkum, A.W.D. 1983. An experimental analysis of factors controlling the standing crop of the epilithic algal community on a coral reef. *Journal of Experimental Marine Biology and Ecology* 69:61–84.

Hickman, L.A. 1995. Techniques of Discovery: Broad and Narrow Characterizations of Technology. In: Pitt, J.C. (ed), *New Directions in the Philosophy of Technology*, pp. 207–218. Kluwer Academic Publishers, Dordrecht, Boston and London.

Hughes, T.P., Reed, D.C. and Boyle, M-J. 1987. Herbivory on coral reefs: community structure following mass mortalities of sea urchins. *Journal of Experimental Marine Biology and Ecology* 113:39–59.

Johannes, R.E. 1981. *Words of the Lagoon: Fishing and Marine Lore in the Palau District of Micronesia*. University of California Press, Berkeley, Los Angeles and London.

Kennett, D., Anderson, A., Prebble, M., Conte, E. and Southon, J. 2006. Prehistoric Human Impacts on Rapa, French Polynesia. *Antiquity* 80:340–354.

Kirch, P.V. and Yen, D.E. 1982. *Tikopia – The Prehistory and Ecology of a Polynesian Outlier*. Bernice P. Bishop Museum Bulletin 238, Honolulu.

Klumpp, D.W. and McKinnon, A.D. 1989. Temporal and spatial patterns in primary production of a coral-reef epilithic algal community. *Journal of Experimental Marine Biology and Ecology* 131:1–22.

Klumpp, D.W. and Polunin, N.V.C. 1989. Partitioning among grazers of food resources within damselfish territories on a coral reef. *Journal of Experimental Marine Biology and Ecology* 125:145–169.

Kroeber, A. 1948. *Anthropology: Race, Language, Culture, Psychology, Prehistory*. Second edition. Harcourt, Brace and World Inc., New York and Burlinghame.

Liddell, W.D. and Ohlhorst, S.L. 1986. Changes in benthic community composition following the mass mortality of *Diadema* at Jamaica. *Journal of Experimental Marine Biology and Ecology* 95:271–278.

Lieberman, M., John, D.M. and Lieberman, D. 1984. Factors influencing algal species assemblages on reef and cobble substrata off Ghana. *Journal of Experimental Marine Biology and Ecology* 75:129–143.

Lieske, E. and Myers, R. 1994. *Coral Reef Fishes. Indo-Pacific & Caribbean including the Red Sea.* Princeton University Press, New Jersey.

Masse, W.B. 1986. A millennium of fishing in the Palau Islands, Micronesia. In: Anderson, A. (ed), *Traditional Fishing in the Pacific: Ethnographical and Archaeological Papers from the 15th Pacific Science Congress.* Pacific Anthropological Records, no. 37 pp. 85–119. Department of Anthropology, Bernice P. Bishop Museum, Honolulu.

McClanahan, T.R. 1998. Predation and the distribution and abundance of tropical sea urchin populations. *Journal of Experimental Marine Biology and Ecology* 221:231–255.

McClanahan, T.R., Nugues, M. and Mwachireya, S. 1994. Fish and sea urchin herbivory and competition in Kenyan coral reef lagoons: the role of reef management. *Journal of Experimental Marine Biology and Ecology* 184:237–254.

Poupin, J. 1996. Crustacea Decapoda of French Polynesia (Astacidea, Palinuridea, Anomura, Brachyura). *Atoll Research Bulletin, April* 442:1–114.

Poupin, J. 1998. Crustacea Decapoda and Stomatopoda of French Polynesia (Dendrobranchiata, Stenopodidea, Caridea, Thalassinidea and Stomatopoda, with additions to Astacidea, Palinuridea, Anomura and Brachyura). *Atoll Research Bulletin, September* 451:1–62.

Randall, J.E. 2005. *Reef and Shore Fishes of the South Pacific: New Caledonia to Tahiti and the Pitcairn Islands.* University of Hawai'i Press, Honolulu.

Randall, J.E. and Sinoto, Y.H. 1978. Rapan Fish Names. *B.P. Bishop Museum – Occasional Papers* XXIV, 15:291–306.

Rensch, K.H. 1988. *Fish Names of eastern Polynesia.* Pacific Linguistics Series C – no. 106, ANU, Canberra.

Russ, G.R. 1987. Is rate of removal of algae by grazers reduced inside territories of tropical damselfishes? *Journal of Experimental Marine Biology and Ecology* 110:1–17.

Sammarco, P.W. 1980. *Diadema* and its relationship to coral spat mortality: grazing, competition, and biological disturbance. *Journal of Experimental Marine Biology and Ecology* 45:245–272.

Sammarco, P.W. 1982. Effects of grazing by *Diadema antillarum* Philippi (Echinodermata: Echinoidea) on algal diversity and community structure. *Journal of Experimental Marine Biology and Ecology* 65:83–105.

Shunula, J.P. and Ndibalema, V. 1986. Grazing preferences of *Diadema setosum* and *Heliocidaris erythrogramma* (Echinoderms) on an assortment of marine algae. *Aquatic Botany* 25:91–95.

Skinner, H.D. 1942. A Classification of the Fish-hooks of Murihiku – with notes on allied forms from other parts of Polynesia. *Journal of the Polynesian Society* 51:208–221.

Stokes, John F.G. n.d. Ethnology of Rapa. Manuscript on file. Bernice P. Bishop Museum, Honolulu.

Stokes, John F.G. 1955. Language in Rapa. *Journal of the Polynesian Society* 64:315–340.

Szabó, K. 2007. An assessment of shell fishhooks of the Lapita cultural complex. In: Anderson, A.J., Leach, B.F. and Green, K. (eds), *Vastly Ingenious*, pp. 227–241. Otago University Press, Dunedin.

Szabó, K. 2005. Technique and Practice: Shell-working in the Western Pacific and Island Southeast Asia. Unpublished PhD thesis, The Australian National University, Canberra.

Tegner, M.J. and Levin, L.A. 1983. Spiny lobsters and sea urchins: analysis of a predator-prey interaction. *Journal of Experimental Marine Biology and Ecology* 73:125–150.

Walter, R. 1991. Fishing on Ma'uke: An Archaeological and Ethnographic Study of Fishing Strategies on a Makatea Island. *New Zealand Journal of Archaeology* 13:41–58.

Walter, R. 1988. Archaeology Beyond the Reef: Koperu Fishing on Ma'uke. *Archaeology in New Zealand* 31(4):222–227.

Weisler, M. 1993. Long Distance Interactions in Prehistoric Polynesia: Three Case Studies. Unpublished PhD thesis, University of California, Berkeley.

10

Palaeobotany and the early development of agriculture on Rapa Island

Matiu Prebble

Department of Archaeology and Natural History, The Australian National University, and Nga Pae o te Maramatanga Trust, University of Auckland, New Zealand, matiu.prebble@anu.edu.au

Atholl Anderson

Department of Archaeology and Natural History, The Australian National University

Introduction

Palaeobotanical studies in tropical and subtropical Remote Oceania have established broad records of vegetation and climate change covering the past 6000–7000 years. They mostly have used sedimentary deposits from large, closed depositional basins such as high-elevation bogs or volcanic caldera lakes in the tropical Hawaiian Islands (Selling 1948; Selling in Massey 1979; Athens and Ward 1993) and subtropical Easter Island (Flenley 1979; Flenley and King 1984; Flenley et al. 1991), and numerous bogs in northern New Zealand. While these records have provided good regional pictures of vegetation change, including the effects of fire and increases in seral pollen and charcoal particles that have been interpreted as indicating human activity, rarely have they revealed more direct evidence of the introduction of agriculture. As a result, many palaeoecological studies that argued the case for or against evidence of agriculture, and its associated age, came under criticism for a lack of direct proxies of human activity, imprecise chronology, and the sensitivity of the biological proxies to natural disturbance (e.g. Anderson 1994, 1995; McGlone and Wilmshurst 1999).

For these and other reasons, views on the significance of agriculture to Remote Oceanic colonisation have tended to be polarised. Kirch and Green (2001), primarily on linguistic grounds, argued that when humans first expanded into Remote Oceania around 1000 BC they brought a complete roster of domestic animals (dog, pig and fowl), plus commensal rats and other small vertebrates, and oceanic crops including taro (*Colocasia esculenta*), yam (*Dioscorea* spp.), bananas (*Musa* spp.) and breadfruit (*Artocarpus altilis*). These were thought essential to the colonisation process, particularly in the islands east of the Solomon Group, where the number of plant genera and the natural distribution of economic plants declines dramatically, forming what Jones and Spriggs (2002) have described, somewhat extravagantly, as a 'green desert'. The necessity of agriculture to colonisation of Remote Oceania has been questioned (Davidson and Leach 2001) and asserted (Addison 2008) on nutritional grounds.

The concept of 'transported landscapes' (*sensu* Anderson 1952) has been employed by Kirch (1982, 2002) to emphasise the motivation behind ecological transformation of islands in Remote Oceania, in which a newly occupied ecosystem was rapidly reshaped to operate in much the same way as the homeland ecosystem. Anderson (2003, 2009a, b), conversely, has argued that the distribution of oceanic crops and domestic animals is very patchy across Remote Oceania, especially in the more remote islands, and that this is a function of the increasing difficulty of transportation eastward and southward. As a result, some islands had no access, or limited access, to agriculture, and others in which it was well established by the historical era had probably created such landscapes by long-term accumulation of taxa rather than during initial colonisation. Of course, some islands, largely by geographical circumstance, were able to institute agricultural economies from almost the beginning of settlement.

Models aside, it remains the case that the importance and sources of vegetable carbohydrates to early populations in Remote Oceania are poorly known and enigmatic, even in very well-studied instances, such as in Vanuatu where stable isotope records from the Teouma burial site on Efate indicate that around 800 BC the diet was dominated by terrestrial and marine protein sources, with only a minor contribution from vegetable foods (Valentin et al. 2010). Whether these were of introduced taxa is uncertain because the identification of starch grains, found on stone tools and pots from archaeological deposits in Vanuatu (Horrocks and Bedford 2005; Horrocks et al. 2009), is open to question on several methodological grounds (e.g. Hardy et al. 2009; Wilson et al. 2010).

Turning to the role of terrestrial palaeoecological records, it is necessary to acknowledge that, in tropical regions especially, the nature of fossil proxies, the state of preservation, the degree of chronological resolution and the completeness of the deposits can be highly variable. Prebble and Wilmshurst (2009) argued that multiple proxies for human activities, primarily agricultural production, are more often preserved in sites close to where such activities occurred and that site selection is critical for addressing questions about agricultural expansion. In considering active taro (*Colocasia esculenta*) gardens built on deep organically rich sedimentary deposits underlying Maunutu Swamp on Rimatara (Austral Islands, French Polynesia), they found that such deposits needed to be treated like archaeological profiles, as the various proxies accumulated under different sets of conditions influenced by human activity. Artefacts, including garden stakes and animal tethers, from the Rimatara deposits emphasised the inherent archaeological character of the deposits. The physical mixing of sedimentary strata by digging, both in the past and present, has increased the likelihood of obtaining unreliable radiocarbon chronologies. Despite these potential problems, the array of fossil proxies available from these sites can reveal important insights into the changing biodiversity of garden systems.

Rapa Island offers a case study of the initiation of agricultural activity in the early phase of human colonisation. Kennett et al. (2006), Prebble and Dowe (2008) and work as yet unpublished have identified multiple proxies for ecological change from Tukou Swamp, on Rapa, spanning the past 7500 years. Preserved *Pandanus tectorius* syncarps and high concentrations of *Pandanus* pollen characterise the pre-human swamp record. A coastal swamp forest developed on top of estuarine sediments between 2000 BC and AD 1000. In the past 750 years, unprecedented increases in charcoal particle concentration and seral fern spores, plus a rapid decline in *Pandanus* pollen, indicate early forest clearance. A number of plant species became extinct, including a palm tree (Prebble and Dowe 2008). The interpretation of cultural activity after about AD

1200 is strengthened by the near-synchronous appearance of pollen from the introduced plant cultigen *Colocasia esculenta,* and of weeds indicative of the expansion of agricultural activity.

Here we extend this analysis by outlining the availability of indigenous food plants and historical evidence of agriculture, and then focus on the development of agriculture at Tukou Swamp by examining the chronology of introduction and expansion of *Colocasia* across the site. We highlight some of the complexities and the potential of palaeobotanical analyses for understanding the role of agriculture in the colonisation of one of the more remote islands of Remote Oceania.

Indigenous carbohydrate sources on Rapa

Understanding the extent of indigenous carbohydrate-rich plants (i.e. those plants that have not been introduced) is one means of assessing the potential of indigenous food sources to sustain growing human populations. The natural distribution of some of the main oceanic root and tree crops is limited to the Western Pacific. Most of the remote Pacific Islands, including Rapa, lacked bananas (*Musa* spp.), yams (*Dioscorea* spp.), taro (*Colocasia esculenta*), rhizome crops including the gingers (e.g. *Curcuma longa* and *Hedychium flavescens*) and tree crops including *Syzygium malaccense*, *Burkella obovata*, *Barringtonia edulis* and *Inocarpus fagifera*. What, then, was available on Rapa?

Based on a summary of the pre-human fossil data from Tukou Marsh (Prebble unpublished data) and survey data of the existing flora of Rapa (Meyer 2002), the variety of indigenous carbohydrate, fat and sugar sources from vascular plants available at initial human arrival can be defined (Table 10.1). Which species would have provided an adequate staple food or supplement to an otherwise protein-rich diet at the advent of people cannot be deduced from this list, and some plants that potentially served as important fat and carbohydrate sources are missing from it. This is merely a partial guide to the potential sources.

Coconut trees are indigenous on many islands in Remote Oceania at least as far east as Tubuai in the Austral Archipelago, but they are not indigenous to the Hawaiian Archipelago or Rapa (Prebble and Dowe 2008). The distribution of coconut trees is partly controlled by rainfall, as fruits remain unviable in areas or in years with less than 1000 mm annual precipitation (Fosberg 1956). The distribution of pigs in the initial colonisation of Remote Oceania may have been limited in part by the distribution of coconut, particularly the domesticated, large-fruited trees. Most of the wild-type indigenous coconuts that were established on the more remote Pacific Islands would have possessed very small fruits with minimal endosperm (Prebble and Dowe 2008) and they may not have provided an adequate source of protein, vegetable fat and carbohydrate to sustain pig husbandry and growing human populations (Kirch 2002). Dried coconut meat (endosperm) from domesticated coconut consists of around 20% carbohydrate, including soluble sugars, sucrose and starch (Jayalekshmy and Mathew 1990). Large servings to satisfy daily requirements of carbohydrate would require domesticated large-fruit varieties. Coconuts occurred rarely (Chapter 2), if at all, prehistorically on Rapa.

Another carbohydrate and fat source would have been provided by the seeds of *Pandanus tectorius*, which, from fossil pollen, appears to have been very common across the remote Pacific Islands including Rapa, particularly on islands that lacked mangroves in estuaries and backswamps. Generally, *Pandanus* forms monospecific stands with a sedge/herb-dominated understorey (Ash and Ash 1984), but no 'true' mangrove species occur east of the Cook Islands (Ellison 1991). On Rapa, *P. tectorius* appears to prefer a mangrove habitat, forming dense stands along the few margins of tidal flats where human activity has not been prominent. Other *Pandanus* species may be indigenous to Rapa; for example, St. John (in Fosberg and St. John

Table 10.1. Fossil taxa with potential food value identified from Tukou deposit in pre-human aged sediments older than AD 900 are listed. Also listed are the possible representatives of the fossil taxa found in the modern flora of Rapa and the biogeographic affinity of taxa. Extant indigenous taxa without fossil records that may provide some food value are also listed (data sources from Meyer 2002).

Fossil taxa	Family	Indigenous representatives in modern flora	Biogeographic affinity	Carbohydrate, sugar and fat sources
Angiopteris	Angiopteridaceae	*Angiopteris rapensis, A. longifolia*	Indo-Pacific/endemic	pith and root
Apiaceae	Apiaceae	*Apium australe*	Indo-Pacific	root
Arecaceae: Arecoideae type	Arecaceae, subfamily Arecoideae, tribe Iguanurinae	extinct	?	fruit and young shoots?
Celtis	Ulmaceae	*Celtis pacifica*	Indo-Pacific	fruit
Coprosma	Rubiaceae	*Coprosma cookei, C. rapensis Coprosma* spp. Possible extinct species	Pacific/endemic	fruit
Cyathea	Cyatheaceae	*Cyathea affinis, C. medullaris, C. rapensis, C. stokesii*	Indo-Pacific/endemic	pith
Cyperaceae-	Cyperaceae	numerous species	pan-tropical, cosmopolitan	root
Davallia/ Histiopteris	Davalliaceae/ Dennstaedtiaceae	numerous species	pan-tropical, cosmopolitan	root
Dryopteridaceae	Dryopteridaceae	numerous species	pan-tropical	root
Freycinetia	Pandanaceae	*Freycinetia arborea*	Indo-Pacific	fruit and root
Hypolepis	Dennstaedtiaceae	*Hypolepis punctata, H. tenuifolia*	Indo-Pacific/Pan-tropical	root
Malvaceae undifferentiated	Malvaceae	numerous species	?	shoots?
Monolete Psilate	?	numerous species	?	root
Monolete undiff.	?	numerous species	?	root
Myrtaceae undiff.	Myrtaceae	numerous species	?	fruits?
Pandanus cf. *tectorius*	Pandanus	*Pandanus tectorius*	Indo-Pacific/endemic?	fruits
Pteris	Pteridaceae	numerous species	?	root
Polypodiaceae	Polypodiaceae	numerous species	?	root
Rubiaceae	Rubiaceae	numerous species	?	fruit?
Trilete Psilate	?	numerous species	?	root
Trilete undiff.	?	numerous species	?	root
Urticaceae/ Moraceae	Urticaceae/Moraceae	numerous species	?	shoots?

Extant indigenous taxa without fossil records

Tetragonia tetragonioides	Aizoaceae	*Tetragonia tetragonioides*	temperate/sub-tropical Pacific	leaves
Capparis sp.	Capparaceae	*Capparis sp.*	Indo-Pacific	fruit
Leptecophylla rapae	Ericaceae	*Leptecophylla rapae*	endemic	fruit
Vaccinium rapae	Ericaceae	*Vaccinium rapae*	endemic	fruit
Astelia rapensis	Liliaceae	*Astelia rapensis*	endemic	fruit
Macropiper puberulum	Piperaceae	*Macropiper puberulum*	indigenous	fruit

1934) recorded 13 species of *Pandanus* in 1934, although Smith (1979) and Stone (1988) suggest many of these are simply varieties of *P. tectorius*. In examining the genus on Tahiti, Stone (1988) could not discount the human introduction of additional *Pandanus* species or *P. tectorius* varieties and this also may have been the situation on Rapa.

Fern roots and pith could have served as an important substitute for tropical root crops at the time of initial Polynesian arrival, especially in sub-tropical or temperate environments (McGlone et al. 2005). Tree-fern pith (particularly of *Cyathea medullaris*) is still consumed on Rapa (Freddy Riaria pers. comm. 2002) and it might have provided an important starch source, given the likely former abundance of these trees at the time of human arrival on the island. Other ferns with large piths include *Marrattia* spp. and *Angiopteris* spp., the latter having a restricted distribution in Remote Oceania. It is unclear how abundant ground ferns including *Histiopteris incisa*, *Dryopteris* sp. and *Dicranopteris linearis* were prior to human arrival, but with cultural burning these plants would have become widespread along forest margins, providing an abundant but rudimentary starch source.

Algae may have provided a source of carbohydrate to the first colonists of Remote Oceania. Algal material is found in some archaeological middens in Remote Oceania (e.g. Kirch et al. 1995), but the extent of consumption is unclear (Conte and Payri 2006). Small fragments of algae were found in the Tangarutu deposit on Rapa, but the possibility that they were blown in cannot be excluded.

Historical observations of agriculture on Rapa

Although nobody landed from the *Discovery* in 1791, the vessel spent some time close inshore and Vancouver thought Rapa conspicuous by the lack of *Cocos nucifera* (described as the 'cocoanut' palm). He did not see any *Colocasia esculenta* pondfield production systems, perhaps because observation of the inland valleys was obscured by thick vegetation along the coastline. Vancouver (in Lamb 1984:215) recorded that:

> ... they [the islands] were chiefly clothed with shrubs and dwarf trees. Neither the plantain [Musa spp.] nor other spontaneous vegetable productions common to the inhabited tropical islands, presented themselves.

Menzies (in Shineberg 1986:65–66) noted some plants that were used in the clothing of Rapan men who came out to the ship:

> The only cloathing they wore were a narrow slip of cloth made from the bark of a tree [prob. *Talipariti tiliaceum* syn. *Hibiscus tiliaceus* but potentially *Broussonetia papyrifera*] which passed round their waist & between their legs, this cloth appeard to be a very scarce article amongst them as many of them had not sufficient of it to cover their nakedness, it was evident however that they generally wore something for that purpose, as some of them had bunches of leaves of a species of Dracena [prob. *Cordyline fruticosa*] suspended to a girdle round their middle for that intention.

Only three or four plant species may be inferred from the descriptions provided in both accounts. More general comments were made regarding the status of the island's vegetation, including the impoverished state of the forests and absence of coconut palms, as summarised here by Menzies (in Shineberg 1986:67–68):

> The valley round the bottom of the Bay is tolerably pleasant when compard with other parts of the Island being scattered over with Bushes among which we could perceive the habitations of the Natives & some little signs of Cultivation, the hills behind & on the South Side of it appeard thinly coverd with some verdure & here & there wooded with some scrubby Trees particularly in the hollow places between

---

the hills, but they seemed of no great magnitude. Towards the North end the hills are not so rugged & rocky but ascend with a smooth surface coverd with grass & destitute of Trees or bushes of any kind. We observed no Cocoa Nut Trees [*Cocos nucifera*] anywhere on the Island.

In 1924, Stokes (m.s. Group 2 Box 7.1) spent most of the year compiling an ethnography of the island but also recorded the recollections of the islanders and made many useful observations of agricultural systems. He remarks that 'in early days cultivation was confined almost entirely to the wet-land taro'. He quotes Davies (1827), who in 1826 'inspected the plantations of taro, which were all laid out, and display a degree of skill and contrivance evinced in nothing else we saw'. He also quotes Davies who found that: 'One coconut palm was reported as present from a drift and was not recognized by the local natives.' Stokes (m.s. Group 2 Box 7.2) also reported in 1924 that:

> There are now many coconut palms scattered through the island, which though vigorous and grown to a fair height, according to report, drop their fruit before it matures. Other introductions at Tupuaki, on the northern coast, are said to have borne fruit that was 'killed by thunder' perhaps to a cold storm. A white man who has tried to grow coconuts for commerce at the northern end of the harbor apparently abandoned the venture as a failure. It is evident that Rapa is too cold for the successful production of coconuts, but that the palms will grow in many parts of the island, and will occasionally produce fruit. The non-recognition of the coconut palm by the natives, reported by Davies, points very suggestively to the fact that the palm was unknown to the ancestors of the Rapa people.

Of taro agriculture, Stokes provides an intriguing account of hand digging of pondfields, commenting that 'most taro cultivation was done with the bare hands a method still used to a remarkable extent. Once the pond is prepared, the hand is really more suitable for taro cultivation than any tool.' He also suggests that many areas of the island 'are dry and well-suited for the cultivation of sweet potato, which though present in the early days, was evidently of very little importance'. He goes on to comment on the cultivation of other crops:

> Opinions differ as to the cultivation of bananas. Of other useful plants, there seem to have been cultivated only koali (gourd) and aute (paper mulberry). Seeds of the gourd are set in the ground with little preparation, and the plants are left to look after themselves. The growing of aute has been given up, but apparently in former days it was definitely cultivated. A dry-looking hill slope bordering the shore at Aupapa, Angairao Bay, is said to have been an aute field; the patches are small, narrow, irregular terraces following the contour of the land. At the bottom of the slope the soil is retained by a rough stone wall.

The benchmark for botanical observations of the island comes from an unpublished report of the B.P. Bishop Museum Expedition of 1934 by Harold St. John and Raymond Fosberg, but they made little comment about the varieties of plant cultigens or about the state of gardens on the island. Additional information about the distribution and character of modern taro pondfields is provided by Bartruff et al. in Chapter 13. From interviews with local gardeners in 2002, Motley (unpublished data) recorded 25 varieties of *Colocasia esculenta* known on Rapa. Of these, 20 were regarded as Polynesian introductions and the remaining five of recent introduction. A number of varieties are known to have been lost as a result of disease and probably neglect over the past decade, including 10 Polynesian varieties, as well as two recent varieties. Around six varieties are currently grown for *popoi*, a type of cooked taro formed by pounding and fermenting to create a thick paste that can be stored.

Study site: Tukou Marsh, Ha'urei Harbour, Rapa

Ha'urei Harbour on Rapa represents the remnant of one of the original volcanic calderas formed during island orogeny in the Pliocene. The shallow bathymetry of the harbour suggests the entire area was exposed during glacial lowstand sea levels. The exposed reef at the harbour entrance, backed by calcareous reef shoals along the interior, currently restricts wave action from the sea, to the degree that the harbour could be described as a lagoon. At low tide, fine-grained sediments of a mixture of alluvial sediments, shell and coral detritus are exposed to reveal three prominent bird's-foot river deltas and tidal flats extending out from the high-tide shoreline (see Figure 10.1). Water depth surrounding the Tapuki (Tapu'i) basaltic islet in the centre of harbour is no more than 1.5 m below low-tide level.

Shoreward of the exposed deltaic sediments is a series of levee-backed marshes positioned at Tukou, Matataa and Aitoke (Figure 10.2). All of these sites have been heavily modified by human activity and grazing by cattle, horses and goats. A map of Ha'urei Harbour sketched in 1864 by John Vine Hall (1869) shows the position of a number of coastal pondfield systems

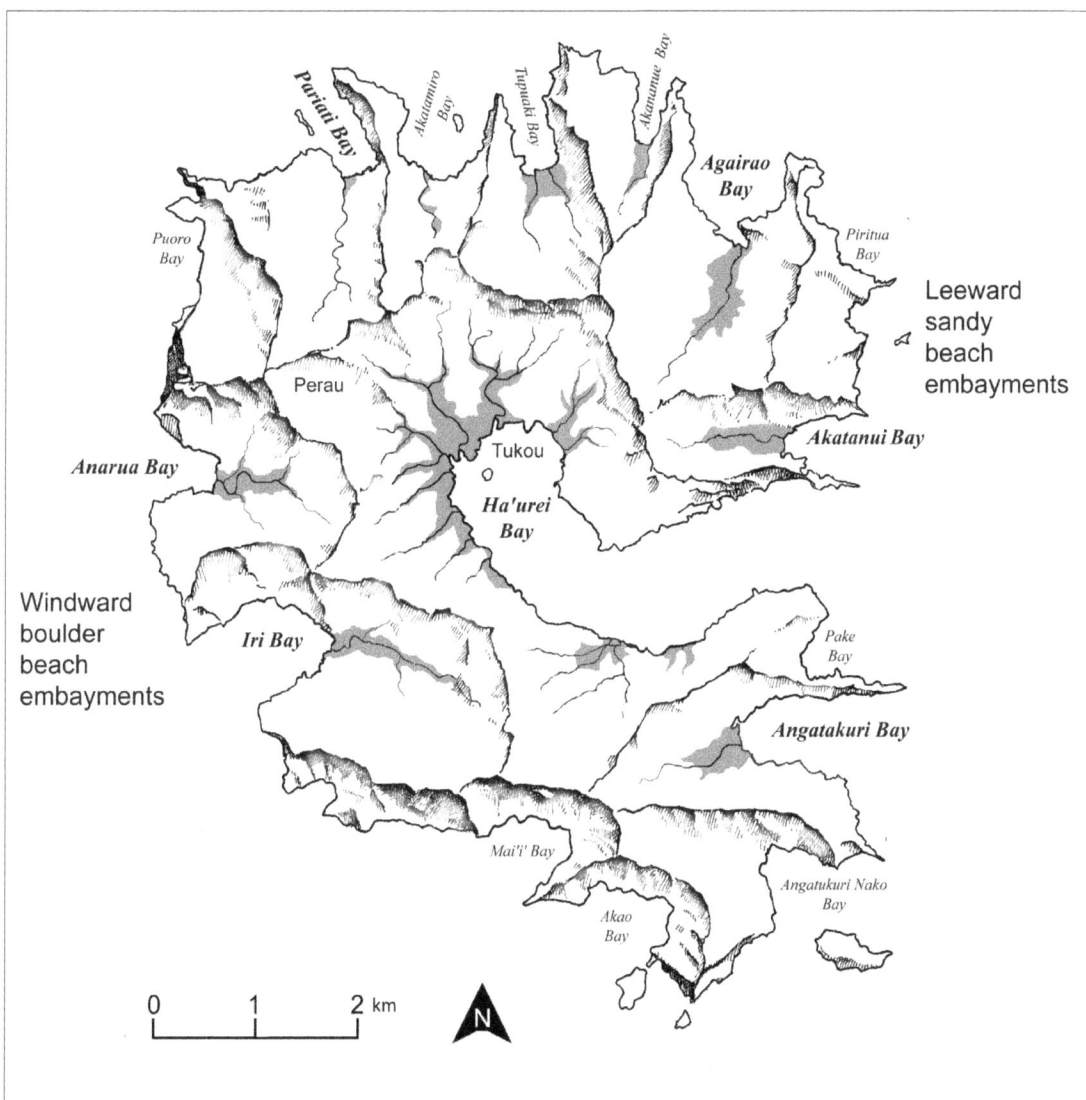

Figure 10.1. Map of Rapa showing the main windward boulder-beach and leeward sandy-beach embayments. The position of Tukou and the highest mountain peak (Perau, 650 m) are also indicated.

that were used for *Colocasia esculenta* cultivation (Figure 10.2). Remnant dry-stonewall terrace features are now interspersed within many of the levee-backed marshes, along the margins of riverbeds, or along the present shoreline. At certain points, these marshlands extend more than 100 m inland and rise to an elevation of more than 2 m. On the most inland side, these marshes are bound either by river levees or steeply rising embankments of the surrounding hill slopes that appear to have been cut by a previous, probably mid-Holocene, sea-level high stand (Figure 10.3).

Tukou Marsh lies on the south side of the broadest river delta and associated tidal flats of Ha'urei Harbour. The marsh is banked and divided by two smaller prograding river channels, forming two waterlogged depressions. The central-most marsh depression was chosen for this palaeoecological study, and sediment cores were taken in 2002 (June–August). The modern marsh appears to have developed behind the southern levee of the main river, and the northern levee of the smaller river bounded the marsh to the south. The marsh extends from the estuarine shoreline, marked at high tide (ca. 0.4 m above mean sea level) by driftwood and estuarine detritus, ca. 135 m to the embankment of the surrounding hill slope. Below the embankment the marsh reaches a maximum elevation, based on laser transit measurements, of 3 m above the high-tide mark. The remains of an agricultural terrace complex rise an additional 50 cm or more above the marsh surface.

Overall, the climate on Rapa is subtropical to warm temperate. It receives around 2500–3000 mm annual rainfall, based on measurements taken from Ha'urei village, also at sea level (Rapa Meteo unpublished data). Tukou is fed by two permanent streams that drain the eastern catchment of the Perau–Namuere range, with water flow gradients averaging above 30 degrees. Hydrological data are unavailable for this catchment.

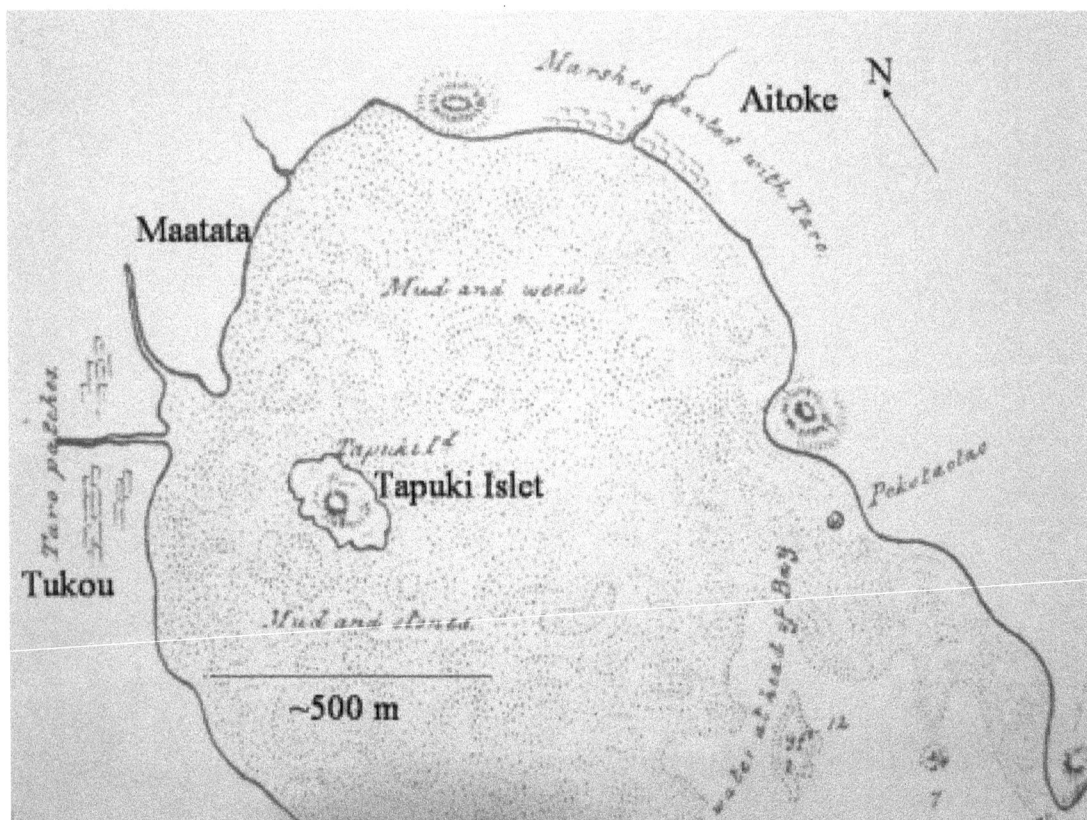

Figure 10.2. Section of a sketched map of the head of Ha'urei Harbour, Rapa, by John Vine Hall (1869a), showing the location of the main marsh systems ('*Taro patches*'), including Tukou.

Figure 10.3. Approximate position of mid-Holocene high stand maximum marine incursion after sea-level stabilisation at Tukou (black line). Up to ca. 3 m of organic rich sediment has accumulated at this location above present high tide/spring tide line, marked by the interface between the marsh and the tidal flats.

The vegetation of the waterlogged marsh surface has been described by Prebble (In press). The marsh is currently dominated by introduced agricultural grasses (e.g. *Paspalum subjugatum*) and adventive herbs (e.g. *Commelina diffusa* and *Ludwigia octovalvis*), with some indigenous sedges (e.g. *Carex* spp.) and rushes (e.g. *Schoenoplectus subulatus* subsp. *subulatus*; some authors suggest that this may have been introduced to French Polynesia). The embankment on the periphery of the marsh is largely open grass with some naturalised *Syzgium jambos* and *Psidium* spp. trees (all in the Myrtaceae). Some indigenous trees are found at the site, including *Talipariti tiliaceum* syn. *Hibiscus tiliaceus* (Malvaceae) and *Metrosideros collina* (Myrtaceae). Hall's (1869) sketch of the site indicates that stone-wall terraces lined the upper portion of the marsh and were focused along the banks of the adjacent river channels. Some of these terrace features remain, but in a degraded state. Only one feral *C. esculenta* specimen was located at Tukou, with no other plant cultigens identified. The marsh is currently left for cattle and horse grazing.

Methods

Multiple profiling at Tukou Marsh

In order to determine the range of taphonomic processes affecting the pollen assemblages, and also the initial establishment of *Colocasia* agriculture and its spatial expansion from palynological and sedimentary proxies, a multiple profile approach was chosen. This allows for direct pollen stratigraphic correlation (*sensu* Clark et al. 1986). Due to the complexities of palynological analyses, multiple profiles are rarely analysed for palynological signatures. Instead, palynologists tend to either increase the temporal resolution of a single profile, or take single profiles in order to compare between individual depositional settings within a region. The multiple profile approach allows local or extra-local spatial variations in pollen representation to be examined in more detail (Dumayne-Peaty and Barber 1998). If a reliable absolute chronology is obtained, it also allows palynological signatures to be more precisely linked to stratigraphic processes, both spatially and chronologically.

Six cores were taken at 20 m intervals along a transect running through the centre of the marsh from the first core site (Core 1) at the shoreline to the embankment behind the marsh. The five cores were all taken with a D-Section corer. An attempt was made with each coring point to reach bedrock or a depth where compacted basal clays prevented further penetration. The relative position to high-tide sea level was determined from laser transit measurements. The main parameters of each core are outlined in Table 10.2.

Laboratory and numerical method

A composite stratigraphic diagram (Figure 10.4) was constructed using the program C2 Data Analysis version 1.6 (Juggins 2010). In this diagram, each core profile is vertically aligned according to relative sea level (at high tide) and its relative position from the original core site. Calibrated radiocarbon age ranges and the Bayesian depositional age/depth models are presented for each core in this diagram. Each model was processed using the program OxCal version 4.1 (Bronk Ramsey 2008). The palynological data for all of the Tukou Cores are presented in this

Table 10.2. Tukou Marsh multiple profile summary. Main features of each core are presented, including mean Bayesian ages for the key listed events. All ages were modelled using the program OxCal 4.1 (Bronk-Ramsey 2008) of calibrated radiocarbon determinations. Mid-point estimates refer to the average age of the mean Bayesian ages presented for each event recorded at Tukou. For more details of the radiocarbon chronology and event stratigraphy see Prebble et al. (In press).

Core features	Core 3	Core 6	Core 2	Core 5	Core 4	Core 1	Age
Depth of core (cm)	318	250	400	250	250	652	
Basal clay reached	yes	no	yes	no	no	yes	
Depth above high tide (cm)	300	243	196	161	111	20	
Distance from shoreline (m)	105	85	65	45	25	5	
number of AMS radiocarbon determinations	3	4	5	2	4	6	
Events							
Depth (cm) of post-European plant introduction	30–32	70–72	60–62	48–50	48–50	–	after AD 1825
Colocasia end (AD)	1685	1920	1852	1816	1554	–	AD 1800
Colocasia onset (AD)	1170	1392	1024	1286	1098	–	AD 1210
Earliest unprecedented Microcharcoal peak (AD)	1016	1117	1024	1073	1098	1193	AD 1105
Microcharcoal onset (BC/AD)	241	585	-130 (BC)	1073	1002	1193	pre-human arrival AD 1263
Pandanus decline >30% from peak (AD)	1016	1254	1510	1393	1376	1401	
Pandanus peak (AD)	550	1117	1364	1180	1287	1297	AD 957

same composite stratigraphic diagram. This examination of the Tukou core transect focuses on radiocarbon ages, charcoal particle concentrations, and *Pandanus* cf. *tectorius* and *Colocasia esculenta* pollen as key markers of forest clearance and agricultural expansion at the site. A more detailed analysis of all of the fossil data recorded at Tukou, including the chronological data, is in preparation.

Results

The palynological record of Tukou indicates that coastal *Pandanus* swamp forests expanded after about 500 BC in response to changing sedimentary conditions following a mid-Holocene sea-level high stand (Prebble unpublished data). Within or around the period represented from the basal ages of the Tangarutu archaeological sequence, certainly after AD 1000, between 50 cm and 120 cm of colluvial sediments accumulated at different rates across Tukou Marsh. This period is represented by a rapid increase in sedimentation comparable with the accumulation rates found from deposits in the other embayments (e.g. Akatanui, Anarua and Iri). The *Pandanus* pollen records (Figure 10.4) indicate that swamp forest declined consistently across the site within the past 1000 years. The stratigraphy and chronology of cores 1 to 6 from Tukou have been described in the context of coastal swamp forest development (Prebble unpublished notes). Here, we outline some of the key palynological indicators for human impact and attempt to further define the stratigraphy and chronology for each core. Following this, we explore each of the cores individually in order to define some of the key ecological responses to human impacts at Tukou.

Summary of palynological analysis of human activity at Tukou

The cores are divided into four palynological zones on the basis of the major vegetation changes. In the composite stratigraphic diagram (Figure 10.4) only the upper zone (IV) is marked. This zone has been divided into two subzones (IVa and IVb) on the basis of palynological marker taxa that represent the Polynesian (IVa, shaded in transparent light grey) and European periods (IVb, shaded in transparent dark grey). These subzones and the lower three zones are discussed in more detail in Prebble (unpublished notes).

Charcoal particles

The presence of high concentrations of charcoal particles in Zone IV of Core 1 is not directly tied to sedimentation or preservation. As a working hypothesis, it reflects human-induced burning at the site. In Zone IV of Core 1, counter to what might be expected, increasing charcoal concentrations overlap with increasing *Pandanus* pollen concentrations. These *Pandanus* peaks may be representative of one of the following: sediment compaction in the early part of the zone allowing for pollen to accumulate and become more concentrated with depth; or the opening of forest conditions allowing for more pollen deposition; or the possibility that *Pandanus* responds to burning by increased flowering and pollen production. The decline in charcoal signals in the later part of this zone also corresponds with a decrease in *Pandanus* pollen concentrations. This might represent a decrease in the amount of fuel available at Tukou after an initial period of burning.

The key problem identified from the analysis of the Core 1 data set is establishing the chronology for deforestation represented by *Pandanus* pollen decline and increases in charcoal particles alone. No radiocarbon dates were obtained from Zone IV sediments of Core 1, but the Bayesian depositional model of the radiocarbon ages that were obtained suggests that the base of Zone IV encompasses the radiocarbon chronology established from the archaeological record (indicated by the vertical grey bar within the age model histogram in Figure 10.4).

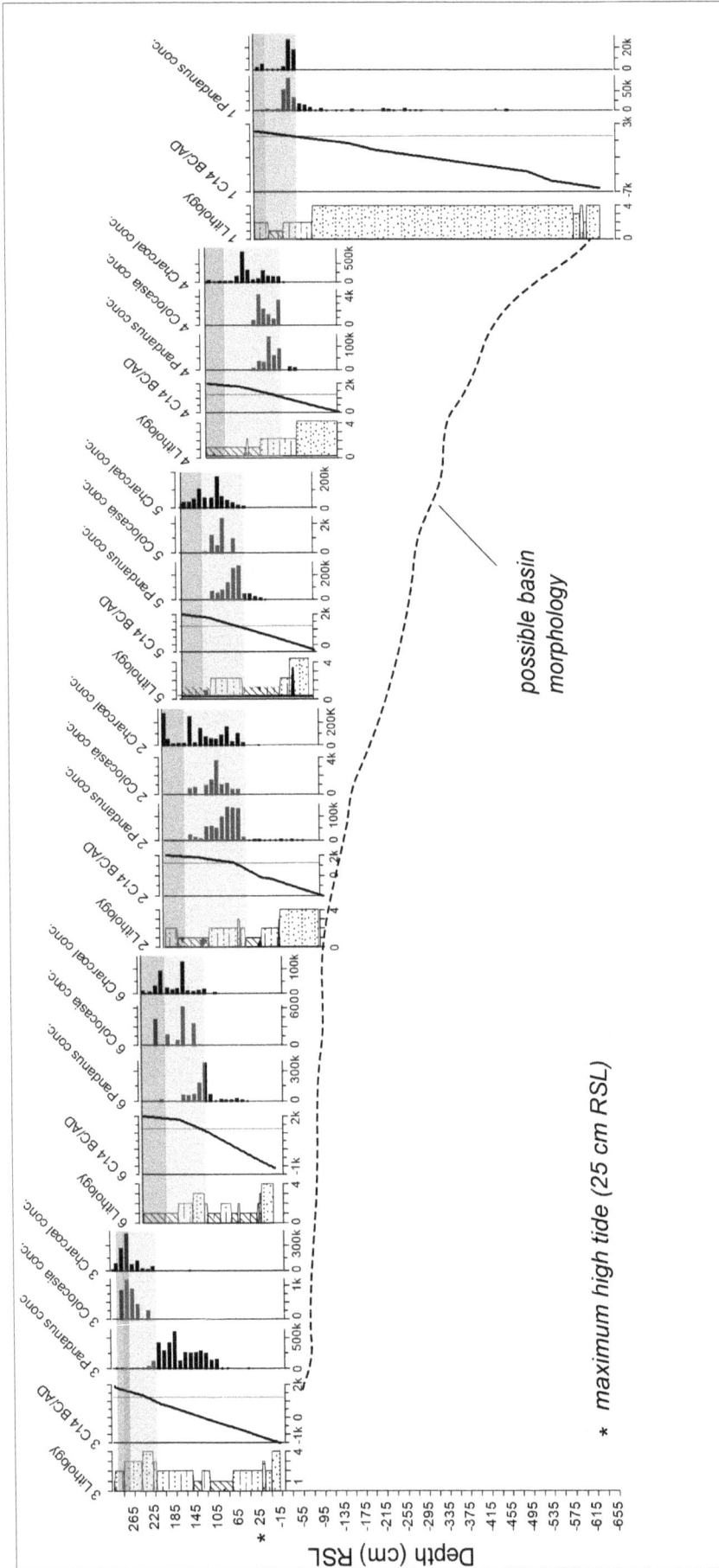

Figure 10.4. Composite stratigraphic diagram for Tukou Marsh, showing the mean Bayesian age models (BC/AD) and bar histograms of charcoal particles, *Pandanus* cf. tectorius and *Colocasia esculenta* pollen concentrations (per cm³). The lithology for each profile is shown, with four being coarse and one being fine sediment. An attempt was made to present the concentration data proportionally, with each single tick mark representing 200k charcoal particles (per cm³), 100k *Pandanus*, 50k *Cyperaceae* and 1k *Colocasia* pollen grains (per cm³). The stratigraphic alignment of each core is displayed, with the modern high-tide level marked at 25 cm relative to mean sea level (RSL). Only two subzones are distinguished on the basis of transitions in the palynological record. Zone IVa is shaded in transparent dark grey and Zone IVb shaded in transparent light grey.

More radiocarbon ages obtained from the five additional Tukou cores (cores 2–6) better establish the chronology of charcoal particle increases, particularly of microcharcoal. The chronology for the onset of microcharcoal particle concentrations identified from pollen concentrates has been modelled using radiocarbon interpolations based on the Bayesian paradigm and generated using the program OxCal 4.1 (see Table 10.2). The earliest age obtained for the initial appearance of microcharcoal particles comes from Core 2 in the centre of the marsh, established from a direct AMS date at 130 BC, with the youngest age determined from Core 1, at AD 1193. The concentration of microcharcoal particles also varies considerably across the site. The highest concentrations occur in Core 6 and concentrations overall are higher in cores 2–6 than in Core 1. Differential fuel loads across the site could explain this variation in microcharcoal concentrations, but the influence of tidal action might also have reduced the amount of particle accumulation. The intensity of human activity at the site is higher towards the inland part of the marsh where evidence for past agricultural activity is most apparent and this may also explain the spatial variation in microcharcoal concentrations.

The mean Bayesian ages for the onset of microcharcoal concentrations from all of the Tukou cores are consistently older than the earliest age determination obtained from the archaeological record of Tangarutu. All of the mean Bayesian ages for peaks in microcharcoal concentrations are recorded within the archaeological chronology established for Rapa. This is quite typical of charcoal profiles in Pacific swamps and it is usually held to represent sporadic low-level charcoal production resulting from infrequent natural fires, followed by abundant charcoal production with a substantially increased rate of ignition on the arrival of people. Thunder and lightning occur infrequently at any time of the year on Rapa and could ignite grass or scrub fires during dry seasons, although such an event has not been recorded.

It is often very difficult to distinguish microcharcoal particles from blackened woody tissue that develops in the reducing environment of estuarine water. The presence of charcoal particles radiocarbon dated from the base of the cores could thus indicate either that there was no burning (the black material not being charcoal), or that burning was part of the pre-human island ecosystem, or, indeed, that charcoal had been produced from an early but transient human visit. In the absence of other human indicators, or of the chemical determination of black particles as charcoal, caution must be observed.

Initiation of agriculture: Colocasia esculenta pollen records

Apart from charcoal particle increases, no plant cultigen pollen or any unequivocal palynological signatures of human presence were identified from Tukou Core 1. Pollen from the cultigen *Colocasia esculenta* was identified from each of the remaining five cores from Tukou, all within Zone IV. The presence of *Colocasia* pollen provides a more secure indication of human presence as it could only have been derived from introduced populations. The distribution of *C. esculenta* in Remote Oceania is restricted by oceanic barriers (Matthews 1995, 2004) and may also be limited by the lack of suitable hydrological environments for it to establish without human intervention. *C. esculenta* pollen has now been identified in numerous pollen records across the Indo-Pacific, suggesting the records from Rapa are not anomalous.

The composite stratigraphic diagram (Figure 10.4) shows that, like *Pandanus* pollen and microcharcoal particles, *C. esculenta* pollen concentrations are differentially represented across the site. The highest concentrations are found in cores 2 and 4 in the central part of the marsh, with the lowest concentrations found in the most inland core (Core 3). This trend could be explained by *Colocasia* cultivation activity whereby plants are actively prevented from flowering during cultivation, mainly by corm harvesting before flowering. *C. esculenta* is known to be a poor pollen producer, and it is relatively rare in the pollen record (e.g. Haberle 1994; Prebble unpublished data). The high concentrations of *C. esculenta* pollen represented in some cores may reflect a response to the increased seasonality of the more subtropical climate of Rapa. Alternatively, high *C. esculenta* pollen concentrations in sediments may reflect the high local presence of feral plant populations outside of immediate cultivation that may have been allowed to set flowers. One hypothesis is that this may have been an integral strategy in the early establishment of *Colocasia* crops, allowing for genetic exchange and the extension of cultivar diversity in an ecosystem different from the homeland of the first Polynesians to arrive on the island.

The mean Bayesian ages for the onset of *C. esculenta* pollen from cores 2–6 (see Table 10.2) all fall in an age bracket that overlaps the earliest age determination obtained from the archaeological record of Tangarutu (Chapter 11). Most of these mean ages are older than expected and this may reflect the loose chronological control for the first appearance of *C. esculenta* pollen in three of the five cores (cores 3, 4 and 5). The onset of *C. esculenta* in Core 2 is constrained by four AMS ages and may provide the most reliable age for the onset of cultivation on Rapa at 1024 AD, but this still appears to be older than expected.

None of the mean Bayesian ages are more than 200 years older than the earliest archaeological determination for the island. They could be correct. It is possible that the process of taro cultivation resulted in the mixing of sediments. Modern digging of wet-fields usually involves the turning of between 20 cm and 30 cm of topsoil and this process could have resulted in older organic material being incorporated into the planting horizon. Yet, it is apparent that no chronological inversions were noted among radiocarbon ages in any of the six profiles examined. This suggests that the swamp was continually accumulating sediment and organic materials and that if sediment mixing did occur, it was minimal.

With the exception of Core 4, all of the peaks in *C. esculenta* pollen occur in the latter part of Zone IVa. With a mean Bayesian age of AD 1231, the sample showing first appearance of *C. esculenta* pollen in Core 4 also has the highest concentrations. If this age is accepted, the early presence of high pollen concentrations of *C. esculenta* in the most shoreward core site might reflect the proposition, above, of high local presence of feral *Colocasia* populations outside areas of immediate cultivation. Later in the sequence, certainly by Zone IVb across most of the cores, *Colocasia* pollen drops out of the record, possibly representing a change in land-use practices at the site. It is possible that harvesting of *Colocasia* intensified to the point where both cultivated and feral plants were prevented from flowering. This could also represent the abandonment of taro field cultivation at Tukou, which was apparent by the time Hall arrived on the island in 1864. Another alternative is that with the introduction of feral grazing animals, including goats, cattle and horses, feral populations of *Colocasia* may have been browsed to the point where flowering was prevented. Few feral specimens survive on the island today and no flowers have been recorded or collected on the island by any visiting botanist (Jean-Yves Meyer pers. comm.).

Sedimentary deposits from other embayments on Rapa

Small sedimentary catchments are located at the base of windward boulder and leeward sandy beach embayments of the island (Figure 10.5; see Figure 10.1 for locations). The more deeply incised windward embayments are characterised by higher energy fluvial/alluvial systems, forming in places of extensive swamp deposits adjacent to abandoned *Colocasia esculenta* terraced pondfields. These swamps possess highly organic clay and silt deposits, preserving botanical remains. The sedge *Schoenoplectus subulatus* var. *subulatus* dominates the vegetation of most of these swamp sites. The swamp deposits were cored with the intent of reaching basal clays or bedrock from Akatanui (2 m deep Core 1; Figures 10.5 and 10.6), Iri (3 m deep Core 1; Figure 10.7) and Anarua (1.8 m deep Core 1; Figure 10.8). Magnetic susceptibility (K) measurements from these cores provide some indication of the extent of organic accumulation at each site. Radiocarbon ages were obtained from charcoal or black organic pieces found in the basal sediments of these cores, revealing 2σ ages of AD 1420–1460 (UCIAMS 2194), AD 620–1280 (ANU 12154), and AD 1190–1950 (ANU 12155) respectively. The radiocarbon date from Akatanui Core 1 corresponds to the archaeological chronology established from the Tangarutu rockshelter (Chapter 11) and suggests that these sediments were deposited during the early colonisation phase of the island. The age ranges of the two dates from Iri and Anarua are insufficient to indicate the precise timing of sediment deposition. The sediments found at the base of the 3 m core from Iri are lagoon sediments rich in marine diatoms (Jan Finn pers. comm. 2005), suggesting that the terrestrial organic sediments had accumulated at the site within the past 1000 years. An additional 2.5 m core was obtained and radiocarbon dated from an upland swamp deposit above Anatakuri Bay, at Otaikui (see Figure 10.9). The swamp appears to be formed behind a landslip and little evidence remains of any agricultural features. The vegetation of the swamp consists mostly of *Schoenoplectus*. A fragment of charcoal from the core gave a modern determination (ANU 12157), suggesting these sediments were recently deposited.

Figure 10.5. Photograph of Akatanui, showing the position of two rockshelters, the extent of abandoned agricultural terraces and the location of three coring locations (white dots), only one mentioned in the text. See Figure 10.1 for location of Akatanui Bay. Photograph D.J. Kennett.

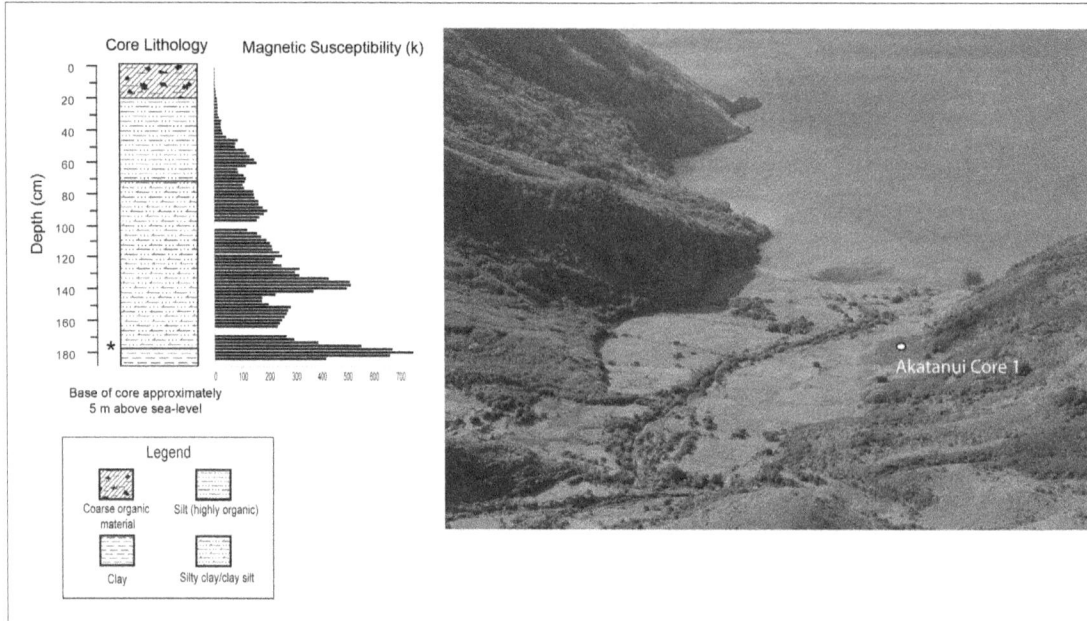

Figure 10.6. Sediment lithology and magnetic susceptibility measurements (K) of the Akatanui Core 1 are shown. *marks location of radiocarbon sample AMS ANU-12157 (charcoal).

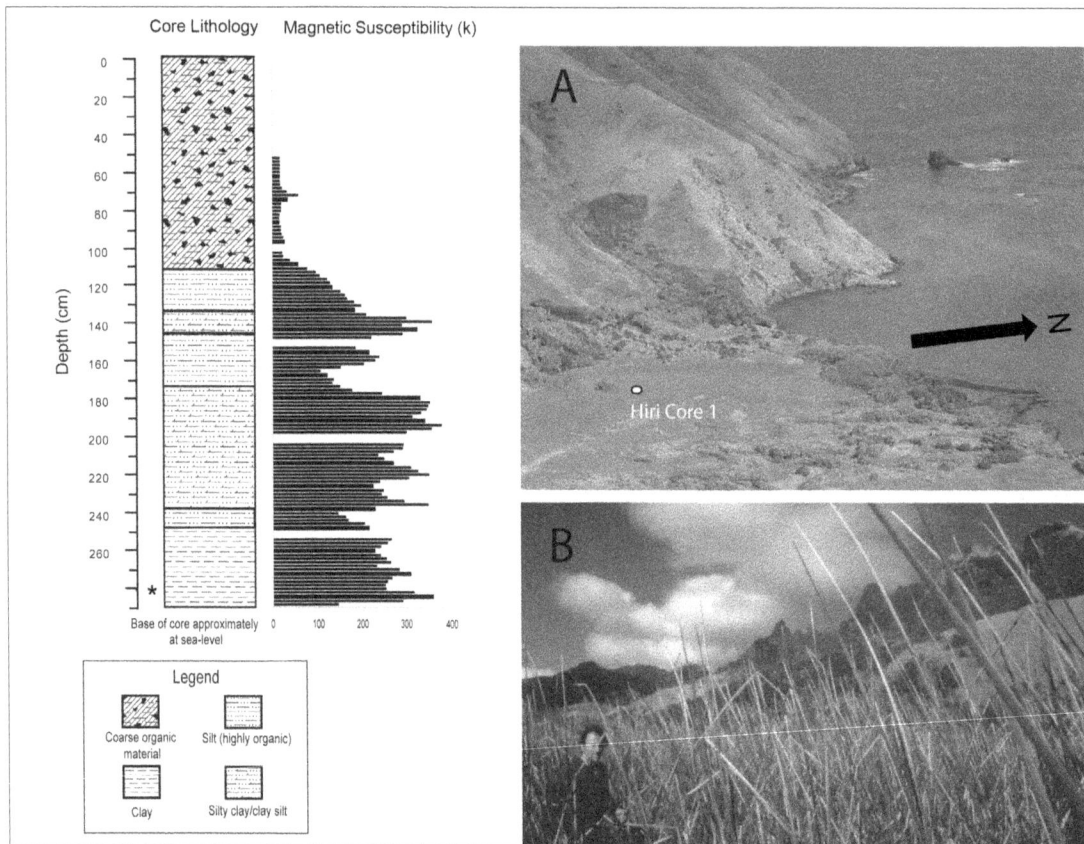

Figure 10.7. Sediment lithology and magnetic susceptibility measurements (K) of the Iri Core 1 are shown (left). To the right are photographs of Iri. A. shows the extent of Iri wetland and the position of Hiri Core 1 (white dot). B. shows the author at the core site among a dense stand of *Schoenoplectus subulatus* var. subulatus. *marks location of radiocarbon sample AMS ANU-12157 (charcoal). See Figure 10.1 for location of Iri Bay. Photographs D.J. Kennett and A. Anderson.

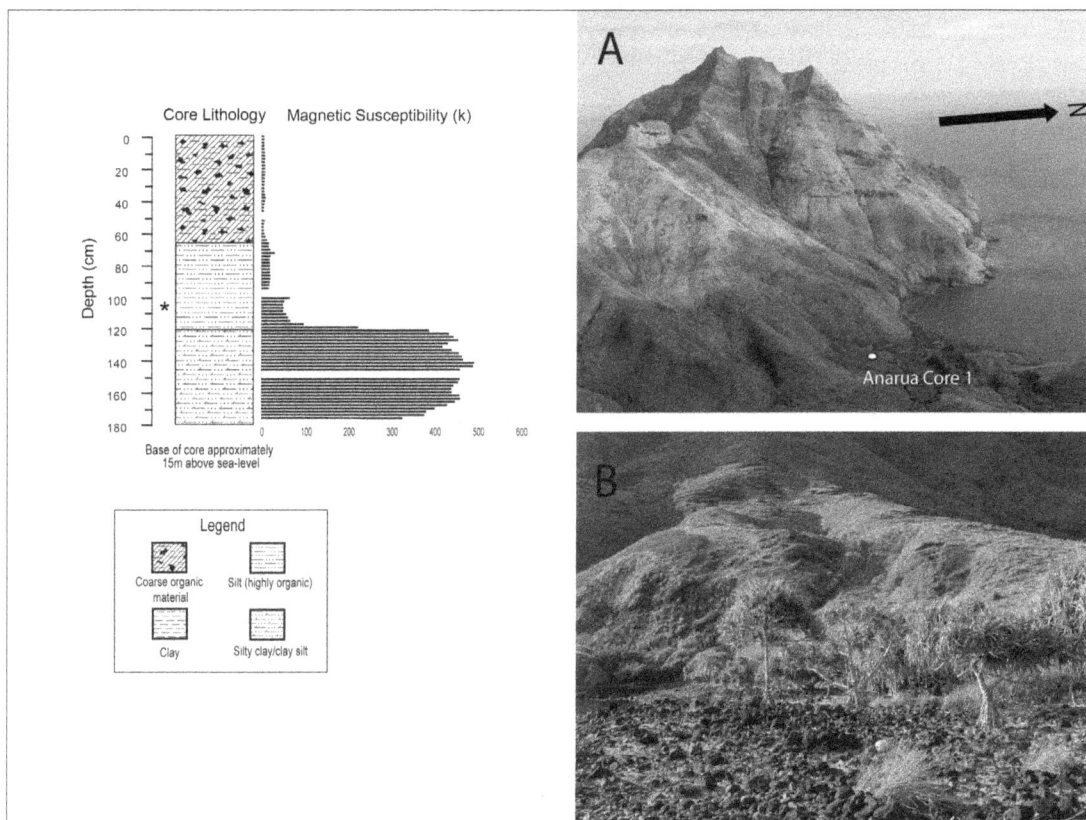

Figure 10.8. Sediment lithology and magnetic susceptibility measurements (K) of the Anarua Core 1 are shown. To the right are photographs of Anarua. A. shows the extent of Anarua wetland and embayment and the position of Anarua Core 1 (white dot). B. shows the boulder beach at the head of Anarua backed by *Pandanus tectorius* trees. *marks location of radiocarbon sample AMS ANU-12157 (charcoal). See Figure 10.1 for location of Anarua Bay. Photographs D.J. Kennett and A. Anderson.

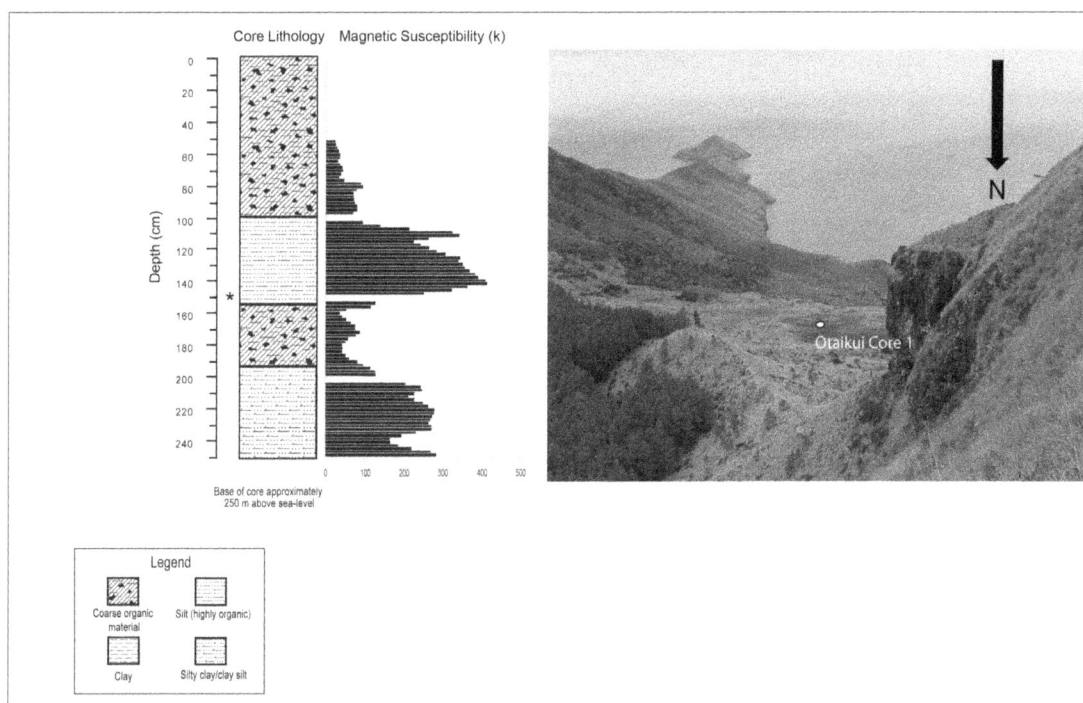

Figure 10.9. Sediment lithology and magnetic susceptibility measurements (K) of the Angatakuri Core 1 (Otaikui Swamp) are shown. To the right is a photograph of Angatakuri that shows the extent of the wetland and the position of the core (white dot). *marks location of radiocarbon sample AMS ANU-12157 (charcoal). See Figure 10.1 for location of Angatakuri Bay. Photograph D.J. Kennett.

Summary

The multiple profile approach revealed an uneven response of pollen deposition to sedimentary influxes, whereby pollen zones could be identified but were represented in differing size units. What is more striking are the direct indications for post-contact introduction of a range of seral weed taxa (Prebble unpublished data). The initial presence of these taxa corresponds to distinctive pollen zones that extend to the modern marshland surface. On Rapa, the earliest anthropogenic pollen zone, described as a Polynesian phase, is characterised by *C. esculenta* pollen, a suite of other potential introduced taxa (e.g. *Aleurites moluccana* and *Erythrina variegata*), the onset of high charcoal particle concentrations, declines in arboreal taxa including the extirpation or extinction of Arecaceae palm pollen, and an associated increase in fern, grass and other herb taxa. The upper European phase palynofacies are characterised by a decline of *C. esculenta* pollen, further local declines or extirpations of arboreal taxa (e.g. *Pandanus tectorius*) and the initial presence and subsequent increase of a range of introduced weed taxa (e.g. *Ludwigia octovalvis*, *Commelina diffusa* and *Sonchus oleraceus*). In addition, high charcoal particle concentrations continue with a further increase in fern, grass and other herb taxa. Such a distinctive pattern of pollen and spore deposition has only been found in a few other sites in island Remote Oceania (e.g. Kawainui Marsh, O'ahu, Ward in Hammatt et al. 1990; Alenaio Swamp, Hawai'i, Wickler and Ward 1992; Maunawili Swamp, O'ahu, Athens and Ward 1997).

Colocasia esculenta at initial colonisation?

We have noted a number of problems in the examination of agricultural swamp profiles from back-beach deposits on Polynesian high islands. The mixing of swamp profiles during the digging and planting process may have resulted in the mixing of organic materials, possibly generating older than expected radiocarbon determinations. This issue could be resolved by further high-resolution radiocarbon dating. Despite these problems, there is great potential for understanding the timing of crop introduction and the rate of expansion using the multiple profiling method employed in this study. It is by no means conclusive, but *Colocasia* may have been planted at Tukou at the time of, or soon after, initial human arrival. The swamp appears to have been planted from near the shoreline to the hillside embankment, covering an area of more than 2 ha. *Colocasia* pollen is continuously represented up to the period of European contact, when the swamp was either infrequently used or overrun by feral animals. Prebble (unpublished data) has identified hydrological changes on the swamp from invertebrate and seed assemblages that may represent the expansion of terraced pondfields.

The work at Tukou Swamp suggests that early deployment of agriculture within the colonisation era in places where it was introduced at that time may not be too difficult to find, contrary to the pessimism expressed by Addison (2008:151):

> Finding archaeological evidence for the sequence of agricultural development … will be challenging. The earliest use of natural wetlands for raised-bed cultivation is unlikely to have left any archaeological signature. Early pondfield systems are likely to have been small, but they would have been built in the easiest areas – areas that have probably seen relatively constant use since initial colonization. This subsequent use will have obscured most traces of the earliest pondfields.

We agree that there are problems in untangling and dating evidence from sites that have often been used repeatedly, perhaps continuously, but taking an archaeological approach to sedimentary history coupled with a multiple profile coring method may help to resolve these. Our work shows that the natural wetlands on Rapa were probably used for *Colocasia* production early, extensively and continuously and that the swamp profiles examined hold informative signatures of agricultural activity. We cannot distinguish raised bed or pondfield systems from the evidence presented, although hydrological proxies do suggest that pondfields were constructed later in the sequence. We agree with Addison that *Colocasia* would have been cultivated in the easiest areas. These were the *Pandanus* swamp forests that were easily and rapidly cleared by fire, creating an immediate soil horizon suitable for crop production.

References

Addison, D.J. 2008. The changing role of irrigated *Colocasia esculenta* (taro) on Nuku Hiva, Marquesas Islands: from an essential element of colonization to an important risk-reduction strategy. *Asian Perspectives* 47:139–155.

Anderson, A.J. 1994. Paleoenvironmental evidence of island colonization: A response. *Antiquity* 68:845–847.

Anderson, A.J. 1995. Current approaches in East Polynesian colonization research. *Journal of the Polynesian Society* 104:110–132.

Anderson, A.J. 2003. Initial human dispersal in Remote Oceania: pattern and explanation. In: Sand, C. (ed), *Pacific archaeology: assessments and prospects*, 71–84. Noumea: Service des Musées et du Patrimoine.

Anderson, A.J. 2009a. The rat and the octopus: initial human colonization and the prehistoric introduction of domestic animals to Remote Oceania. *Biological Invasions* 11:1503–1519.

Anderson, A.J. 2009b. Changing archaeological perspectives upon historical ecology in the Pacific islands. *Pacific Science* 63:747–757.

Anderson, E. 1952. *Plants, man, and life*. University of California Press.

Ash, J. and Ash, W. 1984. Freshwater wetland vegetation of Viti Levu, Fiji. *New Zealand Journal of Botany* 22:377–391.

Athens, J.S. and Ward, J.V. 1993. Environmental change and prehistoric Polynesian settlement in Hawai'i. *Asian Perspectives* 32:205–223.

Athens, J.S. and Ward, J.V. 1997. The Maunawili core: prehistoric inland expansion of settlement and agriculture, O'ahu, Hawai'i. *Hawaiian Archaeology* 6:37–51.

Bronk Ramsey, C. 2008. Deposition models for chronological records. *Quaternary Science Reviews* 27:42–60.

Clark, J.S., Overpeck, J.T., Webb III, T. and Patterson III, W.A. 1986. Pollen stratigraphic correlation and dating of barrier-beach peat sections. *Review of Palaeobotany and Palynology* 47:145–168.

Conte, E. and Payri, C. 2006. Present-day consumption of edible algae in French Polynesia: A study of the survival of pre-European practices. *Journal of the Polynesian Society* 115:77–94.

Davidson, J. and Leach, F. 2001. The strandlooper concept and economic naivety. In: Clark, G.R., Anderson, A.J. and Vunidilo, T. (eds), *The Archaeology of Lapita dispersal in Oceania. Terra Australis* 17:115–124.

Davies, J. Rev. 1827. Extracts from the journal of a visit to the islands of Rapa (or Oparo), Raivavai, and Tupuai etc (July and October, 1927). *Quarterly chronicle of transactions of the London Missionary Society* 3:323–332, 353–361.

Dumayne-Peaty, L. and Barber, K. 1998. Late Holocene vegetational history, human impact and pollen representativity variations in northern Cumbria, England. *Journal of Quaternary Science* 13:147–164.

Ellison, J. 1991. The Pacific palaeogeography of *Rhizophora mangle* L. (Rhizophoraceae). *Botanical Journal of the Linnean Society* 105:271–284.

Flenley, J.R. 1979. Stratigraphic evidence for environmental change on Easter Island. *Asian Perspectives* 22:33–40.

Flenley, J.R. and King, S.M. 1984. Late Quaternary pollen records from Easter Island. *Nature* 307:47–49.

Flenley, J.R., King, S.M., Jackson, J. and Chew, C. 1991. The Late Quaternary vegetational and climatic history of Easter Island. *Journal of Quaternary Science* 6:85–115.

Fosberg, F.R. 1956. *Military geography of northern Marshall Islands*. Tokyo: Intelligence Division Office of the Engineer, Headquarters.

Fosberg, F.R. and St. John, H. 1934. Check list and field notebook of the plants of Southeastern Polynesia: Society Islands, Tuamotus, Austral Islands, Rapa. Honolulu.

Haberle, S. 1994. Anthropogenic indicators in pollen diagrams: problems and prospects for late Quaternary palynology in New Guinea. In: Hather, J.G. (ed), *Tropical archaeobotany: Applications and new developments*, 172–201. Routledge, London.

Hall, J.V. 1869. On the island of Rapa. *Transactions and Proceedings of the New Zealand Institute* 1:128–134.

Hammatt, H.H., Shideler, D.W., Chiogioji, R. and Scoville, R. 1990. *Sediment coring in Kawainui Marsh, Kailua, O'ahu, Ko'olaupoko*. Honolulu.

Hardy, K., Blakeney, T., Copeland, L., Kirkham, J., Wrangham, R. and Collins, M. 2009. Starch granules, dental calculus and new perspectives on ancient diet. *Journal of Archaeological Science* 36:248–255.

Horrocks, M. and Bedford, S. 2005. Microfossil analysis of Lapita deposits in Vanuatu reveals introduced Araceae (aroids). *Archaeology in Oceania* 40:67–74.

Horrocks, M., Bedford, S. and Spriggs, M. 2009. A short note on banana (*Musa*) phytoliths in Lapita, immediately post-Lapita and modern period archaeological deposits from Vanuatu. *Journal of Archaeological Science* 36:2048–2054.

Jayalekshmy, A. and Mathew, A.G. 1990. Changes in the carbohydrates and proteins of coconut during roasting. *Food Chemistry* 37:123–134.

Jones, R. and Spriggs, M. 2002. Theatrum Oceani: Themes and Arguments concerning the Prehistory of Australia and the Pacific. In: Cunliffe, B., Davies, H. and Renfrew, C. (eds), *Archaeology: the Widening Debate*, 245–294. Oxford University Press for the British Academy, London.

Juggins, S. 2010. *C2 Data Analysis*. Newcastle.

Kennett, D.J., Anderson, A.J., Prebble, M., Conte, E. and Southon, J. 2006. Prehistoric human impacts on Rapa, French Polynesia. *Antiquity* 80:340–354.

Kirch, P.V. 1982. Ecology and the adaption of Polynesian agricultural systems. *Archaeology in Oceania* 17:1–6.

Kirch, P.V. 2002. *On the road of the winds*. University of California Press, Berkeley.

Kirch, P.V., Steadman, D.W., Butler, V.L., Hather, J. and Weisler, M.I. 1995. Prehistory and human ecology in Eastern Polynesia: Excavations at Tangatatau Rockshelter, Mangaia, Cook Islands. *Archaeology in Oceania* 30:47–65.

Kirch, P.V. and Green, R.C. 2001. *Hawaiki, ancestral Polynesia: an essay in historical anthropology*. Cambridge University Press.

Lamb, W.K. (ed), 1984. George Vancouver, 1803, *A Voyage of Discovery to the North Pacific Ocean and Round the World 1791–1795*, Volume I. The Hakluyt Society, London.

Massey, J.E. 1979. The diatoms of contemporary and ancient sediments from Lake Waiau, Hawaii, and their geochemical environment. *Review of Palaeobotany and Palynology* 27:77–83.

Matthews, P.J. 1995. Aroids and the Austronesians. *Tropics* 4:105–126.

Matthews, P.J. 2004. Genetic diversity in Taro and the preservation of culinary knowledge. *Ethnobotany Research and Applications* 2:55–71.

McGlone, M.S. and Wilmshurst, J.M. 1999. Dating intial Maori environmental impact in New Zealand. *Quaternary International* 59:5–16.

McGlone, M., Wilmshurst, J.M. and Leach, H. 2005. An ecological and historical review of bracken (*Pteridium esculentum*) in New Zealand, and its cultural significance. *New Zealand Journal of Ecology* 29:165–184.

Meyer, J.-Y. 2002. *Rapport de mission de l'expédition scientifique à Raivavae et Rapa (Australes) du 18 Novembre au 20 Décembre 2002*. Papeete.

Prebble, M. In press. The palaeobotanical record of Rapa (French Polynesia): phytogeographic implications for the Austral Archipelago. In: Meyer, J-Y. (ed), *Biodiversity of the Austral Islands*.

Prebble, M. and Dowe, J.L. 2008. The late Quaternary decline and extinction of palms on oceanic Pacific islands. *Quaternary Science Reviews* 27:2546–2567.

Prebble, M. and Wilmshurst, J. 2009. Detecting the initial impact of humans and introduced species on island environments in Remote Oceania using palaeoecology. *Biological Invasions* 11:1529–1556.

Prebble, M.P., Anderson, A. and Kennett, D.J. In press. Forest clearance and agricultural expansion on Rapa, Austral Archipelago, French Polynesia. *The Holocene*.

Selling, O.H. 1948. *Studies in Hawaiian pollen statistics, Part III: on the late Quaternary history of the Hawaiian vegetation*. Vol. 39. Honolulu.

Shineberg, D.E. 1986. Archibald Menzies' account of the visit of the Discovery to Rapa and Tahiti, 22 December 1791–25 January 1792. *Pacific Studies* 9:59–102.

Smith, A.C. 1979. *Flora Vitiensis Nova*. Vol. 1. Pacific Tropical Botanic Garden, Lawai.

Stokes, J.F.G. n.d. Ethnology of Rapa. B.P. Bishop Museum, Honolulu.

Stone, B.C. 1988. Notes on the genus Pandanus (Pandanaceae) in Tahiti. *Botanical Journal of the Linnean Society* 97:33–48.

Valentin, F., Buckley, H.R., Herrscher, E., Kinaston, R., Bedford, S., Spriggs, M., Hawkins, S. and Neal, K. 2010. Lapita subsistence strategies and food consumption patterns in the community of Teouma (Efate, Vanuatu). *Journal of Archaeological Science* 37:1820–1829.

Wickler, S. and Ward, J.V. 1992. *Archaeological and paleoenvironmental investigations of Alenaio stream flood control project, Hilo, Hawai'i Island*. Honolulu.

Wilson, J., Hardy, K., Allen, R., Copeland, L., Wrangham, R. and Collins, M. 2010. Automated classification of starch granules using supervised pattern recognition of morphological properties. *Journal of Archaeological Science* 37:594–604.

11

A Bayesian AMS ^{14}C chronology for the colonisation and fortification of Rapa Island

Douglas J. Kennett
Department of Anthropology, The Pennsylvania State University, University Park, PA, USA, djk23@psu.edu

Brendan J. Culleton
Department of Anthropology, The Pennsylvania State University

Atholl Anderson
Department of Archaeology and Natural History, The Australian National University

John Southon
Department of Earth Sciences, University of California, Irvine

Introduction

One of our primary objectives on Rapa was to establish a settlement chronology. Although we encountered a range of archaeological sites and cultural features during our short time on the island, our chronological work was focused on determining the likely age of colonisation, with investigations of coastal rockshelters, and the age of hilltop fortifications and their proliferation (Figure 11.1). Heyerdahl's Norwegian expedition to Rapa occurred during the 1950s, shortly after Libby's breakthrough development of radiocarbon dating. Early applications of radiocarbon dating in archaeology were often limited, and in this tradition, Mulloy (1965:59) acquired two radiocarbon dates from the fortified site of Morongo Uta. One date of 310 ± 300 bp (bp = uncalibrated result) came from a hearth in the middle of a centrally located terrace (Enclosure 2) and a second date of 210 ± 200 bp was obtained from the 'floor level' of another terrace on the eastern side of the site (Enclosure 85). These dates were considered to be associated with the last phase of occupation of this fortification, rather than the age of first construction, but when the dates are calibrated they span AD 1260–1500 and AD 1400–1950, respectively. The results place the known age of fortification on the island in the later stages of East Polynesian prehistory, but they are of limited use due to the small sample size, lack of analytical detail and low precision.

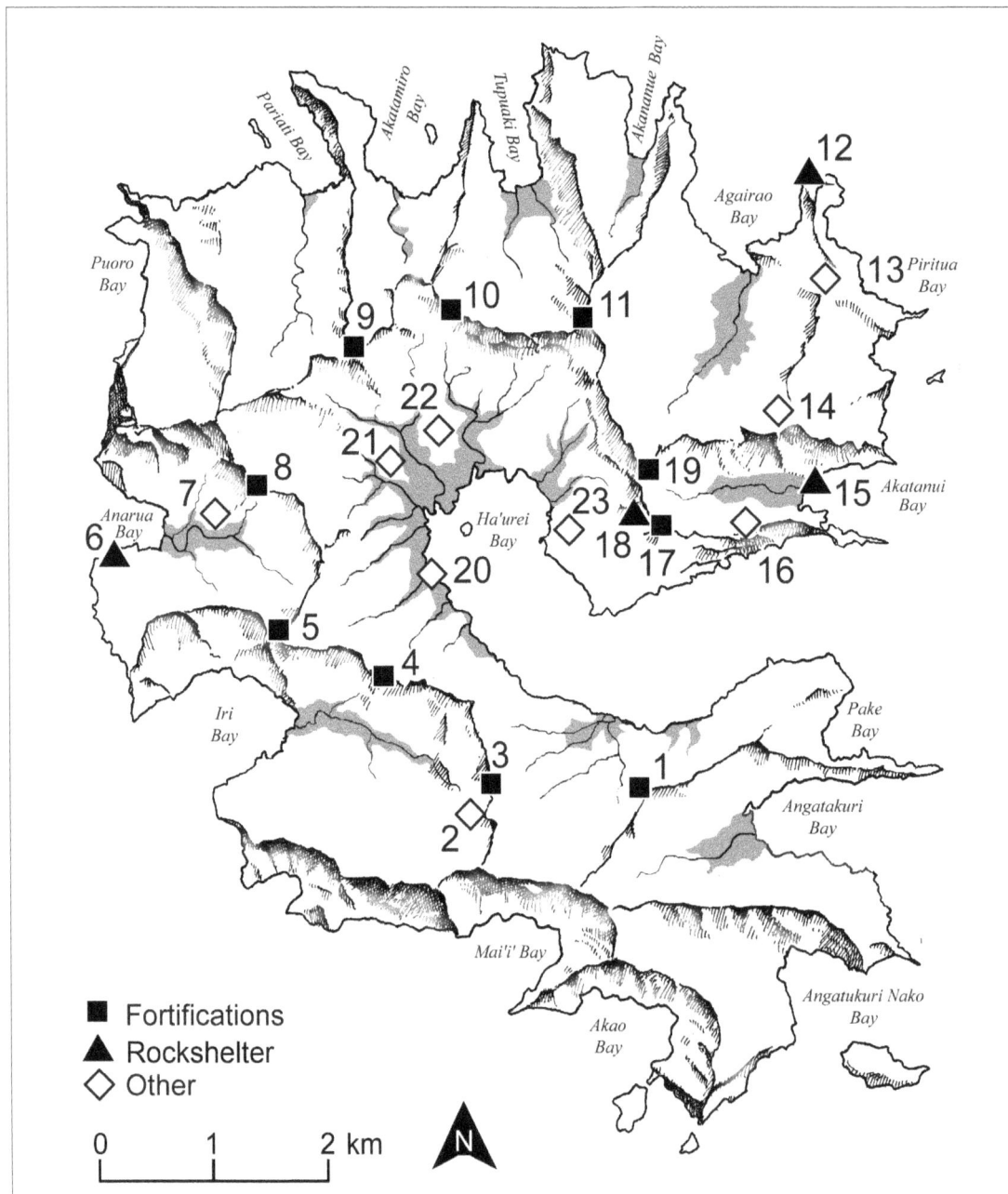

Figure 11.1. Locations of archaeological sites with AMS radiocarbon dates mentioned in text. Drafted by R. Van Rossman. 1 = Ororangi (R-20); 2 = Ngapiri (R2002-50); 3 = Tevaitau (R-18); 4 = Morongo Uta (R-1); 5 = Pukutaketake (R2002-42); 6 = Tangarutu; 7 = R2002-49; 8 = Noogurupe (R2002-43); 9 = Kapitanga (R-5); 10 = Ruatara (R-17); 11 = Vairu (R-3); 12 = Angairao, Shelter E; 13 = Taua (R2002-40); 14 = Pukumia (R2002-39); 15 = Akatanui, Shelter 3; 16 = Pukutai (R-19); 17 = Tapitanga (R-4); 18 = Taga Rockshelter; 19 = Potaketake (R-2); 20 = R2002-48; 21 = R2002-11; 22 = R2002-16; 23 = R2002-20.

The Norwegian expedition focused on the enigmatic fortifications on Rapa and not the age of colonisation. More recent work by Walczak (2001) identified the Tangarutu rockshelter as a possible early site. From deposits exposed in the cave he obtained two radiocarbon dates, of 330 ± 45 bp (Ly-8578) and 495 ± 40 bp (Ly-8577), which calibrate to AD 1460–1670 and AD 1400–1500, respectively. These dates overlap in age with Mulloy's dates from Morongo Uta and are quite late in the East Polynesian sequence.

In this chapter, we describe the results of our ^{14}C dating program. We AMS ^{14}C dated materials from stratigraphic excavations at various coastal rockshelters and fortifications; the contextual information for these dates is described elsewhere in this volume. In this chapter, we combine these data with additional AMS ^{14}C dates on material collected opportunistically from exposed stratigraphic deposits and test probes (augers and 25 cm circular sample test pits) on fortifications, terraces and ovens. We use this AMS ^{14}C survey technique in combination with Bayesian statistical analysis to establish a chronology for broader patterns of landscape use during the colonisation and fortification process. These observations will be valuable for defining future work on Rapa.

Sample selection and analytical methods

We analysed 25 samples from four rockshelters, 30 samples from 10 different fortifications and 10 additional samples from other types of contexts (e.g. ovens, domestic terraces). All of the radiocarbon samples from the four coastal rockshelters come from excavations detailed in Chapter 3. Datable materials were reasonably well preserved in these contexts and carbonised plant remains were recovered from most stratigraphic units of interest. This was particularly the case at Tangarutu rockshelter, where preservation was exceptional and artefacts made of perishable materials were recovered (e.g. fish hooks, cordage). Carbonised wood fragments were most commonly recovered, but we radiocarbon dated carbonised seeds and smaller twigs preferentially if they were available (see discussion below regarding the old wood problem).

Obtaining datable materials from fortifications and other open-air sites was more challenging. The volcanic soils on the island are highly acidic and do not favour the preservation of organic materials. Hilltop fortifications are the most exposed site types and therefore highly susceptible to water erosion and wind deflation, both substantial in Rapa's subtropical location. Compared with rockshelters, fortifications are also larger and more difficult to assess with the limited excavations that our time allowed on Rapa. Regardless of these challenges, we encountered pockets of organic rich sediment containing artefacts, faunal materials and carbonised materials for radiocarbon dating on the terraces surrounding the central tower at each large fortification. Some of the deepest and richest midden soils were encountered on the flattened tops of the central towers themselves. We selected the richest areas for larger excavations and the details of this work are provided in Chapter 12. We also used smaller test units (augers and 25 cm circular sample test pits or STPs) to explore the distribution of midden soils across these terraces. Carbonised plant materials were usually encountered and samples were selected from the deepest intact deposits, which were often only 25 cm to 30 cm in depth. Analysis of these samples was limited by funding, but we tried to analyse at least two samples from each fortification. While visiting the hilltop fortifications, we encountered other domestic terraces on ridges and agricultural terraces in valley bottoms and surrounding hillslopes. Although these were not the focus of this project, we sampled them if exposures were present, in order to get an initial sense of their age.

Most of the AMS radiocarbon dates in this study were prepared chemically at the University of Oregon's Archaeometry Facility (now moved to The Pennsylvania State University) and analysed at the Keck Carbon Cycle Accelerator Mass Spectrometer at the University of California, Irvine (KCCAMS; methods below). Our study also includes seven radiocarbon dates run at The Australian National University and three run at the Waikato Radiocarbon Dating Laboratory (New Zealand). At the ANU facility, all charcoal samples were physically cleaned to remove adhering sediment, then washed in hot 10% Acid-Base-Acid (ABA), rinsed and dried. At Waikato, charcoal samples were washed in hot 10% HCl, rinsed and treated with hot 0.5%

NaOH. The NaOH insoluble fraction was treated with hot 10% HCl, filtered, rinsed and dried. The ANU radiocarbon determinations were made at a time when the laboratory was experiencing technical difficulties that resulted in several instances of demonstrable discrepancy in results. As the extent and nature of the problems remains unknown, it would be prudent to treat the ANU results cautiously. The results from Waikato and KCCAMS are considered reliable. We also include in our analysis two AMS radiocarbon dates collected during previous excavation at the Tangarutu rockshelter (Walczak 2001) and prepared at the radiocarbon laboratory in Lyon, France, using comparable preparation techniques. We exclude Mulloy's two radiocarbon dates from Morongo Uta due to a variety of analytical uncertainties (laboratory used, half-life used, etc) and the high error margins associated with each date.

Methods UO Archaeometry and UCI-AMS

The carbonised plant material analysed at KCCAMS was selected under a microscope to minimise errors associated with old wood (e.g. by selecting twigs or seeds; Kennett et al. 2002). The old-wood problem is thought to be minimal in this context, given the relative absence of long-lived tree species (no older than 20-year inbuilt age) on the island during the interval of interest (see Chapter 10). Sediments adhering to the samples were removed manually, then soaked in a series of acid/base/acid (ABA) baths (1 N HCL and NaOH for 30 minutes each). The HCL removes carbonate contamination and the NaOH extracts humic acid contamination signalled by discolouration of the solution. Base washes were continued until the solution was clear, indicating the near absence of contaminating humic acids.

A final acid wash removed secondary carbonates that could have formed during the base treatment. Samples were then returned to neutral pH with two 15 minute baths in Nanopure water at 70°C to remove chlorides, and dried on the heater block. Sample CO_2 was produced by combustion at 900°C for six hours in evacuated sealed quartz tubes using a CuO oxygen source and Ag wire to remove sulfur and chlorine compounds. Sample CO_2 was reduced to graphite at 550°C using H_2 and a Fe catalyst, with reaction water drawn off with $Mg(ClO_4)_2$. Solid graphite samples were pressed into AMS cathodes and loaded onto the target wheel with OX-1 (oxalic acid) and other known-age standards, together with calcite and Queets wood blanks for AMS analysis. Radiocarbon ages were $\delta^{13}C$-corrected for mass dependent fractionation with measured values (Stuiver and Polach 1977).

Calibration and phase modelling

All AMS ^{14}C dates were calibrated with OxCal 3.10 (Bronk Ramsey 1995, 2001, 2005), using the Southern Hemisphere atmospheric curve for terrestrial samples (McCormac et al. 2004). We assumed, based on ethnohistoric records, that each date preceded the Mission Period, so each probability distribution was truncated using AD 1825 as a *terminus ante quem* model in OxCal. The resulting 1-σ (68.2%) and 2-σ (95.4%) calibrated ranges are reported with probability distributions given for discontinuous distributions. In a few cases, discontinuous ranges containing small gaps (e.g. five to 10 years) were collapsed into a single interval for clarity.

The chronology of Rapa's colonisation and settlement expansion underpins the studies of resource use, landscape transformation and social change presented in this volume. This complex settlement history unfolded within a relatively short period (ca. 800 years), during a time of pronounced fluctuations in atmospheric ^{14}C production, which leads to broad and discontinuous calibrated age ranges (Blackwell et al. 2006). The timing and pace of key events on Rapa (e.g. the initial establishment and subsequent proliferation of fortifications) are therefore difficult to know precisely. To constrain these possible dates, we used Bayesian models provided by OxCal to estimate the beginning and end of five overlapping phases in the settlement history: Initial Colonisation; Expansion of Rockshelter Use; Initial Fortification; First Expansion of Fortifications; and Final Expansion of Fortifications. The *Boundary* command essentially proposes an event that has not been directly dated – the first fire built in a rockshelter, for example – and estimates a probability distribution for its occurrence based on the known dates included in the phase (Bronk Ramsey 2000, 2005). The resulting start and end dates for each phase are presented with 1-σ and 2-σ ranges, similar to calibrated ^{14}C dates.

Table 11.1. Radiocarbon dates from Rapa Island.

Lab #	Provenience	Site type	Material	^{14}C	Error
UCIAMS-2197	Tangarutu, E2, 123 cm	rockshelter	charcoal	465	25
ANU-11849	Tangarutu, NS1, base layer	rockshelter	charcoal	570	70
UCIAMS-14771	Tangarutu S3, 112 cmbs	rockshelter	charcoal	600	15
ANU-11847	Tangarutu, base	rockshelter	charcoal	650	100
ANU-11848	Tangarutu, E2, Spit 23–25	rockshelter	charcoal	710	70
UCIAMS-14769	Tangarutu T1, 150 cm	rockshelter	charcoal	905	20
ANU-11850	Tangarutu, Quarry Pit Core 1, 158–178	rockshelter	charcoal	1020	180
UCIAMS-2325	Tangarutu, E2, 10 cm	rockshelter	charcoal	380	25
ANU-11924	Tangarutu, E2, Spit 2	rockshelter	charcoal	440	60
UCIAMS-14726	Tangarutu, E1, Spit 4	rockshelter	gourd	320	15
UCIAMS-14768	Tangarutu E2, 23–25 cm	rockshelter	charcoal	475	20
UCIAMS-14772	Tangarutu, E1, Spit 11	rockshelter	Aleurites sp.	345	20
ANU-12100	Tangarutu, E2, Spit 18 (Lower Part of E2)	rockshelter	Aleurites moluccana endocarp.	380	60
ANU-12102	Tangarutu, E2, Spit 19 (Lower Part of E2)	rockshelter	Pandanus, cf tectorius key	660	150
UCIAMS-14770	Tangarutu V1, 90 cmbs	rockshelter	charcoal	350	15
ANU-12101	Tangarutu, E1, Spit 4 (upper part of E1)	rockshelter	Aleurites moluccana endocarp.	410	60
Ly-8577	Tangarutu, Unit 1, Walczak 2001	rockshelter	charcoal	495	40
Ly-8578	Tangarutu, Unit 2, Walczak 2001	rockshelter	charcoal	330	45
UCIAMS-14765	Akatanui, Shelter 3, C1, A1, Spit 2	rockshelter	Aleurites sp.	385	15
ANU-11925	Akatanui, base level, 30–40 cm	rockshelter	charcoal	480	70
UCIAMS-14763	Akatanui, C1, Spit 4, 30–40 cm	rockshelter	charcoal	610	15
ANU-11851	Angairao E, 2nd Oven, Spit 10, 140–150 cm	rockshelter	charcoal	500	50
UCIAMS-14767	Angairao, Shelter E, 2nd oven, Spit 11, 150–160 cm	rockshelter	charcoal	375	15
UCIAMS-14766	Angairao, Shelter E, 2nd oven, Spit 11, 150–160 cm	rockshelter	charcoal	220	20
ANU-11923	Taga, Test pit A, Spit 2, 20 cm (base of deposit)	rockshelter	charcoal	370	150
UCIAMS-14755	Morongo Uta (R-1), Exposure 4, 18 cm	fortification	charcoal	380	20
UCIAMS-2178	Morongo Uta (R-1), Exposure 2, 10 cm (Tower)	fortification	charcoal	350	20
UCIAMS-2177	Morongo Uta (R-1), Exposure 1, 20 cm	fortification	charcoal	145	20
UCIAMS-14773	Morongo Uta (R-1), Exposure 3, 10 cm	fortification	charcoal	130	20
UCIAMS-47240	Moronga Uta (R-1), 8 cmbs, Exposure 4	fortification	charcoal	210	15

Continued on next page

Table 11.1. *continued*

Lab #	Provenience	Site type	Material	¹⁴C	Error
UCIAMS-14762	Ruatara (R-17), Exposure 1, 14 cmbs	fortification	charcoal	345	15
UCIAMS-14774	Ruatara (R-17), STP#2, 15 cm, terrace below tower	fortification	charcoal	210	15
UCIAMS-47243	Ruatara (R-17) Exposure 3, 8 cmbs	fortification	charcoal	630	15
UCIAMS-47244	Ruatara (R-17), Exposure 2, 11 cmbs	fortification	charcoal	170	15
UCIAMS-2181	Potaketake (R-2), Unit 1, Feature 2, 10 cm	fortification	charcoal	210	25
UCIAMS-2188	Potaketake (R-2), Unit 1, Feature 3, 30 cm	fortification	charcoal	240	25
UCIAMS-2184	Potaketake (R-2), Unit 1, Feature 4, 51 cm	fortification	charcoal	240	20
UCIAMS-14757	Kapitanga (R-5), below tower, Exp. 3, 33 cmbs	fortification	charcoal	240	15
UCIAMS-14758	Kapitanga (R-5), upper terrace, Exp. 4, 35 cmbs	fortification	charcoal	195	15
UCIAMS-14760	Pukutaketake (R2002-42), STP#2, 19 cm	fortification	charcoal	145	15
UCIAMS-14759	Pukutaketake (R2002-42), STP#2, 35 cm	fortification	charcoal	235	15
UCIAMS-2190	Ororangi (R-20), Unit 1, Feature 1, RC-3, 12 cm	fortification	charcoal	200	25
UCIAMS-2182	Ororangi (R-20), Unit 1, RC-2, 60 cm	fortification	charcoal	185	20
UCIAMS-80840	Tevaitau (R-18), Unit 1, west side, 8 cmbs	fortification	single nut	240	20
UCIAMS-2186	Tevaitau (R-18), Unit 1, Feature 1, 20–30 cm	fortification	charcoal	195	20
UCIAMS-80841	Tevaitau (R-18), Unit 2, Feature 2, 20 cmbs	fortification	single charcoal	185	20
UCIAMS-2187	Tevaitau (R-18), Terrace E, Exp. 2, 22 cm	fortification	charcoal	140	30
UCIAMS-14725	Vairu (R-3), tower, Auger 7, 5–10 cm	fortification	charcoal	190	20
UCIAMS-14761	Vairu (R-3), Exp 1, 25 cm	fortification	charcoal	180	15
UCIAMS-2180	Tapitanga (R-4), Unit 1, Stratum I/II, S1, 20 cm	fortification	charcoal	145	25
UCIAMS-2179	Tapitanga (R-4), Unit 1, Feature 2, 35 cm	fortification	charcoal	140	20
UCIAMS-14756	Noogurupe (R2002-43), Exposure 1, 20 cm	fortification	charcoal	120	15
UCIAMS-47241	Noogurupe (R2002-43), STP#2, 25 cmbs	fortification	charcoal	615	15
UCIAMS-60739	Noogurupe (R2002-43), STP# 3, 15–25 cmbs	fortification	single charcoal	230	25
UCIAMS-60740	Noogurupe (R2002-43), STP#1, 10–19cmbs	fortification	single charcoal	140	25
UCIAMS-36955	Ngapiri (R2002-50), STP #1, 15cmbs, Rapa	small fortification	charcoal	205	25
UCIAMS-36951	Pukumia (R2002-39), STP 3, 11cmbs, Rapa	small fortification	charcoal	185	25
UCIAMS-36952	Pukutai (R-19), Auger 3, 18 cmbs, Rapa	small fortification	charcoal	195	25
UCIAMS-46300	Taua (R2002-40), FS 114, Exposure 1, 25 cmbs	small fortification	charcoal	250	25
UCIAMS-47242	R2002-49, STP#1, 18 cmbs	domestic terrace	charcoal	380	20
UCIAMS-36954	R2002-49, Exp. 1, E. End, 37 cmbs	domestic terrace	charcoal	485	25
Wk-14889	Ha'urei, R2002-20, Aitoke oven, road cut	oven	charcoal	673	41
Wk-14887	Ha'urei, R2002-11, Tukou oven, road cut	oven	charcoal	677	41
Wk-14888	Ha'urei, R2002-16, Tukou terrace, fill	agricultural terrace fill	charcoal	338	61
UCIAMS-36953	Ha'urei, R2002-48 , Exp 1, 50 cmbs, base	domestic terrace	charcoal	200	25

Uncalibrated AMS radiocarbon results

Four coastal rockshelters produced cultural materials that were AMS radiocarbon dated between 1020 ± 180 and 220 ± 20 bp (Table 11.1). Tangarutu is located on the western side of the island at Anarua Bay, and Akatanui and Angairao are positioned on the northern and eastern side of the island, respectively, with Taga on the eastern slope of Ha'urei Bay just below the Tapitanga fortification. Tangarutu was the largest rockshelter and was the most promising as an early colonisation site given its size and stratigraphic complexity (see Chapter 3). Large sections of the remaining deposits at the site were exposed by the more recent mining of sand from this locality to produce concrete for roads, and Walczak (2001) reported two ages from these exposures at the site; 330 ± 45 and 495 ± 40 bp.

Multiple test pits at Tangarutu were excavated and the stratigraphic sequence is complex, with mixing occurring in some parts of the cave. Basal deposits date to between 1020 ± 180 and 465 ± 25 bp. The upper part of the sequence at Tangarutu produced ages between 320 ± 20 and 475 ± 20 bp and other 'mid-sequence' AMS radiocarbon ages range between 330 ± 40 and 660 ± 40 bp. A majority of ages at Tangarutu falls between 300 and 500 bp.

The deposits at the remaining rockshelters were more ephemeral, indicating less extensive use or a single occupation. Three dates from the Akatanui shelters range between 610 ± 15 and 385 ± 15 bp, and a similar range (500 ± 50 and 220 ± 20 bp) was identified in the Angairao shelter. The thin deposits in the Taga shelter produced an age of 370 ± 150 bp.

We also obtained radiocarbon dates on 10 of the primary fortifications surrounding Ha'urei Bay. These dates range between 630 ± 15 and 120 ± 15 bp. Based on these data, the two earliest fortifications occupied were Ruatara and Noogurupe. Ruatara has a commanding view over the rich agricultural lands at the head of Ha'urei Bay and three (Piriati, Akatamiro, Tupuaki) of the five smaller bays along the north coast of the island. Noogurupe was identified by John Stokes (Stokes n.d.) as on the western side of the island overlooking Ha'urei Bay to the east and Anarua Bay to the west, the latter containing Tangarutu Cave. The earliest date at Ruatara is 630 ± 15 bp, and additional dates from domestic terraces at the site suggest habitation until 170 ± 15 bp. The earliest date at Noogurupe is 615 ± 15 bp, essentially equivalent to the earliest date at Ruatara. Additional dates at Noogurupe similarly suggest persistent settlement through to 120 ± 15 bp. Relatively early and persistent settlement is evident at the Morongo Uta (350 ± 20 to 130 ± 15 bp) fortification that overlooks Iri Bay to the west and Ha'urei Bay to the east. This is one of the largest fortifications on the island and was the focus of the Norwegian expedition (Mulloy 1965). The remaining seven fortifications surrounding Ha'urei Bay date to between 250 and 150 bp. In fact, all 10 of the fortifications have ^{14}C dates in this range and present challenges with respect to calibration and chronology building on the island (see below).

Bayesian chronology

A total of 65 AMS ^{14}C dates form the foundation of our provisional chronology for the colonisation and fortification of Rapa. Much more archaeological work in the future will be required to test and improve this chronology. We take a Bayesian statistical approach to chronology building that takes into account knowledge about the context of AMS radiocarbon dates (e.g. stratigraphic sequencing) and other *a priori* knowledge to establish the likely ages (represented by probability distributions) of a series of developments on the island that include: (1) initial colonisation, (2) coastal expansion, (3) initial fortification, (4) first expansion of fortification, and (5) final expansion of fortification (Figure 11.2). These changes in the distribution and character of settlement are modelled in a series of overlapping phases using the program OxCal (see methods).

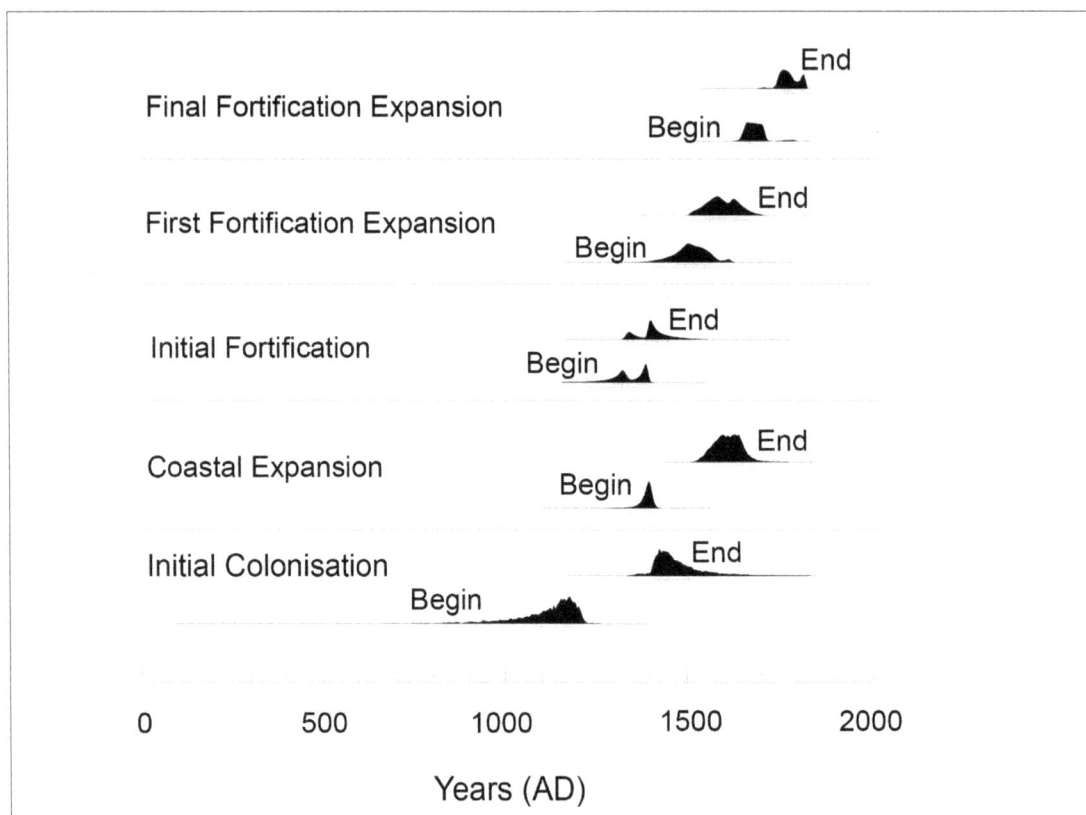

Figure 11.2. Results of Bayesian analysis of radiocarbon dates from Rapa, showing the beginning and end of five phases, starting with initial colonisation and ending with the final phase of fortification before the Mission Period at AD 1825.

The dates within phases were not ordered stratigraphically because these samples often come from different archaeological sites or widely separated test units that do not allow correlation. Stratigraphic relationships between dates are explored in the chapters focused on the excavation of fortifications and coastal rockshelters. We used the historically recorded abandonment of fortified settlements during the Mission Period (AD 1825) to constrain the distribution of the final two fortification phases. We return to this complex question below, but adding this *a priori* knowledge to the model helps resolve several issues related to the poorly behaved calibration curve between AD 1600 and the present.

The initial colonisation phase is represented by a set of dates from Tangarutu rockshelter. All of these dates come from the basal deposits at this site and these levels represent the earliest known cultural materials on the island. The earliest of these dates comes from a small test probe below the base of a modern sand mining pit in the middle of the cave. The large error margins associated with this date from the ANU facility span 800 years between AD 600 and AD 1400 (Figure 11.3, unfilled outline). This is constrained by the other available dates for this phase, between AD 1000 and AD 1400, with peak probability at ca. AD 1000 and AD 1400. It is consistent with the earliest precise AMS ^{14}C date (UCIAMS-14769) on comparable deposits, of AD 1100 to AD 1200. That is consistent, in turn, with the palaeoecological study in which erosion of likely anthropogenic origin has a similar age (Chapter 10; Kennett et al. 2006). The phase boundary for initial colonisation is modelled between ca. AD 800 and AD 1300, with peak probability between AD 1100 and AD 1200. The phase boundary ends between AD 1300 and AD 1600, and peaks between AD 1400 and AD 1500. The fairly wide age distributions for these phase boundaries, compared with later phases, is related to the smaller number of dates used to define the phase.

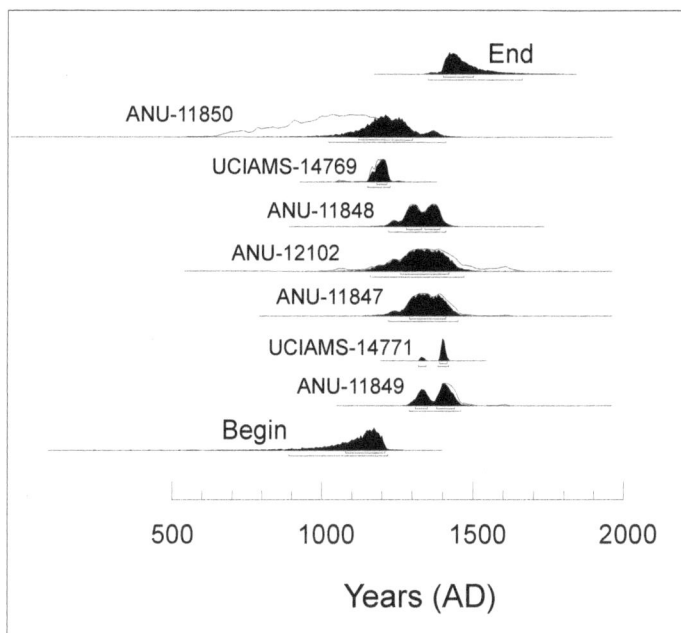

Figure 11.3. Phase modelling results showing probability distributions of radiocarbon dates constraining the early colonisation phase. Prior distributions (routine calibration) are shown in outline, and posterior distributions (modelled in a phase) are solid.

The number of coastal rockshelters with evidence of human use increases between AD 1400 and AD 1600 (Figure 11.4). A majority of the dated components at the Tangarutu rockshelter comes from this interval, indicating more intensive use of this location in conjunction with expanded use of rockshelters elsewhere on the island. Three other rockshelters (Akatanui, Angairao and Taga) show clear signs of human use during this interval and Akatanui was used into the 1700s (UCIAMS-14766), and also later than that, as indicated by the incorporation of European material in the upper stratigraphy of the site (Chapter 3). Taga is one of the few small rockshelters positioned along the mid-slopes of Ha'urei Bay. The deposits were ephemeral and we ran only one exploratory date. It has a high error margin (ANU-11923), but this has been constrained in our model, based on the other dates from the rockshelters in this phase, to between ca. AD 1400 and AD 1600. This is consistent with a handful of AMS dates on other site types (e.g. ovens, terraces) dating to between AD 1200 and AD 1800 along the edge of Ha'urei Bay (Figure 11.5).

Within the context of expanding coastal settlement, we see evidence for elevated settlements (domestic terraces) on ridgelines and the first establishment of fortifications at Noogurupe and Ruatara between ca. AD 1300 and AD 1400 (Figure 11.6), approximately 200 years after the first evidence for island settlement. We suspect there is a historical connection between the people who first occupied Tangarutu rockshelter, those who settled on the ridgeline overlooking the pondfields of Anarua Valley, and those who later established the Noogurupe fortification overlooking Anarua and Ha'urei bays. The contemporary establishment of Ruatara is likely to have resulted from the fissioning of the founding community at Anarua. Our limited stay on the island did not allow for a comprehensive inventory or examination of elevated domestic terraces on ridgelines, although they appear to be fairly common, as noted by Walczak (2001). More work is required to sort out the chronology of these types of sites, but the R2002-20 site suggests their use at the same time as fortifications were first established.

At least two phases of expanded fortification occurred on the island before the Mission Period. Persistent settlement is evident at Ruatara between AD 1400 and AD 1800, and this also appears to be the case at Noogurupe, with a possible hiatus between AD 1400 and AD 1650. Morongo Uta, which developed into the largest fortification on the island, was also established

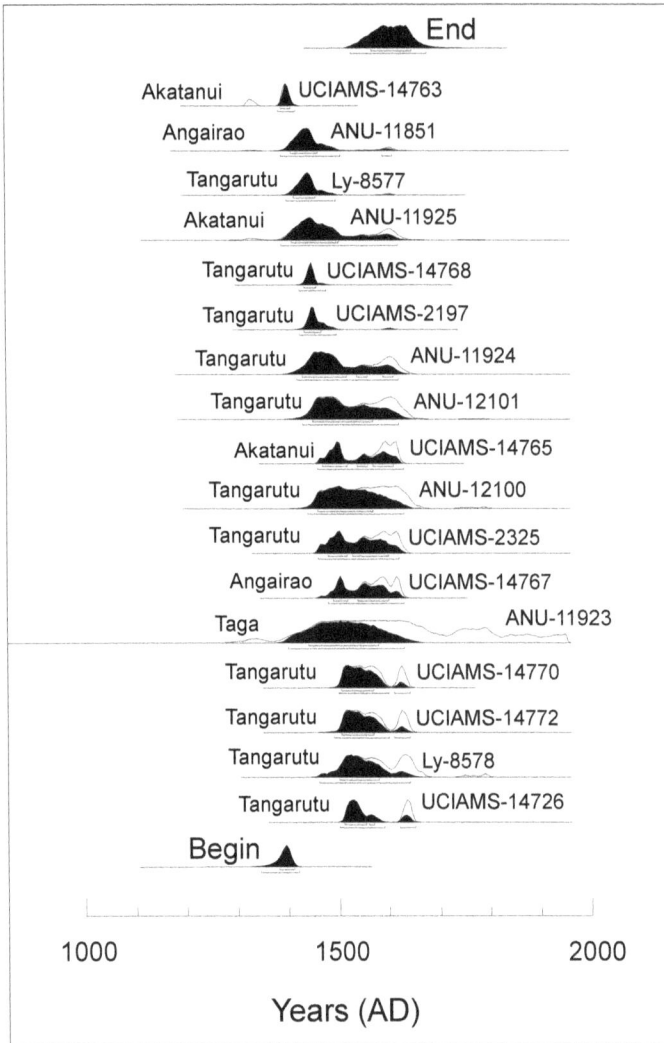

Figure 11.4. (Left) Phase modelling results showing probability distributions of radiocarbon dates constraining the coastal expansion phase. See Figure 11.3 for details about how the figure is organised.

Figure 11.5. (Below) Calibrated AMS radiocarbon dates for miscellaneous archaeological sites and features on Rapa that were not included in the five modelled settlement phases. The posterior distributions (solid) are constrained by the *terminus ante quem* of AD 1825, based on ethnohistoric records indicating the loss of upland settlement by this time.

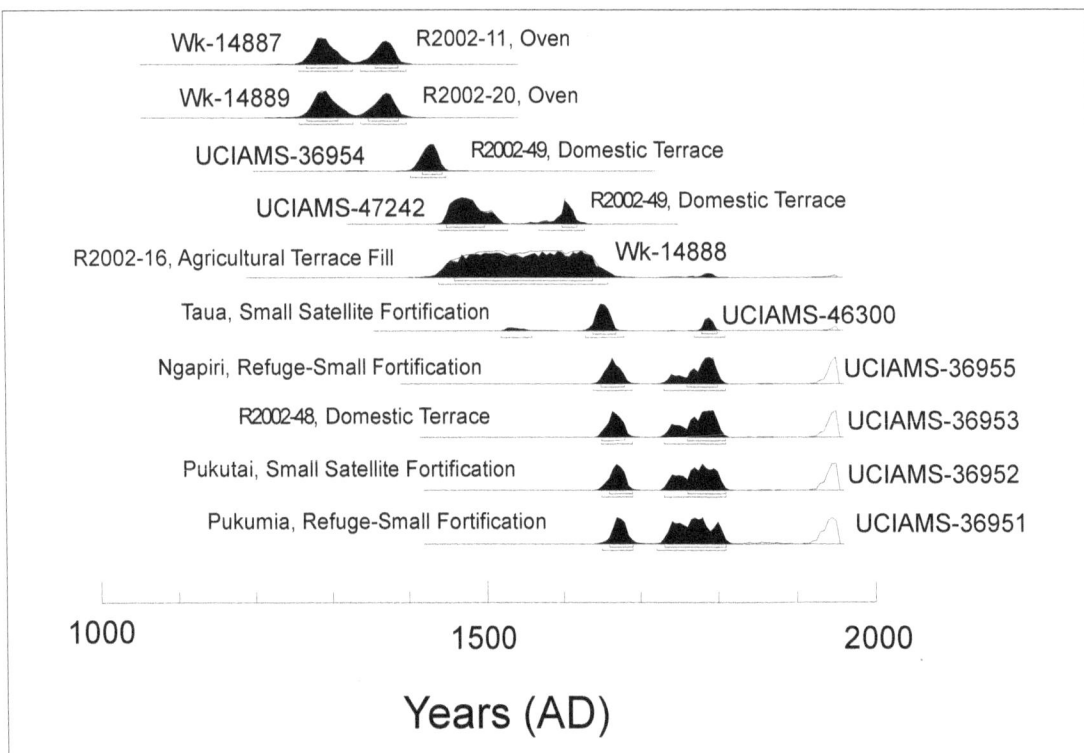

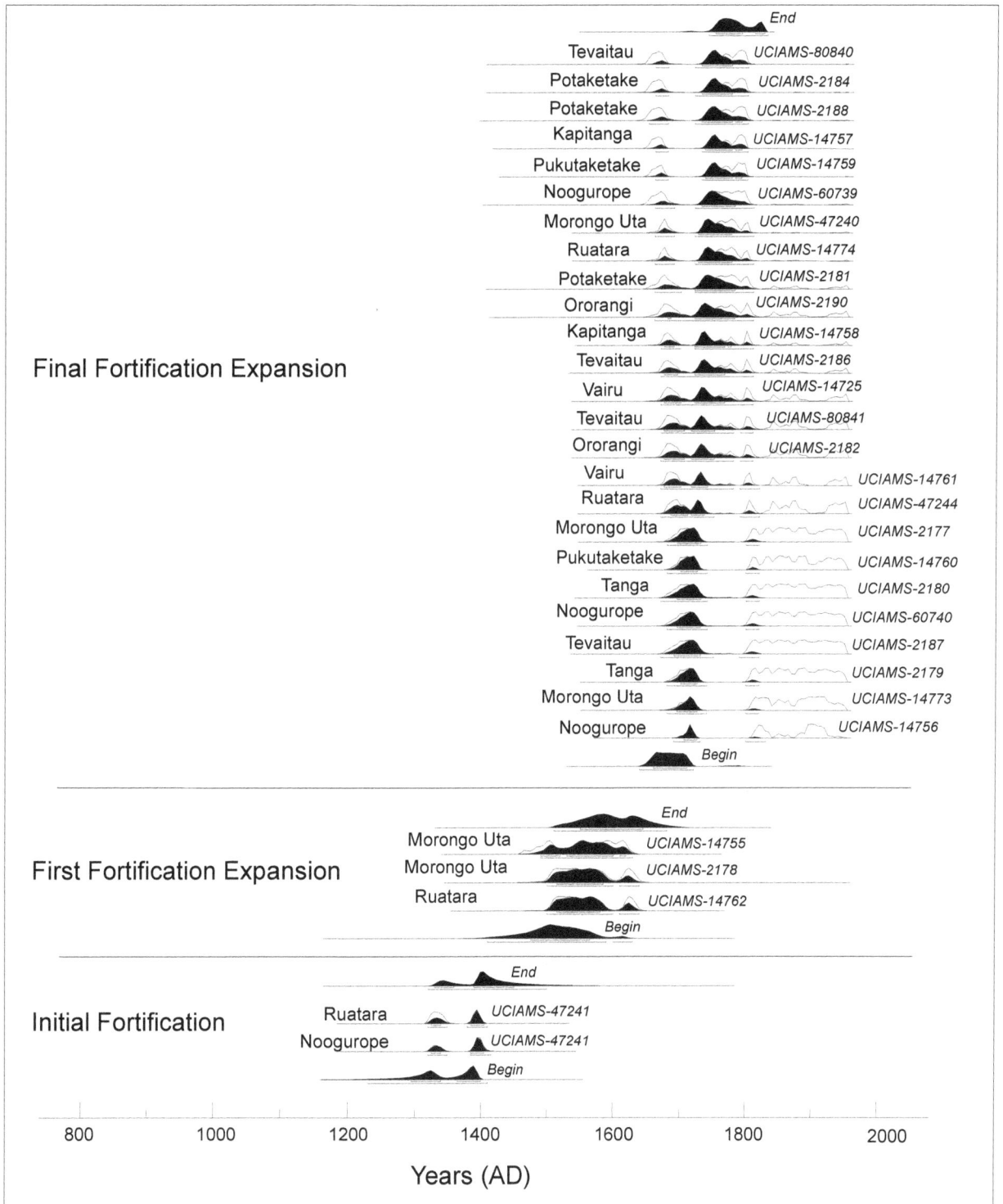

Figure 11.6. Phase modelling results showing the probability distributions of radiocarbon dates forming the basis of the first and final fortification phases on Rapa. See Figure 11.3 for details about how the figure is organised.

during the first fortification expansion phase between AD 1400 and AD 1650. Settlement at Morongo Uta persisted until the early 1800s.

Details of the final fortification phase are marred by major fluctuations in the calibration curve after about AD 1700 (Figure 11.7). All radiocarbon ages starting at about 240 +/- 15 bp are impacted by these fluctuations and cannot be distinguished from those on modern materials. However, we know, based on mission records, that fortified villages were abandoned by AD 1825 when the modern communities of Area and Ha'urei were established. This *a priori* knowledge was built into our Bayesian model and it serves as an important calibration datum (*terminus ante quem*) to help clean up the probability distributions. It truncates the probability distributions at this date and shows a cluster of seven fortifications dating to the early 1700s and at least 10 fortifications in the late 1700s, when Vancouver observed at least six forts in use on the western side of the island (Chapter 2). Smaller satellite fortifications (e.g. refuges) that were probably connected in some way with the larger fortifications nearby also date to the late 1700s (see Figure 11.5, Tauo, Ngapiri, Pukutai and Pukumia). These sites are discussed more fully in Chapter 12.

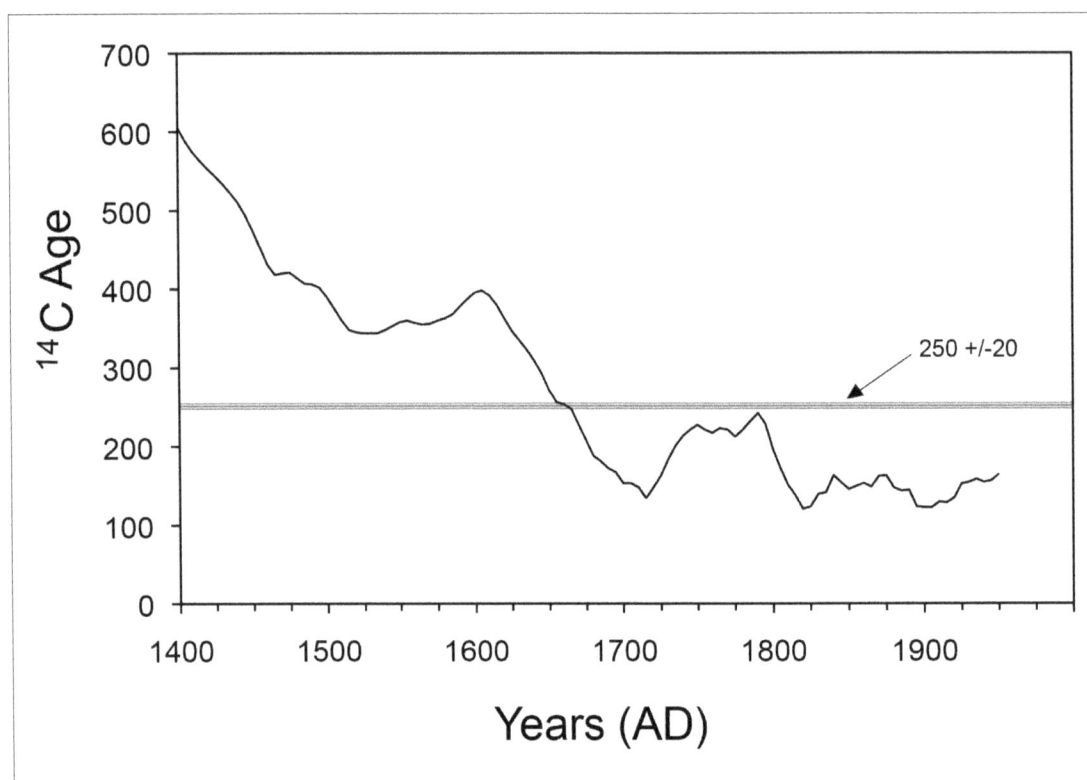

Figure 11.7. Southern Hemisphere atmospheric curve for terrestrial samples (McCormac et al. 2004) between AD 1400 and AD 2000, showing a major plateau and fluctuations between AD 1650 and AD 200 that make calibration challenging.

Conclusions

The systematic use of radiocarbon dating as a survey technique provides a framework for reconstructing a broad pattern of landscape use and how this changed through time. The approach is becoming more commonly used in a variety of coastal and island contexts where erosional processes expose deposits (Erlandson and Moss 1999; Kennett 2005) and it may be particularly useful in East Polynesian contexts where ceramics are absent, along with other temporally diagnostic artefacts used elsewhere to establish preliminary settlement chronologies.

This approach does not serve as a replacement for more intensive stratified excavations, and intensive archaeological work is clearly required to establish more definitive site chronologies. On Rapa, we used the survey technique to establish a broad chronology that can guide future work on the island. Our data suggests that the island was most likely colonised between AD 1100 and AD 1200. This was followed by expanded use of coastal zones and construction of the first elevated domestic terraces between AD 1200 and AD 1600. It is within this context that the first two fortified hilltop settlements (Noogurupe and Ruatara) appear on the island between AD 1300 and AD 1400. The number of fortifications expanded, slowly between AD 1400 and AD 1650 and then more rapidly during the 1700s just before historic contact.

The need for further research, and quite soon, is underlined by the evidence that many of the sites on Rapa are endangered by destructive processes. Hilltop fortifications are heavily wind deflated, and animal grazing has removed much of the vegetation stabilising these sites, leading to erosion, which is also destroying the rock terrace walls. In addition, the mining of sand for road construction from the Tangarutu rockshelter presents a serious threat to these deposits.

References

Blackwell, P.G., Buck, C.E. and Reimer, P.J. 2006. Important features of the new radiocarbon calibration curves. *Quaternary Science Reviews* 25:408–413.

Bronk Ramsey, C. 1995. Radiocarbon calibration and analysis of stratigraphy: the OxCal program. *Radiocarbon* 37(2):461–74.

Bronk Ramsey, C. 2000. Comment on 'The Use of Bayesian Statistics for 14C dates of chronologically ordered samples: a critical analysis'. *Radiocarbon* 42(2):199–202.

Bronk Ramsey, C. 2001. Development of the radiocarbon program OxCal. *Radiocarbon* 43(2A):355–363.

Bronk Ramsey, C. 2005. OxCal v. 3.10. http://c14.arch.ox.ac.uk/embed.php?File=oxcal.html.

Erlandson, J.M. and Moss, M. 1999. The systematic use of radiocarbon dating in archaeological surveys in coastal and other erosional environments. *American Antiquity* 64(1):431–443.

Kennett, D.J. 2005. *The Island Chumash: Behavioral Ecology of a Maritime Society*. University of California Press, Berkeley.

Kennett, D.J., Ingram, B.L., Southon, J.R. and Wise, K. 2002. Differences in ¹⁴C Age Between Stratigraphically Associated Charcoal and Marine Shell from the Archaic Period Site of Kilometer 4, Southern Peru: Old Wood or Old Water? *Radiocarbon* 44(1):53–58.

Kennett, D.J., Anderson, A., Prebble, M., Conte, E. and Southon, J. 2006. Human Impacts on Rapa, French Polynesia. *Antiquity* 80:340–354.

McCormac, F.G., Hogg, A.G., Blackwell, P.G., Buck, C.E., Higham, T.F.G. and Reimer, P.J. 2004. SHCal04 Southern Hemisphere calibration, 0–11.0kyr BP. *Radiocarbon* 46(3):1087–92.

Mulloy, W. 1965. The Fortified Village of Morongo Uta. In: Heyerdahl, T. and Ferdon, E.N. (eds), *Reports of the Norwegian Archaeological Expedition to Easter Island and the East Pacific*, Volume 2, miscellaneous papers. Monographs of the School of American Research.

Stokes, J.F.G. n.d. Ethnology of Rapa, Manuscript on file in the Bernice P. Bishop Museum, Honolulu.

Stuiver, M. and Polach, H.A. 1977. Discussion: reporting of ^{14}C data. *Radiocarbon* 19:355–363.

Walczak, J. 2001. Le peuplement de la Polynésie orientale: Une tentative d'approche historique par les exemples de Tahiti et de Rapa (Polynésie française). Unpublished Dissertation, University of Paris (Panthéon Sorbonne).

12

The archaeology of Rapan fortifications

Douglas J. Kennett
Department of Anthropology, The Pennsylvania State University, University Park, PA, USA, djk23@psu.edu

Sarah B. McClure
Department of Anthropology, The Pennsylvania State University

Introduction

Fortifications were common features in the East and South Polynesian sociopolitical landscape. The initial appearance of defensive features coincides with the first evidence for political hierarchy in West Polynesia (Fiji, Tonga and Samoa, Clark and Martinsson-Wallin 2007; Kennett and Winterhalder 2008) and the competing political systems that they represent. This is roughly coincident with the East Polynesian expansion, and competition for land in West Polynesia may have been one contributing factor stimulating exploration and eventual settlement on increasingly remote islands between AD 800 and 1200. This pulse of migration and settlement to increasingly remote islands was an extension of the Austronesian expansion and provided the agroeconomic context that promoted rapid increases in population, territoriality and competition for limited lands and the periodic use of force to take land and surplus food. It is within this context in Polynesia (and elsewhere) that people focus greater effort on constructing defensive features. Cool and dry conditions in the equatorial Pacific during the Little Ice Age between AD 1450 and 1850 also correlate with a proliferation of fortifications in several parts of the Pacific (Field and Lape 2010).

Rapan fortifications have been used to exemplify defensive sites in Polynesia and have served as an end-member of hyper-fortification and intergroup conflict (Kirch 1984). However, the presence and function of hilltop fortifications on Rapa has been debated since Vancouver (Lamb 1984) reported people living in fortifications on the island in AD 1791. Ellis (1838) questioned the mere existence of these fortifications and argued that the sculpted hilltops and terraces were natural geological features. Stokes (n.d.) dispelled this idea with early ethnoarchaeological work on the island that involved visiting these locations and talking to the Rapan people about their history on the island and how the fortifications functioned. The Norwegian expedition provided the first modern archaeological basis for work on these fortifications and the best descriptions of these sites in existence. They clearly demonstrated that the largest hilltop sites were settlements as Vancouver described and that a range of defensive features (ditches, etc.) was consistent with the idea that they served a defensive purpose. Walczak (2001) has questioned this idea and suggested that these sites were more ceremonial in nature. Our aim in this chapter is to pull together the various strands of archaeological data available from previous studies and add our own observations.

Archaeological observations

We conducted archaeological survey and small-scale excavation at 10 large and four small fortifications on the island (Figure 12.1). All of the larger fortifications are strategically positioned on the highest points along the main ridge surrounding Ha'urei Bay. The sites range in size between 3040 m^2 and 25,237 m^2 and all of them have a central tower carved from the soft basalt ridgelines. The smaller fortifications are often found in close proximity to the larger fortifications and they are considered to be satellite communities or temporary refugia. Two of the four smaller fortifications have central towers. We divided Rapa into southern, western and northern sectors to facilitate our descriptions of the available archaeological data and our own observations. We start with the southern sector because we used the Norwegian expedition's excavations at Morongo Uta to index other observations made on the island during the past century.

Southern sector

Three hilltop fortifications are spaced equidistantly along the primary ridge in the island's southern sector (Figure 12.2). Morongo Uta (R-1, 258 m) overlooks the western side of Ha'urei Bay to the east and west across the rich agricultural lands in the drainage associated with Iri Bay. Tevaitau (R-18, 262 m) is located at a lower elevation along the same ridge. Today it overlooks the modern community of Ha'urei positioned on what would have been highly productive agricultural lowlands. Tevaitau is separated from Ororangi (R-20, 282 m) by a large drainage and a series of high peaks along the main ridge system.

Morongo Uta is one of the largest and most architecturally complex fortifications on the island (10,148 m^2). It is also the best studied. Stokes (n.d.) worked at the site for three weeks in 1921, clearing and recording terraces. Based on interviews with local people, he suggested that the village was originally named Teruta and was occupied by a subdivision of a clan named Kopogoiki that controlled territory between Tekoki and Pukumanga.

Work at Morongo Uta was a focal part of the 1956 Norwegian expedition (Mulloy 1965). Using a large crew of local labour (between 12 and 53 people, see Heyerdahl 1958), the site was cleared of vegetation and excavated between May 21 and June 18, 1956. Controlled excavations were minimal, but the entire site was cleared to expose terrace floors, and formal artefacts (e.g. adzes) were collected as the architecture was examined and mapped. Clearing of the site involved the removal of talus slopes and overburden down to approximately 5–10 cm above terrace surfaces. More careful excavation of terrace deposits was then carried out with smaller hand tools. Excavated sediments were not screened for faunal materials or smaller artefacts and persistent rain during this 28-day period limited identification of subtle features (e.g. post moulds) and stratigraphic control.

Much of Morongo Uta was covered with vegetation during our visit, but all of the terrace units mapped by the Norwegian expedition were visible (Figure 12.3). The site core consists of a tall triangular tower and a surrounding triangular cluster of rectilinear terraces that also points to the south. The tower was carved from the highest peak on the ridgeline and covered with a

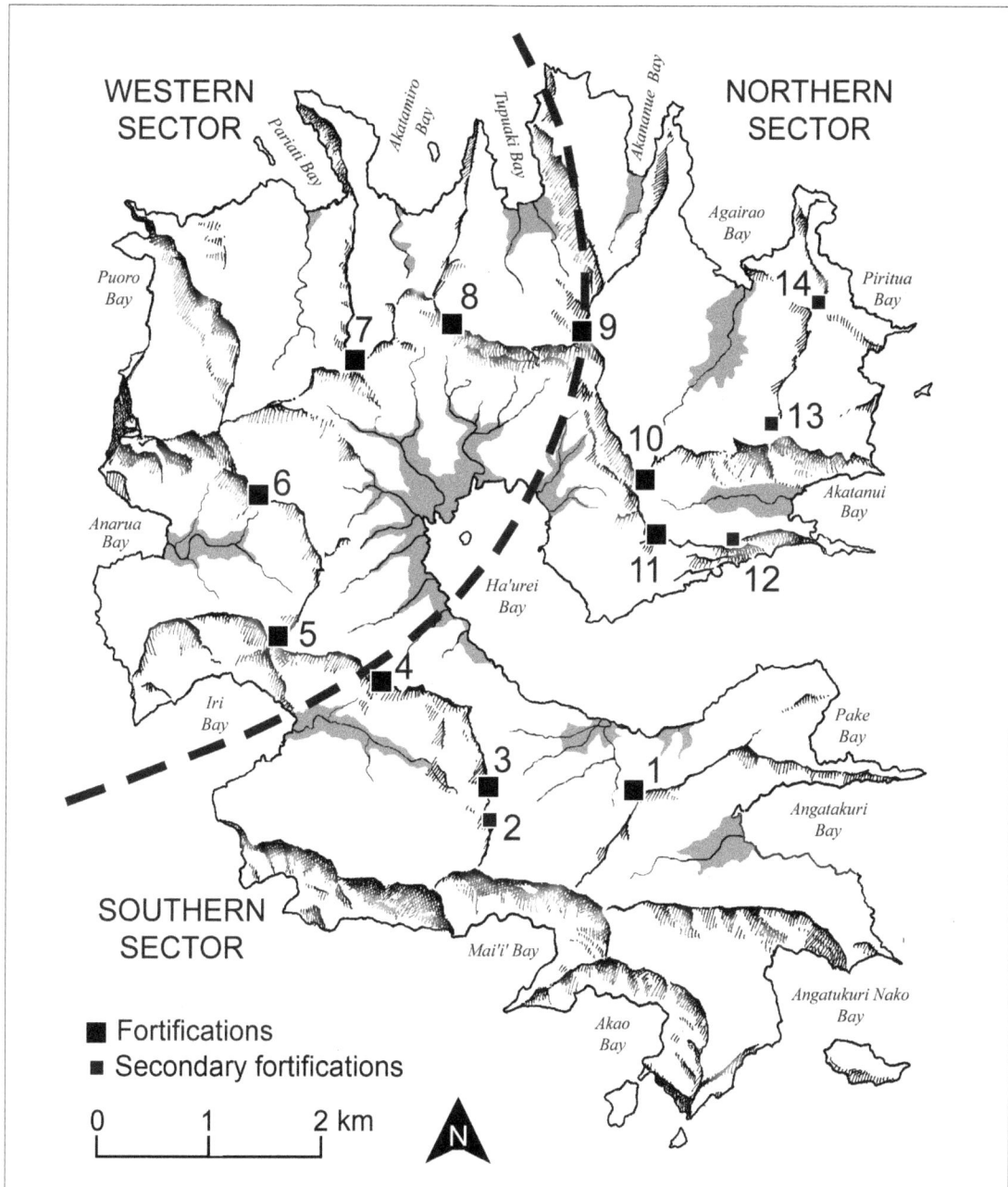

Figure 12.1. Map of Rapa showing the locations of primary and secondary fortifications. The island is divided into southern, western and northern sectors for data presentation purposes and discussion. Drafted R. Van Rossman. 1 = Ororangi (R-20); 2 = Ngapiri (R2002-50); 3 = Tevaitau (R-18); 4 = Morongo Uta (R-1); 5 = Pukutaketake (R2002-42); 6 = Noogurope (R2002-43); 7 = Kapitanga (R-5); 8 = Ruatara (R-17); 9 = Vairu (R-3); 10 = Potaketake (R-2); 11 = Tapitanga (R-4); 12 = Pukutai (R-19); 13 = Pukumia (R2002-39); 14 = Taua (R2002-40).

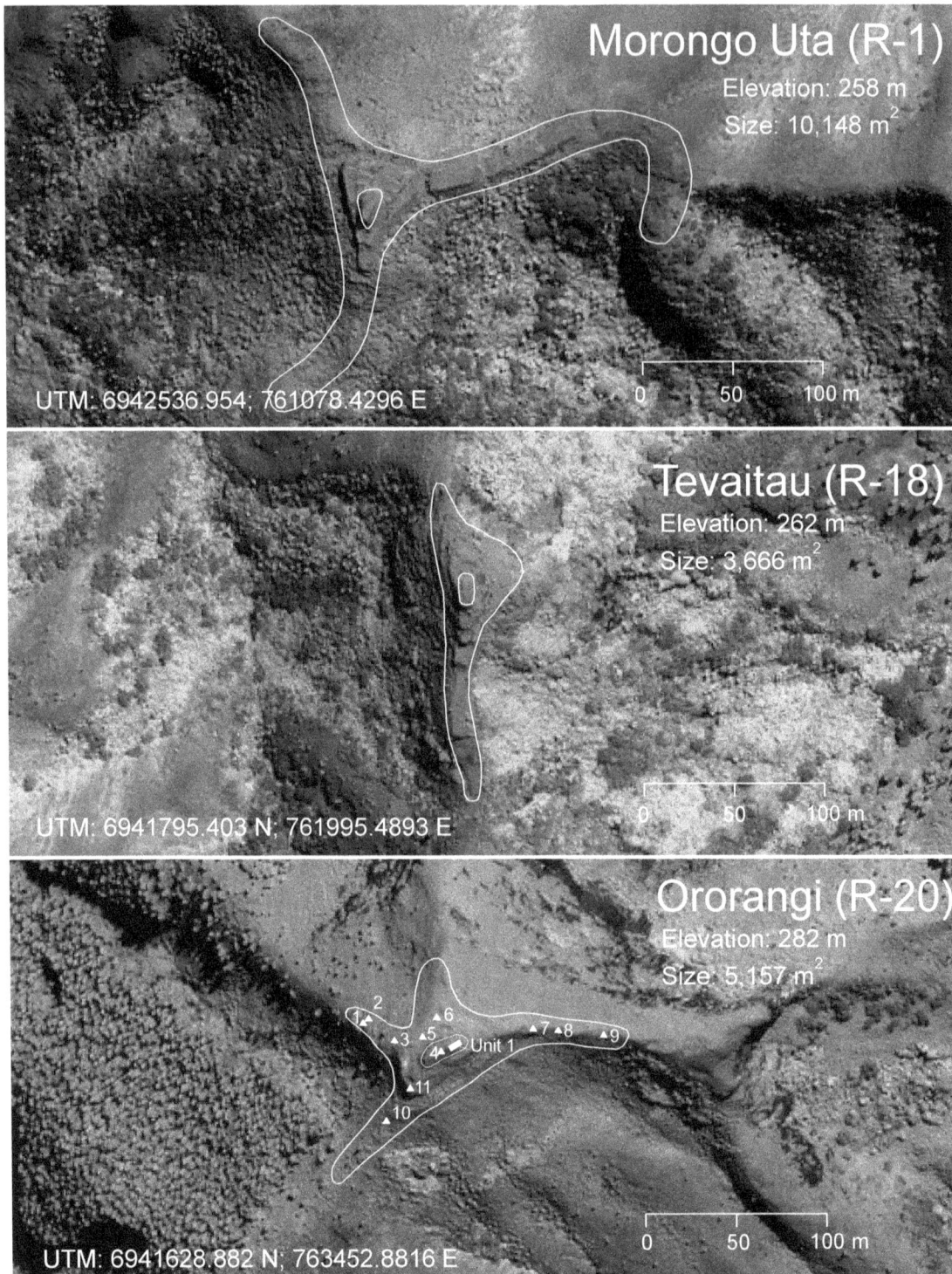

Figure 12.2. IKONOS satellite images of Morongo Uta (R-1), Tevaitau (R-18) and Ororangi (R-20) fortifications. Size estimates, site boundaries and tower orientation are based on field observations and features (e.g. terraces) visible in IKONOS imagery. UTM coordinates are from the centres of each tower. The small numbered triangles on the Ororangi image are the locations of auger tests and the larger rectangle is a 1 m x 1 m test excavation. The locations of test excavations at Morongo Uta and Tevaitau are shown in figures 12.3 and 12.7. Drafted J. Bartruff and D.J. Kennett.

dyke-stone masonry facade. It has a flattened upper surface measuring 10 m x 5.4 m. Stokes excavated the upper flattened surface of the tower and documented a stone-lined oven or hearth in its centre (n.d.:385). At the time, local informants told him that this was the chief's residence and that his closest kin lived in houses positioned on the surrounding upper terrace units. Mulloy (1965) found this implausible, but the upper surface is quite large (34 m²) and dark midden soil containing charcoal and adze flakes is exposed on its northeastern edge (Exposure 2). A charcoal sample from this cleaned exposure was AMS radiocarbon dated to between AD 1500 and 1600 (UCIAMS-2178).

Mulloy (1965:61) mapped 89 terraces at the site, including the enclosure at the top of the tower. The total surface area of these terraces was estimated to be 5406 m². Large numbers of terraces radiate out from the site core along the main ridge and down into the Iri Bay drainage. Dyke-stone walls surround several of the ridgetop terraces and similar walls paralleling the ridge were used as outer retaining walls which were backfilled to create flat surfaces. Many of these walls were reinforced with double interlocking masonry walls filled with a rubble core. Some of the longer terraces were divided into smaller units with walls. The organisation of terraces becomes less formalised with distance from the site core and Mulloy (1965:23) suggested that these were added as populations expanded and clans split into subclans. Stokes (n.d.) also identified additional domestic terraces 300 m to the north of the site core on the same ridgeline and argued that these satellite houses (or *auga*) were also part of the same community. Multiple deep fosses and associated walls cut through the ridgeline at strategic locations point to a large

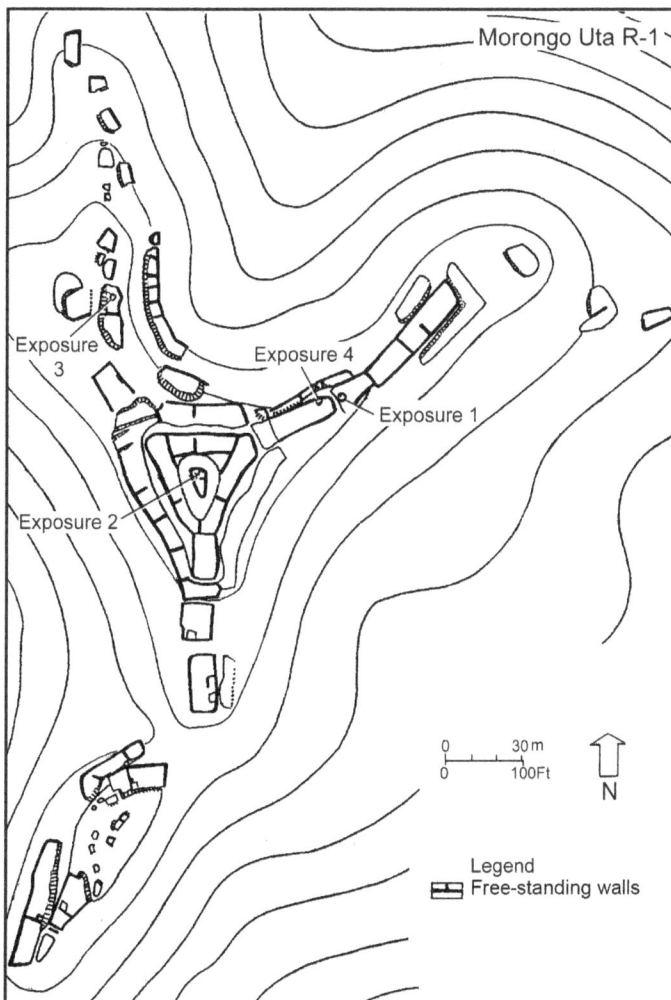

Figure 12.3. Map of Morongo Uta based on the Norwegian expedition's original map, field observations and IKONOS satellite imagery. Exposures were cleaned to examine stratigraphy and collect radiocarbon samples. Drafted R. Van Rossman.

labour investment in defence that is consistent with Vancouver's observations of multiple wooden palisades surrounding these communities (Lamb 1984). Mulloy (1965) suggested that some of these features were excavated after terrace units were in place and indicated heightened aggression later in time.

The Norwegian expedition also documented a number of features and artefacts that provide insight into the types of activities that took place in these communities. Most floors were identified as concentrations of charcoal that were discontinuous across the terrace floor. Terrace walls did not extend above the floor surface and were not designed to support a superstructure. Rectilinear terraces provided platforms for perishable structures made from wood, grass or fronds. Postmoulds were identified, but wet conditions prohibited clear delineation of these structures. Stone-lined cooking pits (ovens) and more formal hearths consisting of three or four tabular stones were identified on many of the terraces (e.g. enclosures 2, 3, 8, 10, 12, 19, 24, 35, 45, 53, 55, 80, 82, Mulloy 1965, figures 7–11). Several smaller d-shaped terraces were interpreted as possible storage features (p. 32) and cylindrical pits of different sizes may have served to store water or taro (see discussion). A group of three prismatic stones driven upright in Enclosure 18 were interpreted by Mulloy (p. 34) as a possible household shrine. Although the Norwegian expedition did not screen and collect faunal and floral remains, Mulloy noted that 'the evidence of daily debris was plentiful', and our observations confirm that dark midden deposits containing charcoal, shell and bone are present at the site. They also collected artefacts indicating a range of daily activities, including 60 whole or fragmented basalt adzes of different types and 60 whole or fragmentary poi pounders (Figure 12.4). Poi anvils were identified and left in place and other types of artefacts were also found in small numbers (circular disk, polishing stones and other groundstone artefacts). This does not include the full range of perishable artefacts that must have been used. Mulloy (1965:53) reports charred fragments of a fish net or netted bag that were identified within a midden in Enclosure 6, but these remains were not recovered intact. We pulled radiocarbon samples from four different midden exposures and these dates suggest persistent use of this site between AD 1600 and 1830 (Figure 12.5).

Our work at Tevaitau was more extensive. The Norwegian expedition recorded this site (R-18), but it does not feature prominently in its 1965 report. It is smaller than Morongo Uta (3666 m²) and, given its overlapping age (AD 1700–1830) and close proximity, it may have developed as a politically connected satellite community (Figure 12.6). Tevaitau has only a distant view of Iri Bay and appears to be more connected visually with the southern part of Ha'urei Bay and the agricultural lands that are now covered with the modern community of Ha'urei. Use of the agricultural lands and access to marine resources via Iri Bay would only have been possible in close consultation with Morongo Uta's chiefly lineage.

Tevaitau is oriented north–south along the main ridge system and consists of a central tower and 14 small surrounding domestic terraces. Most of the terraces were constructed along the ridgeline, but terraces also drop down into the adjacent drainages to the west and east. There is a steep drop into the Iri Bay drainage to the west and only one significant terrace below the core group was identified. Several terraces extend down a steep ridge into the drainage to the east. Morongo Uta is visible to the west and Ororangi is visible to the east. A nice example of dyke-stone masonry covers the tower and several masonry walls are evident within the core. Several foss-like cuts occur between terraces to the north and south of the tower, and steep terrain to the west and east makes the location highly defensible. A free-standing wall divides a long terrace south of the tower. The site was relatively clear of vegetation and we took the opportunity to map it carefully with a laser transit (figures 12.6 and 12.7).

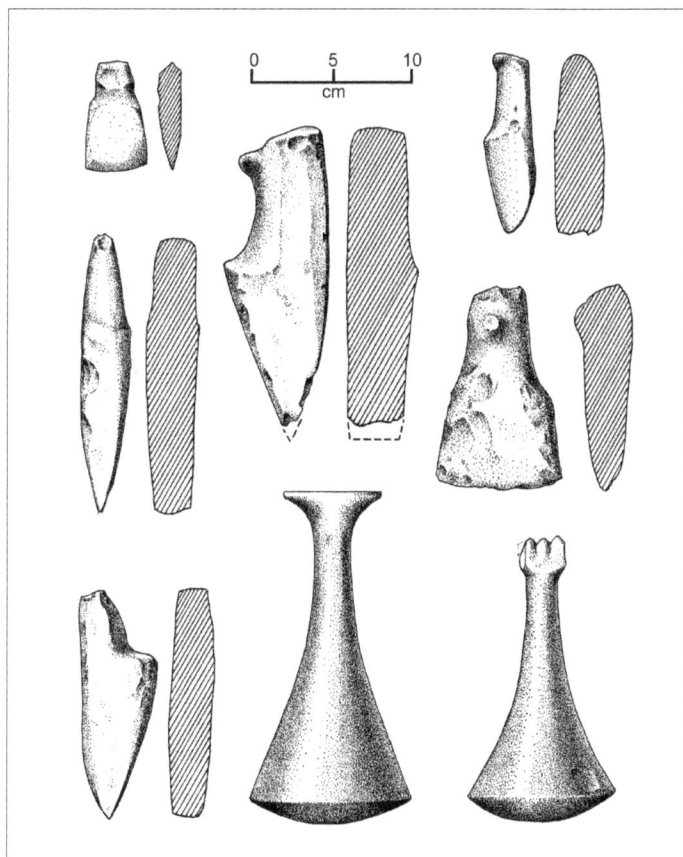

Figure 12.4. Representative selection of adzes and poi pounders collected at Morongo Uta by the Norwegian expedition. Redrawn R. Van Rossman.

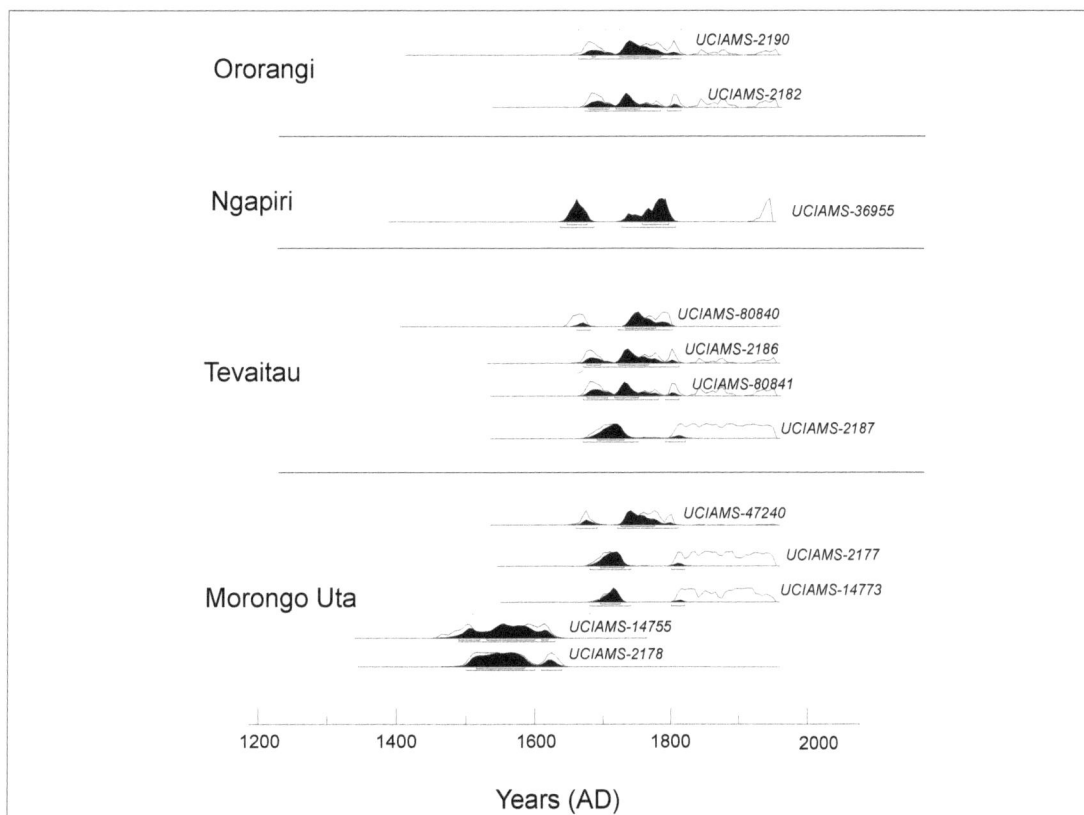

Figure 12.5. Calibrated radiocarbon dates for fortifications in the southern sector based on phase modelling presented in Chapter 11. Prior distributions (routine calibration) are shown in outline, and posterior distributions (modelled within a phase) are solid.

Figure 12.6. Tevaitau (R-18) fortification taken from the south looking north. Photograph D.J. Kennett.

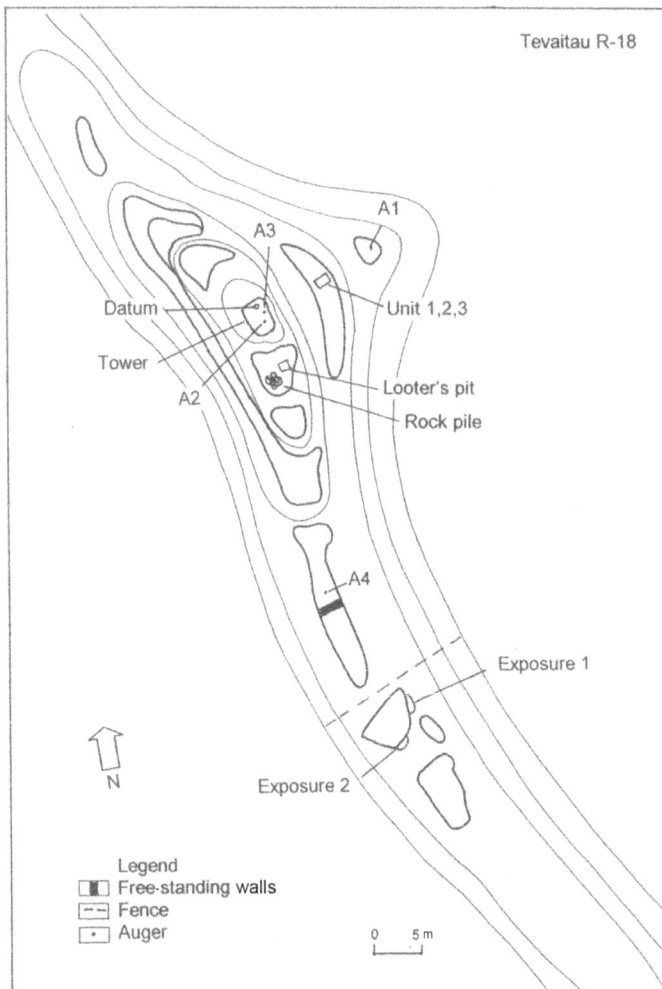

Figure 12.7. Map of the Tevaitau (R-18) showing the locations of excavation units and auger samples.

The site is disturbed by wind and water erosion and there are several looter's pits present in different terraces, the largest just to the south of the central tower. We also learned on the island that Jerome Walczak (2001) had excavated several fortifications in the late 1990s and that he had spent several days at Tevaitau. Documentation of all these excavations is limited (Endnote 1), but he reports excavating a large portion of the upper tower surface of Tevaitau (10 m²) and this large open pit is visible today. He reports finding 922 basalt flakes during this excavation, mostly blanks and adze flakes. These flakes were found in association with wood charcoal, shells and bone, including a goat bone in the surficial deposits that is clearly intrusive given the late introduction of this species. We augered (9 cm diameter) the remaining deposits around this test excavation and identified dark midden deposits that extended from ca.10 cm to 30 cm below the surface.

Similar midden deposits containing basalt flakes, shell, bone and charcoal were evident in two natural exposures and in other auger tests across the site. These deposits range from 30 cm to 80 cm in maximum depth. Based on the density of materials evident in natural exposures and auger tests, we placed three 1 m x 1 m excavation units into undisturbed deposits on a large terrace to the east of the central tower. The deposits are shallow in this location (10–25 cm) and the units bottomed out on the artificially flattened terrace below. Dark midden soils containing charcoal and faunal materials occurred in all these units and there were several small pits that were excavated into the flattened bedrock terrace below. Feature 1 in Unit 2 consisted of two upright tabular stones arranged in a similar fashion to the hearths identified by the Norwegian expedition at Morongo Uta (Figure 12.8). Dark midden soil containing charcoal and faunal materials surrounded Feature 1 and one large concentration (ca. 20 cmbs) was AMS

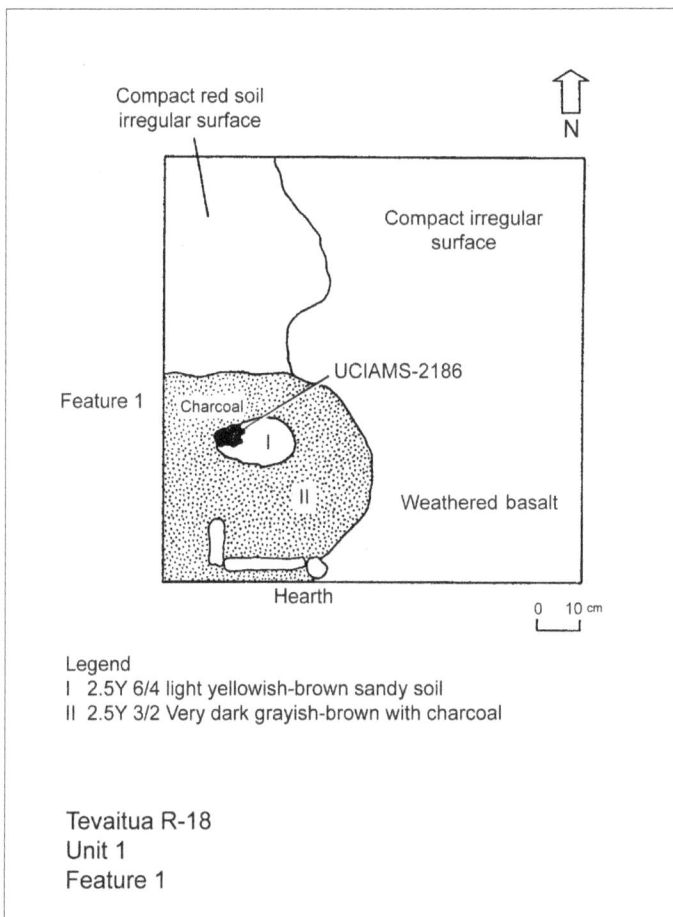

Figure 12.8. Planview map of Unit 1 (20 cmbs) at Tevaitau (R-18). Drafted R. Van Rossman.

radiocarbon dated (UCIAMS-2186) to between AD 1650 and 1750 (see Figure 12.5). A total of 12 basalt adze flakes were recovered in these shallow excavations.

The sediments excavated in units 1–3 were screened in the field with 1/8th inch mesh. Once we determined that sediments contained preserved faunal materials, we also took large bulk samples (six litres in total) for flotation and complete recovery of all faunal and potential floral material. In this way, we recovered the richest faunal assemblage recovered from an island fortification, and associated candlenut fragments that were directly AMS dated (UCIAMS-80840) to between AD 1700 and 1800. The faunal assemblage is composed of nearshore reef fishes that include parrotfishes (Scaridae), damselfishes (Pomacentridae), wrasse (Labridae), pufferfish (Tetraodontidae) and moray eel (Muraenidae). The parrotfishes are the best represented and this may be due to their distinctive character and resistance to decomposition. Rat bones (*Rattus* sp.) were also recovered and are consistent with the observations made by the Norwegian expedition that these hilltop fortifications were also the primary nodes of residence (see Butler, Appendix C). Three AMS radiocarbon dates from these units and one from Exposure 2 on the south end of the site point to occupation between AD 1700 and 1830. Given the substantial overlap in age with the later deposits at Morongo Uta, along with its close and unobstructed proximity, it may have developed as a satellite community of this larger polity.

To the east of Tevaitau at about the same elevation (282 m) is the Ororangi fortification (R-20; see Figure 12.1). It is geographically isolated from Morongo Uta and Tevaitau by a valley that has a steep and impassible ridgeline in its headwaters. The fortification overlooks the modern community of Ha'urei to the west and it is well connected to the exterior of the island via Angatakuri Bay to the east. Tapitanga is visible across Ha'urei Bay and Stokes noted two smaller fortifications in the vicinity (Mititipeiru and Karagarua) and one of these is visible from Ororangi to the southwest.

Ororangi (5157 m^2) is slightly larger than Tevaitau, but substantially smaller than Morongo Uta. The architects at this site took advantage of a high point in the southwest-to-northwest oriented ridge to construct an elongated tower. Two impressive upper terraces surround this elongated tower and together they form the site's core. A total of 43 terraces were documented at the site, but vegetation covers large sections of it to the north and west. The largest number of terraces occurs along the main ridge to the southwest and northeast of the site core. These terraces are rectilinear along the flat portions of the southwestern terrace and more d-shaped down a steeper section of the ridge to the northeast. A cluster of six small terraces (each 5 m x 5 m) occurs on the southwestern flank of the site core and small d-shaped terraces drop down the steep ridges towards Ha'urei Bay. The largest domestic terraces drop down the more gradual slopes towards Angatakuri Bay.

Ororangi does not have the same types of dyke-stone masonry architecture as Morongo Uta and Tevaitau. Terraces were cut directly into the ridgelines and cutting and moving the soft basalt bedrock created flattened surfaces. A sketch map of these terraces was produced and 11 auger samples were taken from across the site (see Figure 12.2). The upper ca. 10 cm of these auger tests consisted of culturally sterile orange sediment that sometimes contained sparse amounts of modern material. Below these upper deposits were prehistoric sediments between 10 cm and 40 cm thick. These sediments were darker and contained charcoal and the occasional adze flake. At the base of these sections, the darker midden transitioned to the underlying soft basalt bedrock that had been flattened to create the terrace. Midden deposits appear to be best developed on the second and third terraces to the north of the tower (augers 5 and 6). Work on the southwestern arm of Ororangi was limited by dense vegetation.

The tower at Ororangi is well preserved and the entire upper surface appears to be intact.

Sediments on top of the tower are dark brown and covered with a thick layer of grass. An auger test near the centre of the tower suggested intact deposits containing charcoal were between 20 cm and 30 cm deep. A small test unit (Unit 1, 1 m x 1 m) was placed near the northwestern side of the tower. Some modern debris was found in the upper 5 cm within sediments that were otherwise culturally sterile. Dark midden soil containing charcoal, fire-cracked rock, adze flakes and faunal material was encountered at ca. 10 cm below the surface. A small cluster of fire-cracked rock was encountered in the eastern part of the unit at ca. 10 cm below the surface (Feature 2) and may be the remnants of an oven. This feature occurred just above the basalt surface of the terrace that had been flattened prehistorically. A much larger fire feature became visible at ca. 10 cm in the northern and western portion of Unit 1 (Feature 1, Figure 12.9). This feature was excavated into the underlying basalt to a maximum depth of ca. 50 cm. The pit contained dark silty sediment with large quantities of charcoal and fire-cracked rock. This is similar in character to the fire feature described by Stokes on top of the tower at Morongo Uta.

Most of these sediments were screened in the field (1/8th inch mesh), but a two-litre flotation sample was taken and examined for floral and faunal remains. Six basalt adze flakes were recovered, along with a small amount of faunal material, including 21 parrotfish (Scaridae) bones and one Elasmobranch (shark or ray) bone (see Butler, Appendix C). A radiocarbon sample taken at the top (UCIAMS-2190) and bottom (UCIAMS-2182) were nearly identical and put Ororangi contemporary with Tevaitau and the later stages of occupation at Morongo Uta (AD 1700 to 1830).

Western sector

The western sector of Rapa is rugged and contains the highest mountain peaks on the island (Perau, 650 m). A ridge running to the south of Anarua Bay and its associated drainage forms the southern boundary of this sector. Tupuai Bay and its associated drainage roughly delineate its eastern boundary. Pukutaketake (R2002-42), Noogurope (R2002-43), Kapitanga (R-5) and Ruatara (R-17) are the four primary fortifications in this area and they are all positioned on

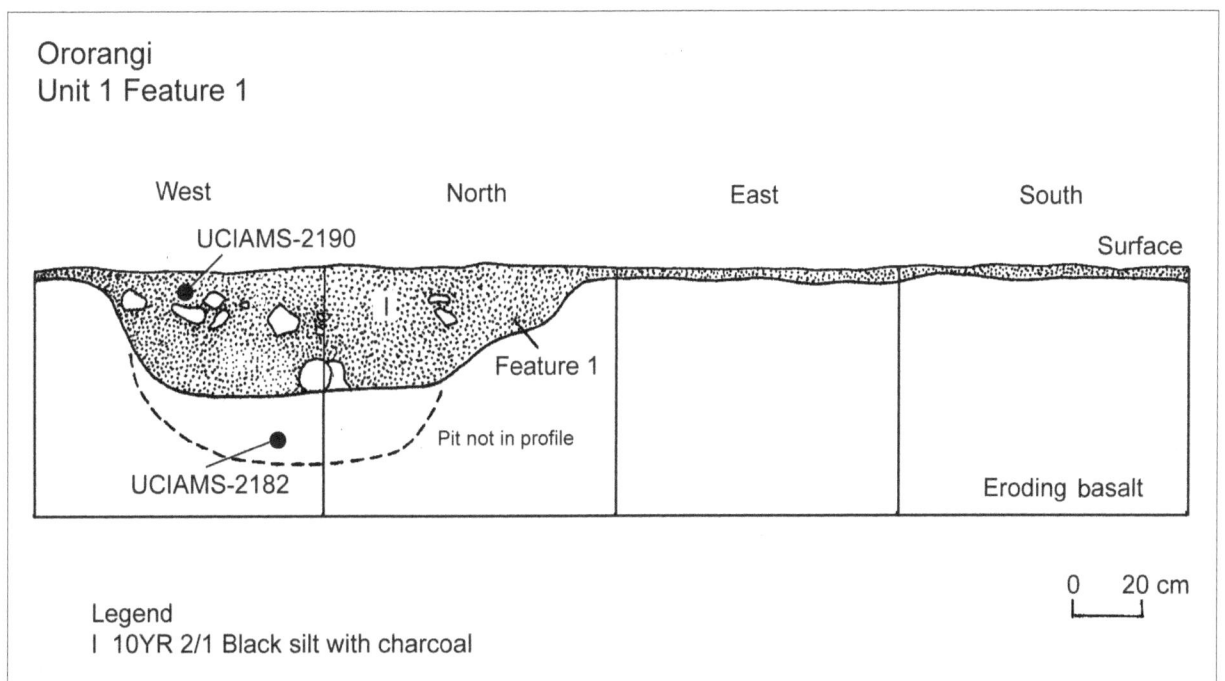

Figure 12.9. Stratigraphy in Unit 1 at Ororangi. Drafted R. Van Rossman.

the main ridge system overlooking the prime agricultural lands at the head of Ha'urei Bay. The Norwegian expedition mapped Kapitanga and visited Ruatara, but it is unclear from its reports whether it examined or visited Pukutaketake and Noogurope. All of these fortifications are clearly identified on Stokes' map from the 1930s. Pukutaketake and Noogurope overlook Anarua Bay to the west. Kapitanga and Ruatara overlook Pariati, Akatamiro and Tupuaki bays along the northern shore. These sites range in size between 3000 m² and 7000 m². This was the least studied part of the island, by us, but our preliminary work suggests that two of the fortifications, Noogurope and Ruatara, were among the first to be constructed on Rapa. Future work at Noogorupe and Ruatara should be a high priority.

Noogurope is the highest elevation fortification on the island (608 m), and Perau (650 m), the tallest peak along the primary ridge system, provides a strong protective barrier blocking easy passage to and from fortifications to the north and west (e.g. Kapitanga and Ruatara). All of the other fortifications on the island are visible from this vantage point. Access from Ha'urei Bay is also limited by a series of rock escarpments and cliffs blocking easy passage. The fortification is small (3040 m²) and consists of 12 terraces surrounding a small circular tower. Nicely formed dyke-stone walls were evident along the eastern and western sides of the upper terrace and a fragmentary segment also occurs along its southern periphery. Unlike Kapitanga to the northwest, the circular tower at Noogurope is not faced with dyke-stone. The longest series of terraces extends to the northwest along the ridge leading towards Perau. Terraces also extend down the subsidiary ridge system to the west towards Anarua Bay and there appear to be several terraces to the east on the ridge dropping down to Ha'urei Bay. Farther down the ridge to Ha'urei were several domestic terraces built with dyke-stone walls. These are associated with a dyke-stone outcrop. A large talus slope is present on the northern side of the outcrop and the large amounts of debris scattered across the surface are suggestive of quarrying activity, but more work is needed to establish the extent and character of this site.

At Noogurope we excavated four STPs (test pits) on the uppermost terrace (Figure 12.10). Charcoal-rich midden soils were encountered in all of these sample test pits and extended down to between 10 cmbs and 25 cmbs. A charcoal sample collected at 25 cmbs in STP #2 returned a date of 650 ± 15 bp (UCIAMS-47241). This is the earliest date at Noogurope and the earliest date associated with a fortification on Rapa. Another date from STP #3 from the basal deposits (15–25 cmbs) returned an age of 230 ± 25 bp (UCIAMS-60739). We also cleared off a natural exposure (Exp #1) on the northeastern side of the second northern terrace. A charcoal-rich midden deposit was defined between 10 cmbs and 37 cmbs, and a charcoal sample recovered from 20 cmbs returned an age of 120 ± 15 bp (UCIAMS-14756). This is comparable in age to STP #1 (10–19 cmbs, UCIAMS-60740) and suggests occupation until approximately AD 1830. Overall, the calibrated dates at this site range between AD 1300 and 1830 (Figure 12.11). Preservation of faunal material was poor in these deposits and only a few adze flakes were recovered during our small-scale excavations.

The imposing site of Ruatara sits on the tallest mountain peak (304 m elevation) on the main ridge system between Vairu and Kapitanga. It is the largest (6940 m²) fortification in the north-central sector and among the largest fortifications on the island. Due to its central position, it has a commanding view of the prime agricultural lands at the head of Ha'urei Bay and of three external drainages and associated bays to the north (Akatamiro, Tupuai and Akanamu). The tower is one of the tallest on the island (5 m) and a step series of four narrow terraces down its western flank adds to the prominence of the tower (Figure 12.12). Sixteen terraces in total radiate from the tower along the primary ridge system and down subsidiary

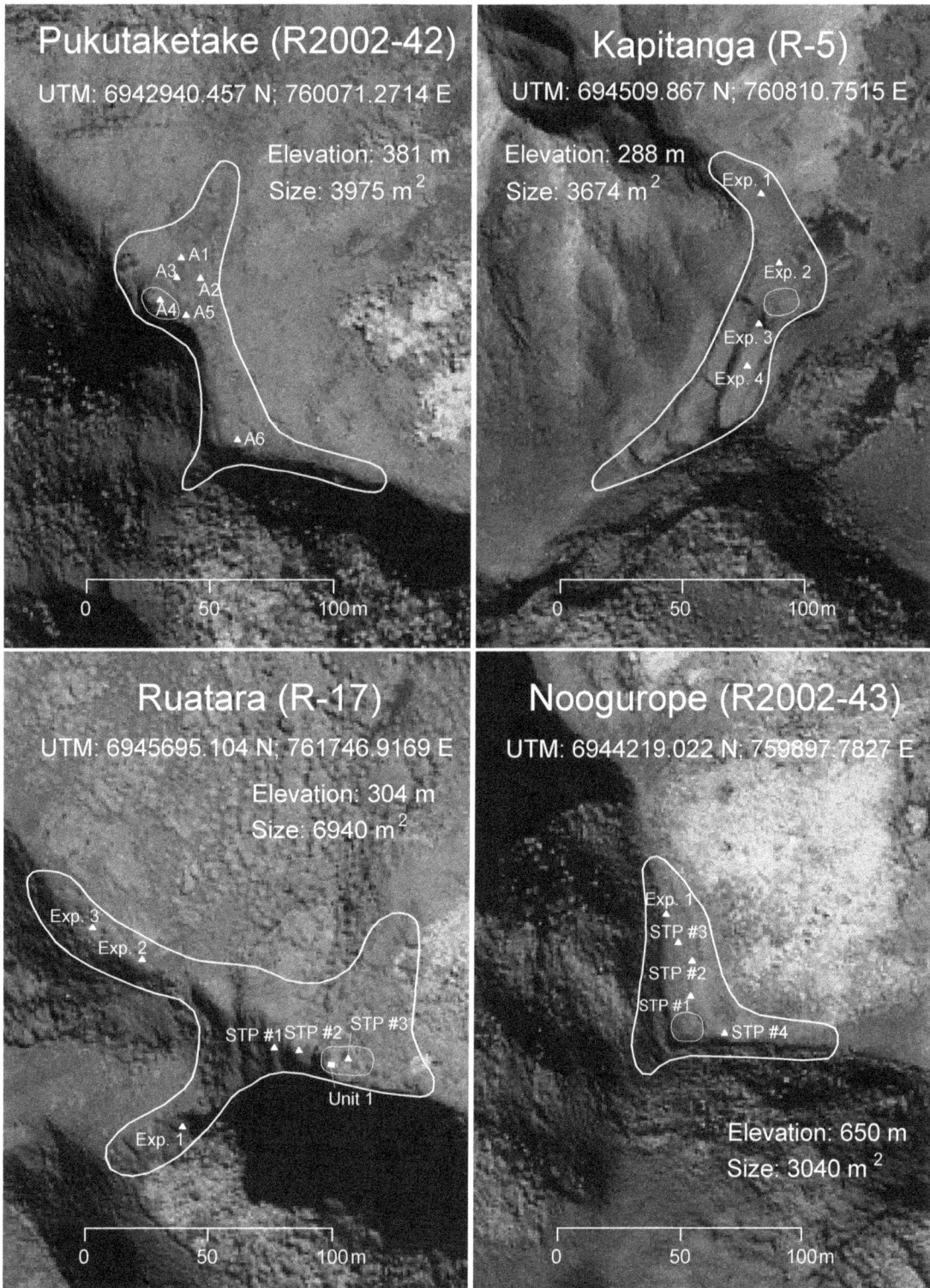

Figure 12.10. IKONOS satellite images of Pukutaketake (R2002-42), Kapitanga (R-5), Ruatara (R-17) and Noogurope (R2002-43) fortifications. Size estimates, site boundaries and tower orientation are based on field observations and features (e.g. terraces) visible in IKONOS imagery. UTM coordinates are from the centres of each tower. The small numbered triangles are the locations of auger tests and sample test pits. A small 0.5 m x 0.5 m test unit was excavated on top of the tower at Ruatara. Drafted by J. Bartruff and D.J. Kennett.

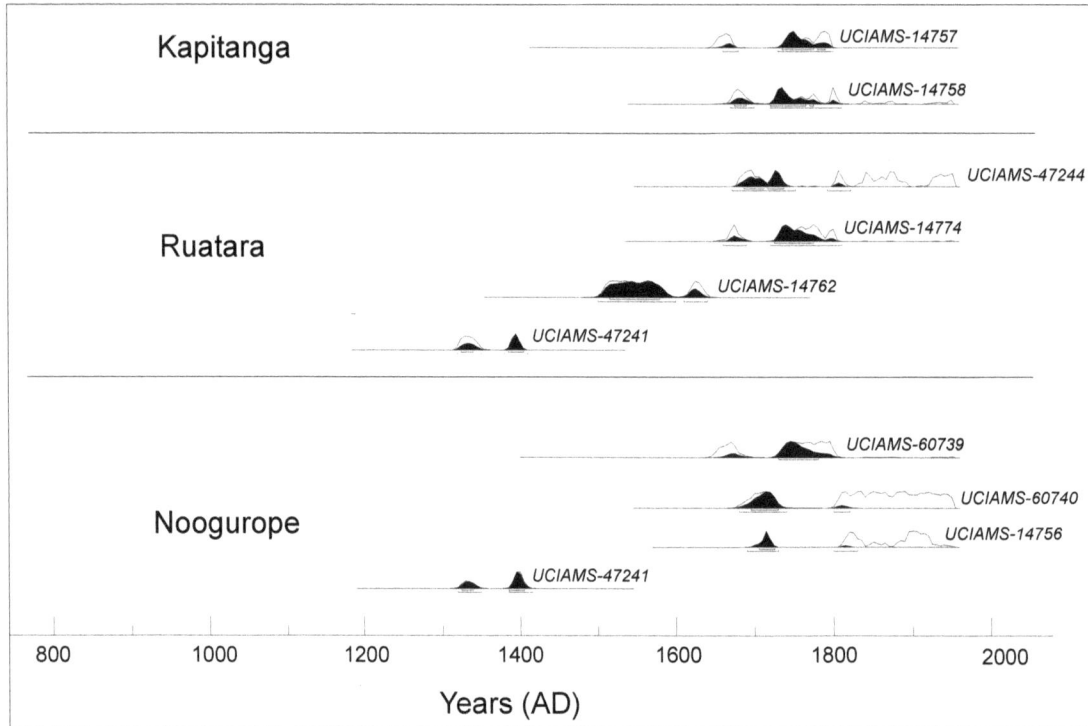

Figure 12.11. Calibrated radiocarbon dates for fortifications in the western sector based on phase modelling presented in Chapter 11. Prior distributions (routine calibration) are shown in outline, and posterior distributions (modelled within a phase) are solid.

ridges to the north and south. Compared with other sites on the island, the use of dyke-stone construction was fairly limited.

One of the unique features of Ruatara is a series of wall-like linear earthen mounds that separate the lower terraces at the site. A series of six well-defined terrace units, often divided by these high earthen mounds, extends from the site core along the primary ridge to the west. These terraces were heavily vegetated during our visit, but a cow trail cuts through and has exposed midden deposits at several locations. Midden soils were shallow, but well developed in both exposures 2 and 3. Exposure 3 occurs along the northwestern terrace wall (8 cmbs) and contained charcoal that dates to 630 ± 15 bp (UCIAMS-47243), comparable in age to the earliest deposits at Noogurope. A similar exposure on the western side of the next terrace to the east produced a much more recent age (11 cmbs, 170 ± 15 bp, UCIAMS-47244). One of the best examples of an earthern wall occurs between two of the most prominent terraces on the southwestern arm of the site. Midden-like deposits were evident in a natural exposure on the eastern side of this earthen mound and this was most likely recycled as construction fill from a previous occupation. A charcoal sample collected from this exposure (14 cmbs) returned an age of 345 ± 15 bp. Calibrated age ranges for the site are AD 1300 to 1830 (see Figure 12.11). Two large pits similar to those found at other fortifications occur in the middle of the terrace just to the west of this earthen mound feature. Future excavations should be undertaken to determine the function of these pits, but they were probably used for the storage of taro, as proposed by Stokes (n.d.).

The tower at Ruatara is impressive and it is unclear whether the thin terraces on its western flank were defensive or domestic features. STP #1 was placed in the middle of the second terrace west of the tower and excavated down to 40 cmbs without encountering midden soils. A second test unit (STP #2) was excavated down to 35 cm and a thin midden soil containing charcoal occurred at about 15 cm and was radiocarbon dated to 210 ± 15 bp (UCIAMS-14774). The tower itself is tall (an estimated 5 m) and is squared off on its northern and western side. Remnants of dyke-stone masonry are evident, but these stones were either recycled elsewhere or the masonry was never as well developed as in other nearby locations (e.g. Kapitanga). The planar upper surface of the tower is 8 m x 3 m in size and is oriented east–west. It was certainly large enough to serve as a residence. Dark midden soil containing charcoal, shell, bone and adze flakes was evident across the surface of the tower. A circular test pit (STP #3, 20 cm diameter) was excavated in the centre of the tower and dark midden soil containing charcoal and adze flakes extended down to 35 cm. Unit 1 (25 cm x 50 cm) was excavated 2 m from the tower's western edge and 50 cm from its southern edge. These deposits were excavated in 10 cm levels down to 35 cm. Faunal materials were reasonably well preserved in these deposits and were dominated by parrotfish (*Scaridae*, see Butler, Appendix C). Other fish (*Serranidae*, *Labridae*) and rat (*Rattus* sp) bones were also identified in these deposits.

Kapitanga (288 m elevation, 3674 m²) is located between Noogurope and Ruatara in the northern section of the island. Compared with the earlier fortifications in this sector, it is highly consolidated with dyke stone-lined domestic terraces similar to Potaketake (R-2). The Norwegian expedition was drawn to this location because of its hyper-fortified position and its well-formed oval tower covered with a beautiful dyke-stone masonry facade. They considered it the best example on the island. Defensively, this fort was enhanced relative to other locations because of a steep rock precipice 100 m tall on the east side of the fortification. The western

Figure 12.12. Ruatara (R-17) fortification taken from the southwest looking northwest. Photograph D.J. Kennett.

side of the fortification is also well protected by a series of steep ridges. Eleven domestic terraces occur in three compact tiers. Rubble-filled double retaining walls bound the upper terrace. Multiple pit features similar to those at Potaketake were also identified and two fosses were strategically placed on the western and southern flanks to cut off the only two viable entry points into the fortification. Large basalt adze flakes were evident on the surface of the northern exposure at the site.

Pukutaketake is positioned on a high point (381 m) overlooking the mountain pass between Anarua and Ha'urei Bay. Noogurope is visible across the pass to the north and Morongo Uta occurs on the same ridge system just to the southeast. Stokes referred to this site as west Potaketake and people living on the island in the 1920s considered this to be one of the oldest sites on the island. The site was heavily vegetated during our visit, but 23 terraces were identified running along the main and subsidiary ridges. The overall size of the site is small (3975 m²) compared with Ruatara. The site has a well-formed tower, but lacks the dyke-stone masonry evident at other sites. Dyke-stone masonry is rare except for a few remnant sections along the southern and east edge of the upper terrace.

We excavated seven exploratory STPs (each 20 cm in diameter) at the site, and most of these (STPs 1–5) were in the terrace surrounding the central tower (see Figure 12.10). One of these was excavated into the northeastern edge of the tower itself. Dark midden soil containing high concentrations of charcoal was encountered in all of these units at approximately 10 cmbs. Adze flakes were more commonly encountered in these deposits than in other locations on the island. These midden deposits were between 20 cm and 30 cm thick, and charcoal appeared to be more commonly concentrated on the outer edges of these terraces. Midden deposits containing charcoal also occurred on the top of the tower, along with several fire-cracked rock fragments, suggesting that a hearth or oven was located near the excavation unit. Two STPs were also excavated at the end of a long terrace that extends east from the central tower. The deposits were more ephemeral and probably severely wind deflated. The radiocarbon date from one test pit (STP #2, UCIAMS-14760, -14759) places it in the final fortification phase between AD 1700 and 1830.

Northern sector

The northeastern sector of the island consists of land roughly delineated by the ridgeline separating Tupuaki and Akananue bays (and associated drainages) and all of the land on the eastern shore of Ha'urei Bay. Three of these drainages flow outwards to Akananue, Agairoa and Akatanui Bays and one flows inwards to Ha'urei Bay. Sharp ridgelines delineate these drainages and provide the easiest overland paths between fortifications and other upland sites. In certain instances, ridges were flattened or modified (e.g. staircases) to promote movement between locations, but ditches and fosses were also placed in strategic locations to inhibit travel. The remains of three large fortifications occur along the ridge separating the inner and outer parts of the island. Each fortification was strategically placed at the juncture between the main ridge and one or two secondary ridges extending out to the coastline. Vairu (R-3) is positioned at the top of the ridge (369 m) that separates Akananue and Angairao. Potaketake (R-2) overlooks Agairao and Akatanui Bay at the ridge separating these two drainages, and Tapitanga (R-4, 268 m) overlooks Akatanui and Ha'urei bays and sits directly above the modern town of Area. The available radiocarbon dates indicate that they were all established and occupied during the final phase of fortification between AD 1700 and 1830 (Figure 12.13).

All the large fortifications were visited in this sector and limited excavations were carried out at Tapitanga and Potaketake to build on previous work by the Norwegian expedition. Vairu

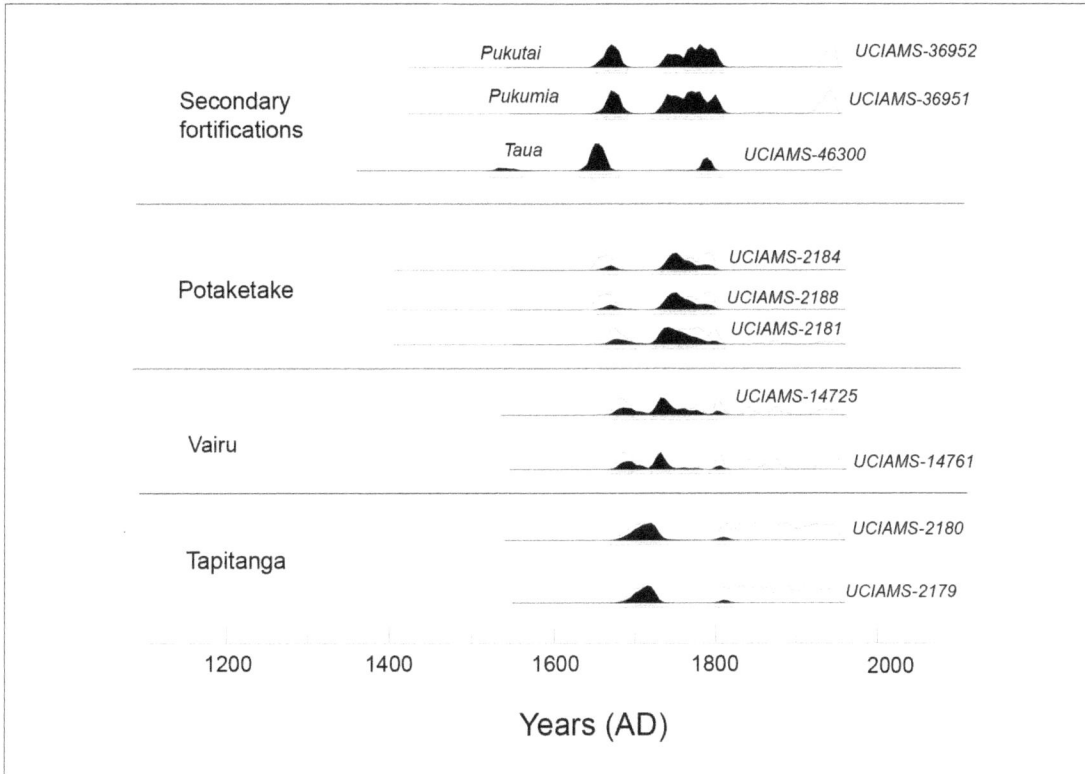

Figure 12.13. Calibrated radiocarbon dates for fortifications in the northern sector based on phase modelling presented in Chapter 11. Prior distributions (routine calibration) are shown in outline, and posterior distributions (modelled within a phase) are solid.

was visited briefly and is estimated to be 4213 m^2 in size (Figure 12.14). As with the other large fortifications, it has a well-formed central tower, and at least 11 domestic terraces extend outwards from the central tower along the main ridge and down the secondary ridge separating Akananue and Angairao. Auger tests on multiple terraces and on top of the flattened tower exposed midden soils containing charcoal and the occasional basalt adze flake. Midden soils were also exposed at the edge of the uppermost terrace on the western side of the site. None of these midden soils were deeper than 30 cm and most were 10–20 cm thick. Two radiocarbon dates, one from Auger #7 (tower) and the other from Exposure #1, suggest occupation between AD 1700 and 1830.

Both Tapitanga and Potaketake sit above the headwaters of Akatanui Bay. AMS radiocarbon work places both fortifications just prior to European contact, with Tapitanga dating earlier, between 1700 and 1750, and Potaketake dating to between AD 1750 and 1830. The Norwegian expedition mapped these two sites in the 1950s and we use its observations as a starting point for describing our work at these sites. Tapitanga is the largest fortification on the island (25,237 m^2), but the site is dispersed and clear evidence of terracing and use is isolated to a much smaller portion of the entire area (Figure 12.15). A poorly developed tower carved from the highest point of the ridge marks the centre of the fortification, and it is surrounded by a consolidated cluster of smaller domestic terraces. Five more distant terrace groups, positioned away from the central group, radiate out along the ridge systems surrounding Akatanui Bay and down the slope towards Ha'urei Bay. Several pit features were visible on the surface of the site, as described by Ferdon (1965), with the best examples in the central and eastern parts of the site.

Free-standing walls and stone-lined terraces are rare at this location and many of the

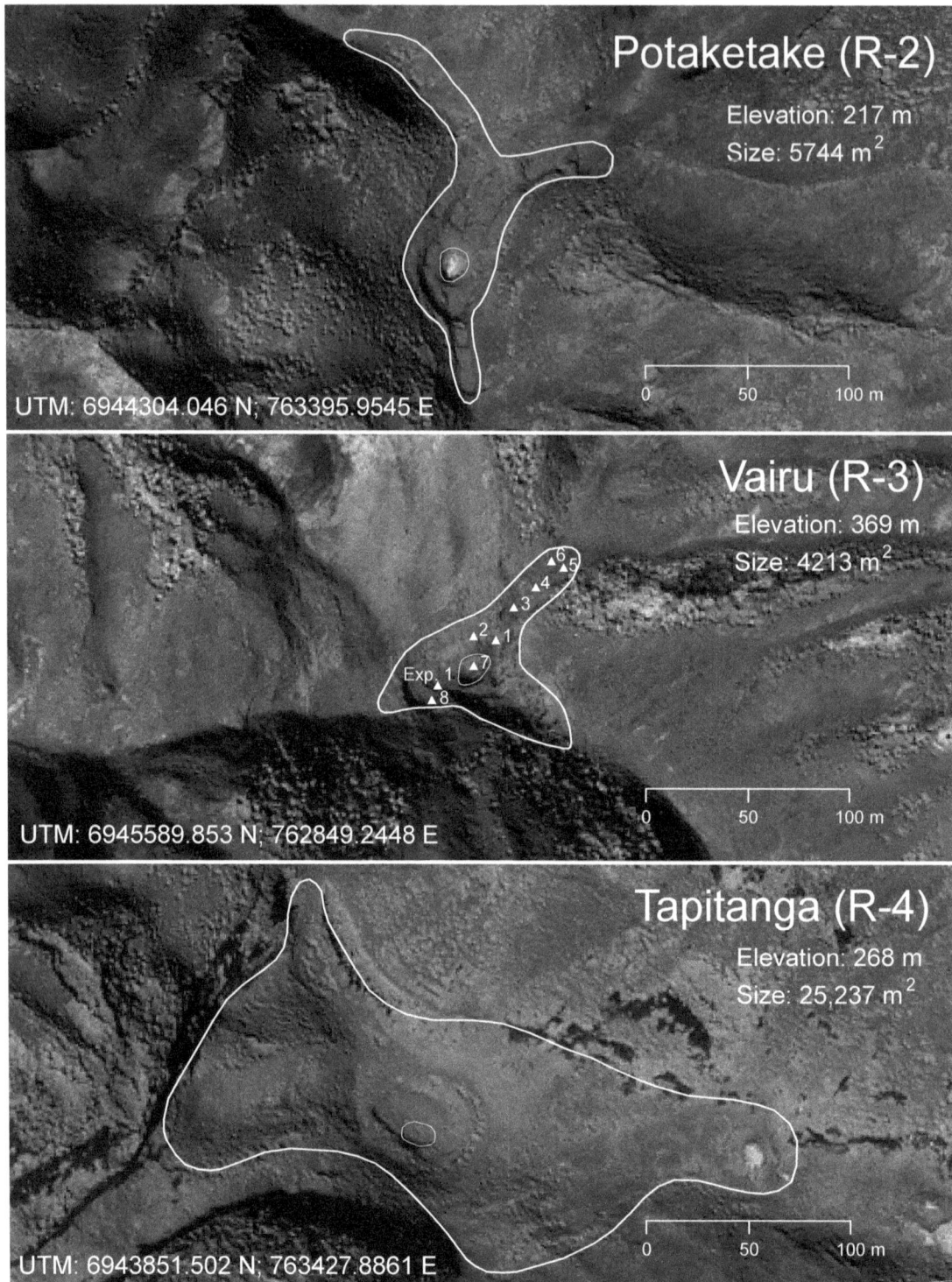

Figure 12.14. IKONOS satellite images of Potaketake (R-2), Vairu (R-3) and Tapitanga (R-4) fortifications. Size estimates, site boundaries and tower orientation are based on field observations and features (e.g. terraces) visible in IKONOS imagery. UTM coordinates are from the centers of each tower. The small numbered triangles are the locations of auger tests and sample test pits. Drafted J. Bartruff and D.J. Kennett.

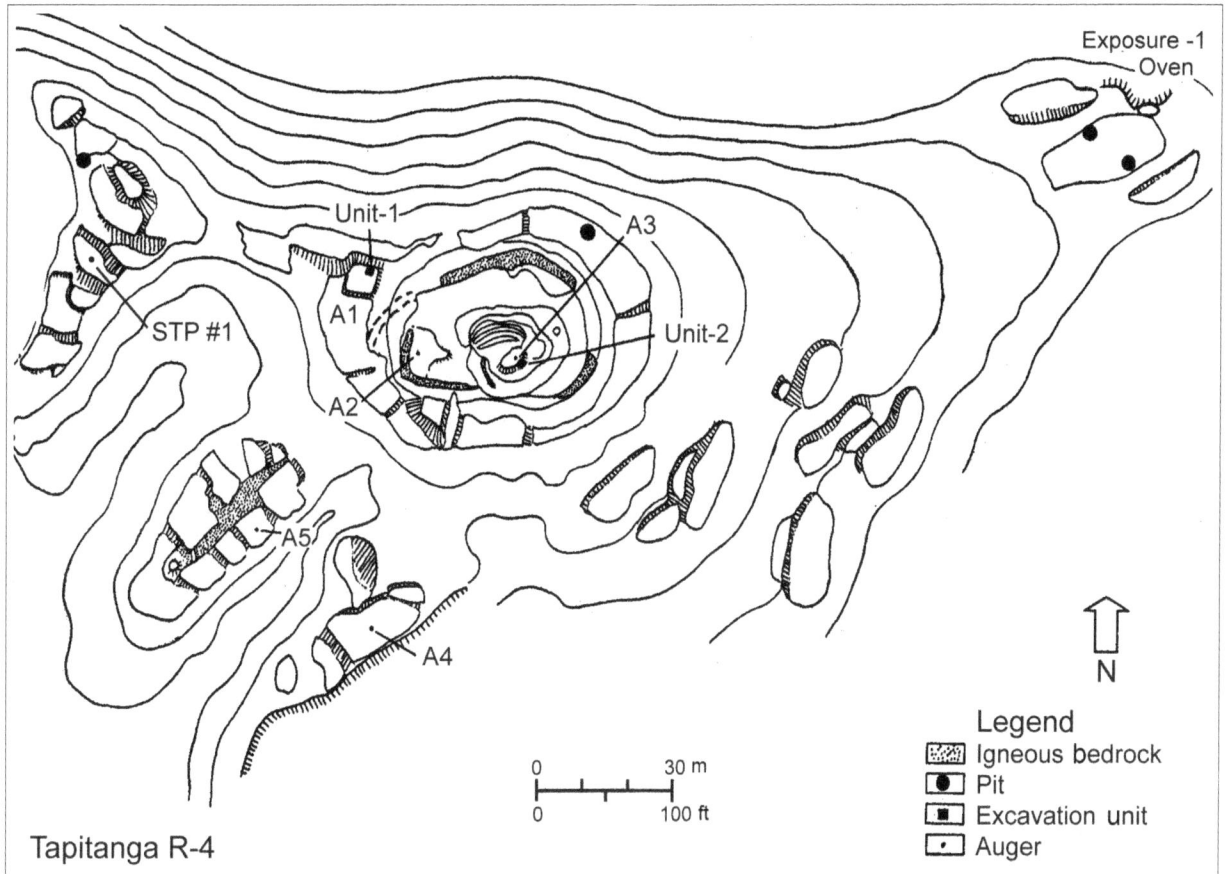

Figure 12.15. Map of Tapitanga showing locations of auger tests and excavation units. The map is based on the Norwegian expedition's original map, field observations and IKONOS satellite imagery. Drafted R. Van Rossman.

structures are heavily eroded. Ferdon (1965) noted more formal architecture, with a few exposed masonry walls exposed in the central precinct and some of the southwestern terrace groups. Terraces were cut directly into the ridge and the distribution of these terraces is skewed towards the Ha'urei Bay side of the ridge, but the upper terrace and tower were clearly positioned to overlook Akatanui Bay. Ferdon (1965) argued for an early occupation of this fortification compared with other forts in the area, based on its dispersed form, its lack of formal walls and defensive features (e.g. fosses), and the heavy erosion it has suffered. It does appear to have been constructed earlier than the other fortifications in the northeastern sector.

Seven augers and one sample test unit (STP) were excavated in terraces on the western side of the fortification and we also examined an exposed oven on the eastern end of the fortification down the ridge towards Akatanui Bay. Dark midden soils containing charcoal and the occasional adze flake were encountered at each location between 5 cm and 10 cm below the modern ground surface. These midden soils were generally between 20 cm and 30 cm deep, but midden soils extended to 60 cm below the surface in the centre of one well-formed rectilinear domestic terrace.

We also excavated two units at this site. Unit 1 (1 m x 1 m) was established on the west side of the tower along the northern wall of a domestic terrace. The unit was placed close to a large basalt boulder that had been heavily battered at some point in the past. Surface collection in the vicinity of the boulder and Unit 1 revealed a large number of primary basalt flakes (N=75). Unit 1 was excavated in naturally occurring levels and all material was screened (1/4" mesh) for maximum recovery. Stratum 1 varied in depth between 5 cm and 10 cm and was a well-developed dark-brown midden soil containing flecks of charcoal and basalt flakes. Removal of this level exposed a stone terrace wall on the north side of the unit and several concentrations of fragmented basalt in the east side of the unit. Stratum II comprised orange-brown soil that contained flecks of charcoal. The cluster of broken basalt visible at the base of Stratum I was revealed to be an oven containing high concentrations of fire-cracked rock, dark brown soil and charcoal (Figure 12.16). An alignment of rocks occurs in the southern side of the unit and was possibly the foundation of an interior wall. A hearth or oven originally excavated into Stratum III was also identified at the base of Stratum II (30 cm) in the eastern side of the unit. It contained large concentrations of charcoal and fire-cracked rock. Charcoal and basalt flakes were recovered while screening (2 mm, 15 litres). Preservation was limited and no faunal remains were recovered, but several burned candlenut (*Aleurites moluccana*) fragments were also recovered from this stratum. Stratum III was an orange-brown soil with a high clay content and contained no charcoal or cultural material. An auger probe in the northern side of the unit indicated that this soil extended down 60 cm to bedrock. The only radiocarbon dates from this site come from the interface between Stratum I and Stratum II (S1, UCIAMS-2180, 145 ± 25 bp) and from the hearth feature (UCIAMS-2179, 140 ± 20 bp).

Unit 2 (50 cm x 50 cm) was excavated on the southern side of the tower near a natural exposure of midden soil containing bone. Midden soil extended to approximately 30 cm below the surface and was excavated in 10 cm intervals. Faunal materials were recovered from all three levels (2 mm mesh) and are dominated by parrotfish (*Scaridae*, NISP of 30, of which 15 are teeth). Larger bones in the sequence are sea turtle, but the bone was poorly preserved and the exact species could not be identified. A large number of unidentifiable vertebrate bones was also recovered (Butler, Appendix C).

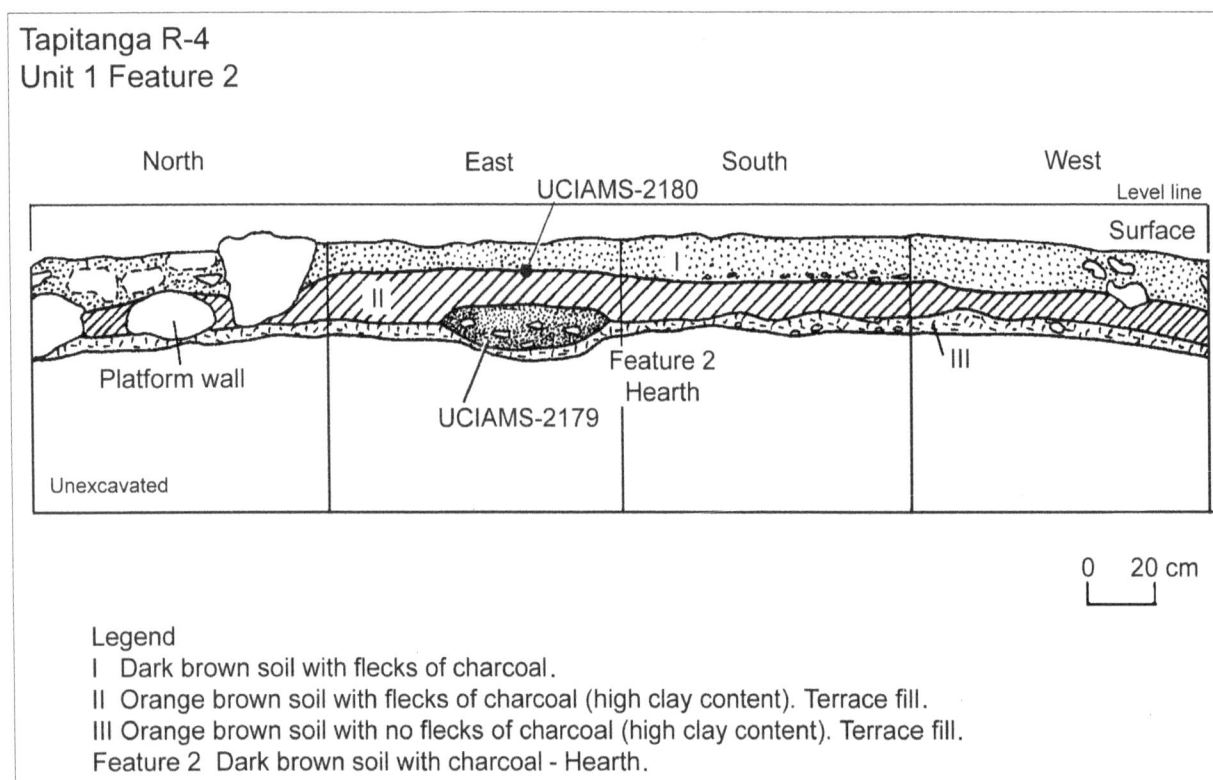

Figure 12.16. Stratigraphy in Unit 1 at Tapitanga. Drafted R. Van Rossman.

Potaketake (R-2) is located at the junction between the ridge lines that form the Akatanui, Angairao and Ha'urei watersheds, at 217 m elevation. From this vantage point there is a commanding view of agricultural lands in two external drainages, Akatanui and Angairao, and the upper portions of the Ha'urei watershed. The hilltop village of Tapitanga (R-4) is located only 0.5 km to the south across a saddle in the ridge at the head of Akatanui Bay. A series of rockshelters with occupation ages between AD 1300 and 1500 are present along the northern shore of the bay, along with several stone fish traps that occur along the edge of the bay.

The heavily wind-blown and eroded remnants of a tower form the centre of Potaketake (Figure 12.17). Well-formed domestic terraces surround this tower in two distinct tiers along the north–south axis of the site. Defensive ditches were cut into three ridges surrounding the residential core. Two of these occur within the residential compound interpreted either as an expansion of the core settlement or a two-part defensive system. Potaketake was surveyed and mapped by the Norwegian expedition in 1956 (Ferdon 1965:13). At that time the tower was intact and composed of a conical bedrock and earthern fill spire reinforced by a masonry wall. Free-standing masonry walls lined the edges of the primary domestic terraces surrounding the central tower. Ferdon noted several large pits within the confines of the site that he interpreted as defensive features. However, local people referred to these as taro pits and the position of some of these features suggests that they were water cisterns or storage pits. Stone slab hearths, most likely for heating room blocks, were also identified on the surface of the northern sector of

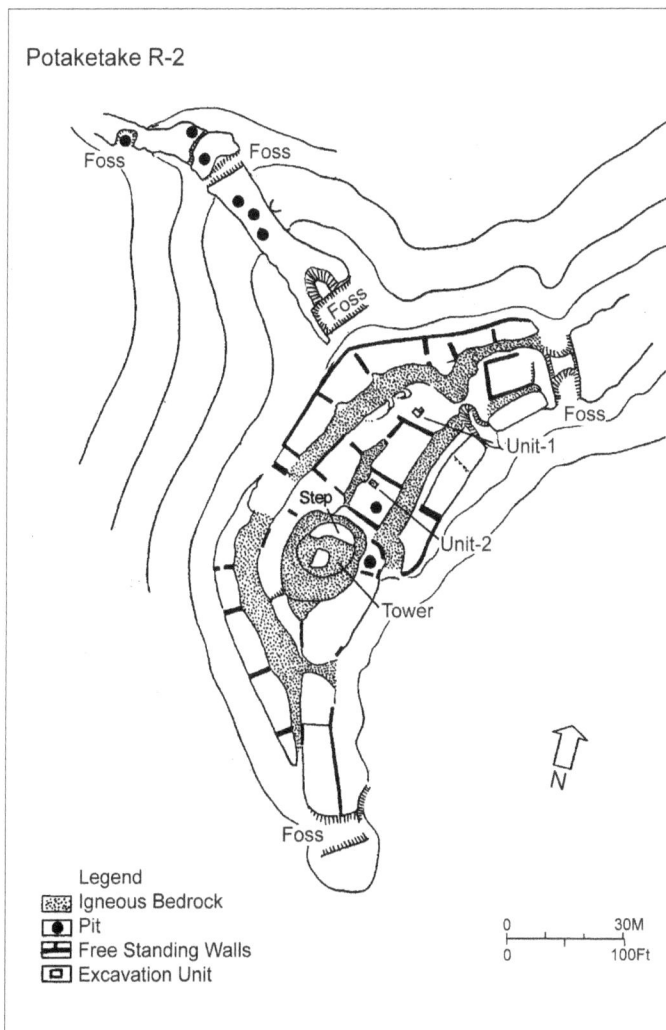

Figure 12.17. Map of Potaketake showing locations of auger tests and excavation units. The map is based on the Norwegian expedition's original map, field observations and IKONOS satellite imagery. Drafted R. Van Rossman.

the site. An eroded face on the northern sector of the site revealed a dark midden soil and bell-shaped poi pounders similar to those found during the excavations at Morongo Uta.

Potaketake (217 m) was covered with low grass during our visit and most of the architecture was visible on the surface (Figure 12.18). The terrace walls and stone-lined hearths described by Ferdon (1965) were clearly visible, along with the dark midden soil eroding from the edges of the stone-lined rectilinear terraces. Double stone walls filled with soil surround most of the terraces in the central precinct. Much of the tower is now destroyed and only a short dyke-stone wall remains surrounding the eroded basalt core. The largest eroded exposure at the site occurs on the northern edge of the central group of domestic terraces. Large flecks of charcoal and fragments of shell were visible in the exposure, including the inner whorl of a large gastropod. The remnants of an oven are also visible in this exposure (fire-cracked rock, burned soil and high concentrations of charcoal). One of our workmen showed us an adze that he had collected from the site (Figure 12.19). Unit 1 (1 m x 1 m) was placed near this erosional face and excavated in naturally occurring levels (Figure 12.20). The uppermost stratum (10–15 cm) consisted of very dark greyish brown (10 YR 3/2) silty soil with sparse amounts of charcoal. The sediment in this stratum is well sorted and contains very few pebbles or small rock inclusions. Soil from this level was screened through a 2 mm sieve and larger chunks of charcoal and eight basalt flakes were recovered. Underlying this stratum is a very dark brown (10 YR 2/2) silty clay containing higher concentrations of cultural material. Charcoal concentrations remain high in this stratum, mixed with sub-angular pebbles and stones.

A series of superimposed oven features (features 2–4) was encountered during the excavation of this stratum and it is visible in the southern and eastern walls of the excavation unit (Figure 12.20). One of these ovens (Feature 4) was excavated into the underlying dark, yellow-brown,

12.18a

12.18b

12.18c

Figure 12.18. Photographs of Potaketake: a) fortification from the south looking north; b) looking north from tower over domestic terraces; c) remnant of dyke-stone facade on tower. Photographs D.J. Kennett.

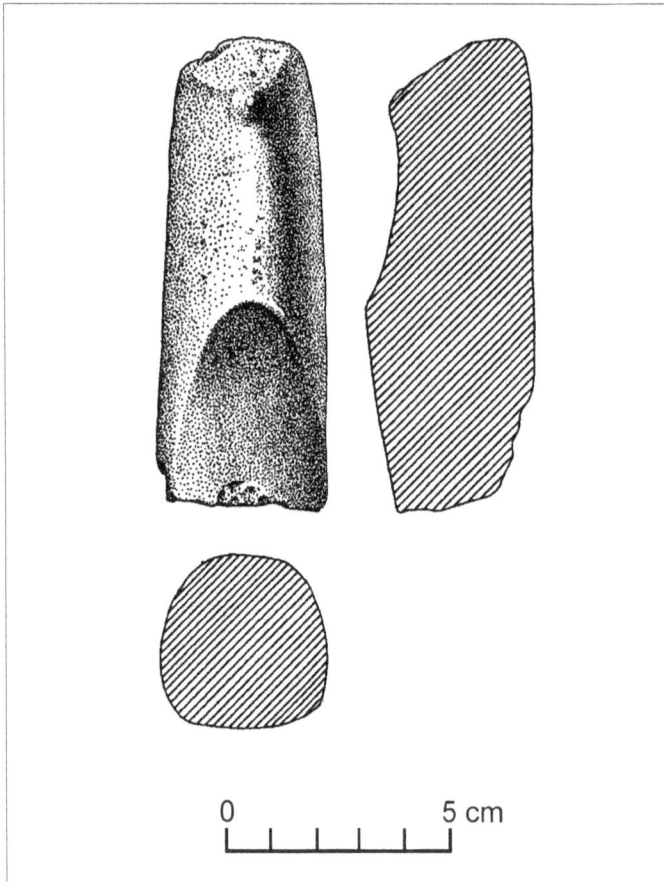

Figure 12.19. Adze fragment found on the surface of Potaketake. Illustration R. Van Rossman.

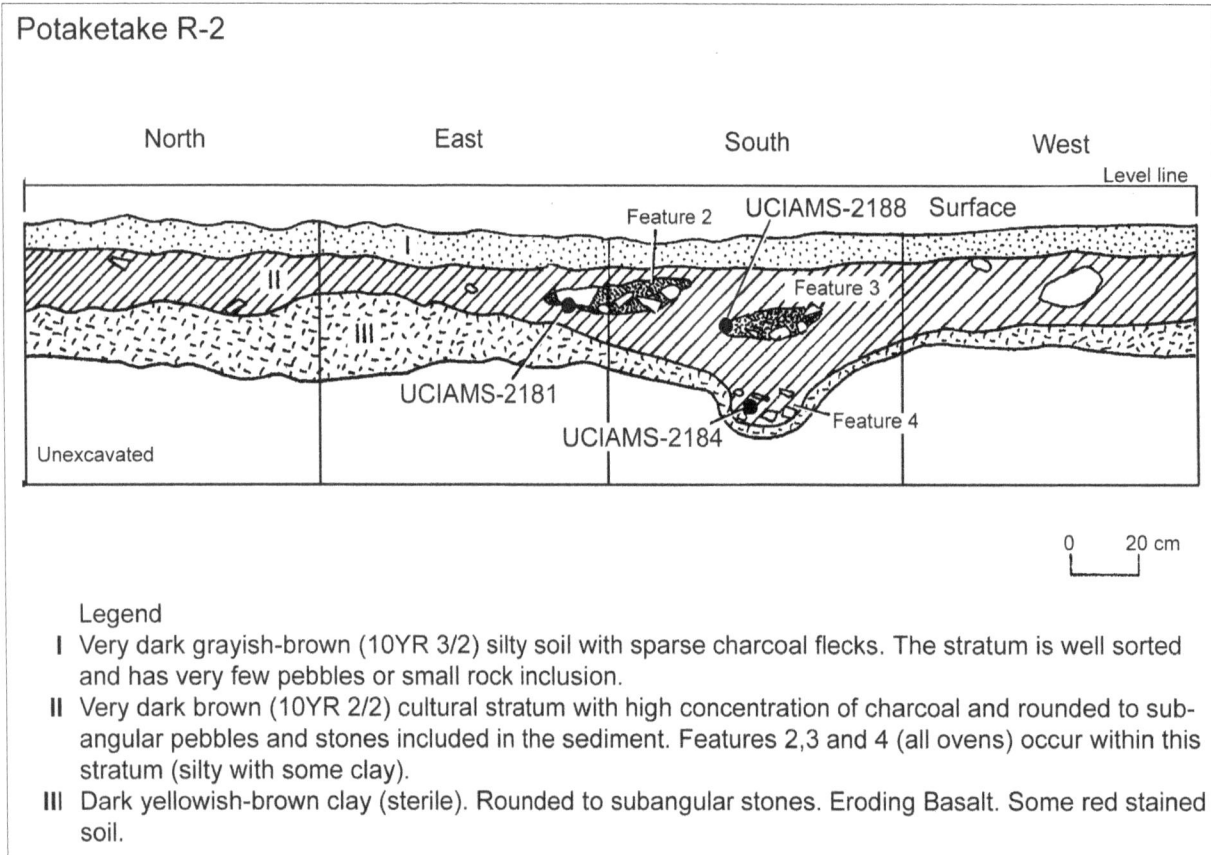

Figure 12.20. Stratigraphy in Unit 1 at Potaketake. Drafted R. Van Rossman.

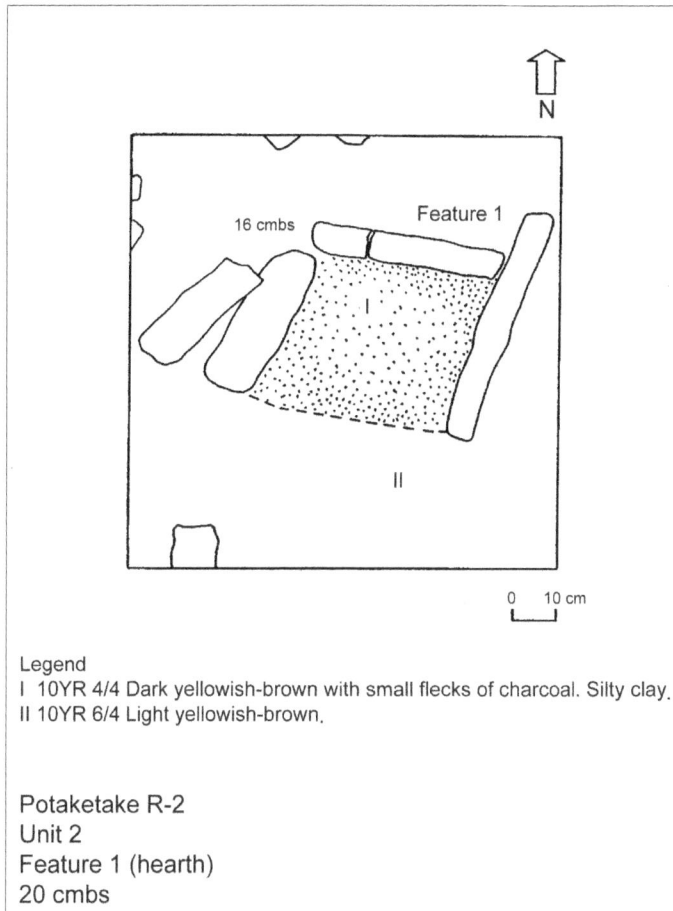

Legend
I 10YR 4/4 Dark yellowish-brown with small flecks of charcoal. Silty clay.
II 10YR 6/4 Light yellowish-brown.

Potaketake R-2
Unit 2
Feature 1 (hearth)
20 cmbs

Figure 12.21. Planview of hearth excavated in Unit 2 at Potaketake. Drafted R. Van Rossman.

sterile, parent soil/rock and it contained eroding basalt. A bifacially flaked basalt tool was found during the excavation of Feature 4, along with four basalt flakes recovered in the 2 mm screens. The three oven features were radiocarbon dated, with the two deepest features (3 and 4 respectively) dating to 240 ± 25 bp (UCIAMS-2188) and 240 ± 20 bp (UCIAMS-2184) respectively, and the uppermost feature dating to 210 ± 25 bp. The calibrated ranges for these dates all fall between AD 1700 and 1800 (see Figure 12.13). Unit 2 (1 m x 1 m) was placed on top of a hearth previously identified by Ferdon (1965) in the northwestern corner of the terrace just north of the tower (Terrace 8, Figure 12.21). Dark yellowish-brown soil and charcoal was found in its centre at 16 cm, but as yet no radiocarbon dates are available for this feature.

Secondary fortifications and refugia

Most of our work focused on the larger fortifications on the main ridge surrounding Ha'urei Bay, but we also visited and sampled several smaller hilltop sites. Additional fortified locations were also observed from a distance, but were not visited. Those at the highest elevation are consistent with what Stokes (n.d.) described as refuges. Others positioned at lower elevations on secondary ridgelines are usually near larger fortified settlements and they were probably the sites of satellite communities that were linked to the larger sociopolitical systems.

Four smaller hilltop sites were investigated on the island during the 2002 field season (Figure 12.22). One of these smaller fortifications, Ngapiri (R2002-50), is located in the southern sector of the island near Tevaitau and Morongo Uta. The other three smaller upland sites are located in the northern sector of the island near Tapitanga and Potaketake. As discussed previously, Tevaitau may have served as a large satellite community of Morongo Uta, given its close proximity and temporal overlap, between AD 1700 and 1830. The site of Ngapiri is smaller than Tevaitau and located higher (320 m) on the same ridge in a more defensible location surrounded by steep-faced boulders. The site consists of eight terraces and some of these occur on a razor-thin ridgeline. Dyke-stone walls are apparent along the edges of two terraces and one of these is close to 1 m high. We excavated three sample test pits and dark midden soil containing charcoal and adze flakes were identified in each. The maximum depth of these midden deposits was 25 cm, but most were about 10 cm thick. One charcoal sample from the uppermost terrace produced a calibrated radiocarbon age similar to those found at Tevaitau and the later dates at Morongo Uta (see Figure 12.5). The site does not have a central tower and, with its elevated position, it was probably a refugium as described by Stokes. Given its age and close proximity to Tevaitau, it was either a satellite community or it may have served periodically as a fortified highland refuge for people living at Tevaitau or Morongo Uta.

The other three small hilltop sites investigated occur in the north sector of the island near Akatanui and Angairao Bay. Two of these overlook Akatanui Bay and are linked by ridgelines to the larger fortifications of Tapitanga and Potaketake. Both of these fortifications were constructed during the final fortification phase between AD 1700 and 1825 (see Figure 12.13), but they were probably not occupied simultaneously given their close proximity, their architectural differences, and the available radiocarbon dates. Tapitanga was more likely occupied in the earlier stages of the final fortification phase, whereas Potaketake was probably occupied after

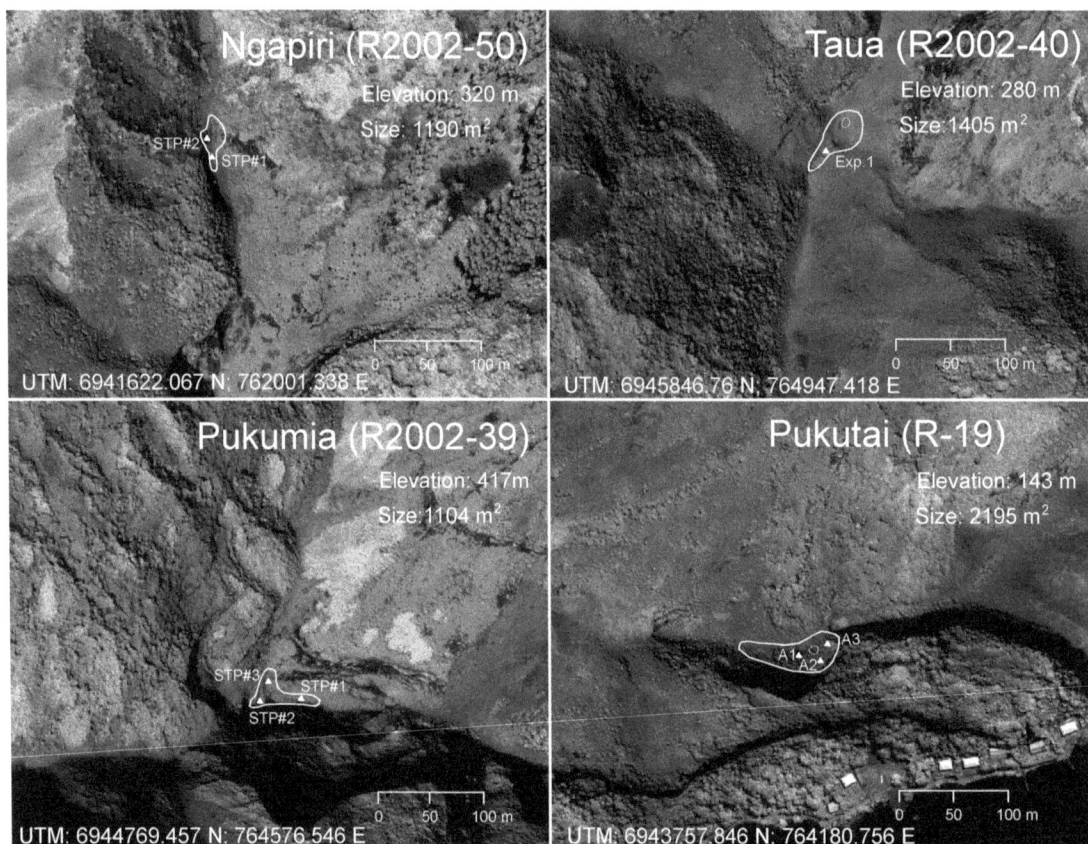

Figure 12.22. IKONOS satellite images of secondary fortifications Ngapiri (R2002-50), Taua (R2002-40), Pukumia (R2002-39) and Pukutai (R2002-19). Size estimates, site boundaries and tower orientation are based on field observations and features visible in IKONOS imagery. UTM coordinates are from the centres of each site. The small numbered triangles are the locations of auger tests, sample test pits or exposures sampled. Drafted J. Bartruff and D.J. Kennett.

this time and into the mission period. The two smaller fortifications date to the latter part of the final fortification phase and therefore appear to be more contemporary with Potaketake.

One of these smaller sites (R-19) was visited and recorded by the Norwegian expedition, but the expedition appears not at have worked at the site. It sits at an intermediate elevation (143 m) equidistant between Point Tekogoteemo and Tapitanga. Today people refer to this location at Pukutai. It overlooks the northern shore of Ha'urei Bay and the flat agricultural lands where the modern town of Area is now located. Compared with Tapitanga and Potaketake, this site is small. Only a few terraces are now visible on its surface, but a tower was purposely carved from the hilltop and remnants of dyke-stone facing are still evident. Three augers were placed on the uppermost terrace surrounding the tower. Organically rich midden soils containing charcoal began at ca. 10 cm and extended down to ca. 20 cm. One radiocarbon sample from Auger 3 (18 cmbs) produced a calibrated radiocarbon age in the later stages of the fortification process between AD 1750 and 1830 (UCIAMS-36952). Pukutai may have served as a moderately fortified satellite community of Potaketake. Access to freshwater, agricultural lands and coastal resources was greater from this location than from the larger fortresses.

The upland site of Pukumia (R2002-39) is quite different from Pukutai. It is located 1 km to the northeast of Pukutai across the drainage associated with Akatanui Bay. Pukumia sits at an elevation of 417 m and has a commanding view of the entire northern part of the island. It is surrounded by steep terrain and several sheer cliffs block access to the site from the south and east. Nine terraces were identified at this upland location. It does not have a central tower and dyke-stone masonry is rare. Stokes appears to have visited this site and classified it as a highland refuge. The small terraces were cut expediently from the ridgeline and were not reinforced with rubble-filled masonry walls. Vegetation was sparse across this site and many of the terraces were exposed and wind deflated. Three test pits were excavated, one on each arm of the refuge. Thin midden soils occurred at all three locations, but were best developed on the northern arm of the refuge. These terraces are larger in this area and there are three extending out towards Point Teruapake to the north. A central hearth-like feature was excavated in the first of these. Large quantities of charcoal were evident at the base of this feature and they produced a date in the later stages of fortification expansion between AD 1750 and 1830 (UCIAMS-36951, STP #3, 11 cmbs).

Taua (R2002-40, 280 m) was the last small fortification site that we examined in the northern sector. It is positioned near Point Teruapake on the ridge extending north from Pukumia. Agairao Bay is visible to the west and the site overlooks Piritua to the east. It is reminiscent of R-19 in that it has a miniature central tower and a series of rectilinear terraces, four to the south and one to the north of the tower. The tower was cut from a natural hillock. Remnant dyke-stone walls line some of these small terraces, but not extensively. A deep fosse was cut into the ridge on the southern end of the site. The location is well protected on the east and north by steep sea cliffs. The terraces are separated by slight differences in elevation and midden deposits were exposed between the two southernmost terraces. Dark midden containing charcoal and adze flakes is best developed between 20 cmbs and 30 cmbs. A radiocarbon age indicates occupation in the beginning of the final fortification phase (AD 1700–1750), suggesting that Taua is more contemporary with Tapitanga than Potaketake.

Discussion and conclusions

Our work at hilltop fortifications builds on previous work by Stokes (n.d.), Ferdon (1965), Mulloy (1965) and Walczak (2001). We examined 10 previously identified large fortifications on the main ridge surrounding Ha'urei Bay. At the core of each fortification is a central tower, carved from a high point in the ridge, which is surrounded by one to two large terraces. Terraces extend out from the site cores along ridges or down into surrounding drainages. The sites range in size from 3040 m² (Noogorupe) to 25,237 m² (Tapitanga) (Figure 12.23).

The number of terrace units varies at these sites and is not directly related to site size. Some locations are more consolidated than others. Potaketake is 5744 m² and has ca. 30 terraces. Tapitanga has a similar number of terraces (ca. 42) dispersed over a much larger area (25,237 m²). There is a tendency for terraces along flat ridgelines to be rectilinear in shape and those on steeper terrain to be d-shaped, a difference due primarily to the natural topography. Towers are commonly covered with dyke-stone masonry facades and rectilinear terraces are often reinforced by dyke-stone masonry walls. Sometimes, parallel series of dyke-stone blocks with a rubble or sediment-filled interior were used to reinforce these platforms. These walls were used to contain

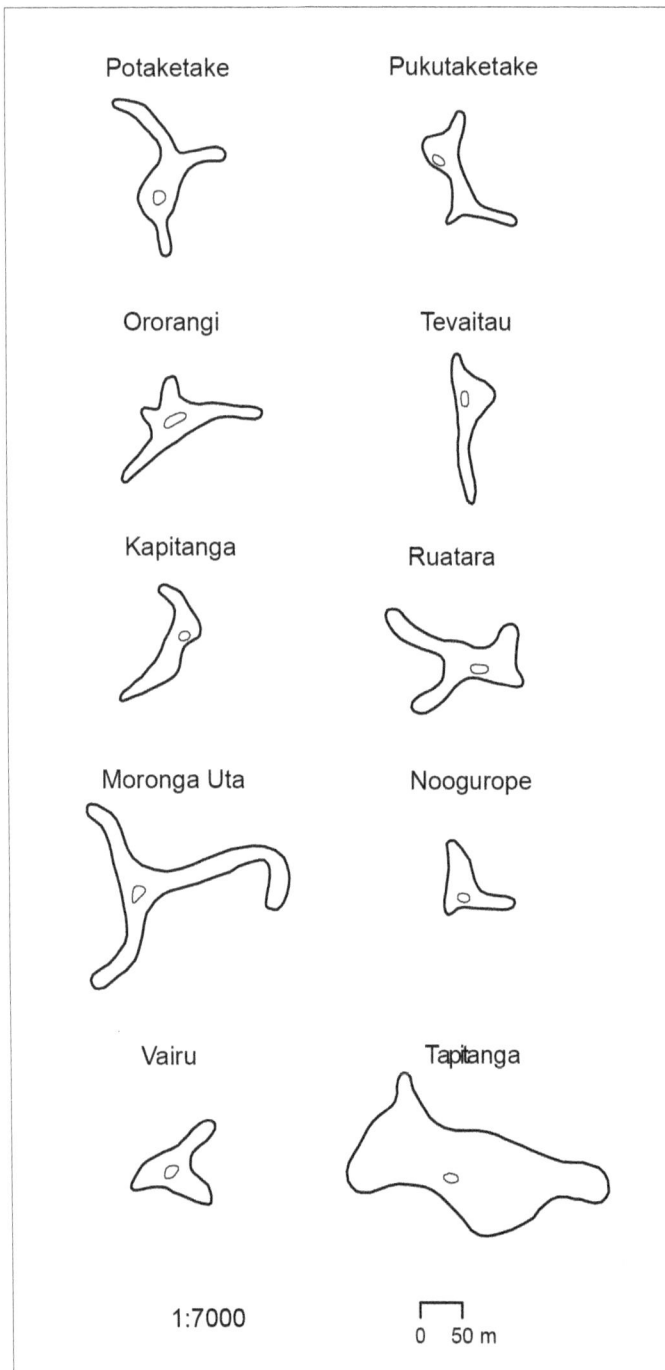

Figure 12.23. Size and configuration of the primary Rapan fortifications. Drafted J. Bartruff and D.J. Kennett.

sediments cut from the ridgeline to create a large level living surface. None of these walls reach above the level of the terrace and they were not constructed to be weight-bearing. Structures made from perishable materials were built in the centres of these platforms, as indicated by the position of hearths (Mulloy 1965). Tapitanga and Ororangi stand out relative to the other fortifications on the island due to the general absence of visible dyke-stone masonry. The most extensive natural dyke-stone deposits are in the vicinity of Noogorupe and there is some evidence that these deposits were quarried. Determining the extent and character of dyke-stone deposits will provide key insights into dyke stone's varied use in fortification construction across the island.

One of our main goals was to build a radiocarbon chronology for the primary fortifications on the island (Kennett et al. 2006). We collected radiocarbon samples from either natural exposures or test excavations at these sites. Thirty AMS radiocarbon dates place the initial fortification at Noogurope and Ruatara between AD 1300 and 1400. Morongo Uta appears to have been established between AD 1500 and 1600. This is followed by the proliferation of fortifications between AD 1700 and 1830. Most of the fortifications on the island were established during this interval and there was a general increase in the number of fortifications on Rapa after AD 1750. Work at Tapitanga and Potaketake (both overlooking Akatanui Bay) suggests that dyke-stone masonry developed after AD 1750 at Potaketake. Most sites with dyke-stone masonry have components that date after this time. Ororangi appears to be the only site dating to between AD 1750 and 1830 where masonry architecture was not used. Mulloy (1965) argued that terrace units were added as populations expanded at each location. Our budget did not allow us to test this hypothesis directly, but the dates at Morongo Uta conform to this expectation. More work will be needed to determine how these sites expanded. Three of the four smaller fortifications tested date to between 1750 and 1830 and support the hypothesis that populations were at a maximum when Vancouver encountered the island in AD 1791. Overall, these data support the hypothesis that populations on the island generally increased through time.

Mulloy (1965) argued that the hilltop sites were residential and not simply used as periodic refuges during times of war. This was based on large-scale cleaning and excavation at Morongo Uta, where he identified house platforms (terraces) with domestic features (hearths and ovens), residential debris (shell, bone, charcoal), and artefacts (e.g. adzes, poi pounders), indicating a range of daily activities. Our work at multiple locations is consistent with the hypothesis that these sites were residential. Hearths and ovens were encountered in most of our excavation units and our auger and sample test-pit excavations indicate that dark midden soils containing cultural materials cover these sites. Preservation in these deposits is poor, and wind deflation and water erosion are diminishing their integrity. Basalt adze flakes were commonly found during our excavations, but formal artefacts were rarely encountered in our units or on the exposed surfaces of these sites. Faunal materials were recovered from most of the sites excavated, but the assemblages are small and poorly preserved (see below). Mulloy (1965:53) estimated the population at Morongo Uta to be ca. 425 people, based on the number of terraces and hearths at the site, along with a conservative estimate of five people per household. This assumes that all 85 terraces were occupied at the time of its maximum extent between AD 1750 and 1830. Future work on the chronologies of individual sites will be required, along with excavations at disassociated terraces on ridges and along valley walls, to determine what percentage of the population lived in these hilltop settlements and whether this changed through time.

We infer from paleoecological data (Prebble and Anderson, Chapter 10) and the remnants of prehistoric pondfields (Bartruff et al., Chapter 13) that the inhabitants of these hilltop settlements had invested heavily in, and were reliant on, wet taro agriculture in lowland pondfields. The limited distribution of lowland environments suitable for this highly productive agricultural practice may be one reason they placed their settlements on ridgetops and ridgelines. However, the cost of transporting taro and other resources (marine foods and water) to upland locations was high and suitable water and food storage within these hilltop settlements would have been essential. Smaller terraces within these complexes may have served as platforms for above-ground storage facilities (Mulloy 1965). Large and small pits are also evident at most of these fortifications. Stokes (n.d.) observed large pits ranging in size between 1.8 m and 4.5 m. Some were as deep as 2.8 m. The best examples that we observed occur at Potaketake, Ruatara and Kapitanga, and in all cases these pits were excavated into terraces on the outer flanks of the radiating terrace units. Based on ethnographic data, Stokes (n.d.) argued that these pits were lined with banana leaves, filled with crushed taro, sprinkled with water, and covered with ti leaves and a layer of sediment (pp. 174–175). Future excavations should target these pits to determine their character and collect sediment samples for microbotanical analysis.

In East Polynesia, agricultural produce was commonly combined with meat from introduced domesticated animals (e.g. chickens, pigs) or marine foods (shellfish and fish). Faunal remains were not well preserved in the acidic soils of these highly exposed sites. The use of 2 mm screens to process sediments in the field helped us identify sediments with reasonable faunal preservation, which were then taken in bulk for flotation. A total of 400 bones representing 10 different vertebrate taxa were identified using this method (see Butler, Appendix C). The results from five different fortifications indicate the greatest reliance on near-shore reef fishes, with parrotfishes (Scaridae) the most represented species. This is consistent with the use of stone fish traps that are common along the shores of the island. The best-recorded example comes from the northern edge of Ha'urei Bay (Ferdon 1965:13). Other carnivorous fish species were also present in small numbers (groupers, snappers, moray eels) and suggest the use of hook and line fishing. The only larger animal identified in these assemblages was an unidentified species of sea turtle in the tower deposits at Tapitanga. Domestic animals were noticeably absent and rats were the only introduced animal species identified in these assemblages. Overall, the faunal data is suggestive of near-shore fishes supplying the primary source of protein on the island.

Political hierarchies and status rivalries were common throughout East Polynesia. Hereditary chiefs controlled access to land and competed with rival chiefs to expand territorial boundaries and improve food security for their kin (Vayda 1976; Kirch 1984). The notion of political and social hierarchy was certainly carried to Rapa, but it only becomes apparent archaeologically with the establishment of the Noogurope and Ruatara fortifications between AD 1300 and 1400. The appearance of two fortified villages signals a status rivalry between two competing polities with chiefly lineages at their core. The structural organisation of these fortifications also reflects this hierarchy. Stokes (n.d.) argued that the flattened tops of each tower served as the platform for the chief's residence and that his closest kin lived in the upper surrounding terraces. We identified dark midden soils on the tops of the intact towers that were similar to those found on lower domestic terraces (e.g. charcoal, adze flakes). Faunal materials were also identified on the tops of Ruatara, Ororangi and Tapitanga. An oven similar to the one identified by Stokes (n.d.) on the tower at Morongo Uta was identified on the northwestern portion of Ororangi's tower. These data are consistent with the idea that the flattened tower tops served as at least one residential component of the chief's quarters. The presence of sea-turtle bones on the tower at Tapitanga is consistent with this interpretation, given their role as chiefly food elsewhere in Polynesia (Anderson pers. comm.). When combined with site distributions and the radiocarbon ages, these data suggest that there were 10 competing chiefly lineages on the island in the century before European contact. Our work on secondary fortifications is also suggestive of subordinate chiefly lineages living in satellite communities that were integrated into larger political systems during the final phase of fortification.

Walczak (2001) has questioned the idea that the hilltop settlements on Rapa were fortifications constructed in the context of inter-tribal warfare between competing chiefdoms. Instead, he argued that these structures were primarily ritual in nature. Certainly, household shrines at Morongo Uta point to the important role of ritual in Rapan society, and the very nature of East Polynesian hierarchies is imbued with a ritual dimension that served to legitimise established social and political orders. But establishing a functional dichotomy between ritual and residence obscures the primary observation that these sites were first and foremost both inhabited and defended. Chiefs were often accomplished warriors (Kirch 1984:196) and struggles over power and land often resulted in war (Williamson 1937). Stokes' (n.d.) ethnographic data from the 1920s, especially his record of Rapan traditions (Chapter 2), make it clear that war for land and food stores was an important part of Rapan life. The strategic position of these sites, combined with the presence of defensive features (e.g. fosses), is consistent with this interpretation. Sites dating to the century before missionisation in 1830 tend to have more defensive features (e.g. Morongo Uta, Potaketake, Kapitanga), and some of these features appear to have been cut through existing architecture, suggesting that the incidence or severity of war was increasing. The higher-elevation refugia sites (Ngapiri and Pukumia) also suggest increased hostilities late in the Rapan sequence. This is consistent with Vancouver's observations that people on Rapa were living in hyper-fortified hilltop communities surrounded by multiple rows of palisades.

Our research was necessarily limited to a few important objectives, notably of chronology and general site function. We have argued that the fortified sites need to be seen primarily in that role, as defended villages, and that the broad history of their construction is consistent with rising levels of population, inter-group competition and hostility, probably most particularly over access to agricultural lands. This situation continued, and possibly was becoming increasingly tense, into the early European era.

Note

1. Walczak (2001) visited and mapped Ngapiri, Namuere, Pukutaketake, Tevaitau, Ungarere, Ororangi and Ruatara in the late 1990s. He also excavated Tevaitau (10 units, 50 cm²), Ngapiri (2 units, 1 m²), Ruatara (1 unit, 2 m²) and Ororangi (1 unit, 2 m²). Only the excavations at Tevaitau are described in detail.

References

Clark, G. and Martinsson-Wallin, H. 2007. Monumental architecture in West Polynesia: Origins, chiefs and archaeological approaches. *Archaeology in Oceania* 42:28–40.

Ellis, W. 1838. *Polynesian Researches, during a residence of nearly eight years in the Society and Sandwich Islands*. Volume III, Fisher, Son and Jackson, London.

Ferdon, E.N. 1965. Report 2: A reconnaissance survey of three fortified hilltop villages. In: Heyerdahl, T. and Ferdon, E.W. (eds), *Reports of the Norwegian Archaeological Expedition to Easter Island and the East Pacific*, Volume 2 Miscellaneous Papers. Monographs of the School of American Research and the Kon-Tiki Museum, 24 Pt. 2. Esselte AB, Stockholm. pp. 9–21.

Field, J.S. and Lape, P.V. 2010. Paleoclimates and the emergence of fortifications in the tropical Pacific Islands. *Journal of Anthropological Archaeology* 29:113–124.

Heyerdahl, T. 1958. *Aku-Aku: The Secret of Easter Island.* Allen and Unwin, London.

Kennett, D.J., Anderson, A., Prebble, M., Conte, E. and Southon, J. 2006. Human Impacts on Rapa, French Polynesia. *Antiquity* 80:340–354.

Kennett, D.J. and Winterhalder, B. 2008. Demographic expansion, despotism, and the colonisation of East and South Polynesia. In: Clark, G., Leach, F. and O'Connor, S. (eds), *Islands of Inquiry: Colonisation, seafaring and the archaeology of maritime landscapes* (Terra Australis 29), pp. 87–96. Australia National University Press, Canberra.

Kirch, P.V. 1984. *The Evolution of the Polynesian Chiefdoms.* Cambridge University Press, Cambridge.

Lamb, W.K. (ed), 1984. George Vancouver, *A Voyage of Discovery to the North Pacific Ocean and Round the World 1791–1795*, Volume I. The Hakluyt Society, London.

Mulloy, W. 1965. The Fortified Village of Morongo Uta. In: Heyerdahl, T. and Ferdon, E.N. (eds), *Reports of the Norwegian Archaeological Expedition to Easter Island and the East Pacific*, Volume 2, miscellaneous papers. Monographs of the School of American Research.

Stokes, J.F.G. n.d. Ethnology of Rapa. Manuscript on file in the Bernice P. Bishop Museum, Honolulu.

Vayda, A.P. 1976. *War in Ecological Perspective.* Plenum, New York.

Walczak, J. 2001. Le peuplement de la Polynésie orientale: Une tentative d'approche historique par les exemples de Tahiti et de Rapa (Polynésie française). Unpublished Dissertation, University of Paris (Panthéon Sorbonne).

Williamson, R.W. 1937. Religion and Social Organization in Central Polynesia. Cambridge University Press, Cambridge.

13

Rapan agroecology and population estimates

Jacob Bartruff

Department of Geography, University of Oregon, Eugene, USA, jbartruf@uoregon.edu

Douglas J. Kennett

Department of Anthropology, The Pennsylvania State University

Bruce Winterhalder

Department of Anthropology, University of California, Davis

Introduction

Colocasia taro (*C. esculenta*) grown in pondfield irrigation systems is the staple of Rapa's subsistence economy. Pondfield irrigation systems are well known in Oceania. Their development usually coincides with the prehistoric expansion of island populations and the associated need to increase crop yields from limited amounts of land (e.g. with intensification, Kirch 2000:317). The primary goal of this type of irrigation system is to create the most favourable growing conditions for *Colocasia* taro, pools of slow-moving water 2.5 cm to 5 cm deep. This involves the construction of artificial terraces, berms and irrigation canals that require a significant investment of time and labour for a pay-off of increased crop yields in the future. Augmentation of the land increases its value and one of the social manifestations of this investment is greater territoriality (Dyson-Hudson and Smith 1978). Hereditary ownership and the need to defend these territories from interested neighbours often develop within this context.

Colocasia taro is not native to Rapa, but was introduced by the early colonists of the island, along with several other commensal species. Wild variants of this plant can be found throughout the Indo-Pacific region from east India to Formosa and south into the Sahul region (Cable 1984). Wild-taro-starch residue identified on stone tools from the Solomon Islands extends its use back to 28,000 years ago (Loy et al. 1992). The traditional view is that domesticated taro was introduced to New Guinea by intrusive Austronesian populations from island Southeast Asia (Bellwood 1975), but recent evidence points to the possibility of an independent domestication 9000 years ago (Golson 1990; Yen 1991). *Colocasia* taro appears in west Polynesia during the late Lapita Period (ca. 3000 BP) and was carried in canoes to more remote islands of east

Polynesia, including Rapa, starting 1500 to 2200 years later (Kennett et al. 2006a).

Oral traditions suggest that *Colocasia* taro was the staple food on Rapa from the time of initial settlement (Hanson 1970; Stokes n.d.), now estimated to be between ca. AD 1100 and 1200 (Kennett et al. 2006b; Chapter 11). Pollen from well-dated stratified lowland sediments indicates its use by at least AD 1200 (Chapter 10). Pondfields dot the alluvial lowlands of Rapa today. Remnant dry stonewall terrace features covering many of the alluvial valley bottoms are indicative of much greater former extent of these agricultural systems. Many of the abandoned or fallow terrace systems remain waterlogged and are now dominated by introduced agricultural grasses (e.g. *Paspalum subjugatum*), sedges (e.g. *Carex* spp.), rushes (e.g. *Schoenoplectus subulatus* subsp. *subulatus*) and adventitious herbs (e.g. *Commelina diffusa*). These terraces are visible in 1 m resolution IKONOS satellite imagery, and the purpose of this paper is to define the former extent of taro production based on this imagery. We also explore prehistoric Rapan population levels based on calculations of potential agricultural yield and maximum sustainable population sizes under different regimes of diverted production.

Colocasia taro production on Rapa

Active and remnant pondfield terraces are visible in all the lowland valleys of Rapa (Figure 13.1). This irrigation method is one of the four types of true irrigation (e.g. diversion of water to fields) in the Pacific, as defined by Spriggs (1981, 1988). Ferdon (1965) conducted a preliminary survey of these terraces and found that almost all of the alluvial valley bottoms on the island were terraced at one time or another, including the land beneath the modern town of Ha'urei. Some of these terraces are still in use today but they represent only a small proportion of the available arable land once under production.

Figure 13.1. A) Modern and remnant pondfields in Akatanui Valley. B) Inset showing *Colocasia* taro growing in a pondfield. Photograph D.J. Kennett.

Information regarding Rapan irrigation techniques comes from Hanson (1970). Rapan terraces are rectangular and about 'forty to fifty feet long [12–15 m] by twenty to twenty-five feet [6 to 7.5 m] wide' (Hanson 1970:70). The terraces are irrigated by narrow ditches. Water from dammed streams runs through notches cut into the curbs surrounding the terraces, descending downhill from the upper to lower levels into the still-water bays surrounding the island. Ideally, each terrace thus is covered with slow-moving water about 5 cm deep.

Taro can be planted at any time during the year but grows best if planted when conditions are warm, especially January through April. Preparations for taro planting generally begin in September. If there are plans for new terraces or repairs on existing ones the work is done by the men of the household during the last months of the year. To prepare an area for taro irrigation, vegetation is cleared and the surface is levelled. The earth is turned to a depth of about a third of a metre and dirt curbs are built around the terrace, with openings for the ingress and egress of water. The irrigation ditch is excavated next and the terrace is filled with water until the soil is muddy. According to Hanson, 'if the soil is especially good, a terrace can produce a high quality of taro for up to thirty years of continuous cultivation. Rapans feel they have a poor return on labor invested if yields are high only for five or six years' (Hanson 1970:71).

In preparation for the planting season, small peripheral plants are harvested from existing terraces between October and December. Instead of being discarded after the edible corm is broken off, the stalk of the plant is saved. The leaves are removed to reduce the chance that wind will uproot the plant, and the stalk is placed in the terraces. After a month or two, these stalks put down roots and start to grow. In January, these stalks are transplanted in the terraces using the correct spacing for optimal production.

The pondfields are planted by men and women after the New Year, between January and April. Rapans say taro grows best if it is planted during a full or new moon. Taro planting is avoided during the first two weeks of March due to the belief that the corm will mature with a hole running through its centre and is likely to develop corm rot (Hanson 1970:72–73).

Corms and cormels (small, younger corms attached to a fully developed corm) of *Colocasia* taro are ready for harvest eight months after planting on Rapa. When planted at the correct time of the year, they can be left to grow for up to two years without rotting. Once removed from the pondfield, though, taro spoils in about five days. Both men and women harvest taro throughout the year. Harvesting and transporting taro is considered the hardest part of the process because of the weight burdens and other travel costs associated with retrieving these bulky tubers. Field processing at the harvest site consists of removing the corm from the stalk (see Metcalfe and Barlow 1992; Bettinger et al. 1997). There is little to discard to reduce the weight of these corms for transport. Individuals may have to trek up and down steep ridges carrying 80 lbs (ca. 36 kg) or more of taro for household consumption. Occasionally, boats are used to reach fields in more distant watersheds.

Today, women prepare taro for household consumption. Taro corms and cormels must be cooked because in raw form they contain inedible calcium oxalate crystals (Hanson 1970:70). Taro is consumed in a variety of ways once it has been boiled, but usually, it is prepared as a fermented paste called *popoi*. The preparation of this paste is labour intensive and usually done by younger women in a household. Corms are first boiled and then mashed on the surface of a flat rock until a rounded mass of paste is created (45–60 cm in diameter). Water and old *popoi* is added to aid fermentation and then strenuously kneaded to the desired consistency. The *popoi* is wrapped in leaf bundles and fermented for one to two days before being consumed by the household (Hanson 1970:73–76) without further preparation.

Remote sensing of pondfield agricultural systems

To explore pre- and post-contact ecology and population levels on Rapa, we estimate the maximum extent of pondfield *Colocasia* taro agriculture using high-resolution IKONOS satellite imagery (1 m). Modern pondfields are clearly visible in IKONOS imagery and appear as distinctive gray to black areas in the panchromatic image, and dark green in the true colour image (Figure 13.2). Multi-spectral data, specifically false colour infrared, were also used to highlight and define older and more subtle agricultural features (e.g. inactive terraces, wall alignments and old canals). The lateral distribution of these features was used to define the maximum extent of ancient pondfield agricultural systems in all viable lowland environments. Due to erosion, sedimentation, modern development and vegetation obscuring these features, we consider this to be a conservative estimate of the maximum prehistoric agricultural extent. Modern pondfields were only identified in five of the 11 watersheds that contained evidence for more ancient systems, and much more land (83.75 ha) was under production in the past compared with the present (3.73 ha; see discussion and results below). The spatial distribution of modern and prehistoric pondfield agricultural systems varies and is discussed in relation to our efforts to model pre-contact population levels described in the following section.

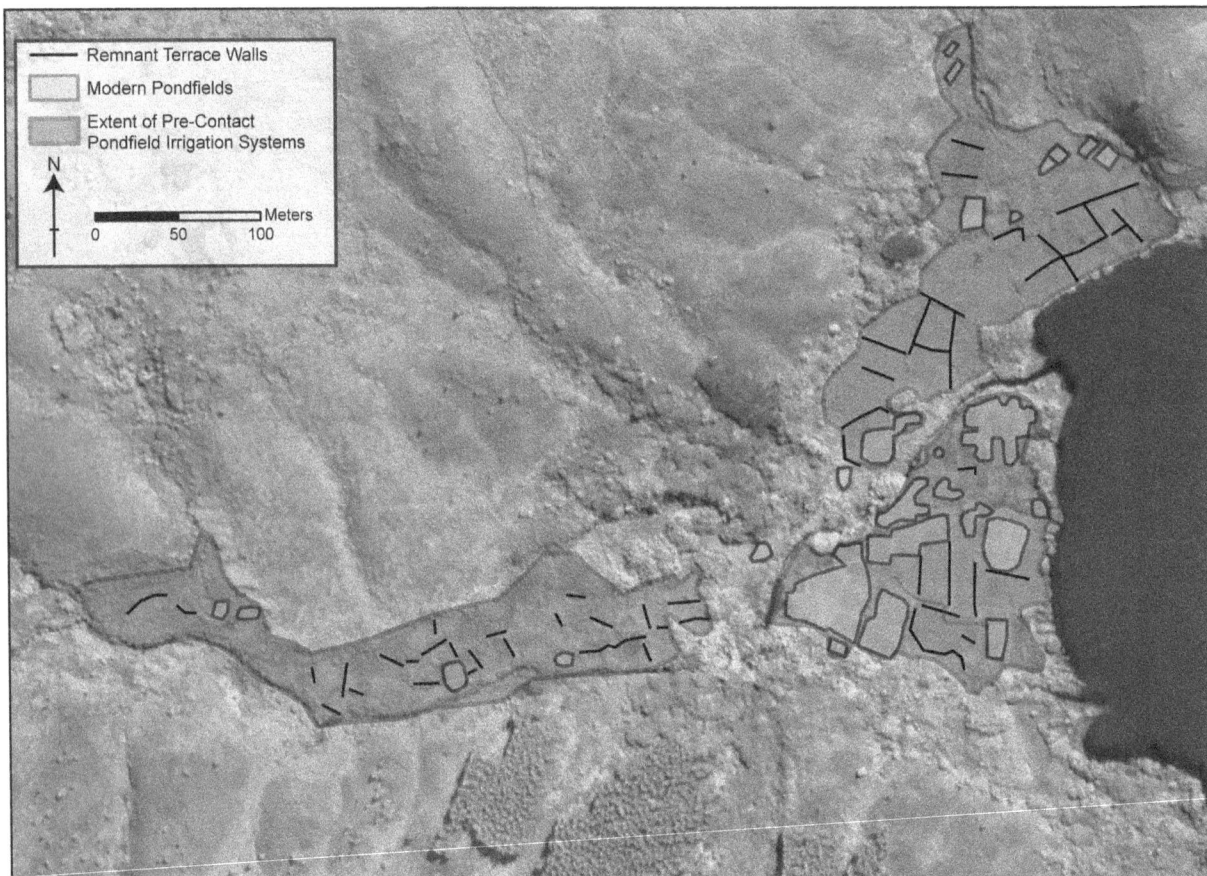

Figure 13.2. Geographic extent of modern and pre-contact pondfield irrigations systems in Angatakuri watershed.

Modelling population size

We employ a model that estimates *Colocasia* taro crop yields and maximum sustainable population sizes based on these estimates, given different levels of diverted production (Bayliss-Smith 1978, 1980). Based on its successful application in other parts of Oceania (Spriggs 1981; Kirch and Sahlins 1992), we implement a simplified version of this model. Model parameters include: 1) total taro production (in kcals); 2) annual consumption of taro per person (in kcals); 3) annual labor costs; and 4) percentage of the population involved in agricultural production. Population estimates based on the extent of these agricultural systems are determined from this information, given that a portion of the crop may have been diverted away from direct consumption into trade or tribute. Our analysis allows for varying degrees of diversion from 0% to 70%. The amount of labour (hours per week) associated with different diversion amounts is also determined.

Parameter 1: Total taro production

We calculate total taro production on Rapa by estimating: 1) the maximum extent of pondfield irrigation systems (in ha); 2) the raw yield of this land (mt/ha/yr); 3) the percentage of the raw yield that is consumable by humans; and 4) the caloric energy provided by taro corms (in kcals). Pondfield agricultural systems were defined in the Rapan lowlands based on the identification of terrace wall alignments and irrigation canals visible in pan-sharpened satellite imagery (See Figure 13.2). Active and inactive pondfields are visible in this imagery and are generally consistent with our observations in the field and Ferdon's independent observations in 1956 (Ferdon 1965). We employ an estimate based on a comparable high-yielding *Colocasia* taro pondfield agricultural system from the Cook Islands to estimate the annual productivity of 1 ha of land (26.67 mt/ha/year; Manarangi 1984). Geographically and environmentally, this is the closest analogous agricultural system and is considered a better productivity measure on Rapa than the more distant and environmentally different island of Maewo (Vanuate; 35.71 and 58.10 mt/ha/year; Spriggs 1981, 1984; Kirch and Sahlins 1992). In determining crop yields, we assume that harvests consist of 34% large corms and 66% small cormels. Approximately 15% of large corms and 40% of cormels consist of inedible peelings (Bayliss-Smith 1980:71–72; Kirch and Sahlins 1992:158). We use 106 kcals to 100 g of edible taro to convert crop yields, based on previous nutritional studies (Bayliss-Smith 1980:72).

Parameter 2: Annual consumption of taro

The total energy requirement for humans used in our calculations is 800,000 kcals/person/year (or ca. 2190 kcal/day). This is based on estimates from elsewhere in Oceania (Bayliss-Smith 1980; Spriggs 1981; Kirch and Sahlins 1992) and is a simplified number that does not take into account variation by age, size, activity level, or the source of the energy. Based on previous research by Stokes (n.d.) and Hanson (1970), along with the limited range of resources available on Rapa (e.g. the island is an inhospitable environment for tropical plants such as coconut, see Chapter 10), we assume that taro comprised 80% of the pre-contact diet. Based on our own estimates of dietary composition (based on anecdotal evidence collected during archaeological fieldwork between June and August 2002), we argue that taro comprises about 20% of the contemporary diet. This is due to the importation of a range of supplemental foods from Tahiti. Given these assumptions, we estimate the pre-contact consumption of taro to be 640,000 kcals per person annually (ca. 1750 kcal/day); 160,000 kcals (ca. 435 kcal/day) is estimated for modern populations.

Parameter 3: Labour costs

Labour costs are based on analogous modern pondfield agricultural systems in Maewo (Spriggs 1981). The labour costs associated with initial preparation, planting, weeding and harvesting *Colocasia* taro growing in pondfield irrigation systems is estimated at 4947 person hours/ha/year using stone tools, and 3296 person hours/ha/year for steel tools. Canal excavation and terrace construction is a large initial investment and Rapans expect to get more than seven years of continuous production from a pondfield, and sometimes up to 30 years. To explore changing labour costs associated with continued field use, we use labour estimates for one and 10-year field usage.

Parameter 4: Labour force

The percentage of the population involved with taro production is more difficult to estimate. On Rapa, men generally prepare pondfields for use and both men and women take part in planting, weeding and harvesting (Hanson 1970). However, we do not know what percentage of men and women took part in these activities in the past and how labour was divided during pre-contact period. Following Kirch and Sahlins (1992), we use a range of estimates for the percentage of people engaged in agricultural activities (80, 60, 40, and 30% of total population).

Population modelling results

Population estimates using the Bayliss-Smith model are presented in Table 13.1. These estimates assume *Colocasia* taro yields of 26.67 tonnes ('mt' in Table 1) each year (per hectare) and it is assumed that the entire system was in use prehistorically. Prehistoric population estimates range from 760 to 2534, depending on the amount of taro diverted away from direct consumption. Given our estimates that the current dietary contribution of taro (20%) and the area of active cultivation taken from the IKONOS imagery would support 135 to 450 persons depending on the degree of diverted production, this range overlaps with the current population on the island. Also shown in Table 13.1 are the person hours required each week given different assumptions about the fraction of the population engaged in taro production (30–80%). Individual labour requirements decrease as the percentage of the population involved increases. Bayliss-Smith (1980:80) argued that subsistence activities in the Pacific consume between 10 and 20 hours a week. Estimates above 20 hours per week are identified in parentheses and are thought to be unrealistic.

Two sets of labour estimates are shown in Table 13.1, the first indicating the necessary hours/person/week if pondfields were used for one year and the second showing use amortised over a 10-year period. These data indicate that individual labour requirements are reduced by more than 50% with multi-year pondfield use. This is because initial field preparation is a large part of production costs. As an example, the model predicts a prehistoric population of 1774 with a 30% crop diversion. If 60% of the population was involved in taro production, then the average producer could expect to work around 7.49 hours each week if fields were used for one year. As a long-term average, weekly labour investment is substantially lower if fields were used continuously over a 10-year period (3.18 hours per week).

Table 13.2 lists the extent of modern and remnant pondfield agricultural systems in each of the 11 watersheds on Rapa, along with population estimates associated with each based on the Bayliss-Smith model. The spatial distribution of these field systems is shown in Figure 13.3. It is immediately evident that even at their maximum extent, these productive agricultural systems comprised only a small portion of the island's total landmass (2.21%) and that these lands were highly circumscribed due to the island's rugged terrain. Modern pondfield agricultural systems

Table 13.1. Carrying capacity model for Rapa (using 26.67 mt/ha/yr as yield).

Surplus (%)	Population	Labor hours/week (one-year field use) Productive % of population				Labor hours/week (10-year field use) Productive % of population			
		80%	60%	40%	30%	80%	60%	40%	30%
Pre-contact taro fields (83.75 ha)									
0	2534	3.93	5.24	7.86	10.48	1.67	2.22	3.34	4.45
5	2407	4.14	5.52	8.27	11.03	1.76	2.34	3.51	4.68
10	2280	4.37	5.82	8.73	11.65	1.85	2.47	3.71	4.94
20	2027	4.91	6.55	9.83	13.10	2.09	2.78	4.17	5.56
30	1774	5.62	7.49	11.23	14.97	2.38	3.18	4.77	6.36
40	1520	6.55	8.73	13.10	17.47	2.78	3.71	5.56	7.42
50	1267	7.86	10.48	15.72	(20.96)	3.34	4.45	6.67	8.90
60	1014	9.83	13.10	19.65	(26.20)	4.17	5.56	8.34	11.12
70	760	13.10	17.47	(26.20)	(34.94)	5.56	7.42	11.12	14.83
Modern taro fields (3.73 ha)									
0	450	0.65	0.87	1.31	1.75	0.39	0.52	0.77	1.03
5	428	0.69	0.92	1.38	1.84	0.41	0.54	0.81	1.08
10	405	0.73	0.97	1.45	1.94	0.43	0.57	0.86	1.14
20	360	0.82	1.09	1.64	2.18	0.48	0.64	0.97	1.29
30	315	0.94	1.25	1.87	2.49	0.55	0.74	1.10	1.47
40	270	1.09	1.45	2.18	2.91	0.64	0.86	1.29	1.72
50	225	1.31	1.75	2.62	3.49	0.77	1.03	1.55	2.06
60	180	1.64	2.18	3.27	4.36	0.97	1.29	1.93	2.58
70	135	2.18	2.91	4.36	5.82	1.29	1.72	2.58	3.43

are even more restricted, occurring in only seven of the 11 major drainages on the island. The extensive lowlands surrounding Ha'urei Bay were divided into three areas for analytical purposes, but in total comprise 60.56% (2.25 ha) of the lands currently under production. Large pondfield agricultural systems are also in use in Angatakuri/Angatakuri Naku (26.02%) and Iri (13.26%) drainages, both located in the southern half of the island, with smaller systems positioned in the Pariati drainage (0.16%) to the north. The model-derived population estimate based on the modern extent of pondfield agricultural systems is 450 individuals. This estimate is based on the assumption that there is little taro diverted away from direct human consumption due to heavy subsidies from the French Polynesian government.

Pondfield agricultural systems were more extensive in the past. Remnant pondfield systems were identified in all of the major drainages examined (n=11) and their overall extent (83.75 ha) was ca. 20 times larger than the modern systems. These abandoned and now fragmentary systems were most extensive around the periphery of Ha'urei Bay (41.12 ha, 49.10%) and were particularly concentrated in the lowlands along its northwestern shore (30.94%; Figure 13.4). Large pondfield systems were also located in Iri (11.35 ha) and Angatakuri (5.38 ha) drainages to the south, and Akatanui (6.48 ha), Agaira (4.85 ha) and Pariati (4.44 ha) drainages to the north (see Figure 13.3). Smaller systems were also identified in several drainages in the north

(Akananu, Akatamiro, Anarua and Tupuai). These data point to much higher and more widely distributed populations in the past. We conservatively estimate an island population of 2027 based on the maximum identifiable extent of pondfield systems on the island (Table 13.1). This estimate is based on an 80% dietary contribution of taro from pondfield systems and does not include other dry farming systems (e.g. terraces) of unknown extent and importance. This estimate includes a diversion of 20% of the production, which we argue to be reasonable given the need to protect against drought, lower crop yields on a year to year basis, and food losses due to war. Taro production is spatially distributed almost evenly throughout the island, with the highest pre-contact production systems occurring in the central to northwest section of the island, followed by the southern section of the island, with the east to northeastern areas of the island a close third.

Table 13.2. Carrying capacity by watershed.

Watershed	Pondfield area (h)	Percentage of total pondfield area	Surplus (%)	Population
Pre-contact taro extents				
Agaira	4.85	5.79%	20	117
Akananu	2.95	3.52%	20	71
Akatamiro	1.07	1.28%	20	26
Akatanui	6.48	7.74%	20	157
Anarua	1.20	1.44%	20	29
Angatakuri	5.38	6.42%	20	130
Angatakuri Nako	2.18	2.60%	20	53
Ha'urei East	6.67	7.96%	20	162
Ha'urei South	8.53	10.19%	20	206
Ha'urei West	25.92	30.94%	20	627
Iri	11.35	13.55%	20	275
Pariati	4.44	5.30%	20	108
Tupuai	2.73	3.25%	20	66
Total	**83.75**	**100.00%**		**2027**
Modern taro fields				
Angatakuri	0.79	21.25%	0	96
Angatakuri Nako	0.18	4.77%	0	23
Ha'urei East	0.78	21.04%	0	94
Ha'urei South	0.36	9.66%	0	44
Ha'urei West	1.11	29.86%	0	134
Iri	0.49	13.26%	0	59
Pariati	0.01	0.16%	0	1
Total	**3.73**	**100.00%**		**450**

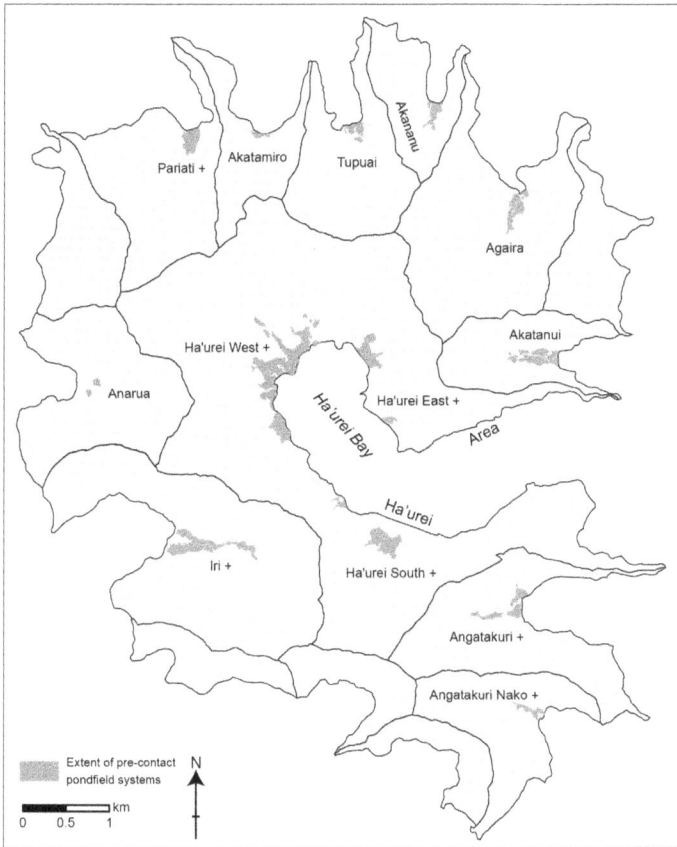

Figure 13.3. Spatial extent of pre-contact pondfield systems for each watershed (+ denotes watersheds with modern pondfield systems).

Figure 13.4. Inactive remnant pondfields on the north shore of Ha'urei Bay. Note the remnants of the prehistoric fortified communities of Morongo Uta and Pukutaketake. Photograph D.J. Kennett.

Discussion and conclusion

Since European contact, the population of Rapa has plummeted from an estimated high of 2000 in 1826 to a low of 120 in 1867 (McArthur 1967:307). Within the past 140 years, the population has slowly increased. It stands at 497, according to the latest official census taken in 2002 (http://www.polynesie-francaise.gouv.fr/hc/iles-australes/dossiers.asp#rapa). Our model prediction of 450 persons – under the assumptions that 3.72 hectares are in production and that taro is 20% of the diet – is quite close to the contemporary census result. Today, Rapan people rely on supplies from Tahiti, imports from abroad and introduced domesticated animals, and this has decreased the importance of taro and taro-based products in the diet. For these reasons, in the present it is more difficult to determine population solely from taro production. Inhabitants of Rapa do not have to depend on taro agriculture for a majority of their diet and the time that would be involved in more intensive agriculture is spent on introduced cash crops such as coffee. Further research on the modern populations is needed to account for all the energy sources that are available and their relative contribution to the diet.

Many of these complexities were absent in pre-contact time due to the heavy subsistence dependence on taro and fish and the lack of imported bulk commodities. This simplification of the pre-contact diet makes it easier to calculate the maximum sustainable population sizes based on taro production. With a diversion of 20%, the model results in a maximum sustainable population of 2027 individuals. This result is supported by early estimates from European sources within the first 30 years of contact, which put the population between 1500 and 2000 individuals. When Vancouver first encountered the island of Rapa in 1791, his ship was confronted at sea by "about thirty" canoes that contained "on a moderate computation, three hundred men, all adult and apparently none exceeding a middle-age; so that the total number of inhabitants on the island can hardly be estimated at less than fifteen hundred" (Vancouver 1801). Stokes (n.d.) thought this number too low, reasoning that Vancouver was probably only met by inhabitants from the north and west of the island. In 1826, John Davies visited Rapa for a second time and estimated the population to be around 2000, even though there had been 'much sickness and death in the island' since his first visit earlier in the year (McArthur 1967:307).

More recently, Stokes (n.d.) estimated the pre-contact population by surveying the fortified and unfortified terraced mountain sites and calculated that if all the sites were occupied at the same time they could house about 3000 inhabitants (see also Anderson, Chapter 2). If Stokes' estimate is closer to the number of people living on Rapa then – with respect to our model estimates – production diversion must have been lower, yield per hectare must have been higher, and/or more land not evident in our satellite imagery was dedicated to taro production. Ferdon (1965) mentions taro terraces further up the valleys of several watersheds. These terraces may have been for dry taro agriculture, but they cannot be seen on the satellite imagery and were not added to the maximum pre-contact extent calculations. It is not known for certain whether these were domestic terraces, similar to the ones Stokes surveyed, dry taro terraces, or a combination of both.

Through the use of the Bayliss-Smith model, we have shown that within the circumscribed environment of Rapa and the limited amount of arable land, the island could have supported population levels in line with or above early European estimates. The use of satellite imagery and the Bayliss-Smith model (Bayliss-Smith 1978, 1980) allows for a cost-effective approach to reconstructing agricultural systems and population levels on Rapa and could readily be used on other islands in the Pacific. Additional ethnographic fieldwork is also needed to help constrain model parameters, and archaeological work to establish the extent of remnant pondfields and other agricultural features (e.g. dry terraces, irrigation canals).

The population estimates presented in this paper are intriguing given the known development and expansion of fortified hilltop communities on the island (Kennett et al. 2006). These communities were strategically located on the highest peaks along the ridge system dividing the primary watersheds on the island. The distribution of these communities suggests that they demarcated territories. The earliest fortifications (Morongo Uta and Ruatara) were established 100 years after the island was colonised (ca. AD 1300–1400, see Chapter 11) and were positioned near the most suitable lands for pondfield agriculture. The number of fortified communities proliferated after AD 1700, just before the first recorded European contact in AD 1791. Population expansion and community fissioning to fortified locations parallels the expansion of pondfield agricultural systems on the island. We suggest that the expansion of pondfield agricultural systems increased the value of land that was highly circumscribed and defensible. This stimulated territorial disputes that were likely one of several interacting contextual variables favouring increased inter-group aggression and greater investment in defence, as has been argued for the Northern Channel Islands of southern California (Kennett et al. 2009; Winterhalder et al. 2010).

References

Bayliss-Smith, T.P. 1978. Maximum populations and standard populations: The carrying capacity question. In: Green, D. Haselgrove, C. and Spriggs M. (eds), *Social Organisation and Settlement*, pp. 129–51. Part 1. BAR International Series (supplementary) 47. Oxford.

Bayliss-Smith, T.P. 1980. Population pressure, resources, and welfare: Towards a more realistic measure of carrying capacity. In: Brookfield, H.C. (ed), *Population-environment Relations in Tropical Islands: The Case of Eastern Fiji*, pp. 61–93. M.A.B. Technical Notes 13. Paris.

Bellwood, P.S. 1975. *Man's Conquest of the Pacific*. Collins, London.

Bettinger, R.L., Malhi, R. and McCarthy, H. 1997. Central place models of acorn and mussel processing. *Journal of Archaeological Science* 24:887–899.

Cable, W.J. 1984. The spread of taro (Colocasia sp.) in the Pacific. In: Chandra S. (ed), *Edible Aroids*, pp. 28–33. Clarendon Press, Oxford.

Dyson-Hudson, R. and Smith, E.A. 1978. Human territoriality: An ecological reassessment. *American Anthropologist* 80:21–41.

Ferdon, E.N. Jr. 1965. A reconnaissance survey of three fortified hilltop villages. In: Heyerdahl, T. and Ferdon, E.N. (eds), *Reports of the Norwegian Archaeological Expedition to Easter Island and the East Pacific*, Volume 2, miscellaneous papers. Monographs of the School of American Research.

Golson, J. 1990. Kuk and the development of agriculture in New Guinea: Retrospection and introspection. In: Yen, D.E. and Mummery, J.M.J. (eds), *Pacific Production Systems: Approaches to Economic Prehistory* pp. 139–47. Australia National University, Canberra.

Hanson, F.A. 1970. *Rapan Lifeways: Society and History on a Polynesian Island*. Little, Brown and Company Ltd, Boston.

Haut-commissariat de la Polynésie française: Subdivision administrative des les Australes: Communes. http://www.polynesie-francaise.gouv.fr/hc/iles-australes/dossiers.asp. Accessed on 20 November 2006.

Kennett, D.J., Anderson, A.J., Prebble, M., Conte, E. and Southon, J. 2006a. The Ideal Free Distribution, Food Production, and the Colonization of Oceania. In: Kennett, D.J. and

Winterhalder, B. (eds), Behavioral Ecology and the Transition to Agriculture, pp. 265–288. University of California Press, Berkeley.

Kennett, D.J., Anderson, A. and Winterhalder, B. 2006b. Prehistoric human impacts on Rapa, French Polynesia. *Antiquity* 80:340–54.

Kennett, D.J., Winterhalder, B., Bartruff, J. and Erlandson, J.M. 2009. An ecological model for the emergence of institutionalized social hierarchies on California's Northern Channel islands. In: Shennan, S. (ed), Pattern and Process in Cultural Evolution, pp. 297–314. University of California Press, Berkeley.

Kirch, P.V. 2000. *On the road of the winds: an archaeological history of the Pacific Islands before European contact.* University of California Press, Berkeley.

Kirch, P.V. and Sahlins, M. 1992. *Anahulu: The Anthropology of History in the Kingdom of Hawaii, Volume Two: The Archaeology of History.* University of Chicago Press, Chicago.

Loy, T., Spriggs, M. and Wickler, S. 1992. Direct evidence for human use of plants 28,000 years ago: starch residues on stone artefacts from northern Solomon Islands. *Antiquity* 66:898–912.

Manarangi, A. 1984. Important taro varieties in the Cook Islands. In: Chandra, S. (ed), *Edible Aroids*, pp. 24–27. Clarendon Press, Oxford.

McArthur, N. 1967. *Island Populations of the Pacific.* The Australian National University Press, Canberra.

Metcalfe, M.D. and Barlow, K.R. 1992. A model for exploring the optimal trade-off between field processing and transport. *American Anthropologist* 94(2):340–356.

Spriggs, M. 1981. Vegetable Kingdoms: Taro Irrigation and Pacific Prehistory. Unpublished PhD dissertation. The Australian National University, Canberra.

Spriggs, M. 1984. Taro irrigation methods in the Pacific. In: Chandra, S. (ed), *Edible Aroids*, pp. 123–35. Clarendon Press, Oxford.

Spriggs, M. 1988. The Past, Present and Future of Traditional Taro Irrigation in the Pacific: An Example of Traditional Ecological Knowledge. SPREP Occasional Paper Series 3. South Pacific Commission, Noumea.

Stokes, J.F.G. n.d. Ethnology of Rapa. Manuscript on file in the Bernice P. Bishop Museum, Honolulu.

Vancouver, G. and Vancouver, J. 1801. *A voyage of discovery to the North Pacific ocean, and round the world.* J. Stockdale, London.

Winterhalder, B., Kennett, D.J., Grote, M.N. and Bartruff, J. 2010. Ideal Free Settlement of California's Northern Channel Islands. *Journal of Anthropological Archaeology* 29:469–490.

Yen, D.E. 1991. Polynesian cultigens and cultivars: The question of origin. In: Cox, P.A. and Banack, S.A. (eds), *Islands, Plants, and Polynesians*, pp. 67–98. Dioscorides Press, Portland, Oregon.

14

The prehistory of Rapa Island

Atholl Anderson

Department of Archaeology and Natural History, Research School of Pacific and Asian Studies, The Australian National University, Canberra, Australia, atholl.anderson@anu.edu.au

Douglas J. Kennett

Department of Anthropology, The Pennsylvania State University

Eric Conte

Université du Polynésie Française

Introduction

Rapa is a small, high and substantially isolated volcanic island lying in East Polynesia at the temperate edge of the subtropical South Pacific. Discovered by Europeans in 1791, Rapa has been the subject of lengthy ethnological and anthropological fieldwork but relatively little archaeology and that directed almost entirely at the hilltop fortifications that dominate the landscape. Our fieldwork, during six weeks in the winter of 2002, has produced sufficient variety and abundance of material from archaeological sites (Appendix D) and palaeoenvironmental research to enable the sketching of a first prehistory of Rapa.

Before turning to that, it is worth noting that we saw no evidence during fieldwork or subsequent analyses of the proposed connection to Easter Island that infused 19th century speculation about Rapan archaeology and drove the only substantial investigations that had occurred previously on Rapa, by the Norwegian Archaeological Expedition (Chapter 1). To the contrary, there is no historical support for the name 'Rapa-iti' as a derived companion to 'Rapa-nui' with colonisation implications; the Rapan language is part of the same southeastern group that includes Mangarevan and Rapanuian, but it is not closer to the latter (Chapter 2); none of the classic Easter Island architectural forms were reproduced on Rapa, nor did Rapa obtain the chicken, sweet potato or most of the other cultivable plants that existed on Easter Island. It is possible that migrants from Rapa reached other islands, including New Zealand, as has been conjectured in relation to the forts, but the evidence is slight, because fortification occurred widely in Polynesia, and New Zealand's typical ditch-and-bank constructions are very different from the stone-faced terraces of Rapa.

This is not to assert that there was no prehistoric movement to or from Rapa. The Rapan traditions suggest some additional arrivals after initial colonisation, and the evident familiarity of Rapans with iron at first European contact also implies external contact (Chapter 2), but evidence of connections is otherwise scarce. Archaeologically, there is no obsidian, which might have come from Pitcairn Island or Easter Island, and no pearl shell, which could have been brought from the more tropical Austral, Society, Tuamotu or Gambier islands. While further research might show evidence indicative of more regular contact, our working hypothesis has been that the development of archaeological features on Rapa through the pre-European era reflects events and contingencies of colonisation followed by adaptation and innovation that occurred very largely in isolation.

Our project focused on questions about the chronology of human colonisation, the nature of settlement and subsistence, landscape change and the rise of fortifications.

Chronology of colonisation

The chronology of colonisation was investigated through sedimentary coring and archaeological research. The palynological record (Chapter 10) indicates that coastal swamp forests expanded on the island after about 500 BC in response to changing sedimentary conditions following a mid-Holocene high-stand in sea level. After about AD 1000, there was rapid sediment accumulation in the embayments around Rapa, and at Tukou in Ha'urei Harbour. At Tukou, sedimentation was associated with a decline in swamp forest, a rise in *Pandanus* and an onset of high concentration in charcoal particles. Radiocarbon ages for the onset of microcharcoal concentrations in the Tukou cores vary from 130 BC to about AD 1200 and are consistently older than the earliest age determinations for human colonisation evident in the archaeological record, although all radiocarbon ages for peaks in microcharcoal concentration occur within the span of archaeological chronology (after AD 1000). This is typical of many charcoal profiles in Pacific swamps and it is thought to represent infrequent natural fires followed by the substantially increased rates of cultural ignition. Radiocarbon ages on charcoal for the beginnings of plant cultivation, as represented by the onset of pollen deposition from taro (*Colocasia esculenta*), generally overlap the beginning of the archaeological chronology. However, the strongest age estimate, from Core 2 at Tukou, is about AD 1020, more than 200 years older than the earliest archaeological determination for the island. This is possibly due to the mixing of sediment by early agricultural activities in these wetland contexts (Chapter 10).

The initial phase of human colonisation is represented archaeologically by a set of dates from Tangarutu rockshelter (chapters 3 and 11), which is by far the largest and most habitable of the rockshelters on Rapa. All the relevant dates are from basal cultural deposits underlain by clean carbonate sand that goes down to the basalt boulders and *in situ* floor of the rockshelter (Chapter 3). The earliest date came from a small test probe below the base of a modern sand mining pit in the middle of the rockshelter floor. The sand was too loose to allow an excavation and even the core sample was difficult to obtain. The date is from the ANU radiocarbon dating laboratory, and as with many later results from that laboratory, it has very large standard errors, extending in this case from AD 600 to 1400. In our Bayesian analysis, this anomalously early date is constrained to AD 1000–1400 based on the other early dates for the island, with peak probability between AD 1000 and 1400. It is, at least, consistent with the earliest precise AMS ^{14}C date (UCIAMS-14769) of AD 1100 to 1200 on comparable deposits. The phase boundary for initial colonisation has been modelled as about AD 800 to 1300, with peak probability between AD 1100 and 1200. The phase boundary ends between AD 1300 and 1600 with peaks between AD 1400 and 1500. The fairly wide age distributions for these phase boundaries, compared with later phases, is related to the smaller number of dates used to define the colonisation phase (Chapter 11).

On these two data sets, the age of onset of human colonisation still remains less precise than was expected. The archaeological data suggest reasonably clearly that the 12th century was the most probable period of human arrival (Chapter 11). The data from sedimentary cores are more problematic, with some evidence indicative of cultural influence in the 11th century and even considerably earlier than that, although the data are few. There are, however, plausible reasons for thinking that the record of microcharcoal concentration in the samples from sedimentary cores includes non-cultural evidence. Some radiocarbon dating samples that had the appearance of charcoal could actually have been, or included, wood tissue blackened in the reducing environment of swamp water, and some microcharcoal concentrations might represent natural firing. As the dates referring to taro pollen were on charcoal samples, the same uncertainty exists (Chapter 10). The span of colonisation could probably be specified more precisely and narrowed further through more radiocarbon dating, but our chronological hypothesis at present is that there was no human colonisation of Rapa before the 12th century AD. Colonisation at that time is consistent with initial human dispersal throughout central East Polynesia (Wilmshurst et al. 2011) and shows that even quite remote islands were reached in this phase.

Coastal settlement and subsistence

Our radiocarbon chronology shows that settlement, measured by occupation of rockshelters, expanded in coastal areas of Rapa between AD 1400 and 1600. Most of the Tangarutu occupational sequence dates to this interval. The second and third largest rockshelter complexes on Rapa, at Akatanui and Angairao, were used first in this period, as were the small Taga rockshelters on the mid-slope of Ha'urei Harbour (Chapter 11). It is very probable that there were settlements on open ground, for example in the coastal flats at the head of the harbour and in most large bays, in the period AD 1400–1600. Earth ovens and terraces around the shores of Ha'urei Harbour, sectioned by road cutting and erosion, or investigated by coring or spade pits, produced radiocarbon dates extending back to about AD 1200. As the terraces are about the size suitable for a domestic unit, often around 8 m by 12 m, and sometimes have remains of ovens or graves, they probably supported individual households. However, neither postholes in section, nor cultural deposits across the floors were found in our preliminary investigations of the Ha'urei sites. In addition, exploratory coring of sand dunes and other sedimentary features in the outer bays did not pick up any evidence of buried occupational levels (Chapter 3).

Judging by excavations in rockshelters (and in hilltop forts, below), subsistence from the beginning of settlement on Rapa was reliant on fishing, foraging and the cultivation of taro.

Coastal fowling, fishing and shellfishing

The list of animal resources available on Rapa was short. Pacific rat bone occurred throughout archaeological deposits, but no dog, pig or chicken bone was found in any context that was plausibly pre-European. No seal bone was recorded and the only reptile remains were from marine turtle. Of 118 birds, identified to 15 species, 90% were seabirds. About half of all bones were from the Kermadec petrel, and that species plus the little shearwater, red-tailed tropic bird, grey noddy, brown noddy, white-bellied storm petrel and white tern, which were also represented in the archaeological material, are still breeding on Rapa. Among landbirds, remains of a *Gallirallus* indicate that Rapa, like most Pacific islands, once had more species of rail. Bones of a large *Ducula* pigeon species and of a *Cyanoramphus* parakeet indicate other extinct taxa (Chapter 6).

Fishing was clearly of primary importance in Rapan subsistence, and fishing patterns were rather unusual. At Tangarutu, the oldest level shows a dominance of Scaridae, which gave way to a dominance by Chaetodontidae and Muraenidae in the middle level, and Muraenidae, plus Scaridae and Serranidae, in the upper level. Muraenidae and Congridae eels are generally very scarce archaeologically in Pacific Island archaeological assemblages, and the high incidence of Chaetodontidae also represents the first positive identification of this family in a Pacific assemblage. Labridae, Serranidae, Muraenidae and Congridae are the other main families represented (Chapter 7). The inter-site differences probably reflect variation between leeward and windward inshore ecologies, but intra-site temporal changes are more difficult to interpret. The rocky coasts of Rapa may have supported comparatively large and accessible populations of marine eels, and large freshwater eels (Anguillidae) are common in streams and taro ponds. The latter were avoided, as they are today, but marine eels are represented in the Rapan middens to an extent matched only on Easter Island. As Rapa and Easter Island have similar inshore ecologies and also are both isolated, the catch in each case may have been shaped by resolutely inshore fishing of taxa in which the major species were those locally common (Chapter 7).

The abundance of Pomacentridae and Chaetodontidae needs to be seen in the context of a generally small size of fish in all families represented in the Rapan assemblages. In the lowest level at Tangarutu there are some remains of larger fish, but as most are small, fish size in the Rapan sites is probably not an effect of over-exploitation. Sampling effects caused by our very small excavations, or social division of catches, cannot be ruled out, but the small fish size occurred both at Tangarutu and Akatanui, and in every other assemblage (Chapter 7; Butler, Appendix C). We suspect that fishing technology was the main factor involved. It is apparent from the absence of trolling lures, of large hooks or points from large composite hooks, and of remains from large benthic or pelagic taxa that open-sea and deep-sea fishing was not common, perhaps because of the danger of being lost in such an isolated location. In turn, this possibly resulted from the absence of a sailing technology capable of bringing canoes back to the island in varied wind conditions. The very small size of most of the Rapan hooks found archaeologically, and known ethnographically, suggests that small fish were being targeted in this method, and it is probable that fine-meshed nets and traps were also employed routinely. Relatively cool ocean temperatures might also have produced smaller mature sizes of fish in families that exhibited larger mean sizes in tropical waters (Chapter 7).

The shellfishing data from Tangarutu show evidence of a transition from hard-shore towards soft-shore collecting within the context of a dominance of algal grazing taxa (Chapter 8). The urchin *Diadema setosum*, in particular, is a prominent algal grazer. As algal-grazing fish such as scarids, pomacentrids and chaetodontids dominate the Tangarutu assemblage, the fish, urchin and shell data from Tangarutu imply, together, that Anarua Bay supported extensive hard substrates on which grew micro-algal turf. Oscillations in frequencies of different algal-grazing molluscs, urchins and fish taxa in the catch data suggest complementary changes among vertebrate and invertebrate algal feeders. Thus, sporadic high levels of *Diadema* occurrence probably resulted from fishing pressure on competing algal-grazing fish; strong initial pressure on Scaridae might have promoted the relative abundance of other algal-grazing taxa and later the pressure on those could have promoted a return to greater numbers of scarids, for which the small candlenut hooks were developed late in the sequence (Chapter 9). Overall, variations in catches within the marine exploitation data suggest a rise in the employment of angling relative to nets and traps, and movement of shellfishing into the soft-shore bayheads, within a pattern of resource use that was changing continually according to complex inter-relationships between algal-grazing taxa (Chapter 9).

Plant foods and fibres

Just as Rapa lacked all of the domestic animals of Remote Oceania, so it lacked key crops, notably coconut, breadfruit, yam and sweet potato, as well as most, if not all, bananas. Pandanus (*Pandanus tectorius* and probably other species) produced edible fruits. Pith of the tree fern (*Cyathea medullaris*) may have been consumed, as it is today, and pith from *Marattia* spp. and *Angiopteris* spp. was also potentially available, but these and the rhizomes of ground ferns such as *Histiopteris incisa*, *Dryopteris* sp. and *Dicranopteris linearis* were rudimentary starch sources at best. Species introduced prehistorically that had food value, as well as other properties of fibre or fruits in some cases were: candlenut (*Aleurites moluccana*), bottle gourd (*Lagenaria siceraria*), taro (*Colocasia esculenta*) and tii (*Cordyline* cf. *fruticosa*). At least two timber trees, the miro (*Thespesia populnea*) and hau or hibiscus (*Talipariti tiliaceum* syn. *Hibiscus tiliaceus*), were probably introduced, and also the coral wood (*Erythrina variegata*), which produced ornamental flowers – along with hibiscus flowers, an essential component of social life in Polynesia. Archaeological charcoals show that tii and hau had been used as firewood in the lowest level at Tangarutu, and candlenuts occurred throughout the sequence and in other rockshelter deposits, being notably abundant at Akatanui (Chapter 4). The existence of these introduced materials in the earliest recorded archaeological levels implies that initial colonisation had occurred earlier still, but perhaps not much earlier.

In the upper level at Tangarutu, lenses of leafy remains produced fragments of plaited *Pandanus* and *Freycinetia* (Pandanaceae) baskets or mats. There were also fragments of bottle-gourd rind, dated earliest to about AD 1600, and many *Pandanus* keys. Knotted cordage made from *Broussonetia papyrifera* (paper mulberry), braided cordage worked from the roots of *Freycinetia* spp. (*kiekie* vine) and twisted cordage from *Hibiscus* also occurred in this level (Chapter 5).

Agriculture

Pollen profiles show that the natural wetlands on Rapa were being used for taro production early and extensively. They seem to have been used continuously throughout Rapan prehistory (starting sometime between AD 1100 and 1200), along with constructed pondfields on higher ground. Remnant pondfield systems can be seen in each of the major bays and the main harbour, and overall they occupy an area (about 84 ha) some 20 times greater than the extent of the modern pondfields (Chapter 13). A general absence of observable charcoal in the pondfield structures and insufficient time or resources to embark on a systematic subsurface investigation prevented our obtaining any information about the development and use of these systems through the prehistoric era. Their distribution through all available bays and the plausible linkage of each system to nearby hilltop forts, or to apparent remnant hamlets at lower levels, suggest that at one stage, if only in late prehistory, they were all in use at once. On that assumption, and given an 80% dietary contribution of taro from pondfield systems, including 20% diverted away from direct consumption (waste, trade, tribute, etc), an island population of around 2000 people could have been sustained (Chapter 13). Lower estimates of the dietary contribution of taro would produce larger population sizes, and some historical data suggest, though very imprecisely, that there might have been around 3000 people living on Rapa before the impact of European disease (Chapter 2).

Chronology, characteristics and purpose of forts

No aspect of the landscape or history has been so widely the subject of commentary as the forts (*pare*) that stand out dramatically along the Rapan skyline. They beg the question of what circumstances drove such an investment in fortification and our research has attempted to answer that by investigating the chronology of construction and material evidence of the purposes served by these structures.

Chronology of construction

Thirty AMS radiocarbon dates, analysed by Bayesian methods, help to put fort construction into a general sequence. As most of the construction occurred after about AD 1700, when the radiocarbon calibration curve has strong fluctuations that obscure precise determination of age, we used the evidence from mission records that fortified villages were abandoned by AD 1825 to constrain the probability distributions (Chapter 11). Radiocarbon dating places initial fortification at Noogorupe and Ruatara between AD 1300 and 1400, approximately 200 years after initial island settlement. There may have been historical connections between the occupants of Tangarutu rockshelter in Anarua Bay, seemingly a colonisation settlement, and those who used the ridgeline above the bay and built the Noogorupe fort, which overlooks Anarua and Ha'urei Harbour. Similarly, the contemporary establishment of Ruatara possibly resulted from fissioning of the founding community at Anarua.

Settlement continued at Ruatara up to about AD 1800, and also at Noogorupe, with a possible hiatus between AD 1400 and 1650. Morongo Uta appears to have been established between AD 1500 and 1600 and it continued until about AD 1800. Most other forts were constructed or occupied between AD 1700 and 1830, with a general increase in construction after AD 1750. Seven forts date to the early 1700s and at least 10 forts to the late 1700s. Smaller forts also date to the late 1700s – e.g. Tauo, Ngapiri, Pukutai and Pukumia (chapters 11 and 12). Investigations at Potaketake suggest that dyke-stone masonry developed after AD 1750 and most sites with dyke-stone masonry have components that date after this time. Ororangi appears to be the only site dating to between AD 1750 and 1830 where masonry architecture was not used (Chapter 12).

Characteristics of forts

Archaeological survey and small-scale excavation occurred at 10 large and four small forts (Chapter 12). All of the larger forts are strategically positioned on the highest points along the main ridge surrounding Ha'urei Bay. The sites range in size between 3040 m² (Noogorupe) and 25,237 m² (Tapitanga). At the core of each fort is a central tower carved from a high point in the weathered basalt ridge and surrounded by one to two large terraces. Terraces extend out from those site cores along ridges or down the slopes at the head of surrounding valleys. The smaller forts are often found in close proximity to the larger forts and they are considered to be satellite communities or temporary refugia. Two of the four smaller forts have central towers.

The number of terraces per fort varies considerably and is not clearly related to site size. Potaketake was 5744 m² and has ca. 30 terraces. Tapitanga has a similar number of terraces (ca. 42) dispersed over a much larger area (25,237 m²). There is a tendency for terraces along flat ridgelines to be rectilinear in shape and for those on steeper terrain to be d-shaped. Natural slabs of dyke stone were used widely in masonry and facing. The most extensive natural dyke-stone deposits are in the vicinity of Noogorupe and there is some evidence that these deposits were quarried. Towers were commonly covered with dyke-stone masonry facades and rectilinear terraces formed by cut-and-fill were usually reinforced with dyke stone laid in parallel series as masonry walls. None of the walls reach above the level of the terrace and they were not constructed to be weight-bearing. Tapitanga and Ororangi stand out as exhibiting very little evidence of dyke-stone masonry (Chapter 12).

Structures made from perishable materials, most probably houses or huts, were constructed on these platforms, their positions indicated by remains of hearths. Around them are scatters of midden comprising charcoal, bone and burnt or flaked stone. The midden is mostly of fish bone, and among it, Scaridae is dominant (Chapter 12; Butler, Appendix C), as at Tevaitau, Orotangi, Ruatara and Tapitanga. Additional taxa are also similar to those found in the coastal sites: Pomacentridae, Labridae, Muraenidae etc. Rat bones (*Rattus* sp.) were also recovered.

The inhabitants of these hilltop settlements were probably also reliant on the wet taro agriculture of lowland pondfields, and the limited distribution of agricultural land may be one reason why settlements moved increasingly to ridgelines and hilltops. These localities were also suitable for storage and protection of harvested crops, probably in the large and small pits that are evident at most of the forts (Chapter 12).

The purpose of forts

Several hypotheses have been advanced to account for the construction of forts on Rapa. Through the telescopes of Vancouver and his officers in 1791 (Lamb 1984) they appeared as fortified habitations with people clustered in them, but in the 19th century, when the structures were manifestly uninhabited, the view prevailed that they were simply fortresses or redoubts used as places of refuge and defence during times of war. In the early 20th century, Peter Buck (1954), with New Zealand experience in mind, thought them rather like Maori pa, which were often inhabited, though not necessarily continuously. The Norwegian archaeological investigations (Heyerdahl and Ferdon 1965), especially the huge effort of exposure and excavation on Morongo Uta, concluded that they were, indeed, fortified villages (Chapter 1).

More recently, however, Jerome Walczak (2003) has argued that the structures served primarily ritual functions. Given that East Polynesian hierarchies had a powerful ritual dimension that served to legitimise established social and political order, it can hardly be doubted that *pare* were localities of ritual function. The same, of course, would have been true of settlements around the coast. If the argument is made in archaeological terms, then slight evidence of ritual activity in the *pare*, such as the small alcoves with upright stones set into walls at Morongo Uta, needs to set against substantial evidence of fortification, habitation platforms, ovens and middens. Our research at multiple locations is consistent with the hypothesis that these sites were, substantially, defended residential complexes.

We argue that as political and social hierarchy is embedded in East Polynesian culture, it was certainly carried to Rapa. It first becomes apparent archaeologically with the establishment of the Noogorupe and Ruatara fortifications between AD 1300 and 1400, the new need for defensive architecture implying the beginning of stronger status rivalry between competing polities than existed at the time of initial colonisation or developed soon afterward. If it is accepted, as ethnographic data suggest, that the flat-topped towers at the centres of large forts were places of chiefly habitation, then 10 competing chiefly polities existed on Rapa by the 18th century. *Pare* at that time tended to have more defensive features (e.g. Morongo Uta, Potaketake, Kapitanga), some of which cut through existing architecture, suggesting improvements to defensive structure. The higher elevation refugia sites (Ngapiri and Pukumia) also suggest increased warfare late in the Rapan sequence. The overall trend in fort construction, from two in the 14th century, gradual increases into the 17th century and an accelerated burst through the 18th century, suggests that conflict and the threat of war increased through the sequence. The most likely reasons for this increase were either direct population growth or indirect population pressure on resources, such as agricultural land.

The subtropical depriment

Rapa is one of a series of Polynesian islands that lie in the subtropical zone below the Tropic of Capricorn. Others are: the Norfolk Islands, the Kermadec Islands, Raivavae, the Pitcairn Group (including Pitcairn, Henderson, Oeno and Ducie) and Easter Island. Leaving aside Raivavae, which has an extensive encircling lagoon, and the two small atolls (Oeno and Ducie), the subtropical islands are distinguished by their virtual absence of coral lagoons.[1] The loss of diversity and biomass in marine resources that this represents is a significant deficit for long-term settlement relative to tropical Polynesia. In addition, the absence for climatic reasons of some tropical Polynesian native food plants and the difficulty or impossibility of growing coconut or breadfruit reduced the value of the terrestrial resource array. Equally, the low number of breeding sea birds (and the virtual absence of seals) was a significant deficit relative to temperate South Polynesia (Anderson 1996). In other words, the subtropical islands lay unfavourably between the lagoonal and agricultural landscapes to the north and the resource landscapes to the south rich in marine birds and mammals (Anderson 2001, 2002). They suffered from what can be called 'the subtropical depriment', i.e. the depression in resource opportunity for human settlement that resulted from subtropical geography and climate.

It was further exacerbated by the fact that most subtropical islands were small (Pitcairn 5 km^2, Norfolk, Raoul, Rapa, Henderson 29–38 km^2), lacking bays or harbours, and notably remote. Pitcairn is 524 km from Mangareva, Rapa 537 km from Raivavae, Norfolk 733 km and Raoul 980 km respectively from New Zealand, and Easter Island 1915 km from Henderson Island. Only the relatively large Easter Island (164 km^2) and Rapa, by the advantage of its large harbour and associated coral reefs in creating a lagoonal surrogate, were inhabited continuously into the European era. Small size meant that population growth soon reached territorial and resource limitations. Remoteness reduced both the range of resources that arrived during colonisation and those that could be readily obtained later. There is no evidence that food crops reached either Norfolk or the Kermadecs in the prehistoric era (although banana was growing on the former by 1788), and they were relatively limited on the other subtropical islands: Rapa had taro, ti, gourd and candlenut, possibly banana; Henderson had coconut, ti, swamp taro and candlenut. Easter Island had sweet potato, taro, yam, banana and sugarcane, a range sufficiently large to suggest that initial colonisation might have involved a number of canoes or some two-way voyaging. Other than the almost ubiquitous Polynesian rat (*Rattus exulans*), the dispersal of animals was slight: possible dog on Norfolk and Easter Island, dog on Raoul, chicken on Easter and pig on Henderson (Anderson 1981; Weisler 1996; Anderson and White 2001; Mieth and Bork 2004).

Overall, then, the subtropical islands were prone to occupational stress caused by a variety of factors and it is difficult to say that the histories of settlement were influenced more by one factor than another. The impact of isolation, either inherent in remoteness or by the decline of early interaction networks (Weisler 1996), was doubtless influential in the prehistoric abandonment of most of the subtropical islands (Norfolk, Kermadecs, Pitcairn, Henderson), but Rapa, and especially Easter Island, were also isolated. Survival on those probably depended on the greater resource availability of a much longer coastline (Easter) or a large harbour (Rapa), coupled with the development of agricultural systems absent or little in evidence elsewhere in the subtropical islands.

Even so, it can be hypothesised that levels of competition for resources had reached quite extreme levels by late prehistory. On Rapa, there may have been 10 competing polities, each the proud lords of, on average, fewer than 4 km^2 of land, nearly all of it steep and largely barren. Perhaps only such a level of competition can have made the labour and inconvenience of building and living in the skyline forts seem at all worthwhile.

Further research

We are well aware of the preliminary nature of our investigations on Rapa and the probability that our results and conclusions will need significant modification in future research. The need for more research is urgent. Increasing development of roads, housing and other facilities has already exposed numerous sites around Ha'urei Harbour; sand deposits needed for concrete are scarce and the largest of them underlies the oldest site on Rapa, at Tangarutu, which is now about 85% destroyed by sand mining; major works, including the development of an airfield, are envisaged. In addition, grazing cattle and, especially, a large population of feral goats have created massive hillslope erosion in many bays. Even without these mechanisms of accelerating site damage, the forts are decaying rapidly. The substrates are mostly saprolitic clays and weathered basalts, which erode quickly in the absence of forest cover and soon bring down masonry and other structures. There is, we suggest, a need for prompt and serious attention to the archaeology of Rapa well beyond that which our resources could meet.

Among those aspects of Rapan archaeology which demand attention are these:

1. Establishing the sequence of cultural landscape development in much more detail. We used AMS ^{14}C dating as a survey technique (Chapter 11) to establish the broad pattern of landscape use, but that is a relatively crude, if initially useful, approach, which, ideally, would be superseded by high-density dating to determine temporal relationships between site clusters, types, localities (such as the individual valley systems), and individual sites and stratigraphy. Some of this research needs to be directed at the major colonisation sites, especially Tangarutu.

2. One particular set of archaeological features, critical to understanding the development of Rapan prehistory, and which has yet to be investigated systematically, consists of the pondfields (Chapter 13) and associated structures. The history of these offers a means of testing conjecture about the trajectory and chronology of population growth and the development of pressure on resources that underlies an economic proposition for the rise of warfare and fortifications.

3. Another set of features, mostly located on low ground behind the coast, or on low hills and ridges, and consisting mainly of terraces, but also ovens, hearths, burial areas defined by stone kerbing, and the ethnographically recorded remains of rudimentary marae, may refer to what is currently a poorly resolved middle phase in Rapan prehistory. We, and others before us, have barely touched on these features.

4. Much more excavation is needed, preferably in large open areas, of the surviving *pare*. Too little is known of how habitation on these sites was organised, whether there were houses of different sizes and locations, to what extent different economic and technological functions were carried out at them, how long settlement lasted at different sites, whether agricultural storage was indeed a major purpose, and whether conjecture about socio-political relationships between major and minor *pare* can be sustained.

Note

1.   There are very small lagoons on Norfolk Island.

References

Anderson, A.J. 1981. The archaeology of Raoul Island and its place in the settlement history of Polynesia. *Archaeology and Physical Anthropology in Oceania* 15:131–141.

Anderson, A.J. 1996. Origins of Procellariidae Hunting in the Southwest Pacific. *International Journal of Osteoarchaeology* 6:1–8.

Anderson, A.J. 2001. No meat on that beautiful shore: the prehistoric abandonment of subtropical Polynesian islands. In: Anderson, A.J. and Leach, B.F. (eds), *Zooarchaeology of Oceanic Coasts and Islands: Papers from the 8th International Congress of the International Council of Archaeozoology, 23–29 August 1998, Victoria B.C., Canada.* Special Issue of the *International Journal of Osteoarchaeology* 11:14–23.

Anderson, A.J. 2002. Faunal collapse, landscape change and settlement history in Remote Oceania. *World Archaeology* 33:375–390.

Anderson, A.J. and White, J.P. (eds), 2001. *The Prehistoric Archaeology of Norfolk Island, Southwest Pacific. Records of the Australian Museum,* Supplement 27, Sydney.

Buck, Sir P.H. 1954. *Vikings of the Sunrise.* Whitcombe and Tombs, Christchurch.

Heyerdahl, T. and Ferdon, E.W. (eds), 1965. *Reports of the Norwegian Archaeological Expedition to Easter Island and the East Pacific*, Volume 2 Miscellaneous Papers. Monographs of the School of American Research and the Kon-Tiki Museum, 24 Pt. 2, Esselte AB, Stockholm.

Lamb, W.K. (ed), 1984. George Vancouver, *A Voyage of Discovery to the North Pacific Ocean and Round the World 1791–1795*, Volume I. The Hakluyt Society, London.

Mieth, A. and Bork, H-R. 2004. Easter Island – Rapa Nui: scientific pathways to secrets of the past. *Man and Environment* 1. Christian-Albrechts-Universität zu Kiel, Kiel.

Walczak, J. 2003. Presentation des données actuelles sur la préhistoire de Rapa Iti (archiple des Australes-Polynésie Française). In: Orliac, C. (ed), *Archéologie en Océanie Insulaire: Peuplement, sociétés et paysages*, pp. 28–45. Editions Artcom, Paris.

Weisler, M.I. 1996. Taking the mystery out of the Polynesian 'mystery' islands: a case study from Mangareva and the Pitcairn group. In: Davidson, J., Irwin, G., Leach, F., Pawley, A. and Brown, D. (eds), *Oceanic Culture History: essays in honour of Roger Green.* New Zealand Journal of Archaeology, Special Publication, pp. 615–629. Dunedin.

Wilmshurst, J., Hunt, T., Lipo, C. and Anderson, A. 2011. High-precision radiocarbon dating shows recent and rapid initial human colonization of East Polynesia. *Proceedings of the National Academy of Sciences* 105:7676–7680.

Appendices

Appendix A: Reference and identification data OAL Reference Collection

Family	Elements not held in collection
Acanthuridae	
Anguillidae	Ceratohyal, cleithrum, epihyal, hyomandibular, maxilla, opercular, palatine, parasphenoid, pharyngeal plate, post temporal, preopercular, scapula, vomer
Balistidae	
Belonidae	Ceratohyal, epihyal, palatine, post temporal, vomer
Bothidae	Parasphenoid, pharyngeal plate, scapula, vomer
Carangidae	
Chaetodontidae	Articular, ceratohyal, epihyal, hyomandibular, maxilla, palatine, parasphenoid, pharyngeal plate, post temporal, scapula, vomer
Chanidae	Pharyngeal plate, scapula, vomer
Cirrhitidae	Ceratohyal, cleithrum, epihyal, hyomandibular, opercular, palatine, parasphenoid, pharyngeal plate, post temporal, preopercular, scapula, vomer
Congridae	Cleithrum, maxilla, palatine, pharyngeal plate, post temporal, preopercular, scapula
Coryphaenidae	
Diodontidae	Ceratohyal, cleithrum, epihyal, hyomandibular, opercular, palatine, parasphenoid, post temporal, preopercular, scapula, vomer
Exocoetidae	Post temporal, vomer
Fistularidae	*reference specimen provided by Dr Marshall Weisler
Gempylidae	Ceratohyal, cleithrum, epihyal, hyomandibular, opercular, palatine, parasphenoid, pharyngeal plate, post temporal, preopercular, scapula, vomer
Holocentridae	
Kyphosidae	
Labridae	
Lethrinidae	
Lutjanidae	
Monocanthidae	Palatine, pharyngeal plate, post temporal
Mugilidae	
Mullidae	
Muraenidae	Ceratohyal, cleithrum, epihyal, maxilla, opercular, palatine, pharyngeal plate, post temporal, preopercular, scapula
Pempheridae	
Pomacanthidae	Palatine, pharyngeal plate, vomer
Pomacentirdae	Parasphenoid, vomer
Pricanthidae	Pharyngeal plate

Continued on next page

Family	Elements not held in collection
Scaridae	
Scombridae	
Scorpanidae	
Serranidae	
Siganidae	Ceratohyal, epihyal, palatine, pharyngeal plate, post temporal, vomer
Syphyraenidae	

Appendix B: Element counts and taxonomic identification of fish

Tangarutu E1/E2 Level III

Family	Element	Left	N/A	Right	Total
Acanthuridae	Palatine			1	1
	Premaxilla	1		1	2
	Preopercular	1			1
	Quadrate			1	1
	Scapula			1	1
Acanthuridae Total		**2**		**4**	**6**
Apode	Ceratohyal	1			1
	Epihyal	1		2	3
	Opercular	2		2	4
	Unidentified element		4		4
Apode Total		**4**	**4**	**4**	**12**
Belonidae	Articular	1			1
	Dentary	1			1
	Opercular			1	1
	Preopercular	1			1
Belonidae Total		**3**		**1**	**4**
cf. Aulostomidae	Articular	1		1	2
	Preopercular	1		1	2
	Quadrate	1		2	3
cf. Aulostomidae Total		**3**		**4**	**7**
Chaetodontidae	Cleithrum	9		9	18
	Opercular	10		6	16
	Preopercular	15		7	22
Chaetodontidae Total		**34**		**22**	**56**
Congridae	Articular	2		2	4
	Dentary	5		4	9
	Hyomandibular	2		1	3
	Premaxilla	3		5	8
	Quadrate	2		1	3
	Vomer		1		1
Congridae Total		**14**	**1**	**13**	**28**

Continued on next page

Tangarutu E1/E2 Level III *continued*

Family	Element	Left	N/A	Right	Total
Diodontidae	Dermal spine		4		4
Diodontidae Total			**4**		**4**
Elasmobranchii	Tooth		6		6
Elasmobranchii Total			**6**		**6**
Exocoetidae	Hyomandibular			1	1
	Inferior pharyngeal plate		1		1
	Scapula			1	1
Exocoetidae Total			**1**	**2**	**3**
Holocentridae	Articular	1		1	2
	Cleithrum			1	1
	Hyomandibular	1			1
	Preopercular	1			1
	Scapula			1	1
Holocentridae Total		**3**		**3**	**6**
Kyphosidae	Articular	1			1
	Post temporal	1			1
Kyphosidae Total		**2**			**2**
Labridae	Articular	1			1
	Cleithrum	2		1	3
	Dentary	4		1	5
	Hyomandibular	2			2
	Inferior pharyngeal plate		4		4
	Maxilla	2		1	3
	Opercular	1		4	5
	Premaxilla	12		9	21
	Preopercular	3		1	4
	Quadrate	1		1	2
	Superior pharyngeal plate			2	2
Labridae Total		**28**	**4**	**20**	**52**
Lethrinidae	Articular	1			1
	Dentary	5		1	6
	Hyomandibular			1	1
	Premaxilla			1	1
	Preopercular			1	1
	Quadrate			1	1
Lethrinidae Total		**6**		**5**	**11**
Mullidae	Articular			1	1
	Dentary			1	1
	Opercular			1	1
	Premaxilla	1			1
	Scapula			1	1
Mullidae Total		**1**		**4**	**5**

Continued on next page

Tangarutu E1/E2 Level III *continued*

Family	Element	Left	N/A	Right	Total
Muraenidae	Articular	8		7	15
	Dentary	20		24	44
	Hyomandibular	8		3	11
	Premaxilla			2	2
	Quadrate	10		4	14
	Vomer		11		11
Muraenidae Total		**46**	**11**	**40**	**97**
NIC 10	Opercular			1	1
NIC 10 Total				**1**	**1**
NIC 11	Opercular			1	1
NIC 11 Total				**1**	**1**
NIC 12	Opercular	2		1	3
NIC 12 Total		**2**		**1**	**3**
NIC 13	Opercular	2			2
NIC 13 Total		**2**			**2**
NIC 14	Palatine			1	1
NIC 14 Total				**1**	**1**
NIC 19	Dentary			1	1
NIC 19 Total				**1**	**1**
NIC 22	Scapula			1	1
NIC 22 Total				**1**	**1**
NIC 23	Scapula			1	1
NIC 23 Total				**1**	**1**
NIC 33	Inferior pharyngeal plate		1		1
NIC 33 Total			**1**		**1**
NIC 34	Superior pharyngeal plate		1		1
NIC 34 Total			**1**		**1**
NIC 45	Vomer		1		1
NIC 45 Total			**1**		**1**
NIC 6	Hyomandibular			2	2
NIC 6 Total				**2**	**2**
Pomacentridae	Cleithrum	7		1	8
	Opercular	2		1	3
	Post temporal			2	2
	Scapula	1		1	2
Pomacentridae Total		**10**		**5**	**15**
Scaridae	4th Epibranchial			3	3
	Articular	2		5	7
	Ceratohyal	2		1	3
	Cleithrum	2			2
	Dentary	7		3	10
	Epihyal	1		1	2

Continued on next page

Tangarutu E1/E2 Level III *continued*

Family	Element	Left	N/A	Right	Total
	Hyomandibular	6		4	10
	Inferior pharyngeal plate	1	13		14
	Maxilla	1		1	2
	Opercular	5		9	14
	Palatine	2		6	8
	Parasphenoid		4		4
	Premaxilla	14		10	24
	Preopercular	7		6	13
	Quadrate	5		1	6
	Scapula	6		5	11
	Superior pharyngeal plate	21	1	19	41
	Toothed element		6		6
Scaridae Total		**82**	**24**	**74**	**180**
Serranidae	Articular	4		11	15
	Ceratohyal	9		3	12
	Cleithrum	5		5	10
	Dentary	11		16	27
	Epihyal	6		3	9
	Hyomandibular	2		3	5
	Maxilla	14		11	25
	Opercular	12		16	28
	Palatine	4		3	7
	Parasphenoid		5		5
	Post temporal	3		5	8
	Premaxilla	12		11	23
	Preopercular	15		16	31
	Quadrate	11		7	18
	Scapula	5			5
	Vomer		2		2
Serranidae Total		**113**	**7**	**110**	**230**
Unidentified	Basioccipital		2		2
	Basipterygium	5		5	10
	Ceratohyal		1		1
	Cleithrum	1		2	3
	Coracoid	9	1	7	17
	Dorsal spine		222		222
	Dorsal spine/pterygiophore		57		57
	Ectopterygoid	8		6	14
	Epihyal		1		1
	Fragments		885		885
	Hyomandibular			1	1

Continued on next page

terra australis 37

Tangarutu E1/E2 Level III *continued*

Family	Element	Left	N/A	Right	Total
	Hypural		4		4
	Hypural 1 and 2		13		13
	Hypural 3 and 4	2	10		12
	Hypural 5		4		4
	Identifiable		209		209
	Interopercular	4	29		33
	Maxilla		2		2
	Mesopterygoid	1			1
	Metapterygoid	6			6
	Misc spines and rays		291		291
	Opercular	1	4		5
	Parasphenoid		1		1
	Preopercular	3		5	8
	Pterygiophore		114		114
	Scale		1360		1360
	Subopercular	7	2	2	11
	Supracleithrum	10	2	4	16
	Toothed element		13		13
	Urohyal		4		4
	Vertebra		728		728
Unidentified Total		**57**	**3959**	**32**	**4048**
Grand Total		**412**	**4023**	**353**	**4788**

Tangarutu E1/E2 Level II

Family	Element	Left	N/A	Right	Total
Acanthuridae	Quadrate	1			1
Acanthuridae Total		**1**			**1**
Apode	Basihyal		1		1
	Ceratohyal	2		1	3
	Epihyal	2		5	7
	Opercular	4		5	9
	Premaxilla	1			1
	Unidentified element		5		5
Apode Total		**9**	**6**	**11**	**26**
Belonidae	Articular			1	1
	Dentary			2	2
Belonidae Total				**3**	**3**
Chaetodontidae	Cleithrum	11		10	21
	Opercular	7		9	16
	Preopercular	2		4	6
Chaetodontidae Total		**20**		**23**	**43**

Continued on next page

Tangarutu E1/E2 Level II *continued*

Family	Element	Left	N/A	Right	Total
Congridae	Articular	3		1	4
	Dentary	5		2	7
	Hyomandibular	1		1	2
	Premaxilla	2		3	5
	Quadrate	1		1	2
	Vomer		2		2
Congridae Total		**12**	**2**	**8**	**22**
Diodontidae	Dermal spine		1		1
Diodontidae Total			**1**		**1**
Holocentridae	Preopercular			1	1
Holocentridae Total				**1**	**1**
Kyphosidae	Cleithrum			1	1
	Maxilla	1			1
	Post temporal			1	1
	Quadrate	1			1
Kyphosidae Total		**2**		**2**	**4**
Labridae	Cleithrum	8		3	11
	Dentary	2		2	4
	Epihyal			1	1
	Hyomandibular	2		2	4
	Inferior pharyngeal plate		4		4
	Maxilla			1	1
	Palatine	1		1	2
	Post temporal	1			1
	Premaxilla	3		8	11
	Preopercular	2		6	8
	Quadrate	2		4	6
	Scapula	1		1	2
	Superior pharyngeal plate	1			1
Labridae Total		**23**	**4**	**29**	**56**
Lethrinidae	Dentary	1		2	3
Lethrinidae Total		**1**		**2**	**3**
Muraenidae	Articular	3		3	6
	Dentary	9		19	28
	Hyomandibular	5		2	7
	Parasphenoid		2		2
	Premaxilla	2		5	7
	Quadrate	2		2	4
	Toothed element		1		1
	Vomer		12		12
Muraenidae Total		**21**	**15**	**31**	**67**

Continued on next page

terra australis 37

Tangarutu E1/E2 Level II *continued*

Family	Element	Left	N/A	Right	Total
NIC 13	Opercular	1			1
NIC 13 Total		**1**			**1**
NIC 15	Palatine		1		1
NIC 15 Total			**1**		**1**
NIC 16	Premaxilla			1	1
NIC 16 Total				**1**	**1**
NIC 17	Premaxilla	1			1
NIC 17 Total		**1**			**1**
NIC 24	Articular	1			1
NIC 24 Total		**1**			**1**
NIC 30	Ceratohyal	1			1
NIC 30 Total		**1**			**1**
NIC 4	Hyomandibular			2	2
NIC 4 Total				**2**	**2**
NIC 41	Scute		1		1
NIC 41 Total			**1**		**1**
Pomacentridae	Cleithrum			1	1
	Preopercular	1			1
	Scapula			1	1
Pomacentridae Total		**1**		**2**	**3**
Scaridae	4th epibranchial	3		3	6
	Articular			1	1
	Cleithrum	1			1
	Dentary	3		4	7
	Epihyal	1		2	3
	Hyomandibular	1		3	4
	Inferior pharyngeal plate		4		4
	Maxilla	1		2	3
	Opercular	1		2	3
	Palatine	2			2
	Parasphenoid		2		2
	Post temporal	2		1	3
	Premaxilla	5		1	6
	Preopercular	1		3	4
	Quadrate	2		1	3
	Scapula	2			2
	Superior pharyngeal plate	12		6	18
	Toothed element		3		3
Scaridae Total		**37**	**9**	**29**	**75**
Serranidae	Articular	2			2
	Ceratohyal			1	1
	Cleithrum	2		3	5

Continued on next page

Tangarutu E1/E2 Level II *continued*

Family	Element	Left	N/A	Right	Total
	Dentary	3		3	6
	Epihyal	1		3	4
	Hyomandibular	4		2	6
	Maxilla	2		1	3
	Opercular	2		1	3
	Palatine	1		1	2
	Parasphenoid		2		2
	Post temporal	2		3	5
	Premaxilla	3		2	5
	Preopercular	4		2	6
	Quadrate	3		1	4
	Scapula	2		1	3
Serranidae Total		**31**	**2**	**24**	**57**
Siganidae	Preopercular			1	1
Siganidae Total				**1**	**1**
Unidentified	Basipterygium	1	2		3
	Ceratohyal			1	1
	Coracoid	3		3	6
	Dorsal spine		158		158
	Dorsal spine/pterygiophore		35		35
	Ectopterygoid	2	1	2	5
	Fragments		670		670
	Hypural 1 and 2		1		1
	Hypural 3 and 4		2		2
	Hypural 5		1		1
	Identifiable		134		134
	Interopercular		12		12
	Maxilla	1		1	2
	Misc spines and rays		340		340
	Parasphenoid		2		2
	Preopercular			1	1
	Pterygiophore		109		109
	Scale		709		709
	Scapula		1		1
	Subopercular	5		6	11
	Supracleithrum	9	1	7	17
	Toothed element		4		4
	Urohyal		3		3
	Vertebra		478		478
Unidentified Total		**21**	**2663**	**21**	**2705**
Grand Total		**183**	**2704**	**190**	**3077**

Tangarutu E1/E2 Level I

Family	Element	Left	N/A	Right	Total
Acanthuridae	Cleithrum	1			1
	Dorsal spine		1		1
	Opercular			1	1
	Pterygiophore		1		1
	Scapula	1		1	2
Acanthuridae Total		**2**	**2**	**2**	**6**
Apode	Epihyal	1		1	2
	Opercular	2		2	4
	Premaxilla			1	1
	Unidentified element		3		3
Apode Total		**3**	**3**	**4**	**10**
Belonidae	Hyomandibular	1			1
	Metapterygoid	1			1
	Preopercular	1		1	2
	Quadrate	1			1
Belonidae Total		**4**		**1**	**5**
Carangidae	Scapula			1	1
Carangidae Total				**1**	**1**
Chaetodontidae	Cleithrum	6		8	14
	Opercular	7		2	9
	Preopercular			3	3
Chaetodontidae Total		**13**		**13**	**26**
Congridae	Articular			2	2
	Dentary			2	2
	Hyomandibular	1			1
	Parasphenoid		2		2
	Premaxilla	1			1
Congridae Total		**2**	**2**	**4**	**8**
Diodontidae	Dermal spine		3		3
Diodontidae Total			**3**		**3**
Kyphosidae	Preopercular			1	1
Kyphosidae Total				**1**	**1**
Labridae	Articular	1			1
	Cleithrum	1		1	2
	Hyomandibular	1		4	5
	Inferior pharyngeal plate		2		2
	Maxilla			1	1
	Premaxilla	2		8	10
	Preopercular			1	1
	Quadrate			1	1
	Scapula	1		2	3
	Superior pharyngeal plate	1			1

Continued on next page

Tangarutu E1/E2 Level I *continued*

Family	Element	Left	N/A	Right	Total
Labridae Total		**7**	**2**	**18**	**27**
Monocanthidae	Cleithrum	1			1
Monocanthidae Total		**1**			**1**
Mugilidae	Premaxilla	2			2
Mugilidae Total		**2**			**2**
Mullidae	Dentary			1	1
	Hyomandibular	1			1
Mullidae Total		**1**		**1**	**2**
Muraenidae	Articular	2		2	4
	Dentary	13		9	22
	Hyomandibular	3		2	5
	Parasphenoid		1		1
	Premaxilla	3		1	4
	Quadrate	3		2	5
	Toothed element		2		2
	Vomer		9		9
Muraenidae Total		**24**	**12**	**16**	**52**
NIC 12	Opercular			2	2
NIC 12 Total				**2**	**2**
NIC 18	Premaxilla			1	1
NIC 18 Total				**1**	**1**
NIC 21	Scapula	1			1
NIC 21 Total		**1**			**1**
NIC 25	Articular	1			1
NIC 25 Total		**1**			**1**
NIC 27	Epihyal	1			1
NIC 27 Total		**1**			**1**
NIC 28	Epihyal			1	1
NIC 28 Total				**1**	**1**
NIC 31	Ceratohyal			1	1
NIC 31 Total				**1**	**1**
NIC 35	Superior pharyngeal plate		1		1
NIC 35 Total			**1**		**1**
NIC 38	Quadrate	1			1
NIC 38 Total		**1**			**1**
NIC 4	Hyomandibular			2	2
NIC 4 Total				**2**	**2**
NIC 42	Hyomandibular	1			1
NIC 42 Total		**1**			**1**
NIC 43	Opercular			1	1
NIC 43 Total				**1**	**1**

Continued on next page

Tangarutu E1/E2 Level I *continued*

Family	Element	Left	N/A	Right	Total
NIC 44	Vomer		1		1
NIC 44 Total			1		1
NIC 45	Vomer		1		1
NIC 45 Total			1		1
NIC 9	Preopercular			1	1
NIC 9 Total				1	1
Pomacentridae	Cleithrum			1	1
	Inferior pharyngeal plate		1		1
	Preopercular	1			1
	Scapula	1			1
Pomacentridae Total		2	1	1	4
Scaridae	4th epibranchial	4		8	12
	Articular	12		9	21
	Ceratohyal			1	1
	Cleithrum	5		2	7
	Dentary	19		18	37
	Hyomandibular	9		10	19
	Inferior pharyngeal plate		29		29
	Maxilla	3		4	7
	Opercular	10		8	18
	Palatine	6		5	11
	Post temporal			1	1
	Premaxilla	20		13	33
	Preopercular	3		7	10
	Quadrate	9		9	18
	Scapula	5		5	10
	Superior pharyngeal plate	33		30	63
	Toothed element		4		4
	Vomer		2		2
Scaridae Total		138	35	130	303
Serranidae	Articular	3		3	6
	Ceratohyal	2		1	3
	Cleithrum	3		2	5
	Dentary			3	3
	Epihyal			2	2
	Hyomandibular	2		3	5
	Maxilla	1		7	8
	Opercular	1		1	2
	Parasphenoid		1		1
	Post temporal	2		3	5
	Premaxilla	5			5
	Preopercular			1	1

Continued on next page

Tangarutu E1/E2 Level I *continued*

Family	Element	Left	N/A	Right	Total
	Quadrate	6		2	8
	Scapula	1			1
	Vomer		2		2
Serranidae Total		**26**	**3**	**28**	**57**
Siganidae	Hyomandibular	1		1	2
	Maxilla			1	1
	Premaxilla	1		1	2
	Preopercular	1			1
	Scapula	1			1
Siganidae Total		**4**		**3**	**7**
Unidentified	Basioccipital		1		1
	Basipterygium	9		4	13
	Ceratohyal		4		4
	Cleithrum	1			1
	Coracoid	2		2	4
	Dorsal spine		92		92
	Dorsal spine/pterygiophore		25		25
	Ectopterygoid	2		2	4
	Epihyal		1		1
	Fragments		1155		1155
	Hypural 1 and 2		6		6
	Hypural 3 and 4		11		11
	Hypural 5		1		1
	Identifiable		163		163
	Interopercular		21		21
	Maxilla		1		1
	Misc spines and rays		279		279
	Opercular		6	1	7
	Parasphenoid		2		2
	Preopercular			2	2
	Pterygiophore		123		123
	Quadrate	1		1	2
	Scale		547		547
	Subopercular	2	2	1	5
	Superior pharyngeal plate		4		4
	Supracleithrum	13		10	23
	Toothed element		2		2
	Urohyal		1		1
	Ventral hypohyal			1	1
	Vertebra		519		519
Unidentified Total		**30**	**2966**	**24**	**3020**
Grand Total		**264**	**3032**	**256**	**3552**

Tangarutu R1 Level III

Family	Element	Left	N/A	Right	Total
Acanthuridae	Cleithrum	1			1
Acanthuridae Total		**1**			**1**
Apode	Ceratohyal	1		1	2
	Ceratohyal			1	1
	Dentary			1	1
	Epihyal			2	2
	Opercular			1	1
	Unidentified element		4		4
Apode Total		**1**	**4**	**6**	**11**
Chaetodontidae	Cleithrum	3		13	16
	Opercular	2		2	4
	Preopercular	1		3	4
Chaetodontidae Total		**6**		**18**	**24**
Congridae	Articular	3		5	8
	Dentary	4		3	7
	Hyomandibular	2		2	4
	Premaxilla	5		1	6
	Quadrate	2		1	3
	Vomer		3		3
Congridae Total		**16**	**3**	**12**	**31**
Diodontidae	Dermal spine		2		2
Diodontidae Total			**2**		**2**
Elasmobranchii	Vertebra		1		1
Elasmobranchii Total			**1**		**1**
Holocentridae	Ceratohyal	1			1
Holocentridae Total		**1**			**1**
Labridae	Cleithrum	2		3	5
	Dentary	2			2
	Hyomandibular			1	1
	Inferior pharyngeal plate		7		7
	Maxilla	3		2	5
	Premaxilla	5		8	13
	Preopercular	3		2	5
	Quadrate	3			3
	Vomer		1		1
Labridae Total		**18**	**8**	**16**	**42**
Mullidae	Dentary			1	1
	Post temporal	1			1
	Premaxilla			1	1
Mullidae Total		**1**		**2**	**3**
Muraenidae	Articular	4		3	7
	Dentary	19		8	27

Continued on next page

Tangarutu R1 Level III *continued*

Family	Element	Left	N/A	Right	Total
	Hyomandibular	2		4	6
	Parasphenoid		2		2
	Premaxilla			4	4
	Quadrate	2		2	4
	Toothed element		1		1
	Vomer		5		5
Muraenidae Total		**27**	**8**	**21**	**56**
NIC 13	Opercular	1		4	5
NIC 13 Total		**1**		**4**	**5**
NIC 17	Premaxilla			1	1
NIC 17 Total				**1**	**1**
NIC 37	Quadrate	1		1	2
NIC 37 Total		**1**		**1**	**2**
NIC 39	Quadrate	1			1
NIC 39 Total		**1**			**1**
NIC 4	Hyomandibular			1	1
NIC 4 Total				**1**	**1**
NIC 40	Quadrate	1			1
NIC 40 Total		**1**			**1**
Pomacentridae	Cleithrum	1		1	2
Pomacentridae Total		**1**		**1**	**2**
Scaridae	4th epibranchial	3		1	4
	Articular	4		3	7
	Ceratohyal			2	2
	Cleithrum			1	1
	Dentary	3		2	5
	Epihyal	1			1
	Hyomandibular	1		1	2
	Inferior pharyngeal plate		4		4
	Maxilla	2		4	6
	Opercular	2		1	3
	Palatine	2			2
	Parasphenoid		1		1
	Post temporal	2		1	3
	Post temporal	1			1
	Premaxilla	3		6	9
	Preopercular	3		3	6
	Quadrate	3		1	4
	Scapula	1		2	3
	Superior pharyngeal plate	4		5	9
Scaridae Total		**35**	**5**	**33**	**73**

Continued on next page

terra australis 37

Tangarutu R1 Level III *continued*

Family	Element	Left	N/A	Right	Total
Serranidae	Articular	3		2	5
	Cleithrum	5		4	9
	Dentary	5		4	9
	Epihyal	2		3	5
	Hyomandibular	2		2	4
	Maxilla	5			5
	Opercular			1	1
	Palatine			2	2
	Parasphenoid		1		1
	Post temporal	1		1	2
	Premaxilla	2		2	4
	Preopercular	2		1	3
	Scapula	1			1
	Vomer		1		1
Serranidae Total		**28**	**2**	**22**	**52**
Unidentified	Basioccipital		3		3
	Basipterygium	2		1	3
	Cleithrum	5			5
	Coracoid	3		4	7
	Dermal spine		1		1
	Dorsal spine		73		73
	Dorsal spine/pterygiophore		31		31
	Ectopterygoid	1	3	2	6
	Fragments		953		953
	Hyomandibular		1		1
	Hypural		1		1
	Hypural 1 and 2		5		5
	Hypural 3 and 4		5		5
	Identifiable		46		46
	Interopercular		6		6
	Misc spines and rays		138		138
	Opercular	1	1		2
	Parasphenoid		2		2
	Post temporal		1		1
	Preopercular	1			1
	Pterygiophore		32		32
	Scale		202		202
	Subopercular	3		2	5
	Supracleithrum	3		4	7
	Toothed element		1		1
	Urohyal		1		1
	Vertebra		233		233
Unidentified Total		**19**	**1739**	**13**	**1771**
Grand Total		**158**	**1772**	**151**	**2081**

Tangarutu R1 Level II

Family	Element	Left	N/A	Right	Total
Apode	Basihyal		1		1
	Ceratohyal	1			1
	Epihyal			1	1
	Opercular	1		1	2
Apode Total		**2**	**1**	**2**	**5**
cf. Aulostomidae	Opercular			1	1
cf. Aulostomidae Total				**1**	**1**
Chaetodontidae	Cleithrum	1		1	2
Chaetodontidae Total		**1**		**1**	**2**
Congridae	Parasphenoid		2		2
	Premaxilla	1			1
	Vomer		3		3
Congridae Total		**1**	**5**		**6**
Kyphosidae	Articular			1	1
Kyphosidae Total				**1**	**1**
Labridae	Cleithrum	1		1	2
	Opercular	1			1
	Premaxilla	1			1
	Preopercular	1			1
Labridae Total		**4**		**1**	**5**
Lethrinidae	Dentary			1	1
Lethrinidae Total				**1**	**1**
Mullidae	Articular	1			1
Family	Element	Left	N/A	Right	Total
	Premaxilla	1			1
Mullidae Total		**2**			**2**
Muraenidae	Articular			2	2
	Dentary	6		9	15
	Hyomandibular			3	3
	Premaxilla			3	3
	Quadrate			1	1
	Vomer		2		2
Muraenidae Total		**6**	**2**	**18**	**26**
NIC 15	Palatine			1	1
NIC 15 Total				**1**	**1**
Scaridae	Ceratohyal	1			1
	Dentary	1		1	2
	Hyomandibular	1		2	3
	Inferior pharyngeal plate		7		7
	Maxilla	1			1
	Opercular			3	3
	Palatine	1			1

Continued on next page

Tangarutu R1 Level II *continued*

Family	Element	Left	N/A	Right	Total
	Premaxilla	3		2	5
	Quadrate			2	2
	Scapula	1		1	2
	Superior pharyngeal plate	2		3	5
Scaridae Total		**11**	**7**	**14**	**32**
Serranidae	Articular			1	1
	Cleithrum	1		1	2
	Dentary	2			2
	Hyomandibular			1	1
	Opercular	2			2
	Palatine			1	1
	Parasphenoid		1		1
	Premaxilla	2		1	3
Serranidae Total		**7**	**1**	**5**	**13**
Unidentified	Coracoid	2		3	5
	Dorsal spine		19		19
	Dorsal spine/pterygiophore		5		5
	Ectopterygoid	3		1	4
	Fragments		398		398
	Hypural 3 and 4		3		3
	Identifiable		32		32
	Maxilla	1			1
	Misc spines and rays		57		57
	Pterygiophore		8		8
	Scale		55		55
	Subopercular			2	2
	Supracleithrum	1		1	2
	Vertebra		53		53
Unidentified Total		**7**	**630**	**7**	**644**
Grand Total		**41**	**646**	**52**	**739**

Tangarutu T1

Family	Element	Left	N/A	Right	Total
Holocentridae	Dentary	1			1
Holocentridae Total		**1**			**1**
NIC 36	Quadrate			2	2
NIC 36 Total				**2**	**2**
Serranidae	Maxilla			1	1
Serranidae Total				**1**	**1**
Unidentified	Dorsal spine		1		1
	Fragments		15		15

Continued on next page

Tangarutu T1 *continued*

Family	Element	Left	N/A	Right	Total
	Misc spines and rays		1		1
	Pterygiophore		1		1
	Scale		22		22
	Vertebra		5		5
Unidentified Total			45		45
Grand Total		1	45	3	49

Tangarutu T3

Family	Element	Left	N/A	Right	Total
Unidentified	Dorsal spine		3		3
	Dorsal spine/pterygiophore		2		2
	Fragments		13		13
	Identifiable		1		1
	Interopercular		1		1
	Misc spines and rays		3		3
	Pterygiophore		2		2
	Scale		72		72
	Supracleithrum	1		1	2
	Vertebra		9		9
Unidentified Total		1	106	1	108
Grand Total		1	106	1	108

Akatanui 1

Family	Element	Left	N/A	Right	Total
Acanthuridae	Parasphenoid		1		1
Acanthuridae Total			1		1
Congridae	Parasphenoid		1		1
Congridae Total			1		1
Elasmobranchii	Vertebra		2		2
Elasmobranchii Total			2		2
Labridae	Inferior pharyngeal plate		1		1
Labridae Total			1		1
NIC 17	Premaxilla	1			1
NIC 17 Total		1			1
NIC 20	Scapula			1	1
NIC 20 Total				1	1
NIC 26	Ceratohyal	1			1
	Epihyal	1			1
NIC 26 Total		2			2
NIC 5	Hyomandibular			2	2
NIC 5 Total				2	2

Continued on next page

Akatanui 1 *continued*

Family	Element	Left	N/A	Right	Total
NIC 7	Hyomandibular	1			1
NIC 7 Total		**1**			**1**
NIC 8	Hyomandibular	1			1
NIC 8 Total		**1**			**1**
Scaridae	4th epibranchial	1			1
	Dentary	1		3	4
	Inferior pharyngeal plate		1		1
	Maxilla	1			1
	Opercular			1	1
	Parasphenoid		1		1
	Premaxilla	4		5	9
	Quadrate			1	1
	Scapula	1		1	2
	Superior pharyngeal plate	1		3	4
	Toothed element		3		3
Scaridae Total		**9**	**5**	**14**	**28**
Serranidae	Articular			1	1
	Ceratohyal			3	3
	Dentary			1	1
	Opercular	1			1
	Palatine	1			1
	Post temporal	2		1	3
	Premaxilla			1	1
	Preopercular			2	2
	Quadrate	1			1
Serranidae Total		**5**		**9**	**14**
Unidentified	Basioccipital		1		1
	Basipterygium	2			2
	Coracoid			1	1
	Dorsal spine		1		1
	Fragments		116		116
	Hypural 1 and 2		3		3
	Hypural 3 and 4		3		3
	Identifiable		25		25
	Interopercular		2		2
	Misc spines and rays		24		24
	Opercular		1		1
	Pterygiophore		12		12
	Scale		33		33
	Subopercular	1			1
	Supracleithrum	2		1	3

Continued on next page

Akatanui 1 *continued*

Family	Element	Left	N/A	Right	Total
	Urohyal		1		1
	Vertebra		54		54
Unidentified Total		**5**	**276**	**2**	**283**
Grand Total		**24**	**286**	**28**	**338**

Akatanui 3 C1

Family	Element	Left	N/A	Right	Total
Acanthuridae	Dorsal spine		1		1
Acanthuridae Total			**1**		**1**
Apode	Epihyal	1		1	2
	Opercular	2			2
	Unidentified element		4		4
Apode Total		**3**	**4**	**1**	**8**
Bothidae	Ceratohyal			1	1
	Epihyal			1	1
Bothidae Total				**2**	**2**
Carangidae	Articular	1			1
	Opercular			1	1
Carangidae Total		**1**		**1**	**2**
cf. Aulostomidae	Articular	1			1
cf. Aulostomidae Total		**1**			**1**
Chaetodontidae	Cleithrum	2			2
	Opercular	2		1	3
Chaetodontidae Total		**4**		**1**	**5**
Congridae	Articular	5		4	9
	Dentary	4		8	12
	Hyomandibular	2		1	3
	Parasphenoid		3		3
	Premaxilla	3			3
	Quadrate	1		1	2
	Vomer		1		1
Congridae Total		**15**	**4**	**14**	**33**
Diodontidae	Dermal spine		1		1
Diodontidae Total			**1**		**1**
Elasmobranchii	Vertebra		13		13
Elasmobranchii Total			**13**		**13**
Exocoetidae	Inferior pharyngeal plate		1		1
	Quadrate	1			1
Exocoetidae Total		**1**	**1**		**2**
Holocentridae	Cleithrum	1			1
	Hyomandibular	1			1
Holocentridae Total		**2**			**2**

Continued on next page

Akatanui 3 C1 *continued*

Family	Element	Left	N/A	Right	Total
Kyphosidae	Ceratohyal	1			1
	Cleithrum			1	1
	Quadrate			1	1
Kyphosidae Total		**1**		**2**	**3**
Labridae	Articular			2	2
	Cleithrum	2		3	5
	Dentary			3	3
	Hyomandibular			1	1
	Inferior pharyngeal plate		5		5
	Opercular	2			2
	Premaxilla	8		2	10
	Preopercular			1	1
	Quadrate			1	1
	Superior pharyngeal plate			1	1
Labridae Total		**12**	**5**	**14**	**31**
Mullidae	Hyomandibular	1		1	2
	Opercular			1	1
	Palatine			1	1
Mullidae Total		**1**		**3**	**4**
Muraenidae	Articular	1		5	6
	Dentary	6		9	15
	Parasphenoid		2		2
	Toothed element		1		1
	Vomer		7		7
Muraenidae Total		**7**	**10**	**14**	**31**
NIC 13	Opercular	1			1
NIC 13 Total		**1**			**1**
NIC 32	Ceratohyal	1			1
NIC 32 Total		**1**			**1**
NIC 4	Hyomandibular			1	1
NIC 4 Total				**1**	**1**
NIC 45	Vomer		1		1
NIC 45 Total			**1**		**1**
Pomacentridae	Cleithrum	23		19	42
	Opercular	11		5	16
	Post temporal			2	2
	Preopercular	1		4	5
	Scapula	4		6	10
Pomacentridae Total		**39**		**36**	**75**
Scaridae	4th epibranchial	1		2	3
	Articular	1		1	2
	Ceratohyal			1	1

Continued on next page

Akatanui 3 C1 *continued*

Family	Element	Left	N/A	Right	Total
	Cleithrum	4		3	7
	Dentary	11		4	15
	Hyomandibular	4		5	9
	Inferior pharyngeal plate		26		26
	Opercular	9		8	17
	Palatine	7		6	13
	Parasphenoid		1		1
	Post temporal			2	2
	Premaxilla	2		5	7
	Preopercular	15		6	21
	Quadrate	6		2	8
	Scapula	1			1
	Superior pharyngeal plate	23		10	33
Scaridae Total		**84**	**27**	**55**	**166**
Serranidae	Articular	4		1	5
	Ceratohyal	4		1	5
	Cleithrum	1		6	7
	Dentary	7		5	12
	Epihyal	3		1	4
	Hyomandibular	2		2	4
	Opercular	1			1
	Palatine	2		3	5
	Parasphenoid		1		1
	Post temporal			2	2
	Premaxilla	5		4	9
	Preopercular	2		4	6
	Quadrate	5		5	10
	Scapula			2	2
	Vomer		2		2
Serranidae Total		**36**	**3**	**36**	**75**
Unidentified	Basipterygium	5		3	8
	Ceratohyal			1	1
	Cleithrum	1		3	4
	Coracoid	4		8	12
	Dorsal spine		117		117
	Dorsal spine/pterygiophore		57		57
	Ectopterygoid	3		1	4
	Fragments		388		388
	Hyomandibular			2	2
	Hypural		3		3
	Hypural 1 and 2		10		10
	Hypural 3 and 4		10		10

Continued on next page

Akatanui 3 C1 *continued*

Family	Element	Left	N/A	Right	Total
	Hypural 5		1		1
	Identifiable		166		166
	Interopercular		32		32
	Metapterygoid		1	1	2
	Misc spines and rays		178		178
	Opercular		2		2
	Parasphenoid		2		2
	Post temporal			2	2
	Preopercular	1			1
	Pterygiophore		69		69
	Scale		792		792
	Subopercular	4	2	5	11
	Supracleithrum	3	2	4	9
	Toothed element		2		2
	Urohyal		2		2
	Vertebra		144		144
Unidentified Total		**21**	**1980**	**30**	**2031**
Grand Total		**230**	**2050**	**210**	**2490**

Akatanui 3 E1

Family	Element	Left	N/A	Right	Total
Acanthuridae	Opercular			1	1
	Parasphenoid		1		1
Acanthuridae Total			**1**	**1**	**2**
Scaridae	Dentary	1			1
	Hyomandibular	1		1	2
	Inferior pharyngeal plate		3		3
	Parasphenoid		1		1
	Post temporal			1	1
	Premaxilla	2		1	3
	Quadrate			1	1
	Superior pharyngeal plate	2		1	3
Scaridae Total		**6**	**4**	**5**	**15**
Serranidae	Hyomandibular	2			2
	Preopercular	1			1
Serranidae Total		**3**			**3**
Unidentified	Dorsal spine		1		1
	Fragments		59		59
	Hypural		1		1
	Identifiable		5		5
	Interopercular		4		4
	Misc spines and rays		3		3

Continued on next page

Akatanui 3 E1 *continued*

Family	Element	Left	N/A	Right	Total
	Parasphenoid		1		1
	Pterygiophore		5		5
	Scale		13		13
	Supracleithrum			1	1
	Vertebra		9		9
Unidentified Total			**101**	**1**	**102**
Grand Total		**9**	**106**	**7**	**122**

Akatanui 3 A1

Family	Element	Left	N/A	Right	Total
Scaridae	Articular			1	1
	Palatine			1	1
	Premaxilla			1	1
	Preopercular	1			1
Scaridae Total		**1**		**3**	**4**
Serranidae	Hyomandibular			1	1
	Preopercular			1	1
Serranidae Total				**2**	**2**
Unidentified	Fragments		2		2
	Identifiable		1		1
Unidentified Total			**3**		**3**
Grand Total		**1**	**3**	**5**	**9**

Angairao C

Family	Element	Left	N/A	Right	Total
Labridae	Premaxilla	2			2
Labridae Total		**2**			**2**
Muraenidae	Dentary	1		1	2
Muraenidae Total		**1**		**1**	**2**
Scaridae	Inferior pharyngeal plate		1		1
Scaridae Total			**1**		**1**
Siganidae	Preopercular			1	1
Siganidae Total				**1**	**1**
Unidentified	Dorsal spine		2		2
	Fragments		17		17
	Identifiable		1		1
	Misc spines and rays		1		1
	Pterygiophore		1		1
	Vertebra		2		2
Unidentified Total			**24**		**24**
Grand Total		**3**	**25**	**2**	**30**

Angairao E Level III

Family	Element	Left	N/A	Right	Total
Kyphosidae	Ceratohyal			1	1
Kyphosidae Total				1	1
Labridae	Cleithrum	1			1
Labridae Total		1			1
Muraenidae	Articular			1	1
	Dentary	1		1	2
Muraenidae Total		1		2	3
Scaridae	Cleithrum	1			1
	Dentary			1	1
	Inferior pharyngeal plate		5		5
	Opercular	1			1
	Palatine			1	1
	Premaxilla	2		1	3
	Preopercular			1	1
	Quadrate	1		1	2
	Superior pharyngeal plate	3		1	4
Scaridae Total		8	5	6	19
Serranidae	Cleithrum			1	1
	Hyomandibular			1	1
	Preopercular	2			2
	Quadrate			1	1
Serranidae Total		2		3	5
Unidentified	Basipterygium			1	1
	Dorsal spine		2		2
	Ectopterygoid			1	1
	Entopterygoid			1	1
	Fragments		67		67
	Hypural		1		1
	Hypural 1 and 2		1		1
	Identifiable		1		1
	Metapterygoid	1			1
	Misc spines and rays		15		15
	Pterygiophore		1		1
	Scale		3		3
	Supracleithrum	1		2	3
	Vertebra		9		9
Unidentified Total		2	100	5	107
Grand Total		14	105	17	136

terra australis 37

Angairao E Level II

Family	Element	Left	N/A	Right	Total
Acanthuridae	Scapula			1	1
Acanthuridae Total				1	1
Congridae	Articular			1	1
Congridae Total				1	1
Labridae	Quadrate	1			1
Labridae Total		1			1
Muraenidae	Dentary	1			1
	Vomer		1		1
Muraenidae Total		1	1		2
Serranidae	Epihyal	1			1
Serranidae Total		1			1
Unidentified	Dorsal spine		2		2
	Fragments		23		23
	Interopercular		1		1
	Misc spines and rays		3		3
	Scale		10		10
	Vertebra		5		5
Unidentified Total			44		44
Grand Total		3	45	2	50

Angairao E Level I

Family	Element	Left	N/A	Right	Total
Elasmobranchii	Vertebra		1		1
Elasmobranchii Total			1		1
Labridae	Parasphenoid		1		1
Labridae Total			1		1
Mullidae	Premaxilla			1	1
Mullidae Total				1	1
Muraenidae	Articular	1			1
	Dentary	2			2
Muraenidae Total		3			3
NIC 29	Epihyal			1	1
NIC 29 Total				1	1
Scaridae	Inferior pharyngeal plate		1		1
	Opercular			1	1
	Preopercular	1			1
	Superior pharyngeal plate	1		1	2
Scaridae Total		2	1	2	5
Serranidae	Post temporal	1			1
Serranidae Total		1			1

Continued on next page

Angairao E Level I *continued*

Unidentified	Dorsal spine		2		2
	Dorsal spine/pterygiophore		1		1
	Ectopterygoid	1			1
	Fragments		42		42
	Misc spines and rays		12		12
	Scale		4		4
	Supracleithrum	3		1	4
	Toothed element		1		1
	Vertebra		3		3
Unidentified Total		**4**	**65**	**1**	**70**
Grand Total		**10**	**68**	**5**	**83**

Angairao N (Noogoriki)

Family	Element	Left	N/A	Right	Total
Carangidae	Dentary	1			1
Carangidae Total		**1**			**1**
Muraenidae	Dentary	1			1
Muraenidae Total		**1**			**1**
Scaridae	Hyomandibular			1	1
	Preopercular			1	1
	Superior pharyngeal plate	3		1	4
Scaridae Total		**3**		**3**	**6**
Serranidae	Ceratohyal	1			1
	Cleithrum	1			1
	Hyomandibular	1			1
	Opercular			1	1
Serranidae Total		**3**		**1**	**4**
Unidentified	Dorsal spine		1		1
	Dorsal spine/pterygiophore		1		1
	Fragments		3		3
	Misc spines and rays		3		3
	Scale		7		7
Unidentified Total			**15**		**15**
Grand Total		**8**	**15**	**4**	**27**

Appendix C: Analysis of faunal remains from upland fortifications sites

Virginia L. Butler
Department of Anthropology, Portland State University

This report summarises the faunal remains recovered during excavation at six upland fortification sites tested in July/August 2002 on Rapa, French Polynesia (Table A). Remains were recovered during field screening (1/8" mesh) and flotation of bulk samples. Materials were identified to the finest taxon possible, using reference materials in Butler's possession at Portland State University. The "probable turtle" specimens were eroded, tabular fragments with porous structure that did not resemble the texture of other large to medium-size vertebrates. These specimens could be from any of the three marine turtles known for the Pacific (leatherback *Dermochelys coriacea*, green turtle *Chelonia mydas*, hawksbill *Eretmochelys imbricata*). All of the bones and teeth collected during field screening were documented and tallied. Unidentified vertebrate specimens – nonfish, include materials which were clearly not from fish, but which could be from other vertebrates, including turtle, marine mammal, pig, dog, or possibly human. None of the remains appear to be from bird, based on texture and robusticity. These remains were extremely fragmentary and poorly preserved. The flotation sample specimens tended to be extremely small (many less than 2 mm in linear dimension) and many could not be distinguished as fish or other vertebrate class. Thus, I only recorded those specimens from flotation samples that could be identified below vertebrate class (e.g. family). Number of Identified Specimens (NISP, Grayson 1984) was used to quantify the specimens.

Results

A total of 400 specimens were documented from the sites. Ten different vertebrate taxa were identified altogether (Table A), including eight fish taxa, rat and probable turtle. Parrotfish far and away dominates the fish fauna. This species was recovered at most sites and has the highest frequency in individual sites. The prominence is partially due to bias in identification, given that parrotfish teeth are more distinctive than those from other taxa. When teeth are excluded from the tallies, the overall frequency (and ubiquity) of parrotfish is reduced (Table A), though it still ranks highest of the fishes.

Method of sample collection needs to be considered in interpreting results. Overall, the flotation samples provided many more identified specimens, especially of fish, than field screening. At Tevaitau (R-18), where both field screening and flotation samples were used, the flot samples generated 36 NISP (21 with teeth excluded); whereas the field screening provided only four NISP (three when teeth were excluded). Fish faunal recovery was especially affected by collection method. At R-18, only two fish taxa were identified in the field screening, whereas seven were identified in the flot samples.

All of the fish could have been taken nearshore. They represent a variety of feeding ecologies and would have likely been taken using different methods (e.g. Leach and Intoh 1984; Leach et al. 1984; Allen 1992; Butler 1994, 2001). Thus the carnivores (groupers, snappers, moray eels) were more apt to be taken with hook and line and the herbivores (parrotfishes, damselfishes, puffers) were more likely taken with nets or traps.

Faunal representation greatly differs across sites. Turtle was only identified at Tapitanga (R-4). Fish is also very scarce at this site, although the scarcity may be due to the fact that flotation samples were not taken from this site. Tevaitau has the richest assemblage, with eight taxa present. This may be an artefact of sampling, however, given the relatively large sample size at the site and the commonly found association between sample size and richness (Grayson 1984).

Table A. Frequency of taxa by site and recovery method. Values in parenthesis are with teeth excluded.

Taxon	R-2		R-4		R-18		R-20		R2002-49		R-17	
	flot	1/8	flot	1/8	flot	1/8	flot	1/8	flot	1/8	flot	1/8
Carangidae (k, pompano)					1							
Elasmobranch (shark, ray)							1 (0)					
Labridae (wrasse)					2						1	
Muraenidae (moray eel)					2							
Pomacentridae (damselfishes)					2							
Scaridae (parrotfishes)	5 (0)			30 (15)	21 (6)	1 (0)	15 (0)				13 (4)	
Serranidae (grouper, sea bass)					2	2					1	
Tetraodontidae (pufferfishes)					1							
Unid Fish						48						
Rattus sp. (rat)					5	1					2	
Probable Turtle				46								
Unidentified Vertebrate (nonfish)				196		1				1		
Total NISP (excludes unid fish, unid vertebrate)	**5**			**76**	**36**	**4**	**16**			**1**	**17**	

References

Allen, M.S. 1992. Temporal variation in Polynesian fishing strategies: the southern Cooks in regional perspective. *Asian Perspectives* 31:183–204.

Butler, V.L. 1994. Fish feeding behaviour and fish capture: the case for variation in Lapita fishing strategies. *Archaeology in Oceania* 29:81–90.

Butler, V.L. 2001. Changing fish use on Mangaia, Southern Cook Islands: resource depression and the prey choice model. *International Journal of Osteoarchaeology* 11:88–100.

Grayson, D.K. 1984. Quantitative Zooarchaeology, New York: Academic.

Leach, B.F. and Intoh, M. 1984. An archaeological fishbone assemblage from the Vitaria Site, Rurutu, Austral Islands. *Journal de la Societe des Oceanistes* 78:75–77.

Leach, B.F., Intoh, M. and Smith, I.W.G. 1984. Fishing, turtle hunting, and mammal exploitation at Fa'ahia, Huahine, French Polynesia. *Journal de la Societe des Oceanistes* 79:183–197.

Appendix D: UTM locations of archaeological sites investigated in the current project

ID	Description	Northing	Easting
R-1 (Morongo Uta)	Fortification	6942536.95	761078.43
R-2 (Potaketake)	Fortification	6944304.05	763395.96
R-3 (Vairu)	Fortification	6945589.85	762849.25
R-4 (Tapitanga)	Fortification	6943851.50	763427.89
R-5 (Kapitangi)	Fortification	6945400.86	760810.75
R-17 (Ruatara)	Fortification	6945695.10	761746.92
R-18 (Tevaitau)	Fortification	6941795.40	761995.49
R-19 (Pukutai)	Secondary fortification	6943757.85	764180.76
R-20 (Ororangi)	Fortification	6941628.88	763452.88
R2002-1	Lithic scatter	6944363.89	761417.44
R2002-2	Domestic terrace	6944922.56	761844.26
R2002-3	Oven	6942355.87	762266.74
R2002-4	Garden soil	6942357.15	762265.81
R2002-5	Oven	6942428.79	762301.56
R2002-6	Garden soil	6943206.33	761630.33
R2002-7	Oven	6943084.84	761772.44
R2002-8	Oven	6942388.64	762239.62
R2002-9	Oven	6942405.36	762231.16
R2002-10	Oven	6944033.31	761177.57
R2002-11	Oven	6944201.57	761149.69
R2002-12	Oven	6944203.04	761197.14
R2002-13	Oven	6944416.30	761145.78
R2002-14	Oven	6944398.69	761180.51
R2002-15	Oven	6944370.32	761299.86
R2002-16	Sectioned terrace	6944429.01	761594.31
R2002-17	Oven	6944478.21	762623.15
R2002-18	Sectioned terrace	6944467.49	762626.94
R2002-19	Oven	6944275.28	762616.22
R2002-20	Oven	6943802.31	762648.68
R2002-21	Domestic terrace	6944360.04	761604.74
R2002-22	Oven	6944565.47	761832.53
R2002-23	Rockshelter	6944563.61	761829.85
R2002-24	Garden soil	6944549.62	761751.07
R2002-25	Garden soil	6943792.39	762655.15
R2002-26	Rockshelter	6944255.20	764831.75
R2002-27	Rockshelter	6944308.95	764914.98
R2002-28	Rockshelter	6944394.56	765075.74
R2002-29	Rockshelter	6943591.20	758682.53
R2002-30	Rockshelter	6942754.43	764938.23

Continued on next page

ID	Description	Northing	Easting
R2002-31	Rockshelter	6940906.57	765096.11
R2002-32	Rockshelter	6940902.14	765124.29
R2002-33	Rockshelter	6941880.04	760167.66
R2002-34	Rockshelter	6947459.35	763650.47
R2002-35	Rockshelter	6947407.65	763668.50
R2002-36	Rockshelter	6946949.59	763755.07
R2002-37	Rockart	6946947.42	763754.02
R2002-38	Rockshelter	6946870.82	764780.06
R2002-39 (Pukumia)	Secondary Fortification	6944769.45	764576.54
R2002-40 (Taua)	Secondary Fortification	6945846.76	764947.42
R2002-41	Lithic Scatter	6943973.67	761677.78
R2002-42 (Pukutaketake)	Fortification	6942940.46	760071.27
R2002-43 (Noogurope)	Fortification	6944219.02	759897.79
R2002-44	Rockshelter	6943923.78	763326.62
R2002-45	Domestic Terrace	6944702.88	761837.02
R2002-46	Rockshelter	6945162.28	765532.68
R2002-47 (Taugatu Cave)	Rockshelter	6944950.65	765466.75
R2002-48	Agricultural Terrace	6943577.40	761368.96
R2002-49	Domestic Terrace	6944068.24	759446.83
R2002-50 (Ngapiri)	Secondary Fortification	6941622.07	762001.34